MW01290427

ALSO BY MARK JONES LORENZO

Affront to Meritocracy: Stories of Overlooked Talents, Ignored Abilities, and Hidden Truths

Not Ok: A Requiem for GW-BASIC

Apophenia's Antidote: A Probability and Statistics Primer

*Its Wildness Lies in Wait: Mathematical Fallacies, Cognitive Traps,
and Debunking the Myths of the Lottery*

*The Paper Computer Unfolded: A Twenty-First Century Guide to the Bell Labs CARDIAC
(CARDboard Illustrative Aid to Computation), the LMC (Little Man Computer),
and the IPC (Instructo Paper Computer)*

Ok: The Resurrection of GW-BASIC

*Endless Loop: The History of the BASIC Programming Language
(Beginner's All-purpose Symbolic Instruction Code)*

ADVENTURES OF A
STATISTICIAN

ADVENTURES OF A
STATISTICIAN

The Biography of John W. Tukey

Mark Jones Lorenzo

SE BOOKS
Philadelphia | Pittsburgh

Ψ

SE BOOKS
5307 West Tyson Street
Philadelphia, Pennsylvania 19107
www.sebooks.com

References to websites (URLs) were accurate at the time of writing. Neither the author nor SE BOOKS is responsible for URLs that may have expired or changed since the manuscript was prepared.

Published in full-throated defiance of Yog's Law.

Library cataloging information is as follows:

Lorenzo, Mark Jones
 Adventures of a statistician : the biography of John W. Tukey /
 Mark Jones Lorenzo.
p. ; cm.
 Includes bibliographical references.
 I. Title
1. Tukey, John W., 1915-2000. 2. Statisticians—United States—Biography.
3. Statistics—United States—History. 4. United States—History—20th century.
 QA273.H374 2018
 519.5322'08—js22
20188703631
ISBN: 978-1-722-01358-5

10 9 8 7 6 5 4 3 2 1

Dedicated to John Tukey's countless intellectual descendants

Some of my critics have amused their readers with the wildness of the schemes I have occasionally thrown out; and I myself have sometimes smiled along with them. Perhaps it were wiser for present reputation to offer nothing but profoundly meditated plans, but I do not think knowledge will be most advanced by that course; such sparks may kindle the energies of other minds more favorably circumstanced for pursuing the inquiries.

—Charles Babbage, *On the Economy of Machinery and Manufactures*, quoted by John Tukey in "How Computing and Statistics Affect Each Other"

The Chinese have a curse: "May your children live in interesting times!"

—John Tukey, in an address to New Bedford High School

CONTENTS

PART THREE: Life Among the Academics

PART FOUR: Exploratory Data Analysis

PART FIVE: The Post-Retirement Years

PROLOGUE

Unless you're a statistician, a mathematician, or a scientist, the name John W. Tukey might not be familiar to you. Even if you have experience in one of those fields, you may have only heard of him through his work: perhaps from the Tukey Test, or the Cooley–Tukey FFT algorithm, or even Tukey's lemma. Although a number of his mathematical discoveries—including the multitudes that were not named after him (he shied away from naming anything after himself)—have stood the test of time, in life, and now in death, Tukey never quite achieved household-name status.

Nonetheless, John Tukey was one the most consequential statisticians and original thinkers of the twentieth century, and certainly the greatest applied statistician of his generation. His academic output was prodigious, turning out scores and scores of papers and several books published over the span of six decades. Frederick Mosteller, his former doctoral advisee and a formidable statistician in his own right, said, "He probably made more original contributions to statistics than anyone else since World War II."

Although he earned his place in history through his groundbreaking accomplishments in statistics, Tukey took the scenic route to get there. The son of educated parents whose high school classmates voted them most likely to give birth to a genius, he learned to read on his own by three years of age, mastered using a hand-crack desk calculator to speed up arithmetical calculations shortly thereafter, and was poring through technical journals in the New Bedford Free Public Library by the time he was a teenager.

His parents homeschooled him, eventually shipping him off to Brown University to study chemistry. From there, multiple degrees in hand, Tukey next enrolled as a graduate student in chemistry at Princeton but switched to studying mathematics—specifically, topology, a pure branch of the discipline requiring the greatest of mental faculties at abstraction. After earning his doctorate in topology and securing an academic appointment at Princeton, Tukey didn't show much interest in statistics or in applied mathematics in general, other than compiling lists of statistical techniques on index cards in the library at Brown University merely because he found them useful or interesting, until after the outbreak of the Second World War; with the U.S. poised to join the war, he was then (in effect) drafted into government work, along with a veritable army of other top-flight mathematicians and scientists. Tukey joined the Fire Control Research Office (FCRO), where, with the stakes never higher, he was exposed to a set of life-and-death problems that bore little resemblance to abstract mathematics: namely, calculating the trajectories of artillery and ballistics and the motions of rocket powder, working with stereoscopic height and range finders, and improving the Boeing B-29 Superfortress bomber. The experiences he gained during the war—and especially those of working with Charlie Winsor, a fellow unconventional thinker twenty years his senior—converted Tukey into a statistician; in the decades that followed, he would arrive at groundbreaking statistical results as well as help build a statistics department at Princeton. In addition, the government continued to come calling and Tukey, ever the faithful, patriotic servant, always answered.

Tukey served as a scientific advisor to several presidents of the United States, though he was adamant that "[y]ou can't expect scientists to solve political problems." In addition to his government work, he held down two jobs, both effectively full time, for decades: professor of mathematics and statistics at Princeton (including as department chair of the statistics department) and Bell Telephone Laboratories researcher and executive. That Tukey was spread thin is an understatement; that he attained long-term success despite the incredible demands on his time and energies is a testament to his otherworldly skills of self-discipline, drive, and focus.

To give you an idea of how astounding Tukey's time management skills were, consider the case of J. Stuart Hunter, a colleague of Tukey's who joined the Princeton mathematics faculty in 1962. Hunter was having a problem: his services were in demand for lectures and public speaking engagements, but he also was a full professor, with all the responsibilities and obligations that came with the role. Being pulled in many directions, and not knowing how to successfully juggle everything, Hunter asked the dean if there was any possibility of a split appointment.

The dean demurred. "If you're going to be a professor at Princeton, you're going to be a professor at Princeton," he said.

"But Professor Tukey is a professor at Princeton but he's also a director at Bell Telephone Laboratories," Hunter responded.

"Stu," the dean explained, "you are no John Tukey"—echoing Senator Lloyd Bentsen's famous "You're no Jack Kennedy" riposte during the 1988 vice-presidential debate.

For decades now, a student couldn't make it to high school without encountering mathematical methods popularized by Tukey. There is the stem-and-leaf plot, for starters, as well as the box-and-whisker plot, both of which were designed to display data intuitively and efficiently—and are startlingly easy even for elementary school kids to construct by hand. (The box-and-whisker plot was not the sole creation of Tukey, as we will later see; the stem-and-leaf plot also had antecedents.) High school mathematics classes introduce students to the identification of outliers in data sets, a process formalized by Tukey in his seminal work *Exploratory Data Analysis* (1977). The book takes its name from an approach to investigating and drawing conclusions from data through a particular kind of detective work: "There is often no substitute for the detective's microscope," Tukey wrote. In college, students in the hard sciences and the social sciences work with multiple comparisons when drawing inferences from sets of data, thus likely employing Tukey's Honest Significant Difference (HSD) test. Students in advanced physics and computer science classes encounter the fast Fourier transform (FFT) algorithm, which he co-created. And through their academic careers, students often hear the terms *bit,* which was coined by Tukey, and *software*, which may have been coined by him (he was the first to use the word in print—at least in the way we understand the term today). Yet Tukey has mostly not received the accolades and attention from the wider public that he's deserved—and that some other mathematicians and scientists, perhaps more focused on garnering publicity and public approval, attained—because of his humility, unprepossessing nature, and, at times, rather eccentric behavior. Tukey was oftentimes the proverbial square peg trying to fit snugly into a round hole. Perhaps it was F. R. Anscombe, Tukey's nephew, who captured his character best: "John W. Tukey challenges holistic appreciation."

As David R. Brillinger, a former student of Tukey's and the statistician most responsible for both curating his vast collection of works and preserving his legacy, writes, "John Tukey's contributions to the field of statistics are massive"; he "merged the scientific, governmental, technological, and industrial worlds more seamlessly than, perhaps, anyone else in the 1900s." You only need page through the eight volumes of *The Collected Works of John W. Tukey*, published over the course of a decade, to get a sense of the copious nature of Tukey's indelible output. An epistemological approach links these volumes together: Tukey makes it clear that the "philosophy that appears…is far more based on a 'bottom up' approach," or an approach that is inductive and experimental in nature, rather "than on a 'top down' one," or a methodology rooted in purely deductive thinking and resulting in the issuing of mathematical diktats. Yet as statistician Colin L. Mallows, who edited one of the volumes, explains, "[A]ny attempt to package Tukey's writings into neat categories must fail; he has worked on too many things!"

The *Collected Works*, unsurprisingly, offers the reader a treasure trove of statistics and mathematics papers; the volumes serve as a valedictory to cap off an especially long and productive career. But the *Collected Works* were also "meant to be more than a collection for the record or for future historians to sort out scientific movements. They can be used right now by researchers, by data analysts, and by students," reads the preface. To that end, there are a number of writings that appear in a heavily revised, polished, "published form" for the first time. Yet the *Collected Works* are not the exhaustive works, since there are some "important subjects, like [statistical] robustness, that escape that series." Interestingly, the overwhelming consensus among statisticians today is that Tukey's work in robustness analysis—the development of statistical methods that still perform well despite not satisfying certain statistical assumptions—mark some of his most important contributions to statistics. In addition to the unpublished works, of which there are many, Tukey was as prolific a writer about statistics as anyone; the importance and volume of his output is perhaps most fruitfully compared to that of the eighteenth century Swiss mathematician Leonhard Euler, who left little of mathematics untouched by his voluminous contributions.

Like Euler, John Tukey was a polymath. Also, like Euler, no mathematics problem was too big or too small to escape his notice. Tukey was never beneath putting in the hard work of "pulling weeds," as he said. According to his former doctoral advisee Karen Kafadar, "Tukey also often left details to the readers, particularly in his later years"; he had worked out the mathematics mentally, "but he left it to others to work out the formal theorems and proofs." Tukey could usually visualize the necessary mathematical paths without having to actually traverse them.

Tukey was also a "joker," as his friend, the physicist Richard Feynman, once referred to him. Tukey's sense of humor was subtle, low-key, suffused with a refined Yankee sensibility. Whereas Feynman could be brash and overt—after all, Feynman's best-selling second memoir was called "*What Do You Care What Other People Think?*", a philosophy which he wore on his sleeve—Tukey was much more deliberate, biding his time until achieving whatever goal happened to be in his sights. For example, after Brillinger described to Tukey a new method that he and seismologist Bruce Bolt arrived at to estimate some statistical parameters of the earth by examining the "free oscillations" resulting from an especially large earthquake, Tukey posed a devastating question to his former student, who was a professor at the University of California, Berkeley: "What if the earthquake is in [nearby] San Francisco?"

In general, Tukey would avoid responding directly to questions, side-stepping offering explicit, paint-by-numbers "answers" and asking his interlocutors questions instead. This technique came about perhaps as a result of his mother, who homeschooled him—and, by her methods of questioning, developed in Tukey an inquisitive mind but a disinclination to answer direct questions. Indeed, he could be evasive and elliptical when you spoke to him. Perhaps the statistician Jimmie Savage best described Tukey's aversion to direct questioning: If you asked Tukey how to milk an elephant, don't expect a response; but if you instead told him that elephants intrigued you, and engaged him in conversation about why, then Tukey might eventually, though circuitously, explain how to milk one.

Tukey, though possessing a relatively cheerful disposition, would pepper his speech with technical terms and phrases he coined, some right on the spot—not necessarily in the name of precision, but to obfuscate and introduce vagueness into the proceedings. He enjoyed fashioning neologisms, reveled in enclosing new terms in what he called "double red quotes." John Chambers, who worked with Tukey at Bell Labs to develop the S statistical programming language, recalls that Tukey "took delight in inventing new words…and saying things in a way that he knew would rankle the audience." The Harvard statistician Arthur P. Dempster classified Tukey's discursive writing style as "frustrating." The Berkeley statistician Erich L. Lehmann said that he "found early encounters with [Tukey] both frustrating and uncomfortable" largely because of the impenetrable vocabulary he used during their conversations. A graduate student of Tukey's, David Freedman, had little patience for Tukey's verbal proclivities. In class one day, he raised his hand to ask Tukey to clarify a fuzzily-defined word: *spectrum*.

"Well," Tukey started, "suppose you've got a radar transmitting signals up and it bounces off an airplane and a signal returns. So you see: well that's a spectrum."

Freedman was satisfied—for the moment. But during the very next class, Tukey kept using the term and Freedman still didn't quite understand what it meant, so he asked Tukey to define it again.

"Well," Tukey began, "suppose you have a sonar system and it bounces a signal off a submarine, or some such…."

Freedman was so frustrated with Tukey's evasions that he never showed up to his class again.

Tukey put up these sorts of barriers to students and faculty alike, perhaps to win an argument, maybe simply to see if the people in question were really serious enough to even remain in the same room with him. Jerome H. Friedman, who worked with Tukey in the early 1970s on the PRIM-9 computer system at Stanford, said, "He always delighted in slightly puzzling you by hiding, not telling you the fundamental reason for whatever he was doing, what lay behind it, what were his reasons." Once, during a lecture, after putting a mass of confusing symbols and terms on the board, Tukey slowly turned back toward his audience, haltingly asked for comments or questions, and then sat back down. Interminable silence pervading the room, he popped prunes in his mouth, one at a time, until someone finally volunteered a question. The number of prunes he managed to eat before anyone spoke up served, in his mind, as a rough measure of the general intelligence of those in attendance.

Tukey could be uncompromising. For instance, he refused to give an inch to the similarly obstinate sex researcher Alfred Kinsey, whose work Tukey publicly analyzed and scrutinized under the auspices of the American Statistical Association. In fact, Tukey so hounded her husband that Clara, Kinsey's wife, decades later described Tukey as "the worst" and expressed an unrelenting desire to poison him along with several other ASA statisticians.

But Tukey was also intellectually generous. He was a quick thinker overflowing with ideas, some of which he brought to fruition himself, many others of which he was happy to pass on to colleagues or students to fully formulate. He arrived at so many ideas, in fact, that a number of his "scratchings" never even made the cut for further study. Once, when Tukey was sitting next to Brillinger at a seminar, he passed his former student a paper. It read, "Measure (?) of 'peakiness' of periodogram: 1) take cepstrum (based on log periodogram), 2) average in octaves, laid 1/2 to the weather." To the best of Brillinger's knowledge, the idea remained dormant—perhaps due to this ominous warning by Tukey: "More lives have been lost looking at the raw periodogram than by any other action involving time series!"

Visiting professors were humbled by the speed at which Tukey could analyze a statistical problem. Consider James R. Thompson, a statistician out of Rice University who visited Tukey in 1977. Although Thompson had an undergraduate degree in chemical engineering, a master's degree and doctorate from Princeton in mathematics, and freelanced regularly for NASA, he thought Tukey's problem-solving abilities otherworldly. "I asked Tukey about this problem, and he devoted all of five minutes to it," Thompson recalled. "I figure five minutes of Tukey time is roughly equivalent to about five weeks of Thompson time."

Clearly, Tukey was an outlier—and unapologetically so. He would drink milk at beer parties, blast classical music from morning to noon in his study while he was working, organize faculty get-togethers in which each spouse would dress as the other, shout "Haw-Haw!", offer a deliberate "Hah, Hah" only if something was very funny, lay supine while working through Princeton's course-scheduling complexities, bird watch, venture out sailing, pluck weeds from his garden, and hold office hours with his students at the oddest of places: while he was chopping wood in his backyard, while his tires were being rotated at a gas station, even while on trips abroad. He would influence his fellow statisticians, and impart his patented statistical wisdom, when traveling to an airport with them, or eating a meal, or during a recess, or when hunting down a used-book store stocked with mysteries—opening up a line of inquiry with the simplest of questions: "What statistical problems have been bothering you recently?" And they knew he wasn't maneuvering to steal their ideas, but only seeking to help add to the greater storehouse of human knowledge; in this way, he was perhaps the ultimate statistical altruist, rarely seeking solo credit or sometimes any credit at all.

Stories about the man are legion: that he slept in his office at Bell using the wastepaper basket as a makeshift pillow; that he stored his notes and transparencies in refrigerator bags. He was careful to never reveal the contents of a transparency to his audience all at once but to instead do it slowly, almost alluringly, covering up the graphs and building suspense for the big reveal. When he traveled, which he did frequently, he carried with him a rather esoteric set of items: a knapsack filled with ping pong balls, a well-worn table-tennis paddle, a *World Almanac*, books of statistical tables, graph paper, transparencies, felt-tip pens in a rainbow of colors, a slide rule (replaced toward the end of his career with a calculator), dried fruit (especially prunes), and paperback fiction books (especially mysteries). He was overwhelmed with things to do but managed to maintain a continual, piercing focus on whatever tasks were before him. In effect, Tukey worked three full-time jobs at once: professor at Princeton, researcher at Bell Labs, and independent contractor to the federal government, at least whenever special projects presented themselves. The physicist and Princeton professor John Archibald Wheeler said of Tukey: "I believe that the whole country—scientifically, industrially, financially—is better off because of him and bears evidence of his influence."

But Wheeler, knowing of Tukey's rather unique disposition and set of skills, also called the statistician "money in the bank"—in the sense that Tukey was there to offer assurance and insurance when it came to thinking statistically—as well as labeling him, rather memorably, "a bouncy beefy extrovert." Tukey was a folk-dance instructor, enjoyed thinking about the combinatorics of square dancing, was an avid collector of several genres of fiction books, had an incredible facility with gardening, and flat-out loved watching professional football and golf on television (at least from the 1970s onward) and playing the card game hearts—and the occasional game of touch football with faculty and graduate students.

Yes, John Tukey was a polymath. But he also was every bit the Renaissance man, every bit the prankster, every bit the odd duck, that Richard Feynman was, just not as blatantly or as obviously so—and, unlike Feynman, he was reticent to write or speak directly about his predilections. As Tukey's nephew noted, "He operated on a discreet, 'need to know' basis," in part because much of what he did for the government was classified, but more so because he was a "self-contained and modest" man.

Tukey could be roused from silence, however, if he thought the cause worth fighting or promoting. For example, he urged scientific statisticians to be proud of what they do, even though the mathematics behind their methods may be "incidental, though perhaps indispensable." He once offered this cutting stereotype of statisticians: as people who draw "straight lines from insufficient data to foregone conclusions." Unfortunately, he knew the stereotypes all too well. As his career took shape, John Tukey repeatedly encountered a barely concealed form of discrimination: that of the typical mathematician's tendency to look down upon statisticians and statistical work, especially if such work wasn't of the mathematical statistics, or theoretical, variety. Sometimes this discrimination took the form of benign neglect; other times it assumed the guise of downright hostility. As someone trained in one of the most abstract disciplines of mathematics, topology, Tukey was able to fight the pervasive disrespect of statistics using the insiders' language of mathematics, thereby, eventually, bringing a sense of respectability to a practice of statistics that put the study of data pride of place—a study of data conforming to the scientific method, rather than one worshiping at the altar of theory. No more would the manipulation of mathematical models divorced from real-world problems be the order of the day.

Like a rising tide lifting all boats, he carved out the intellectual space for data analysis, thereby not only making the data analyst a profession of distinction, but also helping to enlarge the tent of statisticians and bring greater respect to the profession overall. He did this by publishing a great deal and by teaching a great many, but also by being an exemplar, a gold standard by which others could both observe and measure themselves against (though they would usually find themselves lacking). Viewed with the benefit of hindsight, this was perhaps his greatest accomplishment.

ADVENTURES OF A STATISTICIAN is a roughly chronological march through Tukey's life and times, although we will also take a number of detours. Divided into five parts, generally the earlier chapters focus a little more on biographical aspects, while the latter chapters devote more space to mathematical and statistical achievements and their long-term impact.

In PART ONE: The Path to Statistics, Tukey's childhood, early schooling, and journey to Brown University to study chemistry and Princeton University to study mathematics, are covered, as is his shift to statistics during World War II.

In PART TWO: Working as a Statistician, Tukey's time employed at Bell Laboratories and teaching at Princeton is the focus, as are the stories of his astounding achievements in election prediction, time series, Fourier series, statistical computing, and remapping the ontology of statistics. In addition, his intellectual war with Alfred Kinsey is recounted.

In PART THREE: Life Among the Academics, Tukey's work with robustness and the United States Census, as well as the establishment of the Princeton statistics department and his fruitful interactions with students, are detailed.

In PART FOUR: Exploratory Data Analysis, the approach to statistics most associated with Tukey, exploratory data analysis, comes under careful scrutiny.

Finally, in PART FIVE: The Post-Retirement Years, Tukey's accomplishments near the end of his life, in addition to his legacy, are discussed.

Since Tukey was such a prolific fashioner of new words, any time we first encounter a term coined or likely coined by Tukey, it will be printed in italics.

In the final analysis, ADVENTURES OF A STATISTICIAN was written to answer a single question: Who, exactly, was John W. Tukey? Yes, he was a scientist, a scientific generalist, a man versed in the minutiae of chemistry and topology, an environmentalist, a consultant to numerous U.S. corporations, a data analyst (in advance of the existence of the job), an incessant coiner of terms, a man possessed with sharp mental calculating faculties, an advisor to numerous U.S. presidents, an inventor, a top-notch mathematician, a preternaturally creative statistician, a world-class teacher, a prodigious writer, a workaholic, a quick-yet-deep thinker, and an introverted man with an undeniably inexhaustible supply of intellectual energy and curiosity. He was all those things. But he was also so much more.

This is the story of his life.

ADVENTURES OF A
STATISTICIAN

PART ONE

The Path to Statistics

CHAPTER ONE

Origins

"I was just a flash in the pan, my husband was the scholar."
— Adah Tukey

At the turn of the twentieth century, New Bedford, Massachusetts—a large coastal town of roughly 100,000 people—was primarily known for its commercial fishing and textile industries. Originally home to the Wampanoag Native Americans, European explorers settled the land in 1652. Whaling was woven into the fabric of New Bedford at least since the loose confederation of fishing and farming villages were known collectively as Bedford Village. When a Quaker named William Rotch, Jr., arrived at Bedford Village in 1780, he brought with him a whale oil ship named the *Dartmouth*. Although the ship, which was ransacked during the Boston Tea Party in 1773, met an unfortunate fate, within a century New Bedford would emerge as the wealthiest city per capita not just in the United States but in the world, thanks in large part to its bustling whaling port. The novel *Moby-Dick* was born of Herman Melville's experiences at the fabled Seamen's Bethel chapel and aboard the *Acushnet* of Fairhaven, which set sail from New Bedford toward the vast expanses of the Pacific Ocean in 1841.

By the middle of the eighteenth century, the peculiar institution, which was the original sin of America's founding, had increasingly resisted any long-term compromise. The Union was fracturing along geographic, political, and economic fault lines because of tensions over the intractable Slavery Question. Most residents of New Bedford were firmly in the abolitionist camp, strongly against any enforcement of the Fugitive Slave Law; in fact, the Underground Railroad ran right through the town. The abolitionist and fugitive slave Frederick Douglass settled in New Bedford. Other abolitionists, such as Lewis Temple, a blacksmith who invented a specialized whaling harpoon, also settled in the town. A small number of African Americans called New Bedford their home as well. In fact, more than sixty soldiers who served in the 54th Massachusetts Volunteer Infantry Regiment, which was composed solely of African American troops and became more widely known after being featured in the film *Glory*

(1989), resided in New Bedford. The enlistment station was right next to the U.S. Custom House.

The Whaling City, New Bedford's informal moniker, was well equipped to satisfy the high demand for whale oil, but by the late 1850s petroleum had emerged as a viable substitute. That, coupled with a number of whaling ships being lost at sea, precipitated the demise of the whaling industry. To compensate, the residents of New Bedford searched desperately for a new source of economic development. Roughly a decade before the outbreak of the Civil War, a second major industry, textiles, arose—through the founding of a cotton cloth mill. Within a half-century, the town became a leading producer of textiles, with dozens and dozens of mills churning out cotton yarns and positioning the town as an attractive place for both Americans and immigrants seeking skilled employment to settle.

On June 16, 1915, in the midst of a textile-driven economic boom for New Bedford, John Wilder Tukey* was born. He was the only child of two learned teachers, Adah Tukey (née Tasker) and Ralph Tukey. Adah and Ralph met in high school; their classmates had voted them most likely to give birth to a genius. They then attended Bates College together, located in Lewiston, Maine, graduating in 1898 as number one and number two in their class. Adah was the valedictorian, but she was dismissive of her achievement, instead giving the accolades to her husband: "I was just a flash in the pan, my husband was the scholar." In June 1912, after Ralph's mother passed away and also after the couple had relocated several times from Maine, including to Missouri and Massachusetts, Adah and Ralph tied the knot. Shortly before newborn John arrived, the newlyweds settled in New Bedford.

By the time of John's birth, the Tukey name was a mainstay in the New England area as evidenced, for instance, by the names of numerous landmarks, such as Tukey's Bridge (also known as Tukey Bridge), which connects East Deering and Munjoy Hill in Cumberland County, Portland, Maine. Originally constructed in 1796 to serve as a toll bridge, the structure was named for the local toll collector Lemuel Tukey, a native of Portland and proprietor of a nearby tavern, who collected tolls from the bridge until 1837 when he was ordered to cease and desist. Lemuel's brother's, father's, and grandfather's names were all John, three of a handful of men with the name John Tukey that the census records in the Portland and Boston areas at the time. The Tukey surname in the New World stretches back to at least 1744, with the arrival of a John Tukey from England to Portland, who was a common ancestor of John W. Tukey's family.

---

* To prevent confusion going forward: "Tukey" is pronounced "Tuke-ee."

Ralph Hermon Tukey, John W. Tukey's father, was born on May 29, 1876, in Windham, Maine, to Daniel R. Tukey and Carrie Tukey (née Webb). Ralph always had a deep sense of humor and a wonderful way with language and people. He earned a Bachelor of Arts (A.B.) in 1900 and a Master of Arts (M.A.) in 1901, both from Harvard. Then, in 1906, he obtained a doctorate (Ph.D.) from Yale in Latin. Although during most of the first decade of the twentieth century Ralph served as an instructor in Greek, Latin, and the classics at various institutions—such as the Hitchcock Free Academy in Brimfield, Massachusetts; at his alma mater, Bates College; and at the Hopkins Grammar School in New Haven, Connecticut—it was not until 1909 that Ralph landed full-time employment as a Professor of Greek at William Jewell College in Liberty, Missouri. Members of the Missouri Baptist Convention established the institution in 1849. In the early 1900s, when Ralph taught there, William Jewell had an exclusively male student body and a key mission: preparing Baptist ministers. When World War I broke out in 1914, Ralph—along with most of the younger faculty—resigned to permit the established faculty to keep their jobs. After the Great War, he taught at and eventually became the principal of New Bedford High School, which was situated on land that once held the estate of the whaling magnate Charles Waln Morgan.

Adah Mahala Tasker, John W. Tukey's mother, came into the world on Independence Day—fittingly, since she possessed a rich family lineage dating back to Colonial America. Adah was born on July 4, 1877, in bucolic Pittston, Maine, to Joshua Baker Tasker and Nellie May Tasker (née Frost). She was a distant relative of William Pepperrell, the colonial American who was known as "the hero of Louisbourg" because he led the land forces that captured the French fortress of Louisbourg in 1745. After becoming the first American-born baronet, Pepperrell served as acting governor of Massachusetts. Pepperrell's sister married John Frost, who was directly related to Nellie May Frost, Adah's mother.

Tukey was homeschooled by his parents, both of whom had teachers in their families going back generations, and he did not begin any sort of formal education until he was admitted to Brown University. He had learned to read on his own by around three years of age; his parents were only alerted to his premature literacy while on a road trip, when Tukey warned them that a bridge over the Susquehanna River wasn't accessible—something he had read about earlier in a newspaper's legal notices section. He later learned to speed up arithmetic calculations by using a hand-crank desk calculator. Adah did most of the homeschooling since—although her qualifications were second to none—married women were prohibited by law from working as teachers in Massachusetts, though, when her son was growing up, she worked regularly as a substitute teacher at New Bedford High School alongside her husband. Before her marriage, she had been employed full-time as a teacher in Bridgton, Maine (at Bridgton Academy, from 1898 to 1899); Lewiston, Maine (at the local high school, from 1899 to 1901); Quincy, Massachusetts (at the local high school, from 1901 to 1902); and New Bedford (at New Bedford High School, from 1902 to 1912; years later she returned to the high school, but in the role of substitute teacher). Immediately after getting married, she moved to 515 Wilson Street in Liberty, Missouri, since Ralph was employed at William Jewell College at the time.

When Adah grew up in Maine, with its cool, dry air, the facilities were so lacking that she had to break up ice in a bowl and use a pitcher in order to wash herself each morning. But she was a survivor, well schooled in the ins and outs of traditional classroom teaching by the time she returned to New Bedford as a married woman with a child in tow. Ralph's facility with language helped him to land a full-time teaching job at New Bedford High heading up the Latin department (and, as the need arose, other departments). In terms of his intellect and professionalism, Ralph served as a role model to his young son.

Adah, who worked as a substitute at New Bedford High, filled in for teachers of nearly every subject, including Portuguese and typing. Her husband, despite the leadership roles he assumed at the school, also taught numerous classes. In fact, through their many years at the institution, Ralph and Adah ended up teaching nearly every class offered at the high school, save for typing, shorthand, bookkeeping, physical education, and perhaps chemistry. Besides her son, Adah tutored other students too, but nothing came in the way of her son's education.

Though the young Tukey was primarily homeschooled, he traveled to the New Bedford campus for three classes: French (only for one semester), mechanical drawing, and chemistry lab. Adah adopted a Socratic teaching style when homeschooling her son, rather than a more straightforward and conventional "drill and kill" approach. She was convinced that if she simply sent Tukey off to public school full time, he would develop habits of laziness and ultimately turn into a problem child. So, instead, Adah made her son the focus of her teaching life, asking him blizzards of questions as answers to his questions—and his father followed suit, dropping him hints and clues, avoiding directly addressing the topics at hand—fostering an intellectual curiosity in Tukey that would last a lifetime. As Freud said, "If a man has been his mother's undisputed darling he retains throughout life the triumphant feeling, the confidence in success, which not seldom brings actual success with it," which was certainly true of John Tukey, who never regretted being brought up within a relatively isolated environment—sans neighborhood friends, of which he had a few.

To further Tukey's blossoming education, the city of New Bedford fortuitously had one of the most comprehensive public libraries in Massachusetts, the New Bedford Free Public Library, established in 1852, which housed extensive collections of Whaling and Quaker documents as well as a corpus of materials obtained from the New Bedford Social Library; the library even stocked research journals, and Tukey wasted little time in poring through them. (He began a lifelong love of adventure and detective fiction there, too; he also loved reading science fiction.)

Two journals in particular caught his eye: *Journal of the American Chemical Society* and *Transactions of the American Mathematical Society*. As a teenager, Tukey found he could read, parse, and understand the former, but couldn't make heads or tails out of the latter. That set his academic direction for the next several years, as Tukey turned away from mathematics— after dispensing with some required calculus courses prior to starting at Brown (he had worked through many, many calculus problems in a calculus book to prepare)—and turned toward chemistry instead.

CHAPTER TWO

Studying Chemistry at Brown

"Congratulations, you Ketchum."
— Anonymous Brown University mathematics professor

Gaining entry into Brown University required passing College Board exams, which Tukey accomplished effortlessly. But to ease the transition from homeschooling to traditional schooling, Tukey commuted to campus for his first two undergraduate years and then lived on campus during his third.

Tukey entered Brown as a member of the class of 1937 but graduated with the class of '36. While his time at Brown was short, it was nonetheless incredibly productive. Tukey, who worked for two academic years as a lab assistant in freshman inorganic chemistry, managed to earn a Bachelor of Science degree in chemistry and then a Master of Science degree in chemistry only one year later; as his wife, Elizabeth, later explained, prior to securing his bachelor's degree, Brown officials glanced at Tukey's record and encouraged him to simply continue on to secure a second degree.

Tukey's thesis experiments required glass blowing, which William A. Noyes, the organic chemist and editor of *Journal of the American Chemical Society* (the same periodical that spawned Tukey's interest in chemistry), helped him with. Despite his placing out of required mathematics courses (he also received credit for taking a mechanical drawing class in high school, perhaps being "the last person to enter Brown with credit" for the subject, he figured), he didn't forsake the subject by any means: as a freshman, Tukey enrolled in a junior differential equations class, something reserved for the more advanced mathematics students. He even took graduate courses taught by the mathematical luminaries Jacob Tamarkin and C. R. Adams.

Jacob David Tamarkin was born in Chernihiv, Ukraine in 1888. After earning a doctorate at the University of St. Petersburg, Tamarkin was retained there to teach. But he began plotting an escape from Russia after running into a professor of mathematics from Dartmouth in 1924 who was visiting the country. Secret negotiations followed, all culminating in a postcard sent from Hanover, New Hampshire—the location of the

Dartmouth College campus—containing a single line: the "weather is fine in Hanover." Tamarkin had the job, but he needed to escape totalitarianism first. A difficult journey by train and through a river landed him at the doorstep of the American Consul. His wife was thrown into prison; only American intervention at the highest levels of government secured her release. Tamarkin, a nearsighted joyous fellow who could usually be found chomping on a cigarette or cigar, taught for two years at Dartmouth and then landed a position at Brown, where he taught for the remainder of his career. Tukey had him as a professor only several years before Tamarkin, by that point a senior research mathematician, died.

C. R. Adams had a less eventful journey to Brown than Tamarkin. Born in Cranston, Rhode Island, in 1898, Clarence Raymond Adams earned an undergraduate degree from Brown and a doctorate from Harvard. Adams rose to chair the mathematics department shortly after Tukey sat in his classes.

By the end of his time at Brown, Tukey had become acquainted with most of the professors in both the chemistry and mathematics departments as well as spending time with the geologists and physicists, including the chairman of the physics department, Robert Bruce Lindsay who, like Tukey, came from New Bedford (Lindsay was born there in 1900; he earned several degrees from Brown and a doctorate from MIT, as well as studying under Niels Bohr, before returning to teach at Brown). Tukey also took a topology class with the Polish-American mathematician and scientist Stanislaw Ulam in the spring semester of 1937. Ulam, then in his second year as a member of the prestigious Harvard Society of Fellows, had been teaching both elementary mathematics courses (e.g., probability and classical mechanics) and several advanced courses at Harvard. He especially enjoyed teaching the advanced classes, since the best way to obtain a deep understanding of the material was to be forced to present the content to students in a classroom, he believed. Ulam was especially stubborn when it came to grading, refusing to budge from his high standards. (He would later soften up his grading style.)

Ulam, though stationed at Harvard, ended up teaching for a semester at Brown when he got word that Tamarkin was taking a sabbatical. Ulam was directed by Tamarkin only to teach an advanced graduate course, but not supplied with much direction beyond that. "I decided to give the course on the theory of functions of several real variables," he recalled decades later.* "It included a lot of new material—much of it my own

---

* Note that in his autobiography, Ulam never explicitly called the course a "topology class." But both "Quiet Contributor: The Civic Career and Times of John W. Tukey" (2003) by F. R. Anscombe and "John W. Tukey: His Life and Professional Contributions" (2002) by David Brillinger state that Ulam's

recent work—and I was rather proud of it. Every Friday I went to Providence [Rhode Island] by train, taught the course, spent the weekend with Tamarkin at his home, returning to Cambridge [Massachusetts] on Sunday."

Tukey even had his ear to the gossip—or "scuttlebutt," as he more tactfully called it—in the mathematics department at Brown. For example, there was Gertrude Stith, born in 1903 in Vidalia, Georgia, a graduate student in mathematics at Brown, who had left the university in 1930 after earning an assistantship at the University of Illinois at Urbana-Champaign; after only a year at Illinois, she married professor Pierce Waddell Ketchum, born in 1903 in Salt Lake City, Utah, who was a member of the mathematics department at Illinois (he had obtained his master's degree and doctorate from the institution in the mid-1920s). Anti-nepotism rules forbade Ketchum from continuing as a teaching assistant, but she was allowed to finish her studies, earning her terminal (doctoral) degree in 1934 and having a child a year later. After the marriage, a Brown mathematics professor came up with an idea: send an anonymous pithy telegraph to Illinois reading, "Congratulations, you Ketchum." Tukey knew at the time whose idea it was, but for the remainder of his life he never publicly spilled the beans.

Tukey didn't only learn mathematics in a classroom setting. A large portion of Tukey's exposure to mathematics at Brown was through self-directed study, too. His habit of devouring technical books and journals in libraries continued: he read numerous math works in the Brown University Library. In a hint of major intellectual interests to come, Tukey thought it prudent to write down statistical techniques (e.g., tables of critical values) he founds useful or interesting on 3×5 index cards he stored in a small tin container. It was in these self-study sessions that he began developing his statistical intuition, that he came to realize that "[t]he habit of building one technique on another—of assembling procedures like something made of erector-set parts—can be especially useful in dealing with data."[*]

Although his time at Brown was brief, by 1970 Tukey had garnered enough of a national reputation that the president of Brown, Donald

---

class was on topology. Brillinger's citation for this claim is listed as a "Personal communication" between himself and F. R. Anscombe, however, so the topology course information in both aforementioned articles likely stem directly from Anscombe.

[*] A grammatical point worth mentioning: "data" is a plural noun, with "datum" its singular form. The linguist Steven Pinker has argued for keeping data plural, and thus never using the word in this manner: "The data *is* clear...."

Hornig, asked him to join the Brown Corporation, which oversaw the university's activities. Tukey was always sentimental about the institution, having worn his Brown necktie to formal events numerous times in the intervening years, so he readily agreed. Tukey also ended up serving as a member of the Brown Board of Fellows, the Brown Library Committee, and the Brown Committee on Computers in Education.

CHAPTER THREE

Making His Mark at Princeton

"[T]he senior man at a working group there…was an analog type when everybody else was digital."
—John Tukey

Tukey's academic background was in chemistry, a discipline with many real-world applications, so it's no surprise that he later brought a more empirical, inductive, and even pragmatic mindset to bear on statistics. Tukey later recounted his professional path from chemistry to mathematics to statistics, and the unique advantages it conferred on his way of thinking about the world. "Perhaps because I began in a hard but usually non-deductive science—chemistry—and was prepared to learn 'facts' rather than 'proofs,'" he explained, "I have found it easier than most to escape the mathematician's implicit claim that the only real sciences are the deductive ones."

Make no mistake, though: Tukey was no slouch when it came to mathematical proof or mathematics in general. He was so good at abstraction that his friend Richard Feynman—who became one of the most accomplished theoretical physicists of the twentieth century and a world-class polymath in his own right—poked fun at Tukey's (along with stereotypical mathematicians') love of mathematically proving "trivialities," or logical statements that were self-evident even to neophytes—and thus weren't worth expending the brainpower for proof—by mockingly shouting, "It's trivial! It's trivial!" even if Feynman didn't quite recognize the mathematics behind his pronouncements.* Tukey countered Feynman's

---

* Later, when Tukey became a professor at Princeton, he would occasionally encounter the mathematician Salomon Bochner, an Orthodox Jew who had escaped from Germany to accept a position at Princeton the same year as Hitler rose to the chancellorship. Bochner usually had one of two responses to any new mathematics presented to him: either "But zees is trivial!" or "But zees is impossible!" Ralph Boas, a mathematician with whom Tukey's first published paper was co-written, frequently found himself on the receiving end of Bochner's dismissive responses.

dismissive view of math by offering a contrarian take on physics: "all the laws of physics are wrong, at least in some ultimate detail," Tukey maintained, "though many are awfully good approximations." Yet Tukey and Feynman thought more alike than perhaps either would care to admit, if only because they perceived the world very differently than most people. David Brillinger, one of Tukey's doctoral students, said that Tukey "could add two four-digit numbers in ten different ways that no one else in human history would have ever thought of! I mean he was like Richard Feynman. He was of the same ilk."

Three years apart in age, Feynman and Tukey met at Princeton, where Feynman was a doctoral student and Tukey a newly minted mathematics instructor. Tukey had arrived as a student at the predominately male Princeton campus in 1937,* quickly took up residence in the graduate college (where he would live, effectively, until getting married), and enrolled in the doctoral program in chemistry—in fact, Tukey chose to go to Princeton on account of their top-rate chemistry doctoral program— although he also took classes in mathematics in his first year at Princeton. As a first-year graduate student, Tukey split his time attending many chemistry and mathematics seminars and courses. But unlike at Brown, he was not permitted to serve as a laboratory assistant; only Ph.D.s were offered the opportunity to be lab assistants in physical chemistry at Princeton. Tukey had enrolled at the institution expecting to be an assistant (a "demonstrator") in a physical chemistry lab, but he was only permitted to be a laboratory assistant in a sophomore analytic lab, which "perturbed" him—but also helped to alter the course of his career.

Besides his disappointment at the rules of the chemistry department, two things began to attract him toward mathematics: the preternaturally inventive mathematical community at the institution as well as the proximity of Fine Hall, housing the mathematics department, to the Institute of Advanced Study (IAS), housing some of the greatest minds of the age (such as Albert Einstein, whom, despite essentially being a hallway away, Tukey was too intimidated to meet). Named after Henry Burchard Fine, who had been a Princeton professor of mathematics and dean of the faculty in the early 1900s, and positioned on the southeastern corner of campus, the red brick-and-limestone Fine Hall, with its many "closed solid doors" wrapping around the rectangular building, as Tukey recalled years later, beckoned. He was already spending more time in Fine Hall than in the Frick building, named in honor of the industrialist Henry Clay Frick, which housed the chemistry department. So, within six months of enrolling at Princeton, Tukey changed his concentration to mathematics—in characterizing the move, he said he "fell over the fence"—taking

---

* Princeton would remain mostly male for decades to come.

and passing the mathematics qualifying examinations (also called comprehensive exams or prelims) in May of 1938. In fact, he scored so high on the exams that he was awarded the prestigious Porter Ogden Jacobus Fellowship. After his focus shifted to mathematics, Tukey experienced a bit of buyer's remorse, though: he might now never get to work with Henry Eyring, the Wolf Prize-winning Mexican-born Mormon theoretical chemist whom Tukey fondly referred to as the "salt of the salt of the earth." The positive feelings were mutual; Eyring returned from sabbatical only to discover that Tukey had been "stolen away from chemistry" in his absence. Regardless, the University of Utah then stole Eyring away from Princeton.

Feynman, who was studying physics, was only several years away from directing his considerable brainpower to quantum electrodynamics (QED),* formulating theories that would revolutionize the discipline and lead to him winning the Nobel Prize. Born in 1918 in Far Rockaway, Queens, New York City, before he was ten years old Richard Phillips Feynman had garnered a reputation as something of a wizard at fixing radios. Rejected from admission to Columbia University because of a Jewish quota, he ended up graduating from MIT before moving on to Princeton, where he obtained his doctorate in 1942—just in time to join the war effort. Feynman was an integral part of the Manhattan Project at Los Alamos, making important atomic bomb energy-yield predictions and arriving at key results by directing primitive electronic and human computing efforts (one of the people on Feynman's team of young mathematicians and physicists was John Kemeny, who would co-create the BASIC [Beginner's All-purpose Symbolic Instruction Code] programming language and become president of Dartmouth College; Kemeny was only an undergraduate at the time).† Feynman found unique ways to occupy his downtime at Los Alamos, including exchanging coded letters with his first wife (who lived off-site) and cracking the combination locks on safes; he would also spend time with the established physicists and mathematicians who were building the bomb—namely, Edward Teller, Enrico Fermi, and John von Neumann. After the war, besides QED, Feynman would discover a theory for weak interactions, explain the behavior of liquid helium near absolute zero temperatures, and investigate high-energy collisions in a linear accelerator. Feynman would also become one

---

* Note that when a mathematician, rather than a physicist, sees the letters QED, he or she usually takes it to mean *quod erat demonstrandum*, or that which was to be demonstrated—marking the end of a mathematical proof.
† Tukey later had a more direct connection to the programming language: the other co-creator (along with Kemeny) of BASIC was Thomas Kurtz, who was a doctoral student of Tukey's at Princeton and, in his dissertation, made some headway proving Tukey's Conjecture for several cases.

of the great popularizers of physics and science in general, writing entertaining books and releasing lectures that brought his passion to bear on the subjects he loved.

But that lay in the future. At Princeton, Feynman was not afraid to rib Tukey. In the autobiographical *"Surely You're Joking, Mr. Feynman!": Adventures of a Curious Character* (1985), Feynman describes an interaction that he, Tukey, and several other mathematicians had one afternoon in a lounge.

> [I] … overheard some mathematicians talking about the series for e to the x power… [which is] very simple [to calculate]. I mumbled something about how it was easy to calculate e to any power using that series (you just substitute the power for x).
>
> "Oh yeah?" they said. "Well, then what's e to the 3.3?" said some joker— I think it was Tukey.
>
> I say, "That's easy. It's 27.11."
>
> Tukey knows it isn't so easy to compute all that in your head. "Hey! How'd you do that?"
>
> Another guy says, "You know Feynman, he's just faking it. It's not really right."

But Feynman wasn't faking it—he had a trick involving three parts memorization, two parts approximation, and one part blind luck. Feynman's method bore some resemblance to his later famous safe-cracking exploits at Los Alamos.

As their friendship blossomed, Tukey and Feynman, through informal experimentation, came to realize that different people do not keep time in their heads in quite the same way. It was all triggered by an insight of Feynman's: he could read while he was mentally counting—even finding himself somewhat able to comprehend the text—but he couldn't speak while mentally counting. In fact, he could do almost anything while mentally counting: besides reading, Feynman found he could simultaneously count the lines of a newspaper article by grouping them into chunks. But, however much he worked at it, he simply wasn't able to speak. Feynman attributed his speaking paralysis to the way he incremented numbers: by speaking to himself in his head—"1, 2, 3, 4, …"—the mental space for talking aloud was occupied. At breakfast one morning at Princeton, Feynman sat down next to Tukey, a young man with whom he had "had many discussions" by this point, and described for Tukey his mental counting experiments.

Tukey was incredulous. "That's absurd," he told Feynman. "I don't see why you would have any difficulty talking whatsoever, and I can't possibly believe that you could read." But then Feynman demonstrated, and it was Tukey who found himself speechless.

Ever curious, Tukey agreed to try an experiment. First, Feynman had him count, at Tukey's own pace, for sixty seconds; Tukey had been able to count to fifty-two in that timeframe (Feynman was a little faster, counting to forty-eight in a minute). Then, restarting his mental count, Tukey asked Feynman: "All right, what do you want me to say? Mary had a little lamb; I can say anything I want to, it doesn't make any difference; I don't know what's bothering you; blah, blah, blah... Fifty-two!" And, indeed, sixty seconds had gone by—and Tukey had filled up the minute with vocalizations. Now it was Feynman who was incredulous: What could account for the fact that Tukey could speak out loud while mentally counting, while Feynman could not?

They discussed how they counted in their heads, and quickly came to realize their methods were markedly different. When Tukey counted, he imagined a tape with numbers that went "clink, clink, clink; the tape would change with the numbers on it that he could see," as Feynman described it in an interview years later. Tukey used an "optical system," rather than an auditory one; he had the speaking part of his brain freed up—leaving Tukey the capability to speak to his heart's content while the "clink, clink, clink" proceeded apace. But reading while mentally counting?—that Tukey couldn't do. So Tukey and Feynman had opposite limitations while keeping time in their heads: one could speak but not read, while the other could read but not speak. "Tukey and I discovered that what goes on in different people's heads when they think they're doing the same thing—something as simple as counting—is different for different people." Tukey later become fond of saying, "Axiom 1: People are different"—meaning, take people as they are, not as you fancy them to be—a proverb likely originating in these time-counting experiments at Princeton.

"Night after night Feynman and Tukey dazzled all who could crowd around at the graduate school dinner," recalled graduate student Frederick Mosteller, who met Tukey in 1939. But more mathematically serious, and productive, were Feynman, Tukey, Arthur Harold Stone, and Bryant Tuckerman in forming the Princeton Hexaflexagon Committee (also called the Flexagon Committee) devoted to the topological study of hexaflexagons, a subset of flexagons, paper models with multi-triangle faces that can be folded ad infinitum while revealing new and repeating faces with each iteration. It wasn't the only self-selected committee that The

Tuke, as his friends called him, would join—Tukey and some other Princeton peers would also form the *Gegen Tukey Sport und Turnverein*—but it was certainly the most influential, having an almost legendary brain trust.

Arthur Stone, a 23-year-old mathematics graduate student at Princeton who was born in London, England, discovered hexaflexagons in 1939 when resizing American sheets of paper for his English (i.e., British-style) binder; the American sheets he bought at Woolworth's wouldn't fit, being too wide by about an inch. So Stone began folding the trimmed papers, arriving at interesting constructions such as the trihexaflexagon, a flexagon with three faces. Experimenting further, he doubled the number of faces to six, creating the first hexaflexagon (*hex-* for hexagonal, *-flexagon* for their flexible shape). Flexagons were not the first geometric-exploration-by-committee that consumed Stone's time; when he was at Trinity College in Cambridge in the mid-1930s, Stone and three other mathematically gifted friends—Leonard Brooks, Cedric Smith, and William Tutte—pursued the "squaring the square" problem, which involved breaking a large square into smaller squares, all of integral dimensions. In 1942, Tukey and Stone would collaborate again, this time on generalizing the so-called Ham Sandwich Theorem, a mathematical result involving three entities (like two pieces of bread with a slab of ham in between) which can be bisected using a single plane (flat surface) as the "knife"; today, their proof is known as the Stone–Tukey theorem. Stone, clearly fascinated with the mathematical properties of shapes, earned a doctorate in topology from Princeton in 1941 under the guidance of Solomon Lefschetz.

Lefschetz was one of the most influential mathematicians of the mid-twentieth century, not only as a professor at Princeton but also as the editor of the journal *Annals of Mathematics*. Born in 1884 in Moscow, Russia, Lefschetz was raised Jewish by his Turkish parents; his family moved to Paris, where Lefschetz studied mechanical engineering. The dearth of academic opportunities spurred Lefschetz to immigrate to the United States at age twenty-one. By age twenty-three he had lost both his hands, the result of a transformer explosion at the Westinghouse Electric and Manufacturing Company in Pittsburgh, Pennsylvania. His engineering career over, Lefschetz, now outfitted with gloved prosthetic wooden hands, decided to reinvent himself as a mathematician; mathematics had been his first love as a child. Three years after the industrial accident, he enrolled at Clark University in Worcester, Massachusetts, and in the span of only a single year earned a doctorate in mathematics, with a thesis exploring algebraic geometry under the American mathematician William Edward Story; thus, Lefschetz's academic genealogy can be traced back to eminent mathematicians such as Leonhard Euler, Carl Friedrich Gauss,

Siméon Poisson, and Joseph-Louis Lagrange, among many others. Even before joining the faculty at Princeton (he taught at the University of Nebraska and the University of Kansas), Lefschetz's work in algebraic topology was well known; in 1924, he became one of the first recipients of the American Mathematical Society's Bôcher Memorial Prize—and Princeton University snagged him.

Despite his reputation preceding him, those first years at Princeton were difficult. Although he was hired in a permanent position at the institution after serving as a visiting professor for only two semesters, he felt like an "invisible man." As Sylvia Nasar, in her book *A Beautiful Mind* (1998), describes it, Lefschetz "was one of the first Jews on the faculty, loud, rude, and badly dressed to boot. People pretended not to see him in the hallways and gave him a wide berth at faculty parties. But Lefschetz had overcome far more formidable obstacles in his life than a bunch of prissy Wasp snobs." On the other hand, this self-stylized invisible man helped to ensure that Jewish students were literally invisible at Princeton, mostly refusing them entry into the mathematics department. His justification was fashioned of flimsy logic: Jewish students wouldn't be able to secure paying positions after they graduated from Princeton, he reasoned.

Lefschetz's important mathematical results, such as the fixed-point theorem, were legion, but his influence was most greatly seen in his teaching—specifically, in the high standards he imposed and the dozens of top-flight doctoral students he (rather loosely) supervised. He was far from infallible mathematically, however; students joked that he "never wrote a correct proof or stated an incorrect theorem." Lefschetz's personality was loud and brash; he had a tendency to bully others, having little interest in what he considered trivial proofs of obvious results. When a student presented Lefschetz with a much shorter proof of one of his theorems, Lefschetz sniffed, "Don't come to me with your pretty proofs. We don't bother with that baby stuff around here." A short verse, from a faculty song, was circulated about Lefschetz: "Here's to Papa Solomon L. / Unpredictable as hell / When laid at last beneath the sod / He'll then begin to heckle God." The American mathematician John Nash, who attended graduate school at Princeton, had the misfortune to be on the receiving end of a fiery display from Lefschetz. Here is Sylvia Nasar again:

> On Nash's second afternoon in Princeton, Solomon Lefschetz rounded up the first-year graduate students in the West Common Room. He was there to tell them the facts of life, he said, in his heavy French accent, fixing them with his fierce gaze. And for an hour Lefschetz glared, shouted, and pounded the table with his gloved, wooden hands, delivering something between a biblical sermon and a drill sergeant's diatribe.

But his bullying was, in part, a ruse, since he afforded his doctoral students unprecedented freedom to pursue unstructured research independently however they saw fit; Lefschetz was especially enthusiastic about mathematical research. Tukey called Lefschetz one of his most memorable teachers (along with H. Frederic [Henri] Bohnenblust, who earned his mathematics doctorate at Princeton in 1930, as well as game theorist Albert "Al" Tucker, who earned his doctorate under Lefschetz in 1932).

Lefschetz was an algebraic topologist; in fact, he even coined the term "topology," replacing French mathematician Henri Poincaré's rather ungainly "analysis situs." The mathematical study of topology, which was born in the twentieth century, is focused on ascertaining if objects or surfaces are "topologically equivalent," which means that the objects or surfaces can be transformed continuously into one another with all points on the objects or surfaces having a one-to-one correspondence. For example, since a cube and a basketball have no holes in them—they are both classified as "genus zero" for this reason—they can be transformed into each other using a series of topological transformations; thus, cubes and basketballs are topologically invariant objects. A coffee cup and a donut (also called a torus) are also topologically invariant because they can be transformed into one another: both are "genus one," with each object possessing a single hole. We can further generalize that any object with genus one requires one cut to break it apart; any object with genus two requires two such cuts; and any object with genus n needs $n + 1$ cuts. Therefore, on a fundamental level, the study of topological equivalence looks to an object's or a surface's holes and cuts as starting points toward building mathematical taxonomies.[*]

Bryant Tuckerman, also a member of the Hexaflexagon Committee, was born in Lincoln, Nebraska, in 1916. Before attending Princeton, he graduated from Antioch College, a liberal arts institution in Yellow Springs, Ohio. The outbreak of the World War II in 1939 forced Tuckerman put his graduate studies at Princeton on hold; he contributed to the war efforts by working at both the U.S. Office of Scientific Research and the Office of Scientific Research and Development. Returning to Princeton after the cessation of hostilities, Tuckerman earned his doctorate in topology, went on to teach for a short time at Cornell and Oberlin, returned to Princeton to design computer applications with John von Neumann at the Institute for Advanced Study, and then finished out his career work-

---

[*] Feynman observed sardonically that "[t]opology was not at all obvious to the mathematicians."

ing at the IBM T. J. Watson Research Center studying cryptography and data security.

Richard Feynman, excited by the collaboration with like-minded peers and stimulated by the hands-on experimentation, took to the flexagon models right away, drawing diagrams for new designs—diagrams that, as author Les Pook in *Flexagons Inside Out* (2003) observes, "were forerunners to the well-known Feynman diagrams in modern atomic physics." Feynman was the only non-mathematician on the committee. Somewhat ironically, hexaflexagons, and the mathematical study of them, are very abstract—and thus at least somewhat antithetical to the later interests of both Feynman and Tukey, which hewed closely toward the empirical. Nonetheless, Feynman and Tukey scratched out a comprehensive mathematical theory of "flexigation" by 1940, but never published their results. As the popular mathematics writer Martin Gardner notes, their theory "shows, among other things, exactly how to construct a flexagon of any desired size or species." Tukey also worked out a theory of square flexagons. The bombing of Pearl Harbor prematurely broke up the Hexaflexagon Committee, but the theories behind their paper constructions would later be rediscovered and formally documented by others—most notably, Bryant Tuckerman's father, Louis Tuckerman. Gardner would write several articles and a book, *Hexaflexagons and Other Mathematical Diversions* (1959), that took as its foundation the elder Tuckerman's flexagon findings. Tukey had trouble letting a good idea die; in the late 1940s, he pitched the flexagon as a children's toy to at least one toy company, but to no avail.

Like Arthur Stone, Tukey ended up earning a doctorate in topology at Princeton, also under Solomon Lefschetz. Later on, Tukey explained his shift from chemistry to topology to, eventually, statistics by finding a common through line: methodology. All three disciplines are rooted, he realized, in a rigorously methodological approach to everything in their purview; all three seek to carefully systemize large swaths of knowledge. Furthermore, as Tukey waded into the waters of "data analysis"—he was among the first to call it that, in a discussion at a party of one of his student's homes, although he never took credit for its coining[*]—later in his career, he began to see the benefits of *not* having started his academic career in mathematics but in science. As Tukey explained it in a foreword to one of the volumes of *The Collected Works of John W. Tukey*,

> A respectable physical-science education—officially in chemistry, but with large doses of physics and substantial doses of geology—probably

---

[*] We can find the term "data analysis" in use as early as 1956, in a book by the Hungarian mathematician Cornelius Lanczos called *Applied Analysis*.

helped me a lot in understanding the character of the problems to which data brought to me were intended to be relevant. A purely mathematical background would, I believe, have left me at a severe disadvantage. Given a reasonable sensitivity to the underlying issues, seeing many sets of data seems to have made it natural to try to think about techniques in terms of the needs they might fill and the gaps that they left.

Statistics and data analysis were not the same thing. Data analysis was a large field, encompassing much of the pockets of traditional statistics, such as statistical inference, while also bleeding beyond its edges. To that end, major discoveries in statistics typically haven't had a correspondingly revolutionary effect on the practice of data analysis (with notable exceptions like sums of squares calculations). Tukey took to quoting 1 Corinthians whenever asked of his view of data analysis: "All things are lawful for me, but not all things are helpful." But his approach toward data analysis wasn't so easily encapsulated by an aphorism, considering the high degree of personal intuition—sans mathematical proof—he injected into making his statistical inferences. Tukey wanted to be able to *feel* like he was making headway, that he was on the right track, without having to resort to the traditional tool of the mathematician: theoretical proof. To that end, he preferred statistical tools that encouraged some sort of visceral approach. "[T]heorem proving," he noted, "is seductive—and its Lorelei voices can put us on the rocks."

Tukey, a lover of science fiction, found an analogue of himself in an "analog" character—in a short story called "Incommunicado" by Katherine MacLean. Born in 1925 in Glen Ridge, New Jersey, MacLean was fascinated by science fiction from an early age. She earned a degree in psychology from Barnard College but had already begun submitting stories to magazines years earlier. The first story she sold was "Incommunicado," which was printed in *Astounding Science Fiction* the year she graduated from Barnard, although, due to the technical jargon in the story, editor John W. Campbell was initially skeptical that Katherine, rather than her father, who was an engineer, actually wrote it. She sold several more stories to *ASF* as well as to other magazines, gained some national attention for her work in the 1960s, and ultimately found herself drawn to the Dianetics movement of L. Ron Hubbard.

"Incommunicado" is set in an automated space station construction project near Pluto, where the resident workers slowly begin to develop a means of communication with the station's computer—in the form of a complex sort of musical Morse code: "Cliff stood, letting the music flow through him, subtly working on the pattern of his thought…. The station computer translated the data to clicks and scales and twitters, and slowly the picture of the condition of Pluto Station project" came to life.

Much to the surprise of MacLean, the story resonated with scientists, including those at Bell Labs. One of those Bell Labs scientists, of course, was Tukey. But rather than see "Incommunicado" through the lens of a speculative fiction that captured the imaginations of researchers especially interested in the possibilities of the personal computer, Tukey read the story as a conflict between "the senior man at a working group there who was an analog type when everybody else was digital." Tukey's interpretation cast light on how he perceived himself in the realm of data analysis: as a loner who relies on a finely tuned sense of personal intuition when uncovering the truth about data. Yes, he could resort to mathematical proof, but navigating the waters could often only be done successfully by feeling one's way forward.

CHAPTER FOUR

Reaching the Mathematical Summit

"The course ended in a draw."
— Albert Tucker

Stanislaw Marcin Ulam, whom Tukey had as a professor at Brown, penned a revealing autobiography called *Adventures of a Mathematician* (1976). In late 1935, Ulam paid an extended visit to Princeton, a place he described as teeming with "gigantic Kafkaesque frogs" and forests replete with "thin, spindly trees and marshes"; to the Polish expatriate, New Jersey was an "exotic land." In his book, Ulam not only recounts his experiences and meetings with preternaturally talented mathematicians like John von Neumann, but he also attempts to explain, categorize, and generalize the world through a phenomenological lens. For example, when recounting that von Neumann had analogized the "operating systems" of the brain and the computer, Ulam offers his own analogizing about human thought:

> There must be a trick to the train of thought, a recursive formula. A group of neurons starts working automatically, sometimes without external impulse. It is a kind of iterative process with a growing pattern. It wanders about in the brain, and the way it happens must depend on the memory of similar patterns.

At another point in the book, Ulam hypothesizes that von Neumann was a "slave" to technique and force of habit, launching into an examination of the great mathematician's psyche that likely sounded both profound and polished at the time of the book's publication but seems rather shallow and trite upon reading now. Ulam dabbles a bit in outmoded Freudian psychoanalysis as well.

Notwithstanding his flights of fancy into pop neuroscience and psychology, which mostly don't hold up, Ulam's powers of description and observation still ring true. Visiting New York for the first time—he traveled by sea on the *Aquitania*, an English ship, and encountered a few rough patches that sickened him—he tried to contact von Neumann, who was stationed at the Institute for Advanced Study, by walking into a telephone booth and dialing a phone number. The operator told him to "Hold the wire," but Ulam, who was born in 1909 in Lviv, Ukraine, but raised in Poland, didn't understand the expression. "Which wire should I hold?" he replied.

The operator managed to connect him to Solomon Lefschetz, who relayed to him exacting directions to the Princeton campus. There are trains passing by the campus every hour, Lefschetz told him, because Princeton happens to intersect with the main line route from Philadelphia to Washington.

When Ulam arrived at Princeton, he walked to Fine Hall, where the first iteration of the IAS was situated. "A young and pretty Miss Flemming and an older Miss Blake received me. I was greeted with smiles," he recalled. "It surprised me, and I wondered if there was something a little funny about the way I was dressed or whether my trousers were not properly buttoned (there were no zippers in those days)."

Fairly quickly, Ulam noticed that Princeton was "fast becoming a way station for displaced European scientists." This was precisely the milieu that Tukey found himself in as a graduate student: the exotic and foreign coexisting peacefully with the prosaic and banal. In 1938, as he was researching materials for his dissertation and playing some of the ever-present games of Go as well as the chess variant Kriegspiel against other mathematicians at Fine Hall, Tukey began attending too many lectures to count. There was visiting professor—and later Nobel Laureate in physics—John H. van Vleck's series of lectures on magnetic and electric susceptibility, attended eagerly by Tukey purely out of curiosity. Van Vleck, born in 1899 in Middletown, Connecticut, was the son of a mathematics professor; he grew up in Wisconsin and earned his doctorate at Harvard. Van Vleck's key research interest was magnetism, but he also loved trains. Coincidently, one of the guest lectures was in Philadelphia, rather than Princeton, and Tukey had to take three trains there just to see him speak.

Marston Morse's seminar on symbolic dynamics also piqued Tukey's interest. Born in 1892 in Waterville, Maine, Harold Calvin Marston Morse's father was a farmer and a real estate agent. Morse snagged his doctorate from Harvard under the supervision of George Birkhoff; he later taught mainly at Harvard. His best-known result is actually many: a thematic umbrella of topological ideas known collectively as Morse theory.

Morse delivered his symbolic dynamics seminar at Princeton in Fine 113, a cramped lecture room. Tukey decided to have a little fun, conspiring with fellow graduate student and eventual Princeton professor of algebraic topology Norman Steenrod, who, like Tukey, would also earn a doctorate under the loose guidance of Solomon Lefschetz. Tukey planted himself in one back corner of Fine 113, while Steenrod stationed himself at the other; there, through the semester, they "did [their] best to keep Marston Morse honest." Morse was impressed with Tukey, asking him if he was a member of the Institute for Advanced Study or the mathematics department—since the two groups of academics "didn't segregate" at Fine, according to Tukey (the Institute was connected to Fine Hall until 1939)—but, at the time of the seminar, Tukey was still enrolled as a chemistry graduate student.

Another academic impressed with the precocious young Tukey was Albert Tucker, a professor of mathematics. Albert William Tucker, born in 1905 in Ontario, Canada, and best known for putting linear programming (methods of optimizing resources) on firm mathematical footing as well as co-developing the famous Prisoner's Dilemma* to help illustrate game theory, was especially respected as an effective teacher at Princeton. According to Sylvia Nasar,

> Students flocked to Dr. Tucker because of his willingness to back the more independent-minded ones. Dr. [John] von Neumann for example, disapproved of Dr. [John Forbes] Nash's approach to game theory, but Professor Tucker, unfazed by Professor von Neumann's glamour and prestige, encouraged Dr. Nash to pursue his own ideas. "He was extremely flexible as a thesis adviser and as an adviser in general," Dr. Nash said….

In 1938, Tucker gave a topology graduate course on n-dimensional manifolds which was attended by Tukey. "I had a very sharp critic in the audience, John W. Tukey," Tucker recalled. "Every time I came up with a definition of a combinatorial manifold Tukey would come up with a counterexample. The course ended in a draw."

At Princeton in the 1930s, the graduate mathematics program was very unstructured. True, there were prelims, there was an oral exam, and there ultimately was a thesis to submit, but how you prepared—how you managed to build a storehouse of knowledge sufficient to tackle the complexities of higher-level mathematics—was up to you. Certainly you had to know algebra, inside and out. And real variables. And complex variables.

---

* The Prisoner's Dilemma is this: Suppose that two criminals conspire to commit a crime but are captured by the authorities before pulling off their caper—or after, it doesn't matter. Each criminal is locked up in a separate holding cell but faces the same choice: Blame your partner or stay silent. If both criminals point the finger at each other, each is sentenced to two years in jail. If one refuses to cooperate while the other is quick to blame his partner, then the former receives a three-year sentence while the latter is set free. If both criminals don't cooperate, then each is sentenced to one year in jail.

And a bit of statistics, thrown in for good measure. For example, Tukey attended a statistics seminar run by Aurel Friedrich Wintner, who was in residence at the Institute for Advanced Study in 1937-38. But, back then, Tukey hardly knew of "the state of statistics in the [Princeton] mathematics department [as he] learned later," he recalled in a post-retirement interview, adding, "It was a difficult time." Tukey ended up teaching a statistics graduate course *before* ever actually formally taking a course in statistics; in this respect, at the time, this wasn't particularly unusual, since statistics classes, let alone statistics departments, were few and far between.

Classes run by Swiss professor H. Frederic (Henri) Bohnenblust were popular, since the student consensus was that his courses were the best. (Bohnenblust left Princeton after the war.) But there was so much self-directed freedom that there wasn't even a prescribed sequence of courses that required completion for the doctorate. So even though Solomon Lefschetz did indeed supervise many doctoral students, including Tukey, this supervision was only in the most nominal sense. The end result is what mattered, much less so the journey students took to get there.

That journey might even include so-called baby seminars. If a course wasn't being offered but was needed by students, then the graduate students themselves were implored to organize and run a seminar to help them learn the content.

Reflecting on the experience of learning mathematics, Tukey once likened the process to walking the path up a very tall mountain. He had now nearly reached the mathematical summit.

CHAPTER FIVE

Becoming a Specialist in Topology

"Topology should be an analog of modern algebra."
— John Tukey

Tukey's dissertation, defended successfully in 1939 when he was 24 years old (he was also granted an MA in mathematics as part of the deal), was titled *Denumerability in Topology*. At the time, Tukey found the topology he wrote about, such as partially ordered sets and the like, relevant and interesting to him. When he and four other students stood on the dais at graduation to receive their Ph.D.s, the president of the university, Harold W. Dodds (who had once been a professor of politics and was appointed president of the university during the Great Depression), began the time-honored ceremony by reciting in Latin. But the invocation was mistakenly for an honorary degree, rather than a doctorate of philosophy. Tukey, recognizing Dodds' error, interrupted him right in the middle of the recitation as Tukey's fellow mathematics doctorate-awardees Ralph Hartzler Fox and Fritz Joachim "Joe" Weyl looked on. Fox would go on to spend most of his career teaching at Princeton, concentrating on the topological subfield of knot theory, which was the study of classifications and permutations of mathematical knots. Weyl, the son of German mathematician Hermann Weyl, who was in residence at the Institute for Advanced Study, would rise to dean of sciences and mathematics at Hunter College as well as serving as its acting president. Both Fox and Weyl had Lefschetz as their dissertation supervisor.

Tukey's dissertation was modified and published by Princeton University Press a year later, in pamphlet form but without the third chapter (which had too much in common with the published results of mathematician Mahlon M. Day, who had been a graduate student at Brown when Tukey attended the institution), as *Convergence and Uniformity in Topology* in the *Annals of Mathematics Studies*, only adding to the slowly growing number of publications printed in refereed journals that Tukey was amassing;

he already had two—"A Note on Linear Functionals" (with Ralph Boas)* and "On the Distribution of the Fractional Part of a Statistical Variable"—before he finished his doctorate. *Convergence and Uniformity in Topology*, only the second in a series of such mathematics pamphlets, rings in at a little less than one hundred symbol-filled pages, and this *Annals* publication was not simply a carbon copy of Tukey's dissertation. (Tukey's dissertation was later reprinted in Taiwan without permission.)

In the last chapter of *Convergence and Uniformity in Topology*, entitled "Discussion," Tukey puts the symbols aside to wrestle with how, precisely, topology should be defined. "Classically, topology was sometimes defined as 'the geometry whose group is the group of all bicontinuous transformations," he begins.

> I feel that this definition is both too wide and too restricted: it uses the word "geometry," and it insists on invariance under <u>all</u> bicontinuous transformations. Thus it would include combinatorial topology and exclude any discussion of uniformity (as a part of topology).
>
> Topology should be an analog of modern algebra. Modern algebra is concerned with suitably restricted finite operations and relations. Topology should be concerned with suitably restricted infinite operations and relations.

Tukey sees topology as sufficiently abstract and general enough for its notions to be widely applicable to a number of different mathematical disciplines—especially mathematical analysis (which deals with concepts of calculus and differential equations) and topological algebra. Tukey is careful to distinguish between algebraic topology and topological algebra: in the former, "algebra is applied to topological objects," while in the latter, "topology is applied to algebraic objects."

---

* Notably, with the publication of his very first paper, Tukey's Erdös number reached two—which was the highest it would ever go. Paul Erdös was a prolific Hungarian-American mathematician who published copious numbers of mathematical papers, usually with coauthors. Erdös, who loved to travel and spoke in an idiosyncratic way (when he said "epsilon," it referred to a child; when he said "slave," it meant a husband; when he said "boss," it meant a wife), frequently took up residence with fellow mathematicians, usually just long enough to churn out yet another paper. An Erdös number represents the degree of publication separation between a mathematician and Erdös: e.g., Boas published a paper with Erdös, so Boas's Erdös number was one; anyone who published with Boas but never with Erdös directly has an Erdös number of two; and so forth. Tukey would also co-write a paper with Arthur Stone, who had an Erdös number of one, in the 1940s, but he never published with Erdös himself.

His formulation of topological uniform spaces in the dissertation, though he didn't invent the concept, were considered useful by such mathematicians as Norman Howes. And the dissertation also includes the Teichmüller-Tukey lemma,[*] sometimes shortened to the Tukey lemma or Tukey's lemma, formulated by Tukey and independently by the German mathematician Oswald Teichmüller, which states that "every nonempty collection of finite character has a maximal set with respect to inclusion," which is equivalent to the Axiom of Choice (AC).[†] The German logician Ernst Zermelo arrived at the AC in the early 1900s. The AC asks you to imagine a collection of mutually exclusive (non-overlapping) nonempty sets (i.e., sets containing at least one element of some kind); from there, select a single member from every set in the collection. Call this new set of selected members a "choice set." Zorn's lemma, named after German mathematician Max Zorn and also functionally equivalent to the AC, is explicitly connected to the AC in Tukey's thesis.

The Hungarian mathematician Paul Halmos, who coined the ubiquitous mathematical abbreviation iff (if and only if) and an accomplished mathematician—he contributed results to probability theory, mathematical logic, and Hilbert spaces,[‡] among many other sub-disciplines of mathematics, as well as joining the Institute for Advanced Study to work under John von Neumann—claimed that Tukey's thesis was one of the most influential books in topology ever written. "This is a slim volume (90 pages), but it packed a punch in its day, and I am proud to own a copy inscribed by the author [Tukey]," says Halmos—but he also amusingly notes that Tukey attempted to be culturally thoughtful by inscribing Halmos's name in a "Hungarian fashion," but he didn't quite get it right.

Halmos puts *Convergence and Uniformity in Topology* in proper context: as a "competitor to Bourbaki's approach to topology." Bourbaki refers to Nicolas Bourbaki, who was not a single mathematician but a group of them who all published under a collective pseudonym. The twentieth-century French mathematician André Weil is credited with organizing the Bourbaki group, while the Bourbaki group is noted for a wide-ranging influence on mathematics (including introducing the symbol for the empty set, $\emptyset$; Tukey warns his readers not to mistakenly pronounce $\emptyset$ as if it's the Greek letter phi rather than a Scandinavian vowel),[§] ultimately recasting

---

[*] In mathematics, a *lemma* is an intermediate proposition or statement usually used to help prove something else later on.

[†] The term "Tukey's lemma" was coined by the mathematician John Leroy Kelly in his book *General Topology* (1955).

[‡] Named after the prodigious mathematician David Hilbert, about whom we will have much to say later on.

[§] The vowel is "pronounced somewhere between 'uh' and 'urh,'" Tukey explained in *Exploratory Data Analysis* (1977).

the discipline on firmer foundations using set theory. Halmos also criticizes certain sections of *Convergence and Uniformity in Topology* as well, noting that Tukey's definition of compactness in the fourth chapter of the thesis "missed the boat." Regardless, Halmos says, Tukey "was then, and has continued to be, a colorful character whose personality and whose work have had a lot of influence" especially once Tukey left Princeton to become "one of the leaders of the statistical world."

Tukey celebrated being granted his doctorate by hosting a party at the Nassau Tavern in Princeton. But instead of serving beer, he served everybody milk.[*]

---

[*] Robert Eddy, a Tufts professor of chemistry, followed a similar path to his doctorate as Tukey's. Robert Devereux Eddy was born in Providence, Rhode Island, in 1914, earned an A.B. from Brown, and both a master's degree and a doctorate from Princeton. Eddy was also known for preferring milk to beer; he was at that celebratory party at Nassau Tavern, also handing out glasses of milk.

CHAPTER SIX

Navigating World Crisis

"At some time that winter we were told about the mathematical
methods for lion-hunting that have been devised in Göttingen,
and several of us came up with new ones."
— Frank Smithies

At Princeton's sesquicentennial celebration* in 1902, the president
of the university, Woodrow Wilson, delivered a speech that set
the tone for the institution's patriotic mission in the decades to
come. The speech was called "Princeton in the Nation's Service," and
included lines such as these: "Of course, when all is said, it is not learning
but the spirit of service that will give a college place in the public annals
of the nation." Wilson left Princeton's ranks to pursue a career in politics,
ultimately ascending to the presidency of the United States and seeing the
country through the First World War.

By the start of World War II, Tukey left behind the pure deductive
abstractions of topology in favor of bombs and bullets. He also left the
back of the classroom in favor of the front: upon graduation, Princeton
retained his talents, appointing him Henry B. Fine Instructor of Mathematics. The teaching appointment lasted from 1939 to 1941.

As a Princeton graduate student, Tukey had been drafted into what
was then informally called the "Führocracy," a "small group of people
who sat at the near end of the first table on the right as you went into the
dining hall in the graduate college [in Proctor Hall]," he explained; the
dress code for meals was strict: academic gowns worn during dinner were
de rigueur. In those halcyon interwar years, Tukey remembered, there
were

> sad Sunday evening meals when the "Green Pots" appeared; and the
> lunchtime exchange with a waiter: "chiz or frut?"—"what's the frut?"—
> "cupcake," that only a Graduate College resident of those times would
> recognize as referring to mixed fruit, from a can, over a cupcake.

---

* Celebrating the one-hundred-and-fiftieth anniversary of the institution.

Their use of the "Führocracy" moniker predated Hitler's megalomaniacal behavior on the world stage, so the word "Führer" didn't quite have the same negative connotations as it would take on several years later. Who was the "Führer" of these dining proceedings? The indomitable Lyman Spitzer, astrophysicist and theoretical physicist, who sat in the most prominent position of the dining hall table: at the end of it. As Tukey put it, "If spare ice creams needed to be divided it was his responsibility to divide them fairly."

Born in 1914 in Toledo, Ohio, Spitzer had earned his doctorate at Princeton, left for Yale University for a short time, and then returned to Princeton to head the astrophysical sciences department when he was only 33 years old. NASA credits Spitzer's research for the eventual creation and deployment of the space-borne Hubble Space Telescope, although Tukey's later work on the U-2 spy plane also helped lay a path for the technology.

The mathematician Salomon Bochner was also a part of the Führocracy, which was perhaps too ironic by half since Bochner, an Orthodox Jew, had in fact just barely escaped the grasp of the actual Führer. And there were plenty of other noteworthy mathematicians in the Führocracy—such as Frank Smithies (a functional analyst who researched integral equations with G. H. Hardy when he was at Cambridge) and Ralph Boas (he was doing postdoctoral work at Princeton as a National Research Fellow, but he left for Cambridge to work with the Russian mathematician Abram Samoilovitch Besicovitch), whom Tukey tended to socialize with the most, as well as some physicists, a theoretical chemist (Gilbert W. King, who was drawn toward statistics), and even one Romance linguist, who apparently had "permission" to place people into Klein bottles (such topological structures are akin to Möbius strips, which all have only a single side)—metaphorically, of course.

Akin to Nicolas Bourbaki, Smithies and Boas would later fashion their own working-group pseudonym: Ersatz Stanislaus Pondiczery, residing in the ghost town of Ong's Hat, New Jersey. Dizzyingly, Pondiczery published a paper called "The Mathematical Theory of Big Game Hunting" under the pseudonym H. Pétard—meaning that Pondiczery, a nonexistent mathematician, was "writing" as Pétard, another nonexistent mathematician. Smithies explained the inspiration for the strange paper this way:

> At some time that winter we were told about the mathematical methods for lion-hunting that have been devised in Göttingen, and several of us came up with new ones; who invented which method is now lost to memory. Ralph [Boas] and I decided to write up all the methods known to us, with a view to publication, conforming as closely as we could to the usual style of a mathematical paper. We choose H. Pétard as a pseu-

donym ("the engineer, hoist with his own petard"; *Hamlet*, Act III, Scene IV), and sent the paper to the *American Mathematical Monthly*, over the signature of E. S. Pondiczery.

"The Mathematical Theory of Big Game Hunting" reads like something out of *The Journal of Irreproducible Results*. Coming in at a scant two pages, Pétard's central conceit is that the eponymous Theory, which "has a singularly unifying effect on the most diverse branches of the exact sciences," hadn't been given proper attention in published literature and thus the paper is offered as a corrective. Pétard presents a set of algorithms for big game hunting that would be familiar to most working mathematicians and physicists. Restricting attention to only one habitat—the Sahara Desert—and only one animal—lions, although "methods which we shall enumerate will easily be seen to be applicable, with obvious formal modifications, to other carnivores and to other portions of the globe"—Pétard offers the reader a variety of hunting techniques classified into three categories: mathematics, theoretical physics, and experimental physics.

The mathematical techniques center on a key theme: the absurdity of applying abstract mathematical manipulations directly to real life. For instance, consider the steps one must take to perform the "Hilbert, or axiomatic, method":

> We place a locked cage at a given point in the desert. We then introduce the following logical system:
>
> Axiom I. *The class of lions in the Sahara desert is non-void.*
> Axiom II. *If there is a lion in the Sahara desert, there is a lion in the cage.*
> Rule of procedure. *If P is a theorem, and "P implies Q" is a theorem, then Q is a theorem.*
> Theorem 1. *There is a lion in the cage.*

Methods of inverse geometry, projective geometry, topology, and function theory were similarly satiric and proved equally unhelpful in hunting any sort of game at all.

Perhaps the silliest part of the paper lies in the dedication, which reads:

> The author desires to acknowledge his indebtedness to the Trivial Club of St. John's College, Cambridge, England; to the MIT chapter of the Society for Useless Research; to the F o P, of Princeton University; and to numerous individual contributors, known and unknown, conscious and unconscious.

Tukey's nephew, Francis "F. R." Anscombe, writes that Tukey had a hand in writing the Big Game article, but Tukey, in an interview, doesn't take any such responsibility; Anscombe also claims that Tukey would team with Boas and Smithies to submit other "spoof articles to serious journals"—notice the plural.

The creation of Pondiczery was designed to work toward a punchline: Ersatz Stanislaus Pondiczery was said to be from the Royal Institute of Poldavia, thereby resulting in the string of letters "ESP RIP" serving as "his" signature. As Paul Halmos explained it,

> At about the time [Nicolas] Bourbaki was starting up, another group of wags invented E. S. Pondiczery, a purported member of the Royal Institute of Poldavia. The initials (E.S.P., R.I.P.) were inspired by a projected but never written article on extra-sensory perception. Pondiczery's main work was on mathematical curiosa. His proudest accomplishment was the only known use of a second-degree pseudonym. Submitting a paper on the mathematical theory of big-game hunting to *The American Mathematical Monthly*, Pondiczery asked in a covering letter that he be allowed to sign it with a pseudonym, because of the obviously facetious nature of the material. The editor agreed, and the paper appeared (in 1938) under the name of H. Pétard.

But the "ESP RIP" punchline never was delivered in print before the jig was up.

"There was no shortage of interaction," said Tukey, reflecting on the period. For instance, Smithies, Boas, and Tukey would sit in on Aurel Friedrich Wintner's lectures on convolutions, a type of operation on mathematical functions. Wintner, born in 1903 in Budapest, Hungary, had a variety of research interests, including mathematical analysis and number theory. As the three mathematicians sat through Wintner's lectures, they would compile notes, later to be published with the "sympathetic encouragement of Cyrus McDuffie"—the only other "student" sitting through these lectures. "Tukey found himself too busy with other things," Smithies remembered, "so it fell to Ralph and me to do most of the work, though we consulted John occasionally." As a reward for a job well done, when the seminar ended later that spring McDuffie took the three mathematicians on a day trip to North Jersey.

Around the time of the Wintner lectures, Tukey was wrapping up shooting scores of film rolls centering on life at Princeton's campus, making sure to carefully index the pictures; he would end up accumulating around eighty rolls. Tukey had introduced Boas and Smithies to the "art" of "candid camera photography," Smithies wrote. "He got some good shots of [the mathematicians] [G. H.] Hardy, [John Edensor] Littlewood, [Abram Samoilovitch] Besicovitch, [Hans Arnold] Heilbronn, etc."

Tukey also found himself working side by side with Samuel "Sam" Stanley Wilks, who started at Princeton in the early 1930s. Wilks, the oldest of three brothers, was raised on a 250-acre ranch situated in a small town called Little Elm, which was near a large lake in the northeastern part of Texas. His father farmed the land. Like his parents, Sam Wilks was a Texan, through and through, and he never managed to shake a deep Texan drawl when he spoke. As a professor at Princeton, he also never missed an opportunity to travel back home to visit his family, with which he remained close. In fact, he loved his native state so much that he put himself in the running to assume the presidency of his alma mater, the University of Texas—a position he was eventually offered but reluctantly had to turn down.

At the ripe young age of twelve, Sam Wilks built himself a radio. All the more impressive, considering the year he did it: 1918. A budding interest in architecture led Wilks to become a teacher of mathematics and manual arts in a high school in Austin. But higher education came calling, with Wilks snagging a master's degree in mathematics from the University of Texas. At UT, Professor Edward Dodd steered Wilks toward probability and statistics; several years later, Wilks had a doctorate in hand from the University of Iowa. His dissertation centered on certain types of sampling distributions (i.e., all possible samples of the same size from the same host population). Wilks joined the Princeton mathematics faculty in 1933 and brought his love of multivariate statistics and statistics in general with him; he was instrumental in helping to refine the undergraduate program in mathematics as well as developing mathematical statistics courses; he even worked on standardized testing for the Educational Testing Service (ETS), which was located at Princeton. He was also involved with quality control design. But mathematics education was Wilks' passion; when statistical functionality on IBM mainframes became widely recognized, Wilks pushed to obtain the hardware for Princeton's statistical laboratory.

But Wilks encountered much resistance to the study of statistics at Princeton. Opposition came primarily from Lefschetz: he never believed that statistics was "good" mathematics, and his view wasn't particularly uncommon at the time. Perhaps no one explicitly cast aspersions on statistics, but there were persistent rumblings disrespecting the discipline. Luckily, Luther P. Eisenhart, chair of the mathematics department until 1945, was friends with Wilks and believed in him and the work he was doing; Wilks wouldn't have stayed at Princeton without Eisenhart's support. "If it hadn't been for [Eisenhart], I don't think there would have been any statistics in Princeton," Tukey reflected; late in the interwar period, the entirety of the graduate program in statistics was a Sam Wilks' yearlong course. But when Lefschetz was department chair, he would never open the coffers for Wilks' research, so hostile was he toward statistics.

Wilks, like Tukey, had personality quirks. When Wilks wanted you to do something, he wouldn't tell you directly; he would "hint around" at it, according to his former student Frederick Mosteller. "And although tea was a sacrosanct institution at Fine Hall when I was there," Mosteller added, "Wilks almost never appeared except to make an appointment with somebody or to settle something, some kind of business." Though politically conservative, Wilks was very social, with the best-known statisticians always dropping by his house at Princeton. In the early 1960s, Tukey, along with his wife, Elizabeth, threw a come-as-your-spouse party. Elizabeth dressed like John, and John like Elizabeth. Princeton faculty and students, such as David Brillinger, one of Tukey's advisees, arrived dressed as their spouses (Brillinger dressed as his future wife Lori, whom he met on a blind date).* In fact, there was probably a contest held for whichever couple was best dressed. Everyone played along nicely until the Wilkses knocked on the door: Sam didn't dress up as his wife Gena; instead, Sam simply dressed as Sam and Gena dressed as Gena.

Leo Goodman, a co-advisee of Wilks and Tukey, described Wilks as "very friendly and very fair." Goodman continued:

> He was a quiet, penetrating and influential leader in the work of many organizations, especially in mathematics, statistics and social sciences. To these organizations, he brought wisdom, commitment and persistence. He had a remarkable sense of what was important and what was not.

In 1964, when he was only 57 years of age, Wilks passed away in his sleep. Statistician Frederick Mosteller, whose doctoral advisors were Wilks and Tukey, wrote in an expansive obituary that "[a]s a mathematician, [Wilks] found the relation of the mathematical community to the sciences and the nation a matter of intense concern." Mosteller continued:

> Like von Neumann, he feared that the extreme separation of the more theoretical mathematicians from the applied ones and of the mathematical sciences from their fields of application, a noticeable trend in this country for some years, would weaken and sterilize the discipline.

Especially during the Second World War, Wilks was annoyed with those mathematicians who would squander their talents on meaningless abstrac-

---

* Brillinger relayed the details of the party to Jimmie Savage, a professor at Michigan who worked with Tukey during World War II. Quipped Savage, "I know too much Freud to do something like that."

tions instead of on useful applications; he considered such individuals unpatriotic. Tukey, having long been influenced by Wilks' emphasis on practical statistical applications and the connections between mathematics and science, served as an honorary pallbearer at Wilks' funeral. In a piece penned to memorialize his friend, Tukey called Wilks "A Quiet Contributor to Mankind," writing that "[h]is passing leaves an emptiness in so many places that one wonders how one man was so versatile and did so much."

Tukey put some of the blame for Wilks' untimely death on himself: the night before he died, Wilks and a colleague landed in some sort of confrontation centering around graduate school admissions—but Tukey wasn't there, having given a talk at an Atlantic City meteorological conference. He regretted it the rest of his life.

CHAPTER SEVEN

The War, Multiple Comparisons,
and a Seismic Shift

*"In no time at all a stout and genial genius called The Tuke, now
extremely well known as Dr. John Tukey of Bell Labs, decided
that my 'system' should be improved...."*
— Edward Canby

In a short profile published in the 1942 issue of the *American Men of
Science* biographical directory, John Tukey listed two academic interests: point set topology and analysis, mathematical fields at a far re-
move from the applied statistical work of which he would later devote his
life. What led to the shift?

With little interest in statistics before the United States' entry into
World War II, except for his compiling of statistical techniques on 3×5
index cards at the Brown University Library, Tukey did an about-face
when he joined the Princeton Branch of the Frankford Arsenal Fire Control Design Division, Fire Control Research Office (FCRO), located in a
large building at 20 Nassau Street in Princeton, New Jersey, shortly before the December 7, 1941, Japanese bombing of Pearl Harbor. Fire Control Research had nothing to do with controlling fires, as many at Princeton believed. Instead, Tukey explained, the FCRO was focused on
"boom-boom fire control, not hose fire control": calculating the trajectories of artillery and ballistics and the motions of rocket powder, working
with stereoscopic height and range finders, and improving the Boeing B-
29 Superfortress bomber as part of a project called AC-92 (the *Enola Gay*,
which dropped the atomic bomb called Little Boy on Hiroshima, Japan,
was a B-29).

When Tukey was first pulled into the FCRO, he worked on stereoscopic height and range finders. They needed to be *stereo*scopic because
human beings have two eyes; a field with a target appears differently
through a finder stereoscopically than monoscopically. These range finders had to contain reference marks that were accurate under adverse conditions; for antiaircraft fire, the height finders had automatic conversions

of range to height. Naval guns were outfitted with stereoscopic range finders. Testing the efficacy of these range finders was especially difficult, since "if you're going to test height finders and height finder observers, you have to have some way to know how high the target really is," Tukey explained years later in an interview. Rudimentary computers played a part in the analysis, too:

> And so there were recording photo-theodolites which somebody tried to keep pointing at the target. Where the image showed in the frame you could correct and get a good idea of what the angle of the target was. Then we had one of the first IBM multiplying punches and so we actually got IBM calculations of what the true heights actually were.

But their process only revealed more unknowns and raised more questions on the road to producing accurate calculations. For instance, how could temperature errors be obtained? Could the height finder be filled with helium instead of air?—that way, since the thermal conductivity (how well the substance conducts heat) of helium is roughly seven times greater than air's, testing of the device could be conducted at a reasonable height above the ground.

Range finder testing proceeded apace and expanded to other modes of transport, such as armored vehicles. Civil service personnel arrived to help; they could only be ordered around by government employees who were also technically proficient, so Tukey put his nose to the grindstone and became enough of a technical expert to supervise some of the civil service personnel.

At the time Tukey joined the FCRO, it fell under the supervision of the accomplished West Point graduate and MIT-educated Lieutenant colonel Gervais W. Trichel. But Trichel got transferred to a Washington assignment: ordinance department, chief of rocket development. The FCRO then, for a brief time, turned its attention to testing rocket powder until pivoting to the project that would keep them occupied for the rest of the war: improving the B-29 Superfortress bomber.

Chemist Henry Eyring—who, recall, was upset that Tukey had been "stolen away from chemistry"—worked on the B-29, as did the MIT mathematics professor Irving Segal. Code-named the AC-92 project, "which was trying to do all the fixes on the B-29 as an operational device that they could," it afforded Tukey the opportunity to learn to fly airplanes as a member of the coordinating group. Tukey's work on the B-29 primarily involved statistical robustness, the development of statistical methods that still perform well despite not satisfying certain statistical assumptions. (Statistician Frank Anscombe, who was married to Tukey's wife's sister, thought of robustness as a kind of insurance policy, where a payment is made in advance to insure against the possibility of things not working out as anticipated.) Specifically, Tukey was examining predictions made of machine gun fire emanating from the bomber, although he was fairly tight-lipped about the details of his classified war work for the rest of his life.

Nevertheless, Tukey may have left some breadcrumbs in a 1977 book he co-wrote with Mosteller, called *Data Analysis and Regression: A Second Course in Statistics*, under the guise of an ostensibly fictitious example. They begin their example by setting the scene: "During World War II, in investigating aiming errors made during bomber flights over Europe, one of the research organizations developed a regression equation with several carriers (explanatories)." In other words, an equation to accurately model and predict aiming errors was generated; the values of various variables were fed into this equation in order to make the prediction: "Among its nine or so carriers were altitude, type of aircraft, speed of the bombing group, size of the group, and the amount of fighter opposition." Tukey and Mosteller go on to discuss how altitude and speed affect aiming errors as well as fighter opposition (unsurprisingly, there is an inverse relationship between the amount of opposition and the aiming error), even though the fighter opposition "carrier" was merely a "proxy" term in the equation for the degree of cloud cover—and, of course, the more cloud cover, the greater the aiming error.

Whether *Data Analysis and Regression* provided a gateway into Tukey's classified wartime assignments or was simply the creative flourishes of overactive imaginations, the B-29 work triggered in Tukey a lifelong interest in robustness problems; though he would write quite a bit on the topic—including unpublished papers, of which there were some on nearly every statistics subfield—there is no set of "collected works" on Tukey's contributions to robustness available, only some loose strands of organization of the content detailed by the Swiss statistician Peter J. Huber, who worked directly with Tukey during a stint as a visiting professor at Princeton in the early 1970s.

Fortress (Fort) Monroe in Virginia served as the "field laboratory" of sorts for the FCRO. Brockway "Brock" McMillan, who had a doctorate from MIT supervised by Norbert Wiener (often referred to as the father of cybernetics) and briefly worked alongside Tukey at Fine Hall (he was roughly a year ahead of Tukey as a postdoc), joined the Navy and was instrumental in the weapons'-testing work done at Fort Monroe. Born in Minneapolis, Minnesota, in 1915, McMillan, the only child of a civil engineer and a schoolteacher, would go on to have a distinguished career after the war, working with Tukey in the Mathematical Research Group at the

Murray Hill campus of Bell Labs (concentrating in information theory) and for the United States military doing research.

Paul Dwyer also made his home at Fort Monroe for a time; he was in charge of the computing center. Dwyer, born in 1901 in Chester, Pennsylvania, earned his doctorate at the University of Michigan in 1936, and produced work on mathematical statistics through the remainder of his career as a professor at the same institution. During the war, Dwyer became an expert at using an IBM "multiplying punch" punched-card computer; the machine was particularly fickle when performing arithmetic operations, but Dwyer and his team managed to compel the primitive computer to calculate interest rates and mortgage payments as well as war-related computations (e.g., targeting positions).

At the FCRO, Tukey worked with newly christened statistician George W. Brown. Born in Boston, Massachusetts, in 1917, Brown obtained a mathematics degree from Harvard before earning a doctorate from Princeton in 1940 under Wilks. However, as statistician Alexander M. Mood (who also worked with Tukey at the FCRO) later wrote, "That prestigious degree did not bring [Brown] an academic position as he desired, doubtless because institutions of higher education were badly infected with anti-Semitism at that time." So, Brown instead found employment at a department store; he completed statistical analyses of Macy's operations before Princeton came calling during the war. After the war ended, Brown stayed at Princeton in order to build the computer that John von Neumann had conceived, and then transitioned to Iowa State University, where he quickly rose to the position of full professor of mathematics. But Brown's skills were in high demand by both the RAND Corporation and IBM because of his background with computers, so he tendered his resignation from academia to join RAND. (Tukey would later serve as a part-time consultant to the RAND Corporation, which originally began as a project of the Air Force immediately following the Second World War; RAND later attracted top mathematicians from around the world, including John Nash, who, while at RAND, once wrote a question for Tukey to answer. Tukey had earlier, in 1950, served as the second reader for Nash's doctoral thesis on game theory—after first reader Albert Tucker, who submitted a glowing written evaluation of the thesis.)

Tukey also worked with Wilfrid "Will" Dixon at the FCRO. He became fast friends with Will Dixon—a prolific statistician who, after the war, left the University of Oregon to establish UCLA's Biostatistics Division of the School of Public Health—a friendship that lasted the rest of their lives.

But it was Charles Winsor, whom Tukey would quickly befriend at the FCRO, who made the biggest impact on Tukey's professional life.

Charles Paine Winsor, born in 1895 in Boston, Massachusetts, and possessing a similar New England sensibility to Tukey's, is perhaps best known for the process of *Winsorization*, which is a data analysis procedure that serves to smooth out the extremes of a data set by replacing outliers with limiting percentile values. As justified by Tukey, "While the numerical value of an apparently wild observation is untrustworthy, the direction of its deviation (e.g. high or low) is worthy of attention."

Charles Winsor didn't start out in statistics, but rather arrived at the discipline via the circuitous route of an unconventional education. After serving in the Great War as an underage ambulance driver, he arrived at Harvard all set to study engineering. But he was steered away from engineering and toward biology because of his work with Raymond Pearl.

Pearl was born in Farmington, New Hampshire, in 1879. Arriving at Dartmouth College at the tender age of 16, Pearl anticipated studying the classics but instead developed an overriding interest in biology (avocationally, he pursued music). He next obtained degrees from the University of Michigan in biology and zoology and was appointed an instructor at Michigan. In the early 1900s, Pearl would work with the statistician Karl Pearson in London on statistical applications to biology. Although Pearl—along with Pearson—became the associate editor of one of the most storied statistics journals, *Biometrika*, Pearl and Pearson had a falling out by 1910, and their work together discontinued. Pearl journeyed back to the U.S., ultimately landing at Johns Hopkins as a professor of biometry (a precursor to biostatistics) and vital statistics.

Winsor had an opportunity to work with Pearl on biometry, which linked together biology and statistics. Winsor's 1935 Harvard doctoral dissertation was entitled *The Relations of Density of Population to Growth and Reproduction in Pond Snails of the Genus Lymnaea*—which centered on the disciplines of physiology and biology as a whole, not statistics. "Winsor was a Harvard engineer," explained David Brillinger, "but because of his Ph.D. in physiology he was known as an 'engineer-turned-physiologist-turned-statistician.'"

In the foreword to a volume of *The Collected Works of John W. Tukey*, Tukey—who was two decades younger than his mentor—writes of Winsor's considerable influence:

> There [at the FCRO] I met Charles P. Winsor, who taught me much about statistics not known then in books or other literature. It was Charlie, and the experience of working on real data, that converted me to statistics. By the end of late 1945, I was a statistician rather than a topologist.

"Charlie knew an awful lot of statistics that wasn't in the books then, and I am sure a certain amount that isn't in the books yet," Tukey added in a

1995 interview. "So I learned by talking to Charlie and by doing things and by reading," coupled with lots of "Practice!" Winsor also taught Tukey to "beware of extreme deviates, and, in particular, to beware of using them with high weights," Tukey recalled, because "[u]sing second moments to assess variability means giving very high weights to extremely deviant observations." (Moments describe the location and variability of statistical distributions: the mean is the first statistical moment, while the variance is the second.) These "extreme deviates" might have an impact on the efficiency of estimators that target population values, such as the mean (the center of the data), standard deviation (roughly, the average distance of all the data points to the mean of the data set), or variance (the standard deviation squared).

They worked together for most of the war, Tukey spending countless hours over the course of four years with both Charlie and Agnes Winsor, during meals (he ate "an average of 1.9 meals a day" with him, Tukey said) and at all times of the day and night, except for a spell in which the Winsors traveled to Washington—which Tukey retrospectively classified as a "wasted year and a half"—so that Charlie could work in the Mine Warfare Research group. The two worked together so closely during the war that Tukey once said they were "in double harness," which is an informal Americanism meaning married.

In addition to his real-data approach to statistics, perhaps simply seeing Winsor, who had joined the FCRO only months before Tukey, have his hand in so many disciplines inspired Tukey to later avoid the common trap of the academic: that of too-narrow specialization. "The best thing about being a statistician," Tukey said, "is that you get to play in everyone's backyard," since statisticians need to be so well rounded: they must understand statistics, of course, but they also need to be versed in the discipline the statistics is being applied to. According to Tukey, "Most statisticians are used to winning arguments with subject-matter colleagues because they know *both* statistics and the subject matter." For example, at Bell Labs Tukey had a hand in developing the Sound Surveillance System (SOTUS), which was an expensive set of hydrophone arrays installed underwater in the Atlantic and Pacific oceans that could track submarines. Tukey made sure to understand, in depth, the underlying physics of the procedure before working through the mathematics. In the decades to come, SOTUS was improved greatly from the analytic end with the arrival of the fast Fourier transform algorithm, of which Tukey was primarily responsible. Knowing both statistics and the subject matter also resulted in Tukey pulling together experts from seemingly unrelated fields to solve a common problem—a kind of "matchmaking" that increased the store of human knowledge. As epidemiologist Alvan R. Feinstein tells it:

The variable-interval life-table method was created as a result of some "matchmaking" by John Tukey. Knowing about a common interest in time-to-failure events, he brought together workers in two different fields. The workers were Edward L. Kaplan, then at Bell Laboratories, who was studying the "survival" time of vacuum tubes, and Paul Meier, then a biostatistician at Johns Hopkins Medical School, who was interested in analyzing post-therapeutic human survival.

Having a deep familiarity with the subject matter was especially critical when performing statistical simulations. "[T]o be a good user of mathematics in almost any field, one must have some of the 'feel' for the subject matter that is essential if simulation is to be at all safe," Tukey explained. "One must understand something of which aspects of the real situation can be neglected with the least loss of guidance from the behavior of the resulting model."

The SOTUS wasn't the first time that Tukey was involved in audio-related optimization. Decades earlier, he had run into Edward Canby at the Princeton Graduate School in the middle 1930s. Edward Tatnall Canby, born in New Haven, Connecticut, in 1912, was a music writer and choral director who became a specialist in Baroque and Renaissance music. "Finally, by a fluke, I ended up of all places at the math and physics table," Canby recalled. He was surprised at how easily the conversation flowed between him and others at the table. "These people liked music," he immediately realized. Even Einstein, who lived nearby, enjoyed plucking the fiddle. (Canby once nearly ran over the physicist while riding his bicycle.)

Canby encountered a mathematician who would help him approach problems in a new way:

> In no time at all a stout and genial genius called The Tuke, now extremely well known as Dr. John Tukey of Bell Labs, decided that my "system" should be improved—first via a baffle. A baffle, of course, he explained, kept the incurring bass sound waves apart so they didn't cancel out, and the larger the baffle the more effective it would be, i.e., the lower the true bass.

Canby went back to the drawing board, but Tukey did more than just suggest solutions to him—he was actively involved in bring the suggestions to life.

> It was Dr. John Tukey, The Tuke, who persuaded me to try to build my own separate amplifier, of course under his tutelage. By now, the 16-tube radio-and-amplifier was considered a bit passé by the folks I had come to know. What I needed was beam power and push-pull. So I got the nec-

essary parts and started to build, with The Tuke practically hovering over my shoulder.

Despite his seemingly hands-on approach with Canby's amplifier, Tukey cautioned not to take things too far or get too involved with the sources of his data: "The stronger the qualitative understanding the *data analyst* can get of the subject matter field from which his data come, the better—just so long as he does not take it too seriously." Many decades later, Tukey also urged his fellow statisticians to avoid the plague of hubris and unwarranted pride that attends to those who believe that all of the world's problems can be solved courtesy of a lot of data coupled with a generalist's statistician's mindset: "we can help people in many fields, although what we can do is limited," he wrote. And there was another issue he urged his peers to consider: "Difficulties in identifying problems have delayed statistics far more than difficulties in solving problems."[*]

It was in 1944 that Tukey published his first statistics-themed paper— what Tukey more precisely termed a "quasistatistical paper"—which was probabilistic in nature. Called "A Formula for Sample Sizes for Population Tolerance Limits," Tukey is listed as the coauthor along with Henry Scheffé, who was born in 1907 in New York City, New York. Scheffé was the son of German parents, who immigrated to the United States in the early 1900s. Although not interested in mathematics at first, as a young undergrad Scheffé attended the University of Wisconsin-Madison and enrolled in many pure mathematics courses but in only one statistics course. Scheffé stayed at the University of Wisconsin-Madison for graduate and doctoral studies, earning a Ph.D. from the institution in 1935. He then became a journeyman, traveling from university to university to research and teach, until landing at Princeton under Sam Wilks in 1941. By then Scheffé had transitioned to statistics, believing that he could make a more significant contribution where much of the mathematical territory hadn't yet been staked out (Scheffé had, at this point, realized that some of his thesis work he had believed was original had in fact been previously discovered by the mathematician Carl Friedrich Gauss centuries before).[†]

Scheffé collaborated with several statisticians at Princeton, including, eventually, Tukey, with whom he would write two papers in rapid succes-

---

[*] The quotation comes from a 1954 paper titled "Unsolved Problems of Experimental Statistics," in which Tukey sets forth 51 "provocative questions" in statistics to chew on.

[†] Gauss "pre-discovered" much of modern mathematics, such as non-Euclidean geometry; there are several additional examples relating to statistics later on in this book.

sion. Their first paper, only a single page in length, whets the appetite for more:

> In a paper to appear in a later issue of this journal [*The Annals of Mathematical Statistics*] dealing with various results on non-parametric [i.e., distribution-free] estimation, we shall discuss in detail an approximate formula for the numerical calculate of sample sizes for Wilks' population tolerance limits....

Tukey summarized the paper this way: "[it's] a very short note on sample sizes for population tolerance limits." By the time their second paper—"Non-Parametric Estimation. I. Validation of Order Statistics," detailing estimation methods, such as confidence intervals and confidence bands, not requiring the assumption of a specific underlying population distribution—was published in 1945, Scheffé had left Princeton for a mathematics assistant professorship at Syracuse University. Though that second paper was to be their last direct collaboration, an unpublished Tukey discovery would lead to a statistical method for which Scheffé became best known: the Scheffé test.

The idea of multiple comparisons—also called simultaneous inference—involves "making multiple inferences from a single set of data as well as the appropriate interpretation and use of the results," according to Yoav Benjamini and Henry Braun. The "problem" is one of multiplicity: How can we perform multiple statistical tests while controlling for the fact that some of these tests will result in finding statistical significance purely by chance alone? Benjamini and Braun continue:

> Though not always explicitly recognized, the problem occurs widely and often. The proper treatment of multiplicity, which should take into account "the tradeoff between extracting belief from data and payment of error" [Tukey (1991)], is regarded by many as a critical component in a disciplined program of scientific research.

> While the issue of multiplicity was recognized by some investigators long ago, efforts to grapple with the problem were rather scattered until the post-WWII era. John Tukey is rightly considered one of the pioneers of the field.

Benjamini and Braun point to Tukey's 300-page manuscript "The Problem of Multiple Comparisons" (PMC), written over the course of several years (from 1950 or 1951 to 1953), as a "magisterial" work that "did much to shape the philosophy, mathematical development and practical applications of simultaneous inference." They claim that PMC was not only the first time the topic was addressed in considerable depth, but also that the paper established the framework that continues to guide the research and applications of the field decades later, adding, "No other work or writer has had comparable influence."

But here's the kicker: PMC was only available by request, as a mimeographed paper; it was never published. In fact, Tukey didn't publish on multiple comparisons until much later in his career. It was Walter A. Shewhart, one of the first statisticians hired at Bell Labs, who urged Tukey not to publish PMC until such time as Tukey was completely comfortable with the ideas and the approach. Though Tukey later won the American Society for Quality Shewhart Medal for leadership in quality control related to advances in acceptance sampling, he came to regret taking Shewhart's advice—the only time, Tukey felt, Shewhart had given him poor advice.

Tukey, in PMC, wrongly downplayed the significance of his work, thinking it only a restatement of conventional wisdom. He did much in PMC: expressed an inclination toward using confidence intervals (interval estimates of population values) rather than significance tests[*] wherever possible; demonstrated the consequences of ignoring the multiplicity problem when performing scientific studies; demarcated statistical issues arising from different types of scientific investigations (calling these "for the moment" and "for the record"); expressed fruitful ways of accounting and guidelines for controlling multiplicity in a wide variety of circumstances; introduced the *post hoc Wholly Significant Difference* (WSD) procedure, of which the *post hoc Honest Significant Difference* (HSD) test is an outgrowth and extension, designed to perform pairwise comparisons in order to detect any pairwise differences (if they exist); and posed questions and suggestions for future study, such as verifying the so-called Tukey's Conjecture (the partial verification of which ultimately resulted in the Tukey-Kramer procedure—another name for the aforementioned HSD).

In their comprehensive essay tracing the historical development of multiple comparisons, Benjamini and Braun describe how Tukey's work on the topic had two fervent periods: 1947 to 1953 and 1990 to 2000, although in between these periods of activity he never strayed too far from multiple comparisons, usually not missing any opportunity to have healthy debates with the likes of Henry Scheffé and statistician David B. Duncan (who developed the multiple range test). Tukey went back and forth with Scheffé on an abstract mathematical concept called F-projections (their debate was between the utility of the F versus the Stu-

---

[*] The former is a "quantitative conclusion procedure," while the latter is a "qualitative conclusion procedure"; Tukey says that confusion arises when using qualitative conclusion procedures, since decisions and conclusions become inextricably linked, as Lyle Jones summarized it in the third volume of the *Collected Works*.

dentized range statistics) as well as with Duncan on controlling the multiplicity error rate.

Scheffé developed the eponymous Scheffé test, a powerful multiple comparisons test set in opposition to Tukey's HSD. As David C. Howell, emeritus professor at the University of Vermont, explains, "Like much else in statistics, [the Scheffé test] all started with John Tukey." Howell continues:

> In a series of oral presentations beginning in about 1950 and culminating in what might be the most cited unpublished manuscript in statistics [i.e., PMC], Tukey developed the concept of error rates, focusing on the per comparison and familywise rates. Scheffé developed his procedure at the time that Tukey was speaking about his own ideas on multiplicity and, in a footnote to his paper, Scheffé explicitly gave credit to Tukey for the familywise error rate concept that was the basis for his test.

Benjamini and Braun also describe how PMC presages Tukey's later statistical work in a number of areas, such as data analysis, graphics, robustness, and sensitivity curves. But PMC also, they explain, lays the groundwork for Tukey's philosophical approaches toward statistics, namely, the importance of the practicality of results, the value of a scientific approach toward the analysis of data, and the recognition that mathematics, in and of itself, is not a panacea for every real-world problem.

Tukey's interest in simultaneous inference would again be piqued, this time late in his career, with the publication of a paper in *Science* on multiplicity in 1977, a chapter about stepwise multiple testing in a statistics volume, a speech about multiple comparisons (he delivered the Rupert G. Miller Memorial Lecture in 1989), and a flurry of publications about multiple comparisons in the final decade of his life. For instance, significant—quite literally—is Tukey's admonition, in his 1991 paper "The Philosophy of Multiple Comparisons" (reworked from his Miller Memorial Lecture), that cut to the heart of the systemic issues with significance testing—of testing a hypothesis about a population parameter or parameters based on collected sample data: "[s]tatisticians classically asked the wrong question—and were willing to answer with a lie, one that was often a downright lie." Namely, if we're only looking to see if the effects of A and B are different, taken to some decimal place, everything is different; the world is a fuzzy, imprecise place. "Thus asking, 'Are the effects different?' is foolish," he explained. Instead, we should be concerned with the direction of the difference of the effects between A and B, which is an ipso facto endorsement of confidence intervals in place of traditional hypothesis testing:

What we should be answering first is "Can we tell the direction in which the effects of *A* differ from the effects of *B*?" In other words, can we be confident about the direction from *A* to *B*? Is it "up," "down" or "uncertain"?

The third answer to this first question is that we are "uncertain about the direction"—it is not, and never should be, that we "accept the null hypothesis."

The null hypothesis is a best-guess statement about the value of a population parameter; it is an assertion of the parameter's value presupposing that there's "no effect" or "no difference" or that the status quo is maintained in some fashion. The mathematician Ronald Fisher, whom many point to as the father of significance testing, declared that the null hypothesis "is never proved or established, but is possibly disproved, in the course of experimentation. Every experiment may be said to exist only in order to give the facts a chance of disproving the null hypothesis." Every null hypothesis must be paired with an alternative hypothesis, which usually represents a "claim" about the population parameter; implicit in any alternative hypothesis is that there is some sort of "effect" present to be contrasted with the "no effect" bulwark of the null. From the sample data, a *p*-value (probability value) is calculated to help settle the thorny question of every hypothesis test: Is the alternative hypothesis more likely to be true than false? If we obtain a small *p*-value, there is stronger evidence for the alternative than for the null, so we "reject" the null hypothesis; if the *p*-value is large, we have little evidence to support the alternative in favor of the null, so we "fail to reject" the null hypothesis (but we do not "accept" the null). The *p*-value itself is an expression of the likeliness or unlikeliness of observing the sample results by chance alone if in fact the null hypothesis is true.

Why do we "fail to reject" the null, rather than "accepting" the null? Fisher said, "For the logical fallacy of believing that a hypothesis has been proved to be true, merely because it is not contradicted by the available facts, has no more right to insinuate itself in statistical than in other kinds of scientific reasoning…." He also said that the null hypothesis "is never proved or established, but is possibly disproved, in the course of experimentation. Every experiment may be said to exist only in order to give the facts a chance of disproving the null hypothesis." This connects to what Karl Popper, the philosopher of science, wrote about the scientific method: "A scientific idea can never be proven true, because no matter how many observations seem to agree with it, it may still be wrong." Thus, science advances, in part, by offering up conjectures and testing to see whether they survive "falsification." No amount of confirming evidence can ever definitively prove a scientific theory to be true; that's why the qualifier term "theory" is appended even to evidence-rich scientific frameworks such as gravity and evolution. Not every theory, however, can be subjected to falsification. For instance, a number of psychological theories fail the test simply because no empirical evidence can be brought forth to disprove them. As philosopher Daniel Klein writes, "For example, no matter what evidence was put before Freud—a patient who avowedly loved his mother, one who hated his mother, and one who said he was indifferent to his mother," Freud simply claimed that "each of these patients was...displaying a different manifestation of the Oedipus complex." The Oedipus complex couldn't be proven false, but it couldn't be proven true, ether.

Tukey, who viewed statistical reasoning as intimately tied up with the scientific method, cautioned his readers never to "accept the null hypothesis." (Tukey informally conducted this sort of hedging in everyday conversation as well: if he didn't have enough information to refute someone's claim, he might say something along the lines of his not being able to refute a "loud negative.") He also implored his readers to be careful with data collection—whether through sampling techniques or via experimental design—as well as arriving at a formal error rate that makes sense (i.e., the higher the confidence level, the wider the interval—and the less the chance of not capturing the parameter), such as Fisher's standard significance level of five percent. Fisher justified this error rate in a 1929 article published in the *Proceedings of the Society for Psychical Research.**

> In the investigation of living being by biological methods, statistical tests of significance are essential. Their function is to prevent us from being deceived by accidental occurrences, due not to the causes we wish to study, or are trying to detect, but to a combination of many other circumstances which we cannot control.† An observation is judged significant, if it would rarely have been produced, in the absence of a real cause of the kind we are seeking. It is common practice to judge a result significant, if it is of such a magnitude that it would have been produced by chance not more frequently than once in twenty trials [i.e., five percent of the time]. This is an arbitrary, but convenient, level of significance for the practical investigator, but it does not mean that he allows himself to be deceived once in every twenty experiments. The test of significance

---

* As quoted in *The Lady Tasting Tea: How Statistics Revolutionized Science in the Twentieth Century* (2002) by David Salsburg. The Society for Psychical Research is an organization, located in the United Kingdom, with the express purpose of investigating the paranormal.
† Tukey makes the same point in his 1977 magnum opus, *Exploratory Data Analysis*: like with crimes, whose circumstances can be largely accidental, the patterns in data can be the result of pure happenstance or serendipity.

only tells him what to ignore, namely all experiments in which significant results are not obtained.

Statisticians Jerzy Neyman and Egon Pearson, the son of Karl Pearson, further codified Fisher's idea of a significance level, a cutoff through which the statistician could arrive at a preprogrammed decision about the data at hand; the significance level of five percent wasn't necessarily set in stone. (Neyman and Pearson had coined the terms "null hypothesis" and "alternative hypothesis" as well as systemizing the overarching structure of hypothesis testing.) For his part, Tukey wasn't necessarily sold with the "5%, 1%, and the like," as he labeled it. He objected to the regimented nature of significance testing, noting "that one should expect mathematics to provide, not a single best procedure, but rather an assortment of good procedures (e.g., a complete class of admissible procedures) from which judgments and insight into a particular instance…must be used to select the 'best' procedure." Tukey was especially perturbed at the "classical fallacy of significance testing": "The significance level tells you the probability that your result is WRONG," rather than the chance of incorrectly rejecting the null hypothesis when the null hypothesis is in fact true. And, finally, Tukey was frustrated by a misunderstanding of Fisher's five percent level. "The modern test of significance…owes more to R. A. Fisher than to any other man," Tukey admitted. "Yet Sir Ronald's standard of firm knowledge was not one extremely significant result, but rather the ability to repeatedly get results significant at 5%." In other words, the results should be—as it's called in science—reproducible.

Ronald Fisher was especially interested in questions of epistemology—in where our knowledge comes from, in how we know what we know—and he was therefore strongly in favor of replication whenever possible, of repeating the same experiment to minimize the chances of incorrectly concluding statistical significance (or the reverse). Multiple experiments all showing statistical significance at a particular threshold gives the researcher much more evidence in favor of a claim than only a single experiment does—even if the p-value of that single experiment is extraordinarily low, ostensibly indicating that the chances of seeing the sample result by chance alone aren't particularly high.

It costs "coin" to buy knowledge through the chance of error, Tukey wrote, and statisticians need to spend that coin wisely: extra "knowledge" or "belief" comes at the cost of a higher degree of possible error.* There-

---

* Some error, such that comes as a result of poor data collection methods or experimentation techniques, may be out of the statistician's control, and no amount of statistical manipulation can overcome bad data. Think of the aphorism "garbage in, garbage out": if data are collected poorly, then the results obtained from these data aren't likely to bear fruit. In addition, in "The Phi-

fore, Tukey said, a follow-up question must be asked: What "are we confident of concerning the numerical difference [of] effect of A MINUS effect of B," which he rewrites mathematically as $A - B$. Thus, by using interval estimation to obtain information about the degree of difference between A and B, confidence intervals offer the researcher more conclusive information about the population parameter than simply testing a hypothesis in a binary fashion. Tukey compared these binary oppositions (reject or fail to reject the null) to painting only with black or white, unlike confidence intervals, in which one was able to paint in shades of gray.

Tukey went further with confidence intervals than Jerzy Neyman's formulation—Neyman developed confidence intervals in 1934, but the first such interval estimates date back hundreds of years to the work of mathematician Nicolaus Bernoulli—specifically, as Benjamini and Braun point out, by examining the lower and upper bounds in a unique manner. For instance, Tukey further delineated the possibilities for direction, noting that a confidence interval like (–1, 1) is classified as "direction uncertain" whereas an interval like (–1, 100) needs more than the moniker "direction uncertain": "direction uncertain, but plausibly positive" recognizes the magnitude of these endpoints as conveying meaningful information. Furthermore, because Tukey paid attention to the direction of the effects between A and B rather than if A and B were simply different, the traditional errors arising from hypothesis testing—i.e., the Type I error (rejecting a true null hypothesis) and the Type II error (failing to reject a false null hypothesis)—no longer made sense; errors could only be committed in misstating the direction of the differences.

Though the Second World War came to a close, Tukey didn't stop engaging in real-world national-defense projects. In addition to codebreaking (which he engaged in during the war as well), Tukey helped to get the Nike, a surface-to-air antiaircraft guided missile named after the winged goddess of victory in Greek mythology, off the ground. Tukey would travel to "impact parties" or "boondocks expeditions" at the White Sands Proving Grounds in New Mexico, in which he and others would sit around a table with diminutive collection boxes, and, after some missile launches, collect pieces of artillery that had fallen. At Bell Labs, he worked on the paper-and-pencil study for the Nike with a distant cousin of his (somehow, Tukey calculated him to be a ninth-and-a-half cousin): Bernie Holbrook. Holbrook was a switching engineer for the Nike-Ajax project, originally called the Anti-Aircraft Guided Missile 1 (AAGM1);

---

losophy of Multiple Comparisons," Tukey presents three different ways to define the "error rate," which further muddies the waters.

Tukey served as the resident "computer topologist." Together, they calculated trajectories and aerodynamics of the warhead, despite the sorry state (at the time) of the mathematics behind flight at supersonic speeds (some faulty predictions had controls working in opposite directions when speeds reached a certain value, which was somewhere around Mach of the square root of three). They were focused on answering one question: What path could the missile take to both be as far away as possible from its point of origin yet still have sufficient maneuverability? To answer the question, Tukey and Holbrook traveled to Langley, Virginia, to gather more data using wind tunnels, but the mathematics behind the process weren't yet fully developed. Tukey tried to perform integration on some sets of the coupled equations, except the results weren't favorable. So, their work had to be done more empirically than theoretically, by looking at what had been done before and making adjustments and tweaks; to that end, they employed "ladies turning hand calculators who were doing the differential equation integration." "[R]eal problems deserve realistic attention," Tukey later preached. "Which implies it's better to have an approximate solution to the right problem than to have an exact solution to the wrong one."

Tukey devoted his first six months on the Nike project to drawing up a proposal, called "A Study of an Antiaircraft Guided Missile System," and written with Hendrik Bode, Walter McNair, G. N. Thayer, and Holbrook; the next several months would see the Nike's development transition to Bell Labs. All told, Tukey worked on the Nike project for about a year; post-Winsor, his statistical intuition, of which he would come to be renowned, was starting to take shape. He was beginning to view statistics as a sort of dance, a negotiation in which there was give-and-take. "[T]here is always a *quid pro quo* in statistics," and with that understanding came questions that he would model answers to in his head: If the underlying distribution were taken to be normal, how does that affect the statistical power? What about allowing for the possibility of kurtosis—how did that change things?

Radically changed, though, was Tukey's academic focus since the start of the war. Recall that the concise profile issued for the 1942 *American Men of Science* biographical directory hadn't even mentioned statistics underneath Tukey's name. By the 1948 issue, however, his interests had undergone a seismic shift: although point set topology was still listed, there was now military analysis, fire control equipment, and mathematical and applied statistics listed as well. He had transformed into an active member of the statistics establishment, with his election in '48 as the Central New Jersey Representative of the American Statistical Association (ASA)—an organization he would become vice president of less than a decade later—only representing the tip of the iceberg.

PART TWO

Working as a Statistician

CHAPTER EIGHT

A Finger in Every Pie

"There is no great man here. We are ordinary people."
— Elizabeth Tukey

In 1946 Princeton held its bicentennial, with Tukey designated as a reporter for the proceedings. By that point, he had been promoted to Assistant Professor of Mathematics, serving in that position from 1941 to 1948—largely thanks to Wilks urging Tukey to return to Princeton on a part-time basis once he had dispensed with the Nike project. Tukey recorded various bits and interviews for the Princeton bicentennial, hearing what his voice sounded like on the radio for the first time.

Tukey didn't stay an assistant professor for long; many people were beginning to take note of his keen intellect and his prodigious talents. In 1947, he was up for and received a promotion to Associate Professor of Mathematics. The American-Croatian mathematician William Feller submitted a recommendation letter in support of the promotion that read, in part,

> [Tukey] is rich in ideas, has a fifth sense for new possibilities, and develops an infinite amount of energy. He works almost at the same time on supersonic flow, computing machines, theoretical statistics and special biometrical problems. The main value of his papers lie in the lucid exposition, and in the ease with which Tukey popularizes new ideas and combines methods and results from different fields.[*]

With the Cold War heating up in the middle of the twentieth century, Tukey would need to put his "fifth sense" to good use as nuclear weapons' testing proliferated, their use against civilian populations appearing increasingly likely. To help staunch that seeming eventuality, nuclear test ban treaties were negotiated in 1958 in Geneva, Switzerland, at the Con-

---

[*] Quoted by Brillinger in "John W. Tukey: His Life and Professional Contributions," but taken from a "Personal communication" between Brillinger and F. R. Anscombe (Tukey's nephew).

ference on Discontinuance of Nuclear Weapons Tests. In order to ensure a country's compliance, though, scientists had to have some way of differentiating between seismic events caused by earthquakes and those precipitated by atomic blasts (underground or not),[*] so the U.S. created the Panel on Seismic Improvement for just that purpose—and Tukey was instrumental in devising methods for fruitfully examining the time series data of seismograms for underground weapons' detonation, starting in the very late 1950s, although he also believed that nuclear tests could be "masked" somewhat. ("Time series analysis," Tukey wrote, "consists of all the techniques that, when applied to time series data, yield, at least sometimes, either insight or knowledge, AND everything that helps us choose or understand these procedures.") Tukey was then part of a team, with Bell Labs' James Fisk at the helm and which also included the physicist Hans Bethe, that had a key mission: the elimination of all underground nuclear testing. In 1959, Tukey was even made a United States delegate to Technical Working Group 2 of the Geneva Conference in Switzerland on the Discontinuance of Nuclear Weapons Tests, which led to him spending a month in Switzerland; that same year, he also helped to write the paper "Equalization and Pulse Shaping Techniques Applied to the Determination of Initial Sense of Rayleigh Waves," which detailed the process of differentiating between a seismic event due to an explosion and an earthquake. But the high stakes made this work among the most stressful of Tukey's life, since, he felt, slippery politicians implicitly shifted the responsibilities of "[settling] some of the questions that the politicians could not" to the scientists, who, even with Tukey's brainpower, couldn't fully work through the technical details.

By this point, Tukey had been married for more than a decade, and Elizabeth was very concerned about her husband's health. Elizabeth Louise Rapp was born on March 2, 1920, in Ocean City, New Jersey, to Orpha Elizabeth Kelly Rapp and Jesse Rossiter Rapp, a graduate of Pennsylvania State University (class of 1915). She had one sibling, a sister named Phyllis. The Rapps were a very "conventional family," according to Elizabeth. Her parents were devoted members of the local Episcopal church. Her mother descended from a "pioneer family" that first set down its roots in Virginia two centuries earlier; they were forced to fend for themselves, to establish their own traditions, to build their own lives, to be independent—similarly to the pioneers who established colonies in

---

[*] Aboveground nuclear testing wasn't as much of a challenge to detect, since, for example, atmospheric air samples could be obtained for the detection of uranium fission (Tony Turkevitch, a physical chemist, thought of this method).

New England. Her grandparents were Baptists. "[T]here was a lot of eccentricity in my family," she remembered.

Still a teenager, Elizabeth moved to Pennsylvania in order to attend Temple University. She ultimately graduated in 1944 from Radcliffe College in Massachusetts, having been awarded valedictorian honors in business administration. There, she became acclimated to the peculiar mores of New Englanders, finding herself simpatico. After working for a time at Wellesley College and attending graduate school at Harvard, Elizabeth moved to Princeton after being hired for a job at the Educational Testing Service (ETS). It wasn't long before she was promoted to Personnel Director there.*

The ETS's proximity to Princeton University allowed Elizabeth to occasionally attend talks and seminars on campus. It was at one of those talks that she first saw her future husband: he was an audience member needling the speaker with challenging questions. But she didn't approach Tukey at the talk. Rather, in 1949, two years after moving to Princeton, Elizabeth encountered him again at a folk-dance class—Tukey was one of the teachers, having taught folk dancing for over a decade. A representative dance flyer set the scene:

> Old timers and beginners are welcome to the YMCA Folk Dance Group at the Summit YMCA.... This group has been meeting regularly during the season under the direction of John Tookey [*sic*], well-known Princeton folk dance leader. Mr. Tookey and his friends will demonstrate steps for beginners. Newcomers may attend two sessions at 25 cents guest fee, following which they may register as members.

But Tukey didn't limit his folk dancing exploits to New Jersey. He would frequently advise institutions, educational (e.g., Princeton, Brown, Dartmouth) and otherwise (read: the United States government), on the installation and integration of computer systems in their facilities. A nuclear weapons laboratory in Oak Ridge, Tennessee, fell into Tukey's sights for such advising in the 1950s: he traveled to the site enough times to organize folk dancing there, too, in between his time consulting the military on uranium enrichment. Those visits were likely made to serve as a sort of "tech support" for the stored-program computer stationed at the lab, called the JOHNNIAC, which was named in honor of John von Neumann and built by the RAND Corporation.

---

* Prior to her promotion, when her marriage to Tukey was imminent and she told that to the ETS Personnel Director, he relayed to her a statistic that probably didn't surprise her: Tukey "got the highest score on the SATs that we have ever seen."

Such military and defense establishment connections were still legion for Tukey, despite the Second World War ending years prior. From the early to middle 1950s, Tukey was a supervisor of Military Systems Analysis at the Princeton Forrestal Research Center, for example. By 1960, he had helped to establish a branch of the Institute for Defense (IDA) on campus, serving on the IDA Board of Trustees long after IDA was relocated off campus in the wake of Vietnam War protests.

Tukey was an eccentric "New Englander through and through," Elizabeth recalled, complete with that characteristic value system, something that Elizabeth had grown quite fond of, but which her family took a bit of time getting used to. While Tukey's eccentricities attracted her, his unconventional approach didn't always wear well on others. For example, once, early on in their relationship, Tukey arrived at Elizabeth's parents' house to pick her up, but he was dressed in a fake fur, ragged-looking, Teddy bear-like coat, replete with a crumpled-up fedora-style wide-brimmed hat that he had just removed from his pocket because it was cold outside. The Rapp family was shocked at his appearance, but this was only the tip of the iceberg: Tukey was extremely thrifty, reusing a single set of black polos for the majority of his adult life.

"He doesn't say much," Elizabeth told her mother, "but what he [does say is] bang on." Indeed, Tukey wasn't much of a talker, but his wife balanced that out; she was especially comfortable greasing the social wheels. She also evened him out on election days, with Tukey likely voting for Democratic candidates most of the time while Elizabeth voted for Republicans.

Indeed, Tukey played his politics close to the vest. He also wasn't forthcoming about his religious beliefs. In 1966 he co-wrote an article for *The Christian Science Monitor* entitled "Earth—Man's Polluted Spaceship," but that piece focused on the environment, not Christianity. Perhaps the most revealing, yet still mostly opaque, expression of his religious convictions lies in a New Testament quotation appearing on the final page of his masterwork, *Exploratory Data Analysis* (1977). From the *Book of Revelation*, Chapter 13, Verse 18: "Here is wisdom: Let him that hath understanding count the number of the beast, for it is the number of a man; and his number is six hundred threescore and six." That quotation concludes *Exploratory Data Analysis*—not coincidently, on page 666. In the Index, under the b's, one finds this entry: "beast, number of, 666." Is the biblical Easter egg a profound statement of belief? a joke? a clever connection to numerology? Tukey never explained his motivations publicly.

Despite his idiosyncrasies, it didn't take long for the Rapp family to warm up to Tukey. Elizabeth's father, realizing Tukey's prodigious work habits as well as being aware of his impatience, jokingly questioned his future son-in-law: Will you take out a yellow pad to sketch out mathematics while you're waiting for my daughter at the altar?

On July 19, 1950, a year after first meeting, they were married; they eventually moved into a house on 115 Arreton Road in Princeton that Tukey paid for by "putting cash on the barrelhead," as Brillinger described it, meaning that Tukey bought the house outright in cash. The American architect R. W. Bauhan had designed the house, which was enclosed by a number of acres of woodland.

Elizabeth eventually settled into a career as an art and antiques dealer, especially of Asian ceramics and botanical drawings; she also furnished her home with antique American furniture. She tagged along with her husband on his adventures to other countries any chance she could get; on these trips, his eyes were attuned to statistics, while her eyes were focused on exotic artifacts and antiques. She often attended Tukey's academic conferences and enjoyed both fishing and gardening with her husband. Tukey, by his own admission, did only "some" fishing, but certainly not as much as his cousin Chick, for whom fishing was a "pastime." However, Tukey did once manage to earn a citation in the Miami fishing derby, which landed both Tukeys in a picture in a local Key West newspaper. Elizabeth was especially proud of a number of fish she had reeled in over the years when deep sea fishing, including the wahoo, a big game fish, as well as several others, which she had stuffed and mounted in the basement; when she was growing up, her uncle took her fishing, and when she and Tukey landed in the papers next to the large fish, she sent the picture to him.

Gardening also took up the couple's time, but, as Elizabeth said, as they aged, getting up from a kneeling position after working for a while in the soil became more and more challenging. Regardless, Tukey loved gardening and was especially effective at weeding; in his later years, Ralph Tukey visited his son and held long conversations in the garden with him, ripping out weeds as they spoke.

But the couple didn't enjoy doing everything together. Take reading aloud in bed, for instance. To Elizabeth's father's relatives, it was a bit of a family tradition. But when Elizabeth suggested the same to her husband, he demurred. What would be the point of reading aloud, Tukey explained to his wife, when he could dispense with a book quickly when reading it silently—usually in about an hour? It would be a waste of valuable time.

Elizabeth took care of, and worried sick about, her husband. She managed their homes and finances so he could be free to write and think. If he became buried by work or personal commitments, she forced him to cut back or cut loose. And she kept him grounded. One of Tukey's students once strode up to Elizabeth, asking if he could speak to "the great man."

"There is no great man here," she replied. "We are ordinary people."

By the early 1960s Elizabeth was especially worried about her husband, since he wasn't getting very much sleep as the pressure to complete the nuclear testing studies began to mount; in fact, Elizabeth noticed that there was an inverse relationship between Tukey's quantity of sleep and his stress level. While Tukey typically aimed for eight hours of sleep—usually waking up around 3:30 AM (and, in his later years, eating a snack) before falling back asleep—he was sleeping only around five hours when examining the nuclear testing data, and he openly admitted to his wife that he would have been really sick from the stress he was shouldering if not for having recently shed some pounds. Although he worked best in the mornings, he was waking up especially early—around 5:00 AM—to get started. When he came home from work, he usually had no desire to talk about the events of the day: he had lived through these events once, he explained, and there was no need to go through them again; in stressful times, his reluctance to rehash was all the more pronounced. Tukey only wanted to read a good mystery story or two at night to help him fall asleep—reading mysteries stores was one his favorite leisure-time activities, although he would often forget the stories he read—and perhaps read another one to fall back asleep after inevitably waking up in the pre-dawn hours. Elizabeth saw the same sorts of stress-induced, maladaptive behaviors when her husband was laying the foundations of the Princeton Statistics Department as well as in the early years of Tukey's Bell Labs tenure.

His own health notwithstanding, Tukey was well suited to studying the intersection of health and the environment, most notably as a member of the President's Science Advisory Committee (PSAC) from 1960 to 1963. According to Alex Roland of Duke University, who wrote the introduction to *The Papers of the President's Science Advisory Committee, 1957-1961* (1986), which he also edited: "The role of the President's Science Advisory Committee (PSAC) in the Eisenhower administration marked a climax in the spread of science and technology into public life." Tukey participated in one of the first PSAC roundtable discussion, with Eisenhower present, in Newport, Rhode Island, in 1960; interestingly, Tukey later said that his PSAC work involved "no statistics." Whereas the government "exploited science erratically" prior to the onset of World War II, Roland wrote, during the war—"[a]ppropriately called the physicists' war"—there was a burgeoning of scientific organization and discovery, a "harnessing of 'scientists against time,'" culminating in the successful deployment of nuclear weapons as a result of the Manhattan Project.

Their importance now proven beyond doubt, scientists like J. Robert Oppenheimer, who led the atomic bomb effort, and Vannevar Bush, who led the U.S. Office of Scientific Research and Development (OSRD) during the war, were granted unprecedented access to the levers of governmental power. Bush had organized the National Defense Research Committee (NDRC) in 1940 under the auspices of President Franklin Delano Roosevelt. The NDRC's express purpose was to coordinate and centralize scientific research and development with respect to warfare; the organization was quickly absorbed by the Office of Scientific Research and Development (OSRD), an organization with a broader but similar mission. Before the war's end, Bush proposed a National Research Foundation to continue communication and cooperation between scientists and the government in the post-war world. His proposal went through a number of iterations until, during the Truman administration, it finally emerged as the National Science Foundation (NSF), whose mission was narrow in scope, limited only to research funding. Though Bush fell out of favor with Truman, and Oppenheimer fell out of favor with the government entirely because of outspoken criticism of nuclear weapons' proliferation, causing his security clearance to be revoked, President Truman still gave scientists a seat at the table in 1951 by forming the Scientific Advisory Committee, although their influence eroded as the decade wore on.

In 1957, however, a signal event upended the technological and political landscape: the successful launch of the *Sputnik* artificial satellite. Young people flocked to majoring in mathematics, but there had been similar such pivots before in the twentieth century, as Tukey pointed out several years following the launch:

> Why are so many more men and women studying mathematics today? Is it because of some shift in our feeling as to which scientific field is central; chemistry in the twenties, physics in the forties and fifties, biology tomorrow, mathematics some day soon? Is it because of the rise—in size, in complexity of modern computers? Is it a reflection of the needs of the space age?... Surely all the reasons have contributed to the fact that three times as many college graduates majored in mathematics in 1962 as in 1956.

The shock of the Russian's artificial satellite also lit a fire under President Eisenhower. He appointed a science advisor, retained the services of MIT president James R. Killian as special assistant to the president for science and technology, and formed a scientific advisory council: the President's Science Advisory Committee (PSAC), which would work in close cooperation with the nation's chief executive; Killian was appointed director. An approproate response to *Sputnik* was the PSAC's first priority, but the group was tasked with other national security initiatives as well, such as assessing the feasibility of the MIT-designed proto-satellite West Ford system.

Tukey had worked for Killian several years before. In 1954, Eisenhower, shortly after being elected to his first term in office, selected Killian to head a panel to examine the U.S.'s vulnerability in the event of a surprise nuclear attack. Called the Technical Capabilities Panel, it was to be composed of forty-two leading men. Bell Labs sent Brock McMillan, James Fisk, and Tukey, and by 1956 a key recommendation of the panel took flight: the U-2 spy plane, which would stealthily surveil the USSR for years to come, discovering that the Soviets were hard at work constructing long-range ballistic missiles.

Specifically, the subcommittee that recommended building the U-2 was called Project 3, an outgrowth of the initial Killian Committee, with its focus directed toward intelligence gathering; Tukey was one of several scientists on the subcommittee, which was chaired by the cofounder of Polaroid, Edwin H. Land, and included a Nobel laureate physicist, a chemist, and an astronomer. It was perhaps Tukey, Brillinger claims, who first proposed building the bodies of the spy planes using titanium.

Killian was so pleased with Tukey's efforts that in 1955 he wrote the president of Princeton, Harold W. Dodds, telling him as much: Although much of the work of the panel must remain classified, "I can say to you, however, that Dr. Tukey drew upon his insight and abilities as a mathematician and a statistician to join in important creative developments in one of the most pressing aspects of our national program. We are fortunate to have had him as part of the Panel group."

Tukey was also involved with a post-PSAC Killian venture. In 1956, Killian, at the urging of the secretary of defense, established the Institute for Defense Analyses (IDA), a think tank with the express mission to recruit the scientific minds of academia. Tukey served in two capacities for the IDA: as a trustee in the final two decades of his life, and as an associate and/or advisor for the spinoff Communication Research Division (CRD), which was connected with the National Security Agency (NSA). The CRD was housed on Princeton's campus, pulling in academic talent from the university, but, by 1970, with Kent State and student protests dominating the headlines, the CRD was relocated off-campus—over the objections of Tukey, who penned a letter to Princeton's president urging him to not move the CRD.

CHAPTER NINE

Government Science

"John, you got to do something about this!"
— Kai Lai Chung

In the late 1950s, while a member of James Killian's upstart President's Science Advisory Committee, Tukey led a group of scientists to investigate the effects of fluorocarbons in the ozone layer, bringing public attention to the consequences of using aerosol spray cans. There was a bit of pushback, however, especially early on. When civil servants in several government agencies, such as the USDA, got wind that the PSAC was going to write favorably of Rachel Carson's *Silent Spring* (1962)—the landmark book, released during the Kennedy administration, that launched the modern environmental movement by casting light on the ostensible consequences of pesticide use, especially the popular pesticide DDT—"the people from agriculture practically wept in their beer. They didn't think she should receive any mention or notice whatsoever," Tukey said, because of the devastating financial consequences to industry that might result from heeding her advice.

In 1965 Tukey, along with more than a dozen other notable scientists, professors, and officials, assembled a thick report for public consumption entitled *Restoring the Quality of Our Environment: Report of the Environmental Pollution Panel President's Science Advisory Committee*; Tukey chaired the committee. By the time the report was released most of its content had already been leaked, since the PSAC was initially assigned the task, as part of a Great Society initiative under President Lyndon Johnson, of studying the environment and reporting back their findings to the White House— and White Houses, then and now, generally maintain secrecy as well as sieves hold water. *Restoring the Quality of Our Environment*, which took fifteen months to complete, codified a number of ideas that would be considered commonsensical (and thus unnecessary to explicitly state) today, yet were forward-thinking and prescient at the time. For instance, there was recommendation A1:

The public should come to recognize individual rights to quality of living, as expressed in the absence of pollution, as it has come to recognize rights to education, to economic advance, and to public recreation. Like education and other human rights, improved quality of life from reduced pollution will be costly to individuals and governments.

Also consider the corollary of A1, which is recommendation A2:

The responsibility of each pollutor [sic] *for all forms of damage caused by his pollution should be effectively recognized and generally accepted.* There should be no "right" to pollute.

These two recommendations, taken together, put the onus on the polluters to be good stewards of the environment—with the interests of public health and well-being of paramount concern.

Recommendation A7 pays special notice to the automobile, still one of the biggest sources of pollution:

The special importance of the automobile as a source of pollution problems should be clearly recognized. The automobile is our most rapidly growing cause of many and diverse pollution problems.

The committee also explained how pollution could have multifarious effects in and unintended consequences to the surrounding ecology:

As our pollution problems become steadily more serious, it should be generally recognized that we must consider our balances and choices within successively larger and more complex systems.

In a significant nod to Rachel Carson, whose work was not mentioned explicitly in the report, the committee recommended that

Unnecessary use of pesticides should be avoided wherever possible.

They also were one of the first to suggest something like a modern carbon tax that puts in place a system of economic incentives not to pollute:

We recommend that careful study be given to tax-like systems in which polluters would be subject to "effluent charges" in proportion to their contribution to pollution.

Other significant findings and recommendations included warning of the danger of a continuing build-up of carbon dioxide in the atmosphere from vehicles and factories, the need for more facilities and specially trained people to deal with environmental concerns, and changes to natural habitats, such as the shallow waters of coasts and estuaries, having potentially deleterious effects on ecosystems.

President Johnson was satisfied with the work of Tukey's committee, releasing a statement praising their efforts. It read, in part,

> I am pleased at the thoroughness with which the panel has investigated pollution. This report will surely provide the basis for action on many fronts….

> I am asking the appropriate departments and agencies to consider the recommendations and report to me on the ways in which we can move to cope with the problems cited in the report.

Tukey's interest in environmental matters, and Rachel Carson's work in particular, had been piqued by Kai Lai Chung. Born in 1917 in Shanghai, China, Chung, who was a professor at Stanford for the bulk of his teaching career, was considered a leading probabilist who contributed to fields as diverse as Brownian motion and Markov processes. Early on in his tenure at Stanford, Chung was present at a cocktail party with Tukey, whom he had met some years before. Chung, who knew of Tukey's Washington connections (Tukey was a member of the PSAC at this point), sidled up to him—Elizabeth was right beside her husband—and, after describing the import of Carson's work, exclaimed, "John, you got to do something about this!" The "this" was the environment—there was an urgency that Chung hoped to convey to Tukey, who listened intently while sipping ginger ale.

Recall that "the people from agriculture practically wept in their beer" because they believed that Rachel Carson, and her work, had adversely shaped the zeitgeist. Perhaps they were right to weep. When *Silent Spring* arrived on the scene in 1962, it was an immediate sensation. Carson had already established her bona fides as a popular science writer, although she was no scientist, having failed to earn a Doctor of Philosophy. *Silent Spring* was captivating right from the first chapter, "A Fable for Tomorrow": "There was once a town in the heart of America where all life seemed to live in harmony with its surroundings," but a sudden spate of "[m]ysterious maladies" wiped out much of the natural habitat, especially the birds. To top it off, children were dying from leukemia and liver disease; they "would be stricken suddenly while at play and die within a few hours." Carson fingered the likely culprit: pesticides.

At a press conference, President Kennedy was asked what action the government would take in the wake of concerns over the "widespread use of DDT and other pesticides. Have you considered asking the Department of Agriculture or the Public Health Service to take a closer look at this?"

The president quickly responded in the affirmative. "I know that they already are [looking into it]," he said. "I think, particularly, of course, since Miss Carson's book, they are examining the issue."

Silent Spring became an overnight bestseller worldwide, putting Carson and her ideas front and center. She was interviewed in both the print media and on television, and she also served as the key witness during a congressional review of environmental hazards. Arriving to deliver her testimony, the chair of the Committee of Government Operations, Senator Ernest Gruening of Alaska, exclaimed, "You're the lady who started it all!" which recalls Abraham Lincoln's remark upon meeting Harriet Beecher Stowe, the author of *Uncle Tom's Cabin* (1852): "So you are the little woman who wrote the book that started this great war."

But Carson had precious little data to back up her fire-and-brimstone claims; what's more, she misinterpreted the data she did have, leading to a cascade of faulty conclusions that had deleterious effects. Dichlorodiphenyltrichloroethane, or DDT, was first synthesized in 1874 by Othmar Zeidler, a graduate student in Germany, but its insect-killing properties weren't discovered until 1939 when Paul Hermann Müller was experimenting with ways to snuff out moths. DDT took center stage during World War II, when the Allies used it to fight typhus by spraying the chemical on people as a means of delousing them. Proving remarkably effective at staunching the typhus epidemic, DDT was then used after the war to control outbreaks of the malaria parasite, which is spread by the anopheles mosquito; the pesticide again worked wonders, even stemming the tide of dengue and yellow fever as well.

But the publication of *Silent Spring* was a watershed moment: "DDT saw its reputation fade after it was charged with murder by author Rachel Carson," explains Paul A. Offit in *Pandora's Lab: Seven Stories of Science Gone Wrong* (2017). By 1972, DDT use was banned in the United States; like falling dominoes, "support for international DDT programs had dried up. Those inspired by *Silent Spring* had spared mosquitoes from the killing effects of DDT. But they hadn't spared children from the killing effects of mosquitoes." Offit estimates that since the DDT ban took effect, around 50 million people have succumbed to malaria; children constitute a majority of those deaths. Although Carson helped us become "more attentive to our impact on the planet," she also "gave birth to the notion of zero tolerance—the assumption that any substance found harmful at any concentration or dosage should be banned absolutely." Sure, massive quantities of DDT ingested by humans were harmful; but small quantities designated with the express purpose of eradicating mosquitoes were not harmful to human beings. It's the dose that makes the poison, after all.

Roughly a year prior to the U.S. DDT ban, a protracted public hearing was initiated by the Environmental Defense Fund (EDF), an organization strongly opposed to continued use of DDT. Over one hundred experts in a number of science specialties were called to testify. The transcript from the hearing amounted to over nine thousand pages. Judge Edmund Sweeney, the hearing examiner, argued that DDT should not be banned. His opinion read as follows:

> DDT is not a carcinogenic hazard to man. DTT is not a mutagenic or teratogenic hazard to man. The uses of DDT under the registration involved here do not have a deleterious effect on freshwater fish, estuarine organisms, wild birds or other wildlife. The adverse effect on beneficial animals from the use of DDT under the registrations involved here is not unreasonable on balance with its benefit.... There is present need for the continued use of DDT for the essential uses defined in this case.

Carson's work inspired Tukey, the chair of the committee tasked with producing *Restoring the Quality of Our Environment*. Yet it remains surprising and especially disappointing that Tukey, a master of analyzing data if there ever was one, failed to see the obvious: that although *Silent Spring* had a compelling and convincing narrative, it was lacking the data to back up its most sensational claims.

After *Restoring the Quality of Our Environment*, Tukey continued his environmental work, this time as a member of the President's Air Quality Advisory Board (PAQAB) in the early 1970s, where he dealt directly with the first head of the Nixon administration-established Environmental Protection Agency (EPA), William Doyle Ruckelshaus, who was a former lawyer. Tukey thought the EPA head was naïve in his approach toward polluters: Ruckelshaus sincerely believed that he could, through the presentation of compelling facts coupled with the sheer force of his personality, stop the most brazen polluters from polluting the environment. Alas, that approach ultimately didn't pay off.* Regardless, Tukey's PAQAB released a report called *Cleaner Air for the Nation* that summarized the advisory board's findings; the report may have landed Tukey a spot on the U.S. Delegation to the U.N. Conference on the Human Environ-

---

* As EPA head Ruckelshaus also implemented the DDT ban—only two months after Judge Sweeney rendered his opinion, but without even bothering to read the report—arguing that DDT was deadly to human beings. Paul Offit characterizes Ruckelshaus's misguided decision as "political." Though Tukey thought little of Ruckelshaus, his criticism of the EPA head never extended to his banning of DDT.

ment in Stockholm several years later, which had him rubbing shoulders with fellow delegates like child star and humanitarian Shirley Temple as well as anthropologist Margaret Mead.

In the early 1970s, Tukey chaired a 14-member PSAC panel which, for two years, studied the effects of chemicals on human health and assembled a report of their findings entitled *Chemicals and Health*, which noted that individual human beings' health was adversely affected by smoking and alcohol consumption. "We must always live with some risks," Tukey and the panel explained, "both because nature forever confronts us with hazards, and also because the contributions of chemicals to human welfare are so vital." The report also examined the consequences of fluorocarbons being launched into the atmosphere, such as increased ultraviolet radiation due to the depletion of the ozone layer in the stratosphere. Tukey also chaired several NRC committees in the late 1970s devoted to examining the effects of chlorofluorocarbons. Whenever Tukey chaired a committee, he urged its members to be exceedingly prepared—including beginning the mental heavy lifting the night before the meetings if necessary. Sardonically describing his work for one set of meetings in Geneva, Tukey said, "Participating in the meetings when appropriate and participating in the preparation for the meetings, which took you would expect more time than the meetings themselves."

In 1973, President Nixon disbanded the PSAC because of political conflict. Zuoyue Wang, author of *In Sputnik's Shadow: The President's Science Advisory Committee and Cold War America* (2008), writes that "[t]hey [the PSAC] were no longer needed in the Executive Office of the President, Nixon said, because of the growing scientific strength in other parts of the government that they had helped build." Wang continues:

> Thus, a major institution of American science and government, which President Truman initiated during the Korean War, which President Eisenhower revitalized in the aftermath of *Sputnik*, which helped him and Kennedy curb the runaway nuclear arms race with its technological skepticism, and which helped hold American science and state for two decades of the Cold War, ended unceremoniously in the Nixon administration after a steady decline during the turbulent Vietnam War era. PSAC scientists set out to serve both science and the state in the interest of society, but in the end, largely failed to please either side of the partnership.

Tukey, gone from the PSAC by then, had transitioned to working on producing reports for the National Academy of Sciences (NAS)[*]—he chaired the Committee on the Impacts of Stratospheric Change from

---

[*] Upon his election to the NAS, Tukey was presented with a tennis ball signed by his fellow professors in the Princeton mathematics department.

1975 to 1979, which was a joint venture of the NAS and the National Research Council, that examined stratospheric ozone depletion due to the release of chlorine molecules and was prompted by the Rowland–Molina hypothesis—as well as for other organizations. Some of these reports were on the environment (e.g., on the effects of fluoromethane in 1976).

But one committee Tukey was on, the NOAA (National Oceanic and Atmospheric Administration) Advisory Commission on Oceans and Atmosphere, didn't emerge unscathed by the Nixon administration's slash-and-burn political style. Tukey thought of the NOAA committee as a robust, diverse, mostly effective ingathering of talent; for instance, sitting alongside the scientists there was a man from the Seattle's Seaman's Union on the commission who represented a significant commercial shipping firm. Shirley Temple's husband, Charles Alden Black, was on the commission, too; his father was the CEO of the Pacific Gas and Electric Company, and Black himself was an expert in aquaculture and oceanography. But several political blunders by Nixon resulted in the Democrats, who controlled congress at the time, retaliating against the administration by dissolving the committee, only to turn around and reconstitute it with an entirely new cast of characters—Tukey not included. Tukey always maintained a disdain for politicians, who tried to punt the hard policy questions to the scientists. Regardless, "I think a realistic description of things," he said of the NOAA committee in an interview over a decade later, "is that it tried to understand and help resolve those problems which could be resolved without going to legislative questions."

His work on environmental issues continued, especially by serving as an advisor to the Health Effects Institute (HEI), a joint venture of the EPA and the automobile industry based in Massachusetts that studied the effects of automotive emissions. The HEI was divided into two subcommittees: The Health Review Committee and the Health Research Committee. Tukey worked for the latter, with responsibilities that included planning research programs and staffing talent to head the programs.

Lured into the HEI by William Oliver Baker, a Bell Labs president who happened to serve on the HEI board of directors, Tukey served as an HEI advisor from 1981 to 1991. Baker, who met Tukey on a tennis court at the Princeton Graduate College back in 1937 when they were both studying chemistry, thought the world of him, once saying that "[w]e have watched at least four Presidents of the United States listen to [Tukey] and heed his counsel." (In fact, by the end of Tukey's life, the total was five presidents.) Baker, who said Tukey "joined in conceiving and organizing most of the initiatives in communications principles and science research undertaken at Bell Labs since 1955," would help connect Tukey with possible job assignments, such as on government research panels, that suited his interests. Elizabeth said that Baker's "seconding of

John to all sorts of [government] jobs was both masterful and astute," concluding that not only was Baker the best liaison to Washington projects that Tukey ever had, but that he also had a preternatural eye for hiring talent, bringing only the absolute best to Bell Labs in his various leadership capacities over the span of three decades. Baker knew that Tukey was "money in the bank."

Continuing his environmental work, in 1991 Tukey joined the Oversight Review Board of the National Acidic Precipitation Assessment Program. Tukey was tasked with oversight—making sure that the review process was sound. But congress jumped the gun, passing legislation without waiting for the committee's final report. Regardless, through all of Tukey's environmental work, he firmly kept in mind the words of a "wise doctor" who had told multiple EPA administrators that "[i]t is medically demonstrable that it is risky to get up in the morning, but it is also medically demonstrable that it is risky to stay in bed"—meaning that there is no refuge in life from risk. Safety is not, nor will it ever be, guaranteed, and to think otherwise presents an impediment to evaluating and drawing conclusions from data.

CHAPTER TEN

Counting Every Vote

"[Tukey was] the man who destroyed the suspense of election night."
— David Alan Grier

Tukey brought statistics to bear in civic projects centering on the U.S. decennial census and psephology, or election forecasting, thereby ultimately helping to improve estimates and fill in the gaps of incomplete data sets.

Psephology in the United States has a spotty history. Although a victorious President Harry Truman holding up the "Dewey Defeats Truman" front-page headline on the November 3, 1948, issue of the *Chicago Daily Tribune* is certainly the most famous example of faulty election forecasting, mistakes made in predicting an earlier presidential election were more consequential mathematically.

The Literary Digest, a weekly newsmagazine, conducted reader polls prior to each U.S. presidential election from 1916 onward. In 1936, President Franklin Delano Roosevelt was up for reelection; his Republican opponent was Governor Alfred Landon. The magazine conducted its quadrennial poll, sending surveys out to nearly ten million people, of which 2.4 million people responded. The results? Alf Landon was set to crush FDR in a landslide. But when Election Day arrived, the reverse occurred, and FDR cruised to an easy reelection victory. The sampling methods were to blame: *Literary Digest* sent surveys to the addresses of individuals they found in telephone books and from vehicle registrations. But the country was still struggling to recover from the Great Depression, meaning that those who owned cars and even telephones likely had more wealth than the average voter. This systematic exclusion of a large swath of voters resulted in the stunning mismatch between the survey results, which were biased in favor of the Republican candidate, and the Election Day numbers.

Not everyone got it wrong, however. By utilizing a random sampling method coupled with a much smaller sample size, George Gallup correctly predicted an FDR win. And forever after, public opinion polling would have a new master: random sampling.

In 1960, as the Kennedy-Nixon race heated up, the National Broadcasting Company (NBC), in an effort to establish a reliable and advanced election forecasting team, retained the services of the consulting firm CEIR. Tukey, who worked for CEIR, was thereby drafted to the NBC team. Other consultants at CEIR, such as Richard M. Scammon and John Mauchly, were brought onboard as well. Mauchly had co-designed the ENIAC digital computer with J. Presper Eckert, but he only came to election-forecasting prominence courtesy of the UNIVAC in the early 1950s when the UNIVAC I mainframe computer correctly predicted a landslide victory for Dwight Eisenhower over Adlai Stevenson, contrary to the predictions of most other pollsters.

At NBC, Tukey refined and perfected so-called *multilevel modeling* to develop modern "real-time election prediction models that could exploit diverse types of data: polls, past elections, partial results, and complete results from related districts," continuing to refine and improve these statistical models for NBC until the late 1970s, according to the evolutionary ecologist Richard McElreath. At its peak in the late 1970s, the NBC election-forecasting team included nearly 20 statisticians (with doctorates) analyzing data in two locations: the Radio Corporation of America (RCA) Lab located in Cherry Hill, New Jersey, and in New York. Several of the statisticians were stationed in NBC's broadcasting headquarters in New York, but most, including Tukey, were based in the RCA Lab, which had a mainframe computer, as well as a backup computer, busily performing election calculations.

In fact, RCA made sure to leverage the election as an advertising opportunity for its computers. Though known primarily for its radio technology, as early as 1951, starting with the analog Typhoon, RCA also was churning out large mainframe computers. In 1952, they made the transition to digital computing with the BIZMAC, designed for use by the military, which performed calculations utilizing thousands upon thousands of vacuum tubes.

By the late 1950s, RCA introduced the 501 Electronic Data Processing System, which shed the vacuum tubes in favor of transistor semiconductors. The 501 had magnetic core storage, a fast printer, and a centralized control panel, replete with scores of buttons for human operator-to-computer operation. A huge refrigeration unit was also necessary to cool the blindingly hot electronic components, so wherever there was a computer, the ambient temperature nearby was low.

Yet even with the advanced computing power at NBC's disposal, the 1960 Kennedy-Nixon race, one of the closest presidential elections in American history, was especially difficult to call—so difficult, in fact, that Elizabeth recalled that NBC "locked all the analysts up," keeping them sequestered until the next morning, when the results were finalized.* Later elections found the couple inseparable, with Tukey stationing his wife right next to him in front of a computer monitor so she assist the team, too.

But what, precisely, was multilevel modeling? The statistician Stephen E. Fienberg, born in 1942 in Toronto, Ontario, Canada, worked with Tukey on the NBC Election Night team during the tail end of Tukey's tenure with the company (Tukey worked on election prediction for two decades, mostly for the presidential elections, but occasionally in the years in between; NBC had no use for Tukey after 1980, because exit polling had become a better predictor than the statistical methods he had helped to pioneer). Fienberg knew of Tukey's reputation years before he worked with him, thanks to being a doctoral student of Fred Mosteller's at Harvard. Earning a research assistantship at the institution but puzzled by what his responsibilities were, Fienberg stopped by Mosteller's office to find out. At a Harvard Faculty Club lunch, Mosteller described a complicated probability problem to Fienberg over a serving of tough horse steak. It was on something called "assessing probability assessors," and Fienberg had no idea what Mosteller was talking about—and he couldn't ask his advisor to clarify, since he was focusing all his energies on chewing the steak. Mosteller then pulled an envelope out of his pocket. On the envelope's back there were some barely intelligible scribbles.

> It turned out that the scribbles were notes from John Tukey about this problem. In fact, this was a problem that John and Fred were working on for some larger project, and my job was to translate the chicken-scratches on the back of the envelope into something intelligible, when I didn't know anything about what was going on. I worked at it for a

---

* Tukey disagreed pointedly with his wife's recollection of events, leading Elizabeth to slightly amend her story, agreeing with Tukey that it was a later, non-presidential, election in which NBC execs prevented the analysts from leaving until the morning after. I've footnoted Elizabeth's reappraisal, rather than simply papering over the events in the body of the text, because of this rather ambiguous comment Tukey made about the election in question: "that's the election where the river wards in Chicago were crucial." Chicago, and its mayor, Richard J. Daley, came under much scrutiny after the 1960 election, with accusations from Republican camps that he helped to throw the election for Kennedy. Furthermore, Tukey noted that there were some delays that held up "Illinois from [coming] in," implying that the election in which he was "locked up" was a presidential one. Perhaps the coup de grâce for Tukey's version of events is this statement from Tukey's nephew, F. R. Anscombe: "In 1960, they [Tukey and company] may have saved NBC from declaring Richard Nixon the winner in a close contest with John Kennedy." Elizabeth's first take on the events is probably the closest to the truth.

while, and then Fred slowly told me what John's jottings meant, and the key idea was that for assessing probability forecasts, you have to look not just at the equivalent of means, or the bias in them (known technically as calibration), but also at the equivalent of variability (how spread out the forecasts are).

In a written recollection published decades later, Fienberg fingers the three people most responsible for the genesis of multilevel modeling: Tukey, Brillinger, and David Lee Wallace, born in 1928 in Homestead Park, Pennsylvania, who was a professor of statistics at the University of Chicago. What's more, they utilized what would now be called hierarchical Bayesian methods—developed off of the work of the eighteenth-century statistician and theologian Thomas Bayes—but never published their techniques, which involved the notion of *borrowing strength*, later termed an empirical Bayes procedure, from an established distribution of data or from other similar situations in order to "prop up" their predictions (i.e., to literally "borrow strength"); later, statisticians, particularly I. J. Good, Dennis Lindley, and Adrian Smith, formally described the procedure in print. (During his time as a professional psephologist, Tukey refrained from publishing or publicizing his statistical methods, since he thought they weren't developed enough to withstand the scrutiny of academics; what's more, Tukey also strongly believed the techniques were "proprietary" to NBC and, as such, did not belong in the public domain.)[*] Fienberg described the chaotic election night responsibilities of the statistical analysts as one of a back and forth between barrages of incoming data and modeling those data using prior distributions, with "different past elections chosen as 'models' for the ones for which they were creating forecasts," all the while "checking on robustness of conclusions to varying specifications." Each of the analysts was parked in front of a computer terminal and monitored a select group of states and their associated races.

But the comprehensive techniques the ever-expanding team of analysts utilized didn't simply emerge from whole cloth; rather, the process was one of trial and error. Early on, the team made comparisons between election returns streaming in and historical data; later, much complexity, in the form of "stages," was added to the prediction techniques. Simultaneous to the development of more advanced mathematical modeling came advances in precinct reporting—from individual precincts calling their votes in to thousands of precincts aggregated together prior to reporting.

---

[*] Tukey made a habit of pronouncing the word "psephologist" as if the *p* weren't silent—which it is.

The overarching goal of the election team remained the same from the start: to reduce variability as much as possible. As David Alan Grier, in a *Washington Post* piece published on the eve of the 2000 Presidential election—and only months after the death of Tukey—explained it, the techniques to manage variability in elections were of a piece with dealing with variability in other contexts:

> To the study of elections, [Tukey] brought the lessons he had learned during the war, lessons that had taught him how to use mathematics to remove variability. During the war, the mathematicians of the OSRD [Office of Scientific Research and Development] had used mathematics to remove the variability in manufacturing, the variability in supply and even the variability of combat. Under the guidance of mathematically prepared plans, the pilots of D-Day bombed the French coast in a pattern that created the greatest amount of damage while exposing the pilots to the least amount of risk.*

Tukey was "the man who destroyed the suspense of election night," Grier concluded.

Despite the great amount of thought and planning that went into psephology, things didn't always go off without a hitch under the watchful eyes of John Tukey on election night. One year the computers in New York malfunctioned so badly—no amount of cleaning the tape heads helped—that papers, pencils, and adding machines had to be used to frantically compile the results, all under the aegis of political scientist and Director of the Elections Research Center Richard M. Scammon, who joined the NBC team in 1965 and was stationed in front of the camera, eager to explain statistical complexities to a nation hungry for the latest information. And another year, Tukey and the statisticians in Cherry Hill called the governors' races in California and New York early, only to see that incoming vote totals for the next several hours conflicted with their call. Luckily the analysts didn't uncall, because the final tallies agreed with their initial predictions. Although it was a near miss, in the time Tukey worked for NBC the election team never made a bad call.

The team did have one particularly heartbreaking day, however: November 22, 1963, the day of President Kennedy's assassination. News of the tragedy came in while the statisticians and mathematicians were holding a meeting to game plan for the 1964 election. Of course, the meeting

---

* Grier's article is notable not only for publicizing the fact that the 2000 election was the first without Tukey's oversight (of one sort or another) since WWII: Grier also correctly predicted a chaotic popular vote-Electoral College vote split (although he had it in reverse, incorrectly surmising that Bush would win the popular vote).

ended abruptly, and Tukey and the others drove back to Princeton. In the car, concerned about how everyone else was holding up, Tukey addressed the team: "Do [you] people want to talk?"

CHAPTER ELEVEN

Stories from the Birthplace of the Future

"With a characteristic grin, and equally characteristic down-east
inflection, [Tukey] asked, 'Well, isn't the word obviously bit?'"
— Brock McMillan

In Jon Gertner's definitive institutional history of Bell Telephone Laboratories, *The Idea Factory* (2012), John Tukey is mentioned only
twice—and both times it is in reference to Claude Shannon. First,
Gertner traces the etymology of the word *bit*, tracing it to Tukey's oral
contraction of the term "binary digit" in the 1940s. Second, Tukey is
listed, along with William Shockley and Claude Shannon, as writing a "definitive book on a subject"—in Tukey's case, statistics. (With Shockley, it
was semiconductors; Shannon had information theory covered.)

Tukey began as a Member of the Technical Staff at Bell Labs in 1945
and would advance to several key positions over the coming years: in
1958, Assistant Director of Research, Communications Principles; and, in
1961, Associate Executive Director, Research Information Sciences. But
well before Tukey had ever set foot on the Murray Hill campus, Bell Labs
had acquired an impressive reputation as well as quite a storied history.

Bell Labs owes its birth to Alexander Graham Bell. In 1870, he founded what would turn into the American Telephone and Telegraph Company (AT&T); subsidiaries of the company would quickly take root. Independent of AT&T, the late 1800s also saw the rise of the Western Electric Company, an electrical equipment producer based out of Chicago.
The behemoth Western Union, then involved in a legal battle with
AT&T, gobbled up Western Electric Company. A legal settlement between Western Union and AT&T resulted in Western Electric becoming
a subsidiary of AT&T.

Under AT&T, Western Electric flourished, establishing a research laboratory by the early twentieth century. Within only two decades, thousands of people gained employed there, enough to spin off the laboratory.
The newly established Bell Telephone Laboratories, jointly owned by
AT&T and Western Electric, was headquartered in New York City. A

second site, in Murray Hill, New Jersey, was later established to accommodate Bell Labs' continued growth.

Almost from the beginning, Bell Labs had an intimate relationship with the United States government. For example, in 1927 Bell Labs facilitated a long-distance transmission of then-Secretary of Commerce Herbert Hoover. By the onset of World War II, a three-pronged apparatus was set up for war-related research, connecting Bell Labs to academia and academia to government. Through it all, an idea took hold in the public imagination: Bell Labs was the place where the future was being invented, where the ideas of tomorrow were birthed (hence the title of Gertner's book, *The Idea Factory*). The post-war technologies to come out of Bell Labs would be phenomenal: the transistor, which led to the microchip; the binary digital computer; the laser; the solar battery cell; the C programming language; the UNIX operating system; fiber-optic transatlantic cable; and information theory. With the blizzard of discoveries came a downside: controversies and bruised egos, especially centering on the development of the transistor.[*] That was the environment Tukey would work and create in for the next four decades: a hotbed of invention among big-time scientists and mathematics with occasionally even bigger egos holding sway.

As the war wound down and Tukey wrapped up his work at the FCRO—he had served in two official capacities there, first as a Consultant and then an Assistant Director, from 1941 to 1945—he migrated to Bell Laboratories to serve in a part-time capacity, and simultaneously back to Princeton, also part time, to work with Sam Wilks. They would collaborate on a number of projects on campus, including analyzing game statistics for the Princeton Tigers football team.

During the war, Bell Labs was a nonprofit subcontractor for the government; Western Electric was contracting directly for the government. After the war, Bell Labs' links with the government continued with projects such as radar research. One of the people with whom Tukey interacted the most at Bell Labs was Hendrik Bode. Born in 1905 in Madison, Wisconsin, Hendrik Wade Bode worked with Tukey at Bell on the Nike Zeus surface-to-air antiaircraft missile project immediately following the Second World War; in fact, Bode personally hired him for the project thanks to Tukey's stellar performance at the FCRO. Tukey originally thought that he was being brought to Bell Labs to work on the Nike with the two people most involved at that time on the project: Hendrick Bode

---

[*] Walter Brattain, John Bardeen, and their supervisor William Shockley all shared the Nobel Prize for the discovery of the semiconductor, but Shockley felt double-crossed by his subordinates, who had worked independently on the project.

and Walter McNair. The latter worked for the phone company and was responsible for the first "weather machine" (an ancient ancestor of weather websites: place a phone call to the weather machine to obtain the current weather). McNair, who was especially interested in quality control, also built a new kind of radar that tracked the Nike in flight. But Tukey's job responsibilities at Bell Labs expanded over the course of the next year, so he stayed on board. He was one of the few mathematicians at Bell with a decidedly statistical bent.

Bell Labs employed Bode, McNair, and Tukey, but it also had also Paul Olmstead, born in Wilton, Connecticut, in 1898, who was a Princeton physicist interested enough in statistical applications to call himself an "engineering statistician." And it had Milton E. Terry as well, a recently hired full-fledged statistician. But there was no statistics department yet, only an informal group of people with shared statistical interests. That continued for the next decade as the number of mathematicians and scientists with statistics interests increased: Ramanathan Gnanadesikan, an Indian statistician who studied at the University of North Carolina in Chapel Hill, was hired, as was Martin Wilk, a convert from engineering to statistics who spent a year as a postdoc working with Tukey at Princeton during which he transitioned to the Bell Labs research environment. Wilk, according to Brillinger, "was one of the few people who could cause John Tukey to really focus on the topic at hand. (JWT was one of the great multiprocessors and typically focused on several things at a time.)" Anne Freeny, Shirley Reed, Marilyn Huyett, Bill Williams, Liz Lauh, and Colin Mallows were also additions. This motley crew was overseen by Tukey. Gnanadesikan was struck by the independence afforded the Statistics Group at Bell:

> Nevertheless, the group was small and we tended to operate individually. We had our research interests, as well as interactions with other people in the synergistic environment. However, the group didn't have that much of a cohesive mission or a set of goals to reach. That is what started happening with the evolution of the department.

The value of having statisticians on staff in this "synergistic environment" was becoming readily apparent to Bell Labs management. Tukey, as the head of the Statistics Group, was a direct report to Robert C. Prim, a former engineer at General Electric born in 1921 in Sweetwater, Texas, who snagged a doctorate from Princeton after the war and went to work at Bell Labs, becoming best known for rediscovering what ended up being called Prim's algorithm. But, in an interesting case of reciprocity, Prim was also Tukey's direct report, since Tukey was an Associate Executive

Director at Bell. This back-and-forth reporting relationship between Prim and Tukey, termed "bracketing," helped to more quickly communicate the importance of statisticians to the higher-ups. (After retirement, when asked to describe his responsibilities during the last twenty years of his tenure at Bell, Tukey replied, "To assist the executive director, who reported to the vice president for research in the area that was labeled communications principles, at least at one time.")*

By the early 1960s, a more robust statistics department at Bell started to gel: Milton Terry succeeded Tukey as the head of the department, as Tukey began to focus on heading the newly formed statistics department at Princeton. Then, several years later, Martin Wilk took over; Tukey especially appreciated Wilk's attitude toward science: "The hallmark of good science is that it uses models and 'theory' but never believes them." By that point, the size of the Bell Labs statistics department had grown fourfold, from a half-dozen people to around twenty-five. Gnanadesikan would take over next, bringing some much-needed stability to the department; Elizabeth Tukey said that Gnanadesikan's leadership "made a tremendous difference to improving John's life and mine."

Tukey generated masses of innovative mathematical ideas at home, not at his Princeton office,† although he was also productive thirty miles away at Murray Hill, a space designed for the express purpose of research. When Elizabeth asked Tukey why he repeatedly refused to entertain the myriad of job offers attempting to lure him to other academic institutions (besides Princeton University), his rejoinder was, "Where could I ever find another Bell Labs?" Unlike at the research-centered Bell, Tukey's time spent on the Princeton campus was largely geared toward completing administrative and pedagogical duties, such as holding meetings, interacting with faculty, and conducting classes. In fact, Tukey became famous for carrying out a certain administrative task: scheduling classes and ex-

---

* Tukey was a member of the technical staff at Bell Laboratories starting in 1945; he was eventually promoted to assistant director of research communication principles, serving in the position from 1958 to 1962; and, beginning in 1961, he was associate executive director of research.

† The dean of faculty at Brown, concerned that he could never carve out any time to write or conduct research (he was originally a physicist by trade), once asked Tukey about his working habits. Tukey revealed that the creative process occurred for him nearly entirely at home, a place free of the petty distractions of administrative work, and suggested to the dean that he find his own distraction-free space. Why was Tukey still connected with Brown at this late date? In large part because he served on their Board of Fellows from the middle 1970s to the late 1980s.

ams, something he had experience with as far back as during his (limited) time at New Bedford High School; back then, as a mostly homeschooled student, any timetable recommendations Tukey offered to the teachers he presented with the greatest of tact and politeness—an approach, he believed, that served him well later on. At Princeton, as chairman of the Faculty Committee on Schedule, Tukey "would lie flat on his back on a table and people would list the scheduling difficulties and he would reel off solutions," Robert Gunning, a Princeton professor of mathematics who was once chairman of the mathematics department and dean of the faculty, recalled. "He did it quickly and quietly in his head." (Gunning had Princeton connections going back to his graduate school days, having Salomon Bochner as a thesis advisor in 1955.)

And yet, despite the administrative tasks that ate up his time at Princeton, working in a university environment facilitated the sorts of interactions with other top minds that Tukey required as fuel for creative output. As he explained in the subsection called "From Whence Inspiration?", part of the first volume of the *Collected Works*,

> [M]any of the real innovations were stimulated by particular data sets or by the subject-matter problems of particular friends and colleagues. It is not too easy to get such catalysis from real problems—the relative frequency of stimulation is quite low—but I am sure I would have found it harder, and less rewarding, to sit in a pure theorist's ivory tower, and invent the problems that needed to be solved.

Intellectually, Tukey needed to be needed—by friends, by colleagues, and especially by the world at large.

By the late 1960s, Tukey was beginning to work smarter, rather than harder. After interviewing three candidates for an open secretarial position at Bell Labs, he ultimately hired Mary Bittrich—and then had her take over not only Bell Labs tasks, but also much of the administrative work at Princeton that had been piling up (according to Elizabeth Tukey, at that time, secretarial support at Princeton was meager). Perhaps we can term Bittrich a synergistic hire, then; she certainly benefited from Tukey nearly as much as he benefited from her. "[Tukey] was constantly challenging me to learn more, to develop new skills," she recalled. "With his encouragement I've used capabilities I didn't know I had." Tukey encouraged Bittrich to learn and become an in-house expert on the UNIX operating system—and she did, going on to teach a number of Bell Labs employees the ins and outs of UNIX. (According to Bittrich, the *tbl()* function in UNIX was developed in order to correctly format tables on documents for Tukey's written work.)

A big personality whom Tukey interacted with at Murray Hill, nearly from the beginning of his tenure there, was Claude Shannon. Shannon was "a mathematician interested in practical matters" but certainly not a data analyst or statistician, according to Tukey. Claude Elwood Shannon, born in 1916 in Petoskey, Michigan, excelled at mathematics and science at an early age; he had a facility for constructing working mechanical and electrical machines. Shannon graduated from the University of Michigan with degrees in both mathematics and electrical engineering, and set course to MIT; there, he doubled as an electrical engineering student and as Vannevar Bush's laboratory assistant. (Bush, an American engineer who had the ear of top government officials, built the differential analyzer, which was an analog mechanical computer.) By 1938, Shannon had likened Boolean algebra—a nineteenth century creation of the logician George Boole—to electrical switching circuits and logic gates.

After performing cryptographic analysis and fire control[*] during World War II for Bell Labs, Shannon published a two-part paper titled "A Mathematical Theory of Communication" in the *Bell System Technical Journal*, which effectively midwifed the discipline of information theory. Shannon claimed that all information could be encoded in the same way using binary (base 2) digits, thereby eliminating potential errors in transmission. "If the base 2 is used the resulting units may be called binary digits, or more briefly *bits*, a word suggested by J. W. Tukey," Shannon wrote. Shannon had used the awkward term "alternative" rather than "bit" in an earlier paper on his burgeoning "Information Theory" (Shannon's term) after which Tukey made the suggestion, in conversation with Shannon rather than in print, to use the word bit instead. Shannon certainly wasn't averse to taking suggestions from Tukey; for instance, in 1949, it was Shannon who helped to disseminate Tukey's novel ideas on power spectra. Brock McMillan recalled the conversation in which the term bit was coined:

---

[*] While both Shannon and Tukey worked on fire-control problems during the war, Tukey, unlike Shannon, wasn't involved in cryptography—at least according to Shannon. "Now I didn't know that he [Tukey] had any connection with cryptography at all," Shannon said in an interview. Yet a president of Bell Labs whom Tukey worked for years later had a different take: "John was indeed active in the analysis of the Enigma system [the German's wartime encrypting machine] and then of course was part of our force in the fifties which did the really historic work on the Soviet codes as well," he said. "So he was very effective in that whole operation." In the article "Quiet Contributor: The Civic Career and Times of John W. Tukey," F. R. Anscombe fleshes out several plausible scenarios speculating on the degree to which Tukey may have been involved in the Enigma project.

A group of us at Bell Laboratories, probably over lunch, were discussing the awkwardness of, and the hint of internal inconsistency in, the term binary digit. We deplored the lack of a suitable substitute. John Tukey joined us at about this point, and heard our complaint. With a character-istic grin, and equally characteristic down-east inflection, he asked, "Well, isn't the word obviously bit?" And it was.

To the best of his recollection, McMillian placed the following people at that "bit lunch": himself, Tukey, Shannon, and Richard "Dick" Ham-ming.

Shannon was very shy, but he also had a playful side. For instance, he enjoyed riding a unicycle through the Bell Labs hallways, often juggling objects while he rode. Shannon also constructed machines that per-formed odd tasks. There was the THROBAC, a calculator that worked with Roman numerals (it was a THrifty ROman numeral BAckward-looking Computer). And there was also the mechanical maze-running mouse Theseus. Most strangely of all, though, was the Ultimate Machine: a small box with a switch on one of its faces that, when the switch was flipped, would cause a fabricated human hand from inside the box to emerge, slowly move down toward the switch, flip it off, and then retract back into the box. The Ultimate Machine was either a brilliant installation of postmodern art or just an incredibly silly gag—take your pick. But Shannon's fellow Bell Labs employees didn't always look kindly upon Shannon's oftentimes-flippant attitude. When Shannon published a paper in 1954 called "Reliable Circuits Using Crummy Relays," Tukey recalled that some people objected to the "crummy relays" colloquialism in the title. Yet Shannon, in the final analysis, was "a very reasonable person," Tukey concluded.

In 1949, a half-decade into his Bell Labs tenure, Tukey co-wrote a paper with Bode, Winsor, and Mosteller entitled "The Education of a Scientific Generalist" in *Science*. (And when Tukey was listed as one of the coau-thors on a paper, the reader could be certain that Tukey contributed greatly to the work; there was no mere "decorative appearance," he said, in having him as a coauthor.) In it, the authors argue that the "complexi-ties of modern science and modern society have created a need for *scien-tific generalists*, for men trained in many fields of scientists," and thus a new regimen of higher-level courses are necessary to educate these men. And what discipline lies at the nexus of these scientific fields? Statistics, of course: "Statistics, as the doctrine of planning experiments and observa-tions and of interpreting data, has a common relation to all sciences." To successfully train students as scientific generalists, the authors claim, re-quires them to exhibit mastery in at least four semesters of mathematics, chemistry, biology, physics, and statistics. Tukey cited an aphorism originated by Richard Link, a former student of Tukey's who ended up at Oregon State University, as an inspiration for the paper: that statisticians had to be, in effect, schizophrenics, since they had to quickly navigate between the rigidity of mathematics and the looseness of data.

"The Education of a Scientific Generalist" ended up having a wide influence on the graduate program in Computers and Communication at the University of Michigan, according to Arthur Banks.* But Lyle Jones viewed the paper's impact elsewhere as modest at best, writing in the *Collected Works* that in the decades since its publication there have been few changes in undergraduate curricula conforming to the paper's recommendations.

Hendrik Bode, who earned undergraduate and graduate degrees in mathematics from Ohio State University, joined Bell Labs in 1926 and ended up working there for more than forty years; during his first decade of employment, in which he was involved in electrical network theory and filter design as well as long-distance communication systems, he earned a doctorate in physics from Columbia. He also worked in the mathematical research group, and, during the war, helped to build electrical fire control devices—which led directly to his post-war contributions to antiaircraft and antiballistic missile design. By 1952, he assumed the directorship of the physical sciences research group, of which mathematics was a critical part—thus, he became Tukey's boss. By 1958 Bode rose even further up the ranks to the position of a Bell Labs vice president, of which there was only one other; his responsibilities included top-secret military-related projects. Gnanadesikan, who worked under Bode, described Bode's management style this way:

> [T]he essence of the success of Bell Labs was the synergy that brought together people with very different skills, very different approaches, experiences and training and who shared a certain value for this interaction across borders. Statistics was imbedded into that culture.

After retiring from Bell Labs, Bode began a second, albeit part-time, career: as the Gordon McKay Professor of Systems Engineering in the Division of Engineering and Applied Physics at Harvard. There, he taught courses on communication systems and management of technology as well as publishing a treatise on systems engineering for a popular audience. Very much like his friend Tukey, through his long life Bode's

---

* As relayed by David Brillinger.

"advice was much sought after," according to physicist and fellow Harvard professor Harvey Brooks. Moreover,

> not only [was his advice in demand] on technical matters but also regarding questions of organization, management strategy, and even ethics. He was a lucid writer and expositor and was noted for his broad humanistic approach to engineering and technology....

> Although an accomplished mathematician, he never used more mathematics than were necessary to make his point in an explanation, and he was able to translate complex mathematical results into simple physical pictures and analogies.

Besides the Nike, one of Tukey's earliest assignments at Bell involved aerial-tracking radar, being developed by an engineer named Horace T. Budenbom who worked at the Bell Labs Whippany laboratory (and who would go on to accumulate quite a few patents). "He [Budenbom] wanted to go to California [at a "closed meeting," Tukey wrote elsewhere] to give a paper and he wanted a picture to show what his tracking errors were" regarding "the performance of a new radar" that Budenbom was in the process of converting from one format to another, Tukey recalled during the course of two separate interviews. "So it was a question of calculating the spectrum which was done by the best conventional methods (by ladies using desk calculators)." In *The Lady Tasting Tea: How Statistics Revolutionized Science in the Twentieth Century* (2001), author David Salsburg explains the historical import of the problem:

> Budenbom had formulated his problem in the frequency domain but did not know how to get consistent estimates of the frequency amplitudes. Although Tukey, as a mathematician, was familiar with Fourier transformations, he had not yet been exposed to the uses of this technique in engineering. He proposed a method that seemed to satisfy the engineer....

Regardless, Tukey wasn't quite satisfied with his answer, which relied on makeshift "smoothing" techniques (specifically, by smoothing a data series with a quarter, a half, and then a quarter again, which Murray Hill's Dick Hamming had suggested). (To help conceptualize smoothing techniques, think of how rubbing sandpaper on wood removes the ragged edges; likewise, smoothing data removes the noise, allowing the patterns to shine through.) Eventually, from these early brainstorms, the fast Fourier transform, a sophisticated smoothing technique that became an extraordinarily efficient computer algorithm, was born.

CHAPTER TWELVE

The Development of the
Fast Fourier Transform

"I was sitting there scratching."
—John Tukey

The genesis of the fast Fourier transform (FFT) algorithm can be traced to one of the innumerable President's Science Advisory Committee meetings, which were convened in the Old State Department Building in Washington, D.C. At these meetings, Tukey usually sat next to Dick Garwin at the end of a table in an office formerly assigned to the secretary of state—the same office that welcomed Japanese dignitaries prior to the bombing of Pearl Harbor. The two mathematicians sat at the end of the table because, according to Tukey, "we were the junior members of the group."

Richard "Dick" Lawrence Garwin, born in Cleveland, Ohio, in 1928, earned his doctorate in physics from the University of Chicago when he was only 21 years old; Enrico Fermi was his dissertation supervisor. Fermi said that Garwin was the "only true genius he had ever met." Garwin then shifted his career track from one in an academic setting to a semi-corporate one: the IBM Watson Laboratory at Columbia University, considered part of the school's astronomy department, where he was given more freedom to pursue projects to his liking. Garwin's initial job description had him, and other scientists who joined him, using computers to solve problems. Garwin went on to put together a distinguished career, helping to develop new technologies such as GPS, touch screens, and laser printers; he also advised several U.S. presidents.

At one of the PSAC meetings near the end of President Kennedy's tenure, Garwin was, as usual, sitting next to Tukey, who happened to be manipulating some numbers and formulas on a small notepad—specifically, Fourier transform formulas, which reformulate waveforms into sines and cosines. The Fourier transform (FT) is a subset of Fourier series, named after mathematician Jean-Baptiste Joseph Fourier, which decompose functions into the sum of sines and cosines; interestingly, in addition to Gauss and Euler, Fourier is also a scientific ancestor of Lefschetz and thus of Tukey as well.[*]

Garwin glanced down at Tukey's notepad and asked Tukey what he was working on. "I was sitting there scratching,"[†] Tukey recalled, "and Dick [Garwin] wanted to know what [I was doing] and I told him what it was about generally": "a better algorithm for computing the discrete Fourier transform (DFT)." Even apart from Fourier transforms, algorithms were, in many ways, Tukey's preferred way of thinking about all sorts of statistical and mathematical ideas; as the Irish statistician Peter McCullagh notes, this set him apart from the dominant mode in statistics publications at the time, which hewed closely to the mathematical.

As he was scratching numbers on his small notepad while commiserating with Garwin, Tukey, unknowingly, was rediscovering mathematical ideas that Carl Friedrich Gauss arrived at centuries earlier; Gauss's contributions had lain dormant mostly because they were written in Latin. Nonetheless, Garwin was intrigued enough with Tukey's scratching to take notes; Garwin immediately saw applications to computing three-dimensional spin orientations and periodicities of Helium-3 isotopes. So Garwin spoke to Bill Dorn, manager of the computer center, about the far-reaching possibilities of Tukey's algorithm, showing him the notes he compiled. Dorn, who didn't understand the significance of the algorithm, referred Garwin to James Cooley, who also worked at IBM. From Tukey's head, to Garwin's notes, to a discussion with Cooley—Tukey termed this path the "double play."

James William Cooley was born in 1926 in New York City, New York; he served in the Army Air Corps near the end of the Second World War. Leveraging the G.I. Bill, Cooley managed to earn a doctorate in applied mathematics from Columbia University. In the mid-1950s, Cooley programmed von Neumann's computer at the Institute for Advanced Study. In 1962, Cooley joined the IBM Watson Research Center in Yorktown Heights, New York. Shortly thereafter, Garwin spoke to him about Tukey's algorithm.

Cooley had some familiarity with Tukey. Besides encountering him on the square-dancing circuit, Tukey had served as a liaison between Princeton University and IBM, consulting on meteorology problems. Specifically, Tukey had first worked with Cooley on the Blackman–Tukey method

---

[*] Tracing backwards in time: from Tukey to Lefschetz to Story to Klein to Lipschitz to Dirichlet to, finally, Fourier.
[†] By "scratching" or "scratching down" numbers, Tukey essentially means summarizing and organizing batches of values into more convenient and revealing displays (whether they be tabular or graphical).

of spectral analysis[*] in the late 1940s, which was designed to circumvent large Fourier transforms and still differentiate signal from noise (Tukey defined spectrum analysis as "the science and art of frequency analysis" at a dedication address), when Cooley was working at the Institute for Advanced Study. A while later, Tukey assigned Cooley the task of writing a computer program to model wind velocities. (Cooley later reflected on the irony of his and Tukey's collaborations: "Thus, our two collaborations were first on a method for avoiding large Fourier transforms since they were so costly and then a method for reducing the cost of the Fourier transforms.")

When Garwin approached Cooley about the FFT algorithm, Garwin's enthusiasm could hardly be contained; Garwin had with him a yellow pad overflowing with notes. As Cooley later described it, the notes contained the essential idea of the FFT algorithm:

> N, is a composite, $N = ab$, then the Fourier series can be expressed as an a-term series of subseries of b terms each. If one were computing all values of the series, this would reduce the number of operations from N^2 to $N(a+b)$. Tukey also said that if this were iterated, the number of operations would be proportional to $N\log(N)$ instead of N^2.

The importance of computational time, which Cooley is describing in the paragraph above, cannot be overstated, especially in the early days of computers. The typical way to classify time-analysis complexity is with what is called "Big O notation." The "O" stands for order; it describes the growth rate of a function as its inputs increase. Essentially, if a snippet of computer code has no repetition, then its Big O value is 1, expressed as $O(1)$ and called "constant time." Insert a single loop into the code, and the Big O value increases to n, expressed as $O(n)$ and called "linear time." The larger the input value of n into the function, the more steps a computer needs to take to traverse the loop; specifically, the number of steps required is proportional to the value of n. Likewise with $O(n^2)$, called "quadratic time"—a loop within a loop—the number of steps to traverse the code is proportional to the input squared. If a loop is traversed by ever-increasing jumps, rather than incrementing by a constant amount, a computer is instead operating in "logarithmic time," with the notation $O(\log n)$. There are numerous other permutations of time

---

[*] Tukey came to regret calling the method "spectral analysis" rather than "spectrum analysis" in print; though he later advocated substituting in the word "spectrum," "spectral" caught on nonetheless. Out of respect for Tukey's wishes, we will henceforth follow Brillinger's lead and call it spectrum analysis wherever possible.

complexity as well. The FFT algorithm was revolutionary because it reduced computational time from $O(n^2)$ to $O(n \log n)$.

Yet, at first, Cooley, who had met Garwin before, was nonplussed about the FFT algorithm's possibilities. Cooley could devote his time to whatever research he thought was meaningful, and he wasn't interested in pursuing Garwin's, at least at first. So Garwin, sensing that he had to do more to convince Cooley, repeatedly phoned him (and needled his boss), stressing the importance of Tukey's algorithm. Cooley finally acquiesced and got to work in his spare time writing a radix-2 algorithm—now universally known as the Cooley-Tukey FFT algorithm*—that recursively calculated fast Fourier transforms for multiple dimensions, putting into practice Tukey's factorization ideas (which Tukey had been forced to do with paper and pencil alone).

Once completed, Cooley figured his work amounted to only a programming exercise, since Tukey had already polished the mathematics behind the algorithm. Still, Cooley was proud of the program he wrote: to save storage space, the arrays of data in the code were overwritten with the results of the calculations; in addition, space was saved by computing two addresses instead of four, although producing the output required implementing a bit-reversal subroutine. Computations of the algorithm, as shown on a signal-flow graph, resembled a butterfly. The algorithm utilized a "divide-and-conquer strategy to reduce computation," he explained. Cooley thought that the FFT assignment was "kind of forced on me [Cooley] in a way." Yet the successful completion of this assignment ultimately became Cooley's most significant professional accomplishment.

There was an element of subterfuge in the story of Cooley's involvement, however. Garwin was indeed interested in using the FFT to help compute three-dimensional spin orientations and periodicities of Helium-3 isotopes, but he had a greater goal—namely, verification of USSR nuclear

---

* Cooley later considered it an honor to have been formally associated with Tukey. He also thought that people appreciated "the interesting variety of permutations in the sounds in the names [of the algorithm], resulting in names like the 'Cool-Turkey algorithm' and the 'Cookie-Toolie' algorithm.'" People also sometimes inadvertently mangled Tukey's name by itself, referring to the statistician as "J. W. Cutie," for example; Bell Labs mathematician Dick Hamming was probably the first to do this, around the time Tukey published an especially neologism-heavy paper on spectrum analysis. And, at a lunch at Bell Labs, when an informal proposal was made for a Society of Data Analysis (SODA), David Brillinger referred to Tukey as "SODA pop." (In my experience, statistics students often accidently read Tukey's name as "Turkey.")

arms compliance conforming to the Nuclear Test Ban Treaty of 1963. The problem was simple: Russia wouldn't permit inspectors on-site. Garwin realized that compliance could instead be checked through the use of instruments to detect nuclear explosions (seismometers positioned in U.S.-friendly countries adjacent to the Soviet Union) and spectrum analysis calculations, greatly sped up by having computers run the FFT algorithm. What's more, Garwin had a second Cold War-related goal: the detection of submarines from a distance. But Garwin didn't tell Cooley anything of these plans, instead hoping that his research on Helium-3 served as a believable cover story. "Now, this was [Garwin's] incentive [i.e., detecting nuclear explosions], but he didn't discuss that, he came to me and he made up another problem," Cooley said. "He didn't want to tell me about that." Of course, Cooley eventually discovered the truth. (Besides the seismograph analyses, Garwin was genuinely interested in utilizing the FFT algorithm for astronomy calculations.)

In the meantime, questions began to be raised about ownership rights over the algorithm. Cooley, once he had finished writing the code, not only freely shared it with Garwin but also with a number of other interested parties, of which there were few at first; as Cooley remembers it, "[Garwin] went about publicizing [my computer program] and they still didn't think it was very important." But all that changed after Cooley presented the FFT algorithm at a weekly numerical analysis seminar held at the IBM Research Department of Mathematical Sciences, which was run by Larry Horowitz. Howard Smith, an IBM employee, had already used the concise programming language APL (which stands for A Programming Language), developed at IBM in the early 1960s by Kenneth E. Iverson and Adin Falkoff (who were also in attendance at the weekly seminar), to code an FFT algorithm, although APL wasn't fully-formed as a standalone programming language yet since no implementations that ran on any hardware were available. As Cooley and Tukey remember it, "These talks gave the FFT a thorough exposure to a number of mathematicians." However, the seminar, though groundbreaking, hadn't come out of nowhere. At an earlier seminar, which focused on the nascent APL, someone piped up to ask, "Are there any other algorithms that we can illustrate with this?" That's when Cooley offered to give a talk on the FFT, setting the stage for Howard Smith to write his APL FFT algorithm.

A patent attorney named Frank Thomas—who happened to be an expert in mathematics—was also in attendance at the numerical analysis seminar with Cooley and Smith (he was sitting in the back of the room). Thomas raised the issue of patent rights: "This has patent possibilities," he declared. A meeting of mathematicians and lawyers was then convened. At the meeting, the IBM brain trust quickly realized that they first had to get to the bottom of where the antecedent ideas of the FFT originated before being able to determine the patentability of the algorithm—and Tukey, even though he didn't work for IBM, was allowed to assist.

Tukey pointed to Frank Yates, a British statistician, former surveyor, and statistical computing pioneer who specialized in factorial experiment design (with applications to fertilizer experiments), and Irving John "I. J." Good, a British mathematician who had worked with Alan Turing* at Bletchley Park and also written some algorithms which were somewhat similar to the FFT,† as paving the way for the FFT. (In fact, Garwin, who had paid a visit to Good in 1957, joked with him later that "[h]ad we talked about an FFT in 1957, I could have stolen it from you then, instead of from John Tukey in 1963.") Garwin also sought information, asking Cooley's graduate school advisor L. H. Thomas about antecedents to the FFT. Thomas described a paper he had written in which he performed Fourier series calculations on old IBM punched card computers; he had looked up these calculation methods in a "cookbook" of sorts by the mathematician Karl Stumpff.

Years after the publication of his own FFT algorithm, Cooley encountered the work of the Hungarian mathematician Cornelius Lanczos, who in the 1940s did work on Fourier transforms that, at least in passing, bore some resemblance to the FFT, but Tukey hadn't been aware of the connection.‡ Cooley was alerted to this connection by Philip Rudnick, who, while working at the Scripps Institution of Oceanography, wrote a program modeled off of Lanczos's results; Rudnick, however, published his algorithm after Cooley's paper achieved wide circulation. In addition, there was simultaneous invention of the FFT by a mathematician at the Jet Propulsion Laboratory in Pasadena, California, named Lloyd Welch, to virtually no acclaim or publicity. "Perhaps among the ideas discarded before the days of electronic computers, we may find more seeds of new algorithms," Cooley wistfully noted.

Cooley compared the discovery of the FFT to Columbus's discovery of America: it wasn't that Columbus was the first person to set foot in the New World, only that he arrived at a fortuitous time when naval ships were readily available, "commerce had advanced, and Europe was over-

---

* As a Princeton graduate student, Turing, who frequented Fine Hall, once lent Tukey his car, and Tukey drove it to North Carolina with Ralph Boas to attend a meeting.
† Good's version was saddled with the restriction that factors of N had to be mutually prime, meaning that the greatest common divisor of the factors was 1, which dramatically slowed down the algorithm as compared to Tukey's.
‡ After the publication of the FFT, Cooley gave a talk on the algorithm at Yale with Lanczos in attendance. After the talk, Cooley asked Lanczos why he didn't do more to spread his ideas. "Well, at the time, N was not very big," Lanczos said.

populated," so Europeans could take tremendous advantage of the newly available land (by first forcibly displacing indigenous populations, of course); likewise, the FFT's (re)discovery by Tukey and Cooley came at "just the right time," Cooley explained, since computer technology had advanced enough to fully exploit the algorithm. Tukey had a more circumspect view of the FFT's reinvention. "This [the FFT] was the only obvious thing to do," Tukey said. Starting "with a set of samples, the only obvious thing to do was to subsample the samples. So maybe that accounts for why it was invented so many times."

In Tukey's view, his (and Cooley's) contribution was unique enough to be classified as patentable. Tukey already had experience writing patent submissions, having applied for one for a special type of cathode ray along with fellow Bell Labs employees Claude Shannon and the American engineer and science fiction writer John R. Pierce, with whom Tukey was especially simpatico (e.g., they both enjoyed science fiction). However, after raucous discussion of the pros and cons, IBM agreed with lawyer Frank Tezerdian's take: the FFT was simply more suitable for the public domain. Here is Tukey's view on what transpired: "And eventually IBM kicked Jim [Cooley] into publication because they decided they didn't want to try to patent it and they didn't want anybody else to." Cooley agreed with Tukey, adding that IBM "put it in the public domain so we protect the right of IBM to use the idea, before someone else patents it" and "to publicize it and [thus] protect the right of IBM to use it." In the 1960s, as Cooley explained in a 1992 conference, IBM made it a habit to avoid having to patent any software; rather, the company wanted software to be freely distributable—so as to "help sell [their] computers," which were of the large mainframe variety. To advertise the FFT algorithm, and, by extension, its line of mainframes, IBM leveraged the results of geophysicist Lee Alsop, who had successfully run the algorithm through 2,048 samples of a seismograph of an earthquake at Rat Island, New York; IBM placed ads in periodicals such as *Scientific American* boasting of Alsop's research. And Cooley himself helped to publicize the algorithm within IBM, holding a series of seminars with statisticians Peter D. Welch and Peter A. W. Lewis, the notes of which were later compiled and assembled into a set of papers on FFT applications.

At first, however, Cooley had no interest in publishing his algorithm. Nonetheless, he began writing a paper for publication at IBM lawyer Tezerdian's urging, describing the FFT algorithm in detail. There wasn't any available hardware to run the algorithm on, which the IBM legal team insisted was a problem since an unrunnable algorithm couldn't be directly patented then, but a physical device to run an algorithm on could receive a patent. Making such a device, and documenting its construction in a paper, would ensure the public domain status of the FFT and thereby preclude anyone else from receiving a patent. So Cooley commissioned Shmuel Winograd and Ray Miller to build hardware that ran the FFT, and Cooley gave them credit in a footnote of his paper, entitled "An Algorithm for the Machine Calculation of Complex Fourier Series": "A multiple-processing [digital] circuit using this algorithm was designed by R. E. Miller and S. Winograd of the IBM Watson Research Center" (a separate footnote acknowledged the contributions of Garwin).

The paper was co-written with Tukey. Cooley mailed a draft to Tukey for him to peruse and rework; Tukey sent it back to Cooley, with the process beginning anew several more times. Cooley submitted the paper to the journal *Mathematics of Computation* (Cooley knew the editor, Eugene Isaacson, who was based in New York University), and it was published in the April 1965 issue. Cooley's paper is spare, dense, and very short—barely five pages in length—but it remains one of the most cited papers in the history of *Mathematics of Computation*. Even after the paper's publication, Cooley didn't think it was particularly important, let alone believe it to be the citation classic it would become; he didn't even order any reprints to distribute. But Cooley began to understand the import of his work after fielding a call from digital audio pioneer Thomas Greenway Stockham of MIT, who raved about the paper, even suggesting that the FFT could be used to compute convolutions, a method of combining two functions utilized in digital-signal processing. In general, Cooley found that reaction to the paper could be grouped into one of two categories: (1) The FFT was a revolution (e.g., Stockham's sentiment), or (2) The FFT was a modern update of an old idea (courtesy of Gauss, Yates, Good, and so forth).

Even before the release of Cooley's paper, Tukey had no compunction about presenting parts of the FFT, such as his unique factorization algorithms, in his classes. David Brillinger was a student in Tukey's time series class in early 1963, in which Tukey presented an "iterative algebraic approach" to calculating some Fourier transforms; Tukey had, in the previous decade, applied similar time series to the analysis of airplane flight.*

In that same spring semester of 1963, a graduate student named Gordon E. Sande, who was from Alberta, Canada, was inspired enough by Tukey's ideas to independently write a radix-2 algorithm (a "transposed algorithm," different from Cooley's) and a paper to go along with it that he typed up at his Canadian defense research summer job. But, when he presented his work to Tukey, Tukey told his student that such a paper had already been submitted (by Cooley) and Sande withdrew his work

---

* On a related note, Brillinger claims that Tukey's time series results influenced mathematician Leon Warren Cohen, who, during the war, was hard at work on an algorithm to optimize enemy airplane tracking prior to firing.

from publication consideration. Which was unfortunate, since Sande's paper presented the FFT from an alternative perspective than Cooley's, having a different radix-2 algorithm as well as innovative correlation calculations. Tukey regretted what happened. "I sort of floated along and didn't take adequate action to see that Gordon [Sande] got his stuff out, which I always felt bad about."[*] It also didn't sit well with Cooley, who reflected that "[Sande's] paper was actually a far better paper because he described how to use the idea for doing covariance calculations, which was a very important application to this. I hadn't thought of that at all." Regardless, three years later, Sande and the mathematician Morven Gentleman were given an opportunity to present a more thorough and expanded version of Sande's early FFT ideas at the Fall Joint Computer Conference. In addition, Sande eventually published his more developed, fleshed-out version of the FFT algorithm.

As Cooley noted in 1993, the FFT methods that he, Tukey, and Sande discovered are still being used for applications such as digital signal processing (DSP), which were precipitated by analog-to-digital converters, leading to the reliance on algorithms to process signals optimally rather than relying on fine-tuning physical devices. Methods of DSP that worked in theory but were heretofore impossible in practice because they needed too much computing power to function now became feasible with the FFT algorithm; with such barriers torn down, engineers weren't left with a reason not to convert from analog to DSP. For instance, Thomas Stockham demonstrated sound-correction and manipulation techniques such as excising the violin playing out of old Enrico Caruso records. And an MIT graduate student named Norman Brenner, who was working under the auspices of Charles Rader (who had an abiding interest in the FFT), programmed a number of FFT variants that optimized memory storage.

In 1969, Garwin, Cooley, Sande, Stockham, Rader, Brenner, and around one hundred other mathematicians, scientists, and even heart surgeons—who were writing FFTs for postoperative monitoring of their patients—and other interested parties gathered at the Arden House in New York to discuss the state of affairs of the FFT and solve some open problems; Garwin, who gave the keynote, spoke of further publicizing the algorithm. These meetings had by then become something of an annual tradition, and another lasting legacy of Tukey and Cooley's FFT algorithm.

The development of the FFT algorithm had brought together Tukey, who worked at Bell Labs, and Cooley, who worked for IBM, on a major

---

[*] He apologized tacitly to Sande in this interview as well as in the *Collected Works*, saying, "I owe him, and hereby make, a humble apology."

project which IBM had no interest in patenting. But years later, IBM and Bell would feud over a patent; for a period of roughly half a decade, ties were severed between the two organizations. Slowly, relations thawed, eventually resulting in an exchange of talent between IBM (in New York) and Bell (in Murray Hill). Tukey thought that the IBMers were shocked at the large number of industrial statisticians employed at Bell, perhaps enough to reconsider their organizational model.

CHAPTER THIRTEEN

Explorations in Time Series

"The Quefrency Alanysis of Time Series for Echoes: Cepstrum,
Pseudo-Autocovariance, Cross-Cepstrum and Saphe Cracking"
— Title of a 1963 paper by B. P. Bogert, J. R. Healy and J. W. Tukey

S everal years after working on the post-war Nike project, the engineer and accomplished Bell Labs employee Donald Ling attributed
to Tukey a simple calculation involving aerodynamics in an unoffi-
cial draft memorandum. Donald Percy Ling was born in 1912 in Albany,
New York. At first, he studied piano; then, he pursued mathematics,
earning a bachelor's degree at Amherst in 1933 and then a master's and a
doctorate at Columbia. Near the end of the war, Ling joined the National
Defense Research Committee (NDRC) to work on aerial gunnery problems. Immediately after the war, Hendrik Bode hired Ling to work in the
Mathematical Research Department at Murray Hill; he joined Tukey and
others researchers on a study of antiaircraft guided missile systems, which
ultimately bled into the Nike project. As Brock McMillan described it,

> The study broke new technical ground in analyzing the aerodynamic
> control of supersonic vehicles, and it challenged conventional wisdom
> about sensors and about where the control loops should be closed. It al-
> so broke new ground among military "systems analyses" of the period in
> the scope and issues covered and in its penetration of these issues. From
> this study came the Nike series of guided missile systems.

Ling continued at Bell Labs for well over a decade, designing a warhead for the Nike and, after the Mathematical Research Department was
split up, rising in the 1950s to lead a research unit consisting of Sydney
Darlington, R. B. Blackman, and Tukey. The unit was successful at building guidance algorithms for the Nike as well as programs "for the first
digital (and solid-state) bombing and navigation computer (Tradic)," according to McMillan. The TRADIC, or TRAnsistor DIgital Computer,
was the first digital transistorized (i.e., packed with transistors instead of
vacuum tubes) computer. The machine was geared toward military usage;

despite being constructed at Bell Labs, it was commissioned by the United States Air Force, which needed a computer for airborne usage.

Tukey would work again with Ralph Beebe "R. B." Blackman—or "Blackie," as he called him. Blackman, who had a degree from the California Institute of Technology, was an engineer interested in communication theory (as were Tukey and, of course, Shannon). Employed at Bell since the mid-1920s, Blackman's work turned from "physical research" toward the "development of data-smoothing and prediction techniques for antiaircraft fire-control computers, air-to-ground bombing computers, guided-missile computers and satellite launching computers," according to a July 1963 biography printed in *The Bell System Technical Journal*. A number of real-world problems, such as atmospheric measurements affecting airplane flights, were the genesis of the time-series projects that interested Tukey. The 1958 paper "The Measurement of Power Spectra from the Point of View of Communications Engineering," which Tukey wrote with Blackman (and which was expanded and published in book form one year later), was an outgrowth of those interests. So was the Blackman–Tukey method of spectrum analysis, or the Blackman–Tukey Transformation, which utilizes the FFT.

Signal processing methods had as their origin the aggregation and analysis of atmospheric data. Tukey would apply signal processing to detecting echoes and analyzing speech patterns—this he called the power *cepstrum*, which is an anagram of "spectrum"—helping to construct a machine that would relay the pitch of a human being's voice. Careful analysis of the cepstrum would also assist in differentiating between seismic events resulting from underground nuclear explosion tests and naturally occurring earthquakes by looking for specific types of signal delays—a project Tukey was intimately involved with that, as described in a prior chapter, caused him great stress.

The apotheosis of Tukey's word-coining proclivities came in the form of the title of a 1963 paper detailing *cepstral analysis,* the process of estimating the underground depth of seismic activity, which he co-wrote with mathematician Bruce P. Bogert and the British statistician Michael John Romer Healy. Interested in exploring the uses of statistics in an industrial setting, such as with quality control, Healy had arrived at Murray Hill with that objective firmly in mind, but the advent of International Nuclear Test Ban negotiations put his industrial applications on the back burner in favor of cepstral analysis.

The paper the three wrote was called "The Quefrency Alanysis of Time Series for Echoes: Cepstrum, Pseudo-Autocovariance, Cross-Cepstrum and Saphe Cracking." Richard Feynman had engaged in literal safe cracking at Los Alamos; Tukey was now performing *saphe cracking*— analyzing the phase of the cepstrum—at Murray Hill. Furthermore, Tukey wasn't engaging in "analysis," but, rather, *alanysis*. Why the seemingly over-the-top title? The authors' explanation reads as follows.

> In general, we find ourselves operating on the frequency side in ways customary on the time side and vice versa. Experience has made it clear that "words that sound like other words," although strange at first sight, considerably reduce confusion on balance. These parallel or "paraphrased" words are made by the interchange of consonants or consonant groups, as in "alanysis" from "analysis," and are introduced as needed.

The paper was delivered at a conference at Brown on time series. Those in attendance were surely overwhelmed: cepstrum analysis, along with all of its attendant terminology, was unveiled at once. "The audience must have been absolutely amazed," Brillinger said.

Dick Hamming, who also worked at Bell Labs, was inspired by Tukey's work in spectrum analysis. Richard "Dick" Wesley Hamming, born in 1915 in Chicago, Illinois, earned a doctorate in mathematics from the University of Illinois in 1942 and went to work operating primitive computers at Los Alamos for the Manhattan Project. A year after the war ended, Hamming was hired by Bell Labs. Hamming quickly noticed that Bell applied mathematics, of which he considered himself one, were instructed to "do unconventional things in unconventional ways and still get valuable results." Hamming's "Hamming window," a type of digital filter, came about as result of working with Tukey and Blackman.

Tukey's work on time series, which resulted in his advances in spectrum analysis and the fast Fourier transform, weren't performed in a vacuum. In *The Annals of Statistics* article "John W. Tukey's Work on Time Series and Spectrum Analysis" (2002), David Brillinger lays out, in brief, the history of time series analysis prior to Tukey. There was Isaac Newton, who used a glass prism to split the colors of the spectrum; William Herschel, who discovered infrared radiation by placing a thermometer past the red end of the visible spectrum when examining sunlight; and a number of other scientists who made major contributions, such as Lord Kelvin and Sir George Stokes. Especially noteworthy was the harmonic analyzers of Albert A. Michelson[*] and Samuel W. Stratton, which were utilized to study waves of light. Thereafter, Brillinger describes Tukey's contributions, dividing the statistician's work on the topic into two parts:

---

[*] Best known for the Michelson–Morley experiment, conducted with the scientist Edward W. Morley, which measured the speed of light through the theoretical (and ultimately disproven) "luminiferous aether"; their experiment laid the groundwork for Einstein's theory of special relativity.

the "indirect years" (1940s to early 1960s), where spectrum estimation didn't make use of Fourier transforms, and the "direct years" (late 1960s to 1990), where there FFT was utilized for spectrum estimation.

Tukey's first exposure to time series likely came at the FCRO while poring through the work of Norbert Wiener, which was later published as *Extrapolation, Interpolation and Smoothing of Stationary Time Series*. Wiener, born in Columbia, Missouri, in 1894, was a mathematician who became best known for his pioneering work in stochastic processes, the mathematization of a random (as opposed to deterministic) system through time, and cybernetics, the study of how humans, animals, and machines interact. Wiener also published on Fourier transforms. Tukey was interested in taking some of Wiener's ideas, which involved time series, and translating them for statisticians. A 1942 letter Wiener wrote to Tukey[*] offers him detailed technical suggestions on how to properly proceed as well as offering to "write to you more in detail later. We enjoyed your visit very much and hope to keep in touch with you."[†]

Though Tukey probably didn't have a Winsor-like mentor for his time series work,[‡] both Brillinger and Peter McCullagh finger Horace Budenbom as the person most responsible for spurring Tukey's interest in the topic in earnest. Recall that Budenbom, an engineer at Bell Labs, posed a problem related to radar tracking to the mathematics group at Murray Hill, and he requested the calculation of a spectrum from them. But right before heading out to a conference in which he was scheduled to present the details of his findings, Budenbom asked Tukey and Hamming to take a look at a slide of the estimated power spectrum. Hamming and Tukey were intrigued. After finding the Fourier transform, and realizing that the estimate needed a special sort of smoothing—which they quickly fashioned for Budenbom on a new slide that the engineer took to the conference—"Dick (Hamming) and I then spent a few months finding out why," Tukey recalled later on.[§]

Brillinger also named Willard J. Pierson, Jr., a professor of oceanography at New York University and City College of New York, as an influence on Tukey's time series work. An obituary printed in *Eos, Transactions, American Geophysical Union*, describes the import of Pierson's work:

---

[*] Reprinted in "John W. Tukey's Work on Time Series and Spectrum Analysis."

[†] Stanislaw Ulam, though impressed with his technical abilities, categorized Wiener as "childish" because of his constant need for reassurance.

[‡] According to Brillinger; although it is inconclusive as to whether Tukey had a time series mentor, he probably did not.

[§] Tukey details the full technical timeline in "The Future of Data Analysis" (see pages 39 to 40).

In the first half of his professional career, with support provided mainly by the Office of Naval Research, Pierson laid the groundwork for the spectral analysis of ocean waves, the systematic analysis of the motion of ships in a random sea, the generation and propagation of surface waves on the ocean, the methodology of numerical wave forecasting, and the remote sensing of ocean surface winds and sea state....

...Pierson then analyzed the spectral data base for transient conditions to develop quantitative expressions for wave growth consistent with the theories of wave growth of Owen Phillips and John Miles....

A geophysicist and oceanographer named Walter H. Munk, whom Tukey asserted "may well be the most effective practitioner of spectrum analysis the world has seen,"[*] also had an effect on the statistician's thinking. To back this claim up, look no further than this comment by Tukey printed in the first volume of the *Collected Works*: "Through the years, my strongest source of catalysis has been Walter Munk." Tukey wasn't alone in these sentiments; Walter Heinrich Munk, born in Vienna, Austria, in 1917, has been labeled by many as the "Einstein of the oceans."

In 1970, Tukey, who was by now renowned for his time series advancements, was invited to present at the annual Arthur William Scott Lectures at the Cavendish Laboratory in Cambridge University; he followed Werner Heisenberg and Niels Bohr, among many other luminaries of science, who had presented in previous years. Tukey focused on exploratory data analysis, the FFT, and time series. The talks took place over the course of two days, and the audience consisted of "mainly physical scientists." Tukey offered them gems like this: "Often the purpose of good analysis is not so much to do well in catching what you want but rather to do well...in rejecting what you don't want."

Brillinger adds that although some of Tukey's time series techniques were inspired by geophysics problems, it cut both ways: through the early unpublished time series papers of the 1940s (which found a home in the *Collected Works*), ultimately leading to the more mature time series work of the 1950s and beyond, Tukey influenced geophysicists, too, such as with his delivery of an address at the dedication of the La Jolla Laboratories of the Institute of Geophysics and Planetary Geophysics at the University of California—an address that served as a sales pitch for spectrum analysis. In fact, it was in the delivery of this address, called "Data Analysis and the Frontiers of Geophysics," that Tukey most clearly and concisely defined

---

[*] Tukey said this at a seminar held to honor Munk on the occasion of his 65th birthday.

spectrum analysis: as "the science and art of frequency analysis." What's more, Tukey made sure to meet with scientists of note, such as Pierson and Munk, at every opportunity—conferences, seminars, and the like. "The literature of applied time series," Brillinger observes, "contains numerous acknowledgments of [Tukey's] suggestions."

Brillinger also notes that time series analysis set the course for much of Tukey's other work: time series work was linked thematically to numerous other Tukey projects, including robustness, the analysis of variance, and data analysis. In fact, Tukey himself wrote that "[i]t is now clear to me that spectrum analysis, with its challenging combination of amplified difficulties and forcible attention to reality, has done more than any other area to develop my overall views of data analysis." This assertion comes in the *Collected Works*, where Tukey called spectrum analysis an "active catalyst" for his notions on data analysis because both subfields have, as he saw it, similar constraints and a "forcible attention to reality." With all this in mind, it is Tukey's breakthrough formulation of data analysis to which we now turn.

CHAPTER FOURTEEN

The Difference Between Science and Mathematics

"Statistics is a science in my opinion..."
—John Tukey

I n "The Growth of Experimental Design in a Research Laboratory" (1953), a paper he presented at Columbia University for the Third Annual Conference on Industrial Research, Tukey breaks down the three key elements to consider in any experimental research program: measurement (how is the measurement process arrived at and conducted? How is variability of measurement analyzed? How confident are we in the results?), selection (what is to be tested? What makes the most sense to test?), and personnel (who will organize, conduct, and analyze the research?). He also offers this sentiment, which turned out to be one of his most quoted passages:

> Statistics is a science in my opinion, and is no more a branch of mathe-matics than are physics, chemistry and economics; for if its methods fail the test of experience—not the test of logic—they are discarded.

Notice the word "science." How, exactly, could statistics be a science? Wasn't it a math? Well—yes and no. Like physics, chemistry, and eco-nomics, statistics "uses mathematical models as an essential, perhaps its most essential tools." But mathematical statistics isn't synonymous with statistics any more than mathematical physics is synonymous with phys-ics. "Just remember that not all statistics has been mathematized," Tukey warns, "and that we *may* not have to wait for its mathematization in order to use it." (To illustrate his point, consider an analogy: the pharmaceutical industry releases drugs that seem to work wonders despite scientists not always completely understanding how they do so. Likewise, Tukey claims, we can use statistical techniques that have proven effective despite their inner workings not having been laid bare via mathematization.)

With these searing statements, Tukey lays bare the empirical nature of the discipline of statistics: unlike in, say, a geometry class, where the logic of the results is paramount—geometry class is where most mathematics students first see proofs, after all—in statistics it is necessary to see if the mathematical models fit the data well (at least that's what Tukey is saying we should do), rather than treating the real world as an inconvenient distraction to be swatted away in a heady pursuit of abstract mathematical modeling.

True, a mathematical model is useful for guiding the statistician; "these formalized models are *reference situations*—base points, if you like—things against which you compare the data you actually have to see how it differs," Tukey wrote. Perhaps taken to their logical conclusion, the intermingling of the formalized models and the data will overturn what has heretofore been conventional wisdom. Peter McCullagh termed this approach as one of a "constructive scientific anarchist."

The empirical world is "fuzzy" and "imprecise," Tukey added, which is counterpoised by the "precise logic of mathematics"—useful to the statistician for theoretical derivations, but not necessarily a good fit for thinking about the world, replete as it is with imprecision. To drive home this point—that to be an effective applied statistician one needs to be comfortable with uncertainty—Tukey would describe an interaction he had with the Jewish mathematician Walther Mayer, born in 1887 in Graz, Austria-Hungary. In 1946, Mayer, who had collaborated with Einstein in Germany, asked Tukey where his career was taking him. Tukey replied that he was staying at both Princeton and Bell Labs. Mayer expressed surprise at the latter, explaining that while "applied matters" were the order of the day in Germany during World War I, he was overjoyed to return to a high level of mathematical abstraction where "If I say a g_{ik} has certain properties, it does." There is no doubt that Tukey was sympathetic to those like Mayer who were "monastic," or single-mindedly focused on pure mathematical research:

> If one takes this word [monastic] correctly, it is well chosen. Concern with pure mathematical research can be engrossing and satisfying enough to meet the intellectual needs of some of the ablest men of all time. The intellectual challenge of new knowledge, new concepts and new order is as pure and intense a challenge as any we know. The satisfactions from its successes are great; for certain kinds of individuals they are clearly the greatest possible. Many for whom this is so have had stimulating and satisfying lives and have contributed much to human life.

But Tukey believed the greatest utility of mathematics rested not in its purest forms, but in its most applied varieties, where nearly one-to-one correspondences could be made with simulation and real life. Mathematics' "great use," he wrote, "is to simulate some physical, biological, social, or organizational system, or, more precisely, to simulate a carefully select- ed set of aspects of such [a] system, aspects which may be important, and for which we can do an adequate job of finding abstract analogs."

Hungarian-American physicist Eugene Wigner explored the idea of abstract analogs in a famous essay entitled "The Unreasonable Effective- ness of Mathematics in the Natural Sciences" (1960). He gives attention to two related ideas:

> The first point is that the enormous usefulness of mathematics in the natural sciences is something bordering on the mysterious and that there is no rational explanation for it. Second, it is just this uncanny usefulness of mathematical concepts that raises the question of the uniqueness of our physical theories.

While grappling with illuminating questions like "How do we know that, if we made a theory which focuses its attention on phenomena we disre- gard and disregards some of the phenomena now commanding our atten- tion, that we could not build another theory which has little in common with the present one but which, nevertheless, explains just as many phe- nomena as the present theory?"—a question that could just as equally apply to statistics as it does to physics and the other natural sciences[*]— Wigner ultimately comes to an equivocal conclusion: "[F]undamentally, we do not know why our theories work so well. Hence, their accuracy may not prove their truth and consistency." It's a miracle, the Austrian physicist Erwin Schrödinger observed, that "certain regularities" could be discovered despite the mind-blowing complexity of the world.

Statistics was the "foundation" of experimental design, Tukey wrote. Tukey also wrestled with crystalizing an all-encompassing definition of statistics; he knew it was a science, so he knew what statistics was not. After a time, Tukey arrived at this description: "Statistics is the science, the art, the philosophy, and the technique of making inferences from the particular to the general." Yet Tukey remained unsatisfied with the defini- tion, largely because of the practical nature of the discipline—after all, if we dare look at data, we perform statistics. The trappings of what he called "formal statistics" in "The Growth of Experimental Design in a Research Laboratory" (also called Confirmatory Data Analysis—i.e., clas-

---

[*] Perhaps influenced by Wigner's work, Read D. Tuddenham formulated the "statistician's dictum": "that whatever exists can be measured." He also ob- served that the converse—"whatever can be 'measured' must exist"—doesn't necessarily hold.

sical statistics, replete with significance testing and the like), help to steer the experimental researcher between the Scylla of unalloyed optimism and the Charybdis of self-defeating pessimism when poring through experimental results, especially those obtained through some sort of measurement.

But why did Tukey consider statistics a science, rather than a math? In his most influential published article, "The Future of Data Analysis" (hereafter abbreviated FoDA) printed in *The Annals of Mathematical Statistics* in 1962 but written in 1961 with the express purpose of grappling with what he perceived to be the key upcoming challenges of and opportunities for study in data analysis (i.e., a quest for new questions and "growth areas"), Tukey notes that "[t]here are diverse views as to what makes a science," but he nonetheless enumerates three criteria: (1) "Intellectual content"; (2) "Organization in understandable form"; and (3) "Reliance upon the test of experience as the ultimate standard of validity." "By these tests," Tukey claims, "mathematics is not a science since its ultimate standard of validity is an agreed-upon sort of logical consistency and provability."

Prototypical scientists and mathematicians approach their quest for knowledge in decidedly different ways. According to Yuval Noah Harari in his book *Homo Deus: A Brief History of Tomorrow* (2017), if we venture back in time to medieval Europe, the formula for obtaining knowledge was

$$\text{Knowledge} = \text{Scriptures} \times \text{Logic}$$

"If people wanted to know the answer to an important question, they would read scriptures and use their logic to understand the exact meaning of the text," Harari explains. But the Enlightenment and Scientific Revolution decoupled scriptures as source material for knowledge about natural phenomena, if not for all aspects of life (including things like, say, ethical dilemmas). The formula for obtaining knowledge became

$$\text{Knowledge} = \text{Empirical Data} \times \text{Mathematics}$$

Gathering observations and carving up the data with mathematical tools was the order of the day. For instance, as Harari notes, observing the sun, moon, and planets from earth might allow us, with the help of trigonometry, to model the solar system. "In practice, this means that scientists seek knowledge by spending years in observatories, laboratories and on research expeditions, gathering more and more empirical data, and sharpening their mathematical tools so they can interpret the data correctly."

Mathematics—despite often being referred to as the queen of the sciences—bears little resemblance to science, since, in mathematics, if a proposition is proven true using a series of airtight logical steps, the proposition is forever true; statements in mathematics require no empirical justification or verification to ascend to a kind of "immortal truth." With science, however, theories can only ever be disproven, never proven true. As Thomas Kuhn famously argued in *The Structure of Scientific Revolutions* (1962), science progresses through periods of revolutionary discontinuities in which "paradigm shifts," such as the one triggered by the Copernican Revolution, mark tipping points in explaining and understanding phenomena.

Despite sequences of logical steps ostensibly sowing the seeds of "immortal truth," foundationally, mathematics as both a consistent and provable discipline has always been on shaky ground. To understand why, we need to take a brief detour to examine some of the epistemological foundations of mathematics. The case of David Hilbert serves as a cautionary tale. Hilbert, born in 1862 in (probably) Königsberg, Prussia, was one of the most consequential mathematicians of the nineteenth and early twentieth centuries. In 1900, at the International Congress of Mathematicians in Paris, Hilbert set the tone and course of study of the discipline, at least for the immediate future, by proposing a series of nearly two dozen mathematics problems that he believed were critical for mathematicians to tackle.* Hilbert's problems fed into larger notions he had about mathematics—namely, that it could be rigorously and exhaustively formalized, perhaps using set theory. At first, thinkers like Bertrand Russell and Alfred North Whitehead agreed, producing a first draft of this formalization project in the form of a massive, multivolume work called *Principia Mathematica* (1910-1913), a sort of Euclid's *Elements* for the twentieth century. "Mathematics," Russell said, "rightly viewed, possesses not only truth, but supreme beauty." The general consensus was clear: although there

---

* Tukey had his Hilbert moment in 1954, when he posed 51 "provocative questions" on a multitude of topics in experimental statistics for researchers to consider; as Lyle Jones, an editor of the *Collected Works*, explains, Tukey made headway on some of the questions as well as inspiring other individuals to take the reins. However, although he was often asked to prognosticate, Tukey always trod carefully when making predictions. In a chapter of the third volume of the *Collected Works*, which was based on a talk he delivered at a symposium, Tukey says that a telling answer to the question "Where do we go from here?" is "To the psychiatrist!"—meaning statisticians often slip into any number of cognitive traps that can skew their thinking, such as a dependence upon "intellectual parents" and a "retreat from the real world toward the world of infancy."

was plenty of math yet to do, and many outstanding conjectures hadn't been proven yet, a lot of hard work, some preternatural creative thinking, and maybe a dash of good luck could tidy up all of mathematics.

Disaster struck fairly quickly as cracks in using what is called "naïve set theory" as a foundation for all of mathematics became exposed. Russell, in fact, found a foundational problem that he famously called the Barber's paradox. Suppose that in a small town, there is one barber. He only shaves men who don't shave themselves; men aren't permitted to wear facial hair of any kind in the town. Sounds fine, except when we ask ourselves a key question: Who shaves the barber? Russell generalizes from the Barber paradox to illustrate the larger issue:

> [N]ormally a class is not a member of itself. Mankind, for example, is not a man. Form now the assemblage of all classes which are not members of themselves. This is a class: is it a member of itself or not? If it is, it is one of those classes that are not members of themselves, i.e., it is not a member of itself. If it is not, it is not one of those classes that are not members of themselves, i.e. it is a member of itself. Thus of the two hypotheses—that it is, and that it is not, a member of itself—each implies its contradictory. This is a contradiction.

Although Russell evaded responsibility for coming up with the Barber's paradox, its larger implications were devastating: namely, the proposition *the set of all sets which are not members of themselves* began the process of undermining both Hilbert's formalism project and, ironically (since Russell was the coauthor), *Principia Mathematica*. Although Russell and the logician Alfred Tarski tried desperately to patch up set theory with a "ramified theory of types," which addressed such problematic impredicative (self-referencing) definitions, mortal damage to mathematics had already been sustained.

It took two more mathematicians to put the final stakes firmly into the faintly beating heart of the formalism project. Hilbert, who believed all mathematical systems could be made both consistent and complete—i.e., could have an exhaustive set of axioms—had publicly posed three questions: Was any formal mathematical system complete? was it consistent? and was every statement provable? In 1931 Kurt Gödel, with his incompleteness theorems, was able to answer the first two questions with a resounding "no": he showed that any consistent axiomatic mathematical system invariably contained undecidable propositions—propositions that could be proven neither true nor false. Alan Turing, who was only years away from helping to crack the German's Enigma machine during his stay at Bletchley Park, solved the third of Hilbert's questions—usually called the "Entscheidungsproblem," or decidability problem—by conceptualizing his Turing machine, a finite-state precursor to the digital computer that he sketched out only on paper.* "The Entscheidungsproblem is solved," Hilbert said, "when one knows a procedure by which one can decide in a finite number of operations whether a given logical expression is generally valid or is satisfiable." By leveraging a Universal Turing machine, programmed to simultaneously act as a series of Turing machines, Turing proved the existence of what are termed "non-computable numbers" as well as "non-computable functions," thereby supplying Hilbert's formalist program its coup de grâce: that there is no algorithm to solve the Entscheidungsproblem.† Poking fun of mathematical methods in satiric pieces like "The Mathematical Theory of Big Game Hunting" suddenly didn't seem so funny.

The formalist program wasn't the first time in the history of mathematics that the proverbial cart was put before the horse. Negative numbers were used before they were mathematically justified; so was the number

---

* Besides the Turing machine, Turing is perhaps most famous for his eponymous test, which he designed in 1950 to determine if convincing artificial consciousness existed. The basic idea of the Turing test was to station a human in front of a terminal that was networked to two others in another room: one operated by another human, and the other controlled by a computer. A text-based chat between the parties would commence about a selected topic or a series of topics. After an extended dialogue with both the human operator and the computer, if the computer could convincingly fool the human tester into thinking that it was also a human being—meaning the tester couldn't differentiate which one of the conversations was with the computer—the machine would have passed the Turing test.

Fascinatingly, in *Homo Deus*, Yuval Noah Harari posits that Turing's persecution by the British government for his closeted homosexuality—being gay was, quite literally, against the law in the country then, and Turing was forced to undergo chemical castration treatments that ultimately resulted in him committing suicide—was the genesis for the Turing test. "The Turing Test is simply a replication of a mundane test every gay man had to undergo in 1950s Britain: can you pass for a straight man?" Harari explains. "Turing knew from personal experience that it didn't matter who you really were—it mattered only what others thought about you. According to Turing, in the future computers would be just like gay men in the 1950s." But what's the difference between actually having consciousness and only appearing to the outside world that you do? Even though philosophers like René Descartes famously wrestled with this question four centuries ago (e.g., *Cogito, ergo sum*), it remains, frustratingly, unsettled.

† Alonzo Church also solved the Entscheidungsproblem around the same time as Turing, but he used a different approach.

zero,[*] irrational numbers,[†] and imaginary numbers.[‡] The infinitesimals of calculus also came under question in the 1700s: famously, Bishop George Berkeley labeled the then-newly introduced concept of the calculus limit as infinitely small "ghosts of departed quantities" that must certainly rely on religious doctrine for their justification rather than on airtight mathematical logic. Within about a century, with the help of an ε (the Greek letter epsilon), the idea of a limit was mathematically rigorously set—for all time.

The dissolution of Hilbert's program resulted in the balkanization of epistemological approaches to the discipline. With the foundations of mathematics in disarray, plenty of space existed for disagreement on its core truths. Three main philosophical camps emerged to dominate the conversation: Logicism (all of mathematics, which is a subset of logic, can be arrived at deductively), Formalism (all of mathematics is analogical, like a game, and set apart from reality), and Intuitionism (all of mathematics exists solely in the minds of its practitioners). Contrast these approaches with Plato's: he believed that the blueprint to the universe lay in mathematics. "Let no one ignorant of geometry enter" was engraved above the door to Plato's Academy. Plato's Theory of Forms spoke of the perfect world of concepts and objects, discoverable only by philosopher-kings, that lurked behind our imperfect everyday experiences. For those who maintain that the practice of mathematics is one of discovery, there is Platonism. Intiutionists are, in effect, anti-Platonists. Tukey, who was never deeply involved in these debates, took a more sterile view of the discipline, writing that mathematics consisted of "[a]bstraction, calculation, free assembly, logical solidity and security, precision, quantitativeness and symbolism." But he also warned of "the power and the danger of abstraction" of mathematics, which "have the same source, its combination of utter simplicity and utter certainty." "[A]ttaining the simple is often a complex task," he added.

In *Mathematics: The Loss of Certainty* (1980), Morris Kline argues that the history of mathematics is really one of sometimes-successful attempts to clean up earlier carelessness, papering over an ever-growing set of mathematical results that were ontologically questionable to begin with. Is mathematics built on a house of cards? Kline answers in the affirmative:

---

[*] As Alfred North Whitehead observed, "No one goes out to buy zero fish." His point is that the notion of zero is not necessarily intuitive.

[†] Numbers that cannot be written as the quotient of two natural numbers (i.e., the positive whole numbers).

[‡] Numbers that result in a negative product after being squared.

[M]athematics developed illogically.... The creation of these new geometries and algebras caused mathematicians to experience a shock of another nature. The conviction that they were obtaining truths had entranced them so much that they had rushed impetuously to secure these seeming truths at the cost of sound reasoning. The realization that mathematics was not a body of truths shook their confidence in what they had created, and they undertook to reexamine their creations. They were dismayed to find that the logic of mathematics was in sad shape.

Careless logic, errors, and "blunders" served to build up the towering edifice we call mathematics.

CHAPTER FIFTEEN

The Ontology of Statistics

"Statistics lives on the empirical, rather than the
theoretical side of science."
— Paul Velleman

The University of Chicago statistician and historian Stephen M.
Stigler begins his slim volume *The Seven Pillars of Statistical Wisdom*
(2016) by asking his readers, "What is statistics?" After observing
that the question has been in circulation since at least 1838 when the
Royal Statistical Society began publication of a journal, Stigler offers his
own answer: statistics is not a "single subject." Furthermore, statisticians,
who pride themselves on forming partnerships with scientists, position
statistics so as to "[present] different faces to different sciences," Stigler
writes. "In some applications, we accept the scientific model as derived
from mathematical theory; in some, we construct a model that can then
take on a status as firm as any Newtonian construction. In some, we are
active planners and passive analysts; in others, just the reverse." Morris
Kline had his own view of the discipline. He dismissively and reductively
thought of statistics as "the mathematical theory of ignorance."

Statistics as a practiced discipline looks like mathematics as seen
through a funhouse mirror. Statistics, and, even more pointedly, data
analysis, falls under the rubric of science since, according to Tukey in
FoDA, it "passes all three tests"—intellectual content, organization, and a
reliance upon the test of experience—the upshot being that "[d]ata analysis must use mathematical argument and mathematical results as bases for
judgment rather than as bases for proof or stamps of validity." In other
words, let the data do the talking—don't try to shoehorn the data into
mathematical models and "[n]ever believe the man (he is likely to be a
mathematical statistician) who tries to reduce everything to a special case
of any one mathematical model."* After all, just because your only tool is
a hammer, it doesn't mean all of your problems are nails. Tukey did,

---

* This wisdom comes not from FoDA but "The Growth of Experimental Design in a Research Laboratory."

though, turn the definition of "model" on its head when he said elsewhere that "[i]n the sense in which we...use the word 'model'—a means of guidance without implication of belief or reality—all the structures that guide data analysis, however weak and nonspecific, are models—even when they are not explicitly mathematical."

Tukey explained "data analysis is intrinsically an empirical science," more in the vein of geologist Thomas C. Chamberlin's notion of science as "the holding of multiple working hypotheses"—an idea Tukey was fond of citing, repeatedly doing so throughout his career—than logic or mathematics, despite pushes to systematize statistics into a purely rule-driven field of binary oppositions and cookie-cutter algorithms for decision-making (e.g., statistically significant versus non-statistically significant results). Any science practiced well always require at least a touch of art thrown into the mix, Tukey thought.

Chamberlin's influence on Tukey's approach to data analysis extended beyond a mere repeated quotation. Akin to Tukey, Thomas Chrowder Chamberlin, born in 1843 in Mattoon, Illinois, urged a scientific investigator to arrive at his conclusions in a deliberate manner and also warned of the ownership that naturally attends to one's theories. "The moment one has offered an original explanation for a phenomenon which seems satisfactory, that moment affection for his intellectual child springs into existence," Chamberlin warned, "as the explanation grows into a definite theory, his parental affections cluster about his intellectual offspring, and it grows more and more dear to him, so that, while he holds it seemingly tentative, it is still lovingly tentative, and not impartially tentative." This "unconscious selection" of a favored scientific theory results in a sort of confirmation bias, a "special searching-out of phenomena that support it." To counteract such habits of mind, to strive toward "impartial intellectual rectitude" through the course of a scientific investigation, Chamberlin implored the researcher to adopt the method of multiple working hypotheses. Here is his explanation of why: "The effort is to bring up into view every rational explanation of new phenomena, and to develop every tenable hypothesis respecting their cause and history. The investigator thus becomes the parent of a family of hypotheses: and, by his parental relation to all, he is forbidden to fasten his affections unduly upon any one."

Likewise, no statistical model should ever become sacrosanct, beyond reproach. "I believe that conclusions are even more important to science that decisions," Tukey added. In the schematic he drew for the first volume of the *Collected Works*, Tukey made sure to have an entry point of "distilled experience" as part of the "Approaches."

That no statistical model should vault to rarified air, to the status of unimpeachability, brings to mind another key characteristic that statistics has in common with science. Statistics can change; its techniques can be modified or tossed out entirely, depending on the situation or the tasks at hand. Statistics can evolve—and so could, and so does, science, with the detritus of discarded theories littered through the centuries illustrative of this point. Mathematics, however, is entirely a discipline of addition: once a result is proven, once a conjecture is codified into a full-fledged theorem (if logic permits it), the result can never be disproven: it stands ipso facto as true forever more.

"[S]tatistical analysis is a gatekeeper," explains Paul F. Velleman, a former doctoral student of Tukey's who went on to have a very accomplished career as a professor of statistics at Cornell. He continues:

> John Tukey taught that Statistics is more a science than it is a branch of Mathematics. For a mathematics theorem to be elegant, it is sufficient that it be beautiful and true. But Statistics is held to the additional standard imposed by science. A model for data, no matter how elegant or correctly derived, must be discarded or revised if it doesn't fit the data or when new and better data are found and it fails to fit them.

Furthermore, Velleman says, "Statistics lives on the empirical, rather than the theoretical side of science."

Velleman perceived a close connection between the philosophy of data analysis as expounded by John Tukey and the philosophy of scientific inquiry that Francis Bacon wrote about centuries earlier, particularly in his *Novum Organum* (1620). "Indeed," Velleman presses the point, "while I am reasonably certain that Bacon did not write Shakespeare, I sometimes think that he might have written Tukey." Bacon's approach was unique; as author Gavin Kennedy, in *Invitation to Statistics*, explains, though Bacon has been called the father of experimental science, "Bacon was as critical of experiments without thought as he was of thought without experiments." The Renaissance thinker attempted to forge a compromise path between empiricism and rationalism, categorizing the philosophers of his day into three kinds: ants, spiders, and bees. Empiricists are like ants, who "simply accumulate and use; Rationalists, like spiders, spin webs from themselves; the way of the bee is in between: it takes material from the flowers of the garden and the field; but it has the ability to convert and digest them...."

Bacon maintained that experiments were the *sine qua non* of any scientific inquiry, the key source of any project that required the analysis of data. Tukey called data analysis *scientific statistics*, a term of which Velleman strongly approves, "because it conveys the underlying philosophy as well as the immediate focus of the data analyst's attention." And Bacon, like

Tukey, maintained that mathematics is not a science. "Mathematics and Logic, which ought to be but the handmaids of Physic, nevertheless presume on the strength of the certainty which they possess to exercise dominion over it," Bacon wrote.

In a chapter for the book *The Practice of Data Analysis: Essays in Honor of John W. Tukey* (1997), Velleman compares short quotations from Bacon and Tukey centering on related topics (what he calls "aphoristic statements"), convincingly demonstrating how Bacon presaged much of the spirit, if not the details, of a philosophy of data analysis that Tukey later made famous. For instance, here is a data analysis idea Velleman explores:

> *The Process of Data Analysis is inherently subjective. Because the goal is understanding, the path cannot be mechanically or arbitrarily determined a priori.*

An investigator obtaining knowledge through "a priori" means is putting the cart before the horse: presupposing how the world works without the benefit of experience. Statements in Euclidian geometry, such as *A square projected on a plane has four right angles*, derive naturally from a priori reasoning, since no experience hunting many different projections of squares is necessary to confirm such generalized statements about any particular square. *All bachelorettes are unmarried* is another example not necessitating any empirical data collection to establish its veracity. The ancient Greeks were in thrall to a priori, deductive reasoning, believing it could explain the world. The German philosopher Immanuel Kant believed that deductive thinking alone could explicate all of human morality. In *Novum Organum*, Bacon warned of the dangers of a priori reasoning when performing scientific inquiry.

> [M]ere groping, as one does in the dark, testing the ground in every direction in the hope of finding one's way, when it would be sensible…to kindle a light, and only then go forward…. [T]he right order for experience is first to kindle a light, then with that light to show the way, beginning with experience ordered and arranged, not irregular or erratic, and from that deriving axioms….[*]

Contrast a priori reasoning with the "a posteriori" kind, which is arrived at by experience. If a friend hands you a gold coin and claims it's biased (or weighted) toward heads, how can you check her assertion? Construct a free-body diagram to try to map out all the forces acting on

---

[*] Quoted by Velleman in his chapter for *The Practice of Statistics*, which is titled "The Philosophical Past and the Digital Future of Data Analysis: 375 Years of Philosophical Guidance for Software Design on the Occasion of John W. Tukey's 80th Birthday."

the coin? Such a method wouldn't be easy or necessarily fruitful. The surefire way to see if the gold coin is unfair is simply to flip it—many, many times—and record the results. Although a significant bias toward heads after many such flips wouldn't guarantee that the coin isn't fair, this a posteriori approach could produce significant evidence in favor of your friend's assertion. The practice of data analysis must be a posteriori; as Tukey makes clear, "Data analysis is like doing experiments."

In FoDA, Tukey also pointedly addresses how statistics—and, more specifically, data analysis—should be taught: move away from rigidity and what he called *cookbookery* (the pejorative of statistics as merely a "cookbook discipline" is the bane of statisticians everywhere) while admitting that "it [data analysis] uses judgment,"* a "free use of ad hoc and informal procedures," and "weaker [statistical] assumptions" to permit more flexibility. Teachers of data analysis shouldn't be afraid to tell their students, "I don't know." New challenges to students can be introduced with such an admission.

Tukey strived to distance himself from those who would "draw straight lines from inappropriate assumptions to inapplicable conclusions," as he wrote in a technical report.

> If statistical techniques are to be helpful in practice, it will have to be because they work fairly well in real situations. A carpenter has to build a house using boards and timbers that have the shapes they have. No one will be exactly a rectangular parallepiped [*sic*].†

Likewise, since "no one assumption will hold exactly," performing data analysis well involves heavy doses of reasoned and careful judgment applied to real-world phenomena.

The notion of judgment in data analysis, Tukey explained, was guided by deep knowledge and took several forms: (1) Experiential judgment, both with respect to the discipline from which the source data was collected as well as the investigator's past experience with the particular statistical techniques, and (2) theoretical judgment, with respect to the underpinnings upon which the statistical techniques receive their mathematical justification. Data analysis was not a quest for certainty.‡ Akin to oth-

---

* More specifically: the use of knowledge coupled with judgment.
† He clearly meant to write: "a parallelepiped."
‡ "If we really want to make progress" in statistics, Tukey wrote in "What Have Statisticians Been Forgetting" (1967), "we need to identify our next step away from certainty." There simply may not be one "unique appropriate anal-

er scientific disciplines, those practicing data analysis won't always be right; the allowance of some error is part of the deal.

Through observation—examining the data at hand, replete with all its real-world variability—and experimentation—seeing which mathematical models fit the data, a process akin to falsification rather than logical proof, as well as making sure to "[collect] the results of actual experience with specific data-analytic procedures"—Tukey had squarely set the paradigm as science, rather than math, for data analysis and statistics at large—though the abstract mathematical models of statistics, and their underpinnings, still relied on classical proof for justification; the approach to problems, though, had shifted. Probability theory and mathematical proof were deemphasized in favor of simulation (e.g., random sampling via Monte Carlo methods) and flat-out good, sound statistical judgment. Velleman drills home the point that statistics, "as a science, is not algorithmic or deterministic" and is thus rife with uncertainty requiring careful judgment. Although, as statistician Peter J. Huber points out, not everyone is "endowed with a good share of John Tukey's statistical intuition and judgment!" (If for no other reason, Tukey's masterwork *Exploratory Data Analysis* is a fascinating, but difficult, read because you get to see, step-by-step, how Tukey approaches certain kinds of statistics problems.)

Yes, the tools that we use to analyze data are important—whether those tools be of the algebraic or the mathematical analysis variety—but "our attitudes" are equally important: "If algebra and analysis cannot help us, we must press on just the same, making as good use of intuition and originality as we know how." We must keep a positive attitude throughout, but also not attempt to game the system by beginning our exploration with the end result already in mind. "It is not sufficient to start with what is supposed to be desired to estimate, and to study how well an estimator succeeds in doing this," he cautions; statistics must never be viewed as a "monolithic, authoritarian structure designed to produce the 'official' results." To that end, there are no theorems or proofs in the FoDA. If one wants to perform theory-based mathematical statistics, Tukey says, then that work should either further the practice of data analysis—or it shouldn't. If the work isn't related to data analysis, then it should be viewed and assessed as something wholly mathematical, related to pure mathematics.

FoDA set data analysis apart as its own field, entirely worthy of study. But what, precisely, is data analysis? Data analysis, as Tukey defined it in

---

ysis" (and known distribution) for every particular set of data, as Karl Pearson supposed.

FoDA, swallows conventional statistics whole: statistics was only a mere component of data analysis. The most famous passage of FoDA is its first paragraph, which sets data analysis apart from the traditional practice of statistics.

> For a long time I have thought I was a statistician, interested in inferences from the particular to the general. But as I have watched mathematical statistics evolve, I have had cause to wonder and to doubt.... All in all, I have come to feel that my central interest is in *data analysis*, which I take to include, among other things: procedures for analyzing data, techniques for interpreting the results of such procedures, ways of planning the gathering of data to make its analysis easier, more precise or more accurate, and all the machinery and results of (mathematical) statistics which apply to analyzing data.

Statistician Peter Huber recalls first reading FoDA: "Very few people will have realized at that time (I certainly was not among them), and many have not realized even now [1997], that Tukey, while ostensibly speaking about his personal predilections, was in fact redefining the field of statistics." Huber goes on to note that Tukey casts off anything in conventional statistics that is theoretical to the realm of pure mathematics: "to the extent that pieces of *mathematical statistics* fail to contribute, or are not intended to contribute, even by a long and tortuous chain, to the practice of data analysis, they must be judged as pieces of *pure* mathematics, and criticized according to its purest standards," Tukey explains in FoDA. Underscoring this point, Tukey writes that "judgment," rather than "proof," should be the preeminent standard when performing data analysis, and that data analysis can often "precede probability models."

As Peter McCullagh notes, "Tukey relished the grand gesture, and it is no accident that [FoDA] reads in part like the 1776 Declaration of Independence." There were hints of the revolution to come. Tukey had run a seminar from 1957 to 1958 on data analysis at the Center for Advanced Study in the Behavioral Sciences at Stanford, with the revised, mimeographed, notes being distributed several years later. Tukey had also penned and disseminated memos, as far back as the 1940s, detailing proto-exploratory data analysis techniques. But FoDA, published in the first issue of Joseph L. Hodges' editorship of *The Annals of Mathematical Statistics*,[*] crystalized and condensed all of Tukey's data analysis wisdom in a single place.

---

[*] Hodges, born in Shreveport, Louisiana, in 1922, obtained his doctorate in 1949 under the supervision of Jerzy Neyman at Berkeley. Hodges, who served as the editor of *The Annals* from 1961 to 1964, worked most of his career as a professor in the Berkeley statistics department.

In their text *Breakthroughs in Statistics: Methodology and Distribution*, editors Samuel Kotz and Norman L. Johnson assign FoDA pride of place, declaring the piece one of the most important and influential in the history of statistics. "[T]he impetus for including exploratory analysis as a part of statistics seems attributable more to Tukey's initiative, dedication, and persistence than to the efforts of any other individual," they explain. "Indeed, this 1962 paper provides considerable support for this view," because in FoDA Tukey "pleads for novelty in data analysis, as illustrated by 'wholly new questions to be answered,' by 'more realistic frameworks' for familiar problems, and by developing 'unfamiliar summaries' of data that are likely to be 'unexpectedly revealing.'" In addition to this, Tukey lays out many procedures for dealing with "spotty data" coming from a variety of statistical distributions.

William Cleveland, who edited the *Collected Works*, saw Tukey as a "Renaissance man of science and technology," straddling the line between statistics and science. Cleveland attributes Tukey's high rate of intellectual productivity to his equal comfort in both worlds: "Most of the great steps forward in statistical science have been made by those who have been part statistician and part scientist," with FoDA being a case in point.

Peter Huber, for his part, talks of the timelessness of the first several pages and the last couple of pages of FoDA. Indeed, the general consensus on the article is in line with Huber's view: the first several pages and the last several pages stand the test of time, since they elucidate a general philosophy of performing data analysis, while the content presented in the middle has been either superseded or rendered superfluous (or both).

Regardless, Tukey's revolutionary approach to statistics resulted in statistician David Salsburg, in *The Lady Tasting Tea*, nicknaming Tukey the "Picasso of Statistics." As Salsburg points out, "Nothing had been too mundane for Tukey to attack with original insight, and nothing is too sacrosanct for him to question.... Like Picasso going from cubism, to classicalism, to ceramics, to fabrics, John Tukey marched across the statistical landscape of the second half of the twentieth century," leaving little unchanged in his wake.

CHAPTER SIXTEEN

Teaching at Princeton

"I can see that you have a complex problem:
it has a real and an imaginary part."
—John Tukey

By the time *The Annals of Mathematical Statistics* published "The Future of Data Analysis" in 1962, Tukey had been at Princeton for more than twenty years, and a full professor of mathematics more than ten. He was teaching a wide variety of classes—some at the elementary level, such as exploratory data analysis, and others on more advanced research topics. Tukey prepared for his class lectures like a general readying his troops for battle: he woke up early, usually around 6:00 AM, to lay out his plan of attack, as well as to work on his many statistics projects.

Tukey taught courses that straddled the line between applications and theory throughout the 1960s. In the spring of 1963 at Princeton, for instance, Tukey taught a graduate course called Mathematics 596: An Introduction to the Frequency Analysis of Times Series. "An adequate understanding of the frequency analysis of time series," Tukey said in the class, "requires understanding from three points of view: mathematical, philosophical, and (computation) engineering." Most of the students who enrolled in Math 596 were mathematics graduate students with statistics concentrations. Course notes, published twenty years later, show a Tukey as Renaissance man, regaling his audience with application problems, new words, and timely aphorisms, such as this one: "Models should not be true but it is important that they be applicable." Plus, he proffers fascinating philosophical questions. In discussing periodicity, he asks, "Of what human-generated phenomena are we *sure* that they will not repeat exactly after 10 million years? And do we know enough cosmology to be *certain* that the entire physical universe will not be exactly duplicated in 131 billion years?"

Tukey's teaching style was unique, "strikingly original in presentation and content," according to John A. Hartigan, one of his former students at the time. Hartigan tells of the many new words used during lectures, words like *orstat* for order statistic and *hinges* for quartiles (the medians of the upper and lower halves of the data) and *jackknife* for a resampling procedure* that estimates the variance, originally proposed by the mathematician Maurice H. Quenouille in 1956 but named by and improved upon by Tukey two years later. As Stephen Stigler writes in *The Seven Pillars of Statistical Wisdom*, the jackknife, "a method of estimating standard errors of estimation by seeing how much the estimate varied by successively omitting each observation," is a *sine qua non* of what Stigler terms the "intercomparison" pillar of statistics—intercomparison being "the idea that statistical comparisons may be made strictly in terms of the interior variation in the data, without reference to or reliance upon exterior criteria."

Why did Tukey call it the jackknife? Because the statistical procedure "shares two characteristics with a Boy Scout Jackknife: (1) wide applicability to very many different problems, and (2) inferiority to special tools for those problems for which special tools have been designed and built." Plus, he said, "If you had exactly the right tool for the job, you'd use it. But if you don't, then you'd use a jackknife." A jackknife, he mused, could be viewed as "a meat-grinder with some reusable pieces of meat." Plus, the jack-of-all-trades jackknife came in handy when it's not clear what the best statistical tool to use is—or even if there is a best tool: Tukey begins *Exploratory Data Analysis* by writing, "We do not guarantee to introduce you to the 'best' tools particularly since we are not sure there are unique bests."† Tukey would often test out strange terms like "jackknife" verbally, with students or faculty, before committing them to print.

---

* The jackknife was preceded by Fisher's special permutation test but was a precursor to "bootstrapping," introduced by Bradley Efron of Stanford University, which is the more commonly used procedure today. In 1987, Tukey penned a technical report (No. 292) delving into the bootstrap technique. "As I have heard Efron say, the bootstrap was invented, using the jackknife as a model, to be supported by a simpler and more coherent theory and thereby support the jackknive [*sic*]," he wrote. In that same technical report, Tukey also warned of the "ever-present danger…that 'resampling' will come to be thought of as a cure-all." He even labeled a type of bootstrap, in which a 95 percent confidence interval is constructed by culling the 2.5th and 97.5th percentiles of the distribution of resamples, as the *seductive bootstrap*.

† This sentence echoes a passage written by Thomas C. Chamberlin, whom we know informed Tukey's view of science. Chamberlin wrote the following about pedagogical theory and practice: "The search for instructional methods has often proceeded on the presumption that there is a definite patent process through which all students might be put and come out with results of maximum excellence; and hence pedagogical inquiry in the past has very largely concerned itself with the inquiry, 'What is the best method?' rather than with the inquiry, 'What are the special values of different methods, and what are their several advantageous applicabilities in the varied work of instruction?'"

In fact, Tukey and Bruce Bogert, who were two of the three authors of the paper "The Quefrency Alanysis of Time Series for Echoes," once went to a restaurant to have lunch; a customer at a nearby table, curious at what he was hearing but not understanding, came over to Tukey's table and asked: What language are you guys speaking? Nevertheless, "more than the new words, there were new, different ways of thinking about the subject matter. He always aimed to shake you out of old ways of thinking," Hartigan believed, and "No one ever left [Tukey's] class early."

Tukey always invited questions during class, and certainly Hartigan asked him a bundle. Unlike Hartigan's other professors, who were oftentimes visibly annoyed at having to stop their free-flowing lecturing to dispense with the interruptions, Tukey enjoyed the impromptu back and forth of students' questions and was never dismissive of queries that were seemingly off-task or trivial; he would even encourage his students to ask them. In fact, Tukey's questioning style may have come about because he was homeschooled in a way that encouraged the young Tukey to ask many questions, all in an effort to learn the content on his own in an exploratory way.

In class, Tukey would warn his charges of the *over-utopian* nature of textbook problems and how a random sample of values—a *batch of values*—oftentimes *fail to be utopian*. In other words, idealized, non-real-world, pre-constructed data typically aren't realistic data. Data taken from real life won't necessarily be what we expect, so there might not be a blueprint for how to proceed. To wit: "Most batches of data fail to tell us exactly how they should be analyzed," according to Tukey.

And there was also *head banging*, which helpfully smoothed the rates of cancer mortality in U.S. counties, brought about by an uproar among second-year statistics graduate students in 1977 who were eager to work on more "meaningful" (their word, taken from a formal letter they drafted) projects. In the seventh chapter of *Exploratory Data Analysis*, Tukey demonstrates how robust smoothing techniques can bring forth a truer picture of the shape of the data, somewhat akin to how Michelangelo purportedly sculpted the statue of David: "You just chip away the stone that doesn't look like David," he said.* In *Exploratory Data Analysis*, Tukey first displays a scatterplot of the annual precipitation in New York City, from 1872 to 1958; the plot looks randomly scattered, like raindrops falling outside a windowsill. But then Tukey begins chipping away at the stone, clearing the "fog" that clouds the deeper structure of the plot, by using a robust smooth. What's left is an oscillating, periodic, curvilinear shape with distinct peaks and valleys that clearly relays long-term periods of heavier and lighter participation through the roughly eight decades

---

* Probably apocryphal, but a great quote nonetheless.

observed. He performs the same smoothing trick—peeking underneath the blurry mass of points to reveal the signal buried beneath the noise—with scatterplots displaying the production of wheat in the U.S. from 1897 to 1958 and the production of gold in the U.S. from 1872 to 1956.

Words were important to Tukey, both spoken aloud and in print. Precision with these words was especially important—since there is always *fuzz*, or noise and uncertainty, to contend with that is inherent in our knowledge or beliefs about real-world phenomena—and he rarely used a single word to stand for more than one concept. Terms shouldn't be made to multitask, he believed. Late in his life, Tukey offered this succinct apologia for his precision with language in response to a (imagined) statistician who admits that he isn't careful with terminology yet claims he always "act[s] in the proper way":

> Unless we learn to keep what we say, what we think, and what we do all matching one another, and matching a reasonable picture of the world, we will never find out way safely through the thickets…—and we will not serve ourselves, our friends, and our clients adequately.

Especially important was being careful with terminology during a lecture or a class.

In FoDA, Tukey asks: "How might data analysis be taught?" Like biochemistry, he answers. There would be "laboratory work," where trials of empirical sampling and presentation of proofs would be completed, while traditional class time would be reserved mostly for post-lab debriefing. Tukey was, of course, comfortable with the archetypical science lecture-lab setup from his days as a chemistry student at Brown. That he envisioned a statistics course taught more like a science class than a mathematics class shouldn't be surprising. But wouldn't such a course structure simply be a recipe for disaster? Wouldn't teaching the discipline this way result in instructors offering a proverbial cookbook of statistics recipes in a laboratory setting? Not if Tukey had anything to say about it: it wouldn't be cookbookery but rather, implemented properly, the "art of cookery," since students would become intimately familiar with the ingredients.

Students would ascertain practical tips on how to perform research simply by "watching" the master, according to Brillinger. To wit:

> things like carry-on baggage for air flights, gallon-size refrigerator bags for protecting notes and transparencies, coloring and displaying view-graphs, employing two overhead projectors in tandem, telephone usage,

multi-colored pens, multi-tasking at seminars, quality of remarks, student supervision, learning the basic science, assistance of others.

Tukey would sometimes joke with his students, too. When one sketched out a potential thesis topic for the statistician, he replied, "I can see that you have a complex problem: it has a real and an imaginary part."[*]

And Tukey would go out of his way to help students, even meeting with them at his home on the weekends; he might even assign his charges gardening activities like weeding and mowing, while Tukey was busy multitasking: cultivating plants and dispensing statistical direction simultaneously. Sometimes that direction took a downright Eastern-style turn, replete with profound aphorisms like this one: "Doing statistics is like doing crosswords except that one cannot know for sure whether one has found the solution." He even brought this meditative idea to life. At Christmastime one year, he gifted crossword puzzle books to some of his students, but with a catch: the answer pages were ripped out. In their stead, printed in bold letters, was the aphorism.

Doctoral advisee Leo Goodman especially appreciated what he called Tukey's "elliptical" way of nudging students toward mathematical truth. Leo A. Goodman was born in 1928 in New York City, New York. He enrolled at Syracuse University, initially majoring in sociology. One of the requirements for satisfactory completion of the major was a course in statistics. At the time, Robert Faris, a sociologist with a limited statistics background, was given the unenviable task of teaching the required stats course. Faris admitted to his class, right from day one, that statistics wasn't his strong suit—I hope you'll all be able to help me muddle through the material, he told them.

Goodman stepped up to help Faris—the young undergrad found he had an innate ability in statistics, and Faris agreed, urging Goodman to take more mathematics courses in order to acquire a stronger mathematics background. So Goodman did, taking classes with such mathematical heavyweights as Lipman "Lipa" Bers. Several years later, Goodman graduated from Syracuse with a double major in mathematics and sociology. Faris told Goodman to apply to graduate school at the University of Chicago. But Bers had different plans for the budding statistician: go to Princeton to study mathematics, he said, even though no Syracuse undergraduate student majoring in math was ever accepted into the graduate school there. Goodman applied and was accepted into both institutions,

---

[*] The premise of this analogical joke is that complex numbers are each composed of a real part and an imaginary part in the form $a + bi$.

eventually selecting Princeton after a visit to the New Jersey campus led to a surreptitious encounter with Sam Wilks.

After Goodman stepped off the train at Princeton Junction, he walked to Fine Hall. Overwhelmed by the beauty of the campus and the living history within Fine Hall's walls, he walked laps through the hallways, passing by the same rooms repeatedly. Finally, a secretary stepped out into the hall and asked Goodman if she could assist in any way. "I [am] an undergraduate senior at Syracuse University, and [I] [have] applied to Princeton for graduate study in math," he told her. Please wait here for a moment, she said. After stepping into a nearby office, she walked back out with Sam Wilks.

They spoke for an hour. Goodman was taken by Wilks' Texas twang, his "floor to ceiling" wooden shelves overflowing with books, an imposing conference table, a welcoming fireplace, and the overall homey feel of his wood-paneled office. But the undergrad also felt like he was imposing, so he stood up and got ready to walk out—but Wilks stopped him in midstride. Just let me make a phone call first, Wilks said. Wilks called Fred Stephan, a Princeton sociologist, told him about the talented young undergrad sitting in his office, and then instructed Goodman to make a beeline to Stephan's office so he could meet with him too. Things went so well that a distracted Goodman stepped on the train heading to Philadelphia, rather than the one traveling back to New York.

But in his first semester at Princeton, Goodman felt increasingly insecure. His cohort, he believed, had much more experience with studying mathematics than he had; after all, he realized, he had taken the absolute fewest number of courses in both mathematics and sociology necessary in order to snag the dual degree from Syracuse. That hardly constituted deep intellectual exposure—to either math or sociology, for that matter. Plus, John Nash was also a freshman student at Princeton, and comparing oneself to the future "Beautiful Mind" would have been anything but confidence inspiring.

But Goodman's fortunes began to change courtesy of a second serendipitous encounter in the hallowed hallways of Fine Hall, this time with John Tukey rather than Sam Wilks. "I happened to be walking in the Fine Hall hallway, and Tukey happened to be walking in the hallway too, and our paths happened to cross," Goodman recalled.

"How are you doing?" Tukey asked him. "I don't know how I'm doing," Goodman responded. "Follow me," Tukey said, as he led the first-year graduate student to an empty classroom. Tukey made himself comfortable in the back of the room[*] and asked Goodman to walk to the

---

[*] Tukey would usually situate himself at the back of rooms and lecture halls during presentations and seminars, by turns appearing to be asleep, distracted-

blackboard in the front. The statistician posed a math query for Goodman to tackle, which he tried to by sketching out the logistics of the problem on the board while the multitasker Tukey busied himself writing an article completely unrelated to the mathematical content of the oral questioning session.

Once Goodman finished, Tukey paused only long enough to deliver a second question to his young charge—without bothering to offer him any feedback. When Goodman wrapped up his second response, Tukey didn't give him a break, immediately presenting him with a third problem. And a fourth. And a fifth. Over an hour's worth of problems streamed from Tukey's brain to his mouth to be processed by the greenhorn in the front of the classroom.

Then, finally, silence. Tukey rose from his seat, walked slowly toward Goodman, and stood before him. He cupped his chin and assumed a contemplative pose.

"Well," Tukey started. He paused.

"What I really think you need…"—Tukey paused again—"…is some folk dancing."

Making sense of the curious interaction sixty years later, Goodman said the following:

> [T]his comment by Tukey is a good example of his special kind of sense of humor and his at times elliptical manner of speech. He was telling me, in his own way, that I was doing fine, that my ability to answer math questions was fine, and that I ought to take time out for folk dancing or for whatever else might please me. He then told me when and where the folk dancing would take place, and he invited me to come to it, which I then did.

When Goodman showed up to dance, he was surprised that Tukey was in charge; somehow, Tukey had neglected to inform the graduate student of that. It was 1949, and Tukey was only months away from meeting his future wife at one of those folk dancing classes.

Deep into that first year at Princeton, Goodman had another beneficial interaction with Tukey. Walking by the statistician, who had been check-

---

ly scribbling away on a trusty yellow pad, reading the newspaper, solving a crossword puzzle, editing papers, and reading mail. At any time, though, he could perk up and interject fruitfully about the statistical goings-on at the front of the room—and he would not hesitate to do so. Alan Gross recalls that some graduate students once tried to imitate the master by also sitting in the back of a room during a presentation while working through crosswords, but they couldn't simultaneously focus on the mathematics at hand since none of them had the preternatural multitasking abilities of Tukey.

ing his faculty mailbox, Tukey stopped Goodman and showed him a postcard he had just received. On it was a statistics problem. Allen Wallis, who headed Columbia's Statistical Research Group during the Second World War, had sent the postcard. Tukey said but a single sentence regarding the problem, and then handed Goodman the postcard. Goodman chewed on the statistical query for around a month, struggling to understand what, precisely, Tukey had meant in that one explanatory sentence. He wrote up a paper summarizing his findings and shoved it in Tukey's mailbox.

Stop by my office, Tukey told Goodman later that week. When Goodman arrived, Tukey was adamant: the paper should be published in the *Annals of Mathematical Statistics* immediately! He then scrawled Goodman's name at the top of the paper, but Goodman demurred—we're both the authors, he said. Tukey disagreed. This is your work, he insisted.

The paper was published in the *Annals* in late 1949.

"Tukey was a New Englander," Goodman reflected, "and he spoke with a sort of 'down-east' accent. He also spoke in an elliptical, enigmatical, oracular fashion, and he liked to coin his own words." And he also helped Goodman, who ended up with both Tukey and Wilks as his doctoral thesis advisors, gain a measure of mathematical confidence when he needed it most.

Advising students and conducting classes were one thing; academic lectures, which also allowed Tukey to communicate multifarious ideas in front of mostly rapt groups of people, were quite another. One of the best descriptions of what sitting in one of Tukey's lectures must have been like comes from statistician Peter McCullagh, who was a graduate student at Imperial College in London when Tukey was invited to give a seminar there.

After being introduced, "Tukey ambled to the podium, a great bear of a man dressed in baggy pants and a black knitted shirt.... An array of coloured pens bulged from his shirt pocket," which were necessary for his "scratching" with data on paper. (Tukey had a large set of black polo shirts he reused for decades.) He scratched some headings on the blackboard, with the words delivered from Tukey's mouth like "overweight parcels" at a deliberate, "slow unfaltering pace." The words made sense, examined individually; but taken together, the sentences were impenetrable.

When he finished writing on the board, Tukey pivoted toward the audience, paused for a moment, and very slowly said, "Comments, queries, suggestions?" He then carefully shifted his body atop the podium and placed one leg over the other. A full minute passed since Tukey had addressed the audience, but no one had said anything yet. As the silence prevailed, Tukey reached into his pocket to grab a bag of dried prunes and proceeded to eat them, slowly, one at a time; he had started eating the fruit later in life as part of a dieting regimen, often bringing boxes of prunes to distribute at meetings.

After popping prunes into his mouth for a minute or two, a man in the front row finally punctuated the silence to ask Tukey a question, and the considerable tension that had developed in the seminar room eased.

To many in the room that day, the number-of-prunes-till-a-question had seemed a test of the audience's intelligence: the more prunes eaten, the lesser the average smarts in the room. "My impression is that [Tukey] liked to play games his way to get people to figure out for themselves the things that he already knew.... Whatever the explanation, he was much more successful with individual students than in seminars or formal lectures."

Some of his lectures went rather well, however. Having a closer look at one of those lectures will help us take the measure of the man.

CHAPTER SEVENTEEN

Statistical Computing and the PRIM-9

"[Tukey] had the rare ability to think like a mathematician or like an engineer, depending on what the problem at hand required."
— Jerome Friedman and Werner Stuetzle

It is November of 1964. Tukey is invited to give a talk at the 125th Anniversary Meeting of the American Statistical Association (ASA), held in Boston. The ASA was founded in Massachusetts in 1839; as such, it is one of the oldest such professional organizations in the United States.

Many mathematicians and statisticians are present at the anniversary banquet. Tukey sits at the head table and consumes his by-now customary portion of skim milk (he also sometimes drank cider).* "Have you ever seen a spherical milk bottle?" he wonders.

After the dinner, Tukey rises to the podium and speaks. His talk, later given the title "The Technical Tools of Statistics" when reprinted in *The American Statistician*, is customary for its prescience, sprinklings of pithy aphorisms, and use of neologisms (since Tukey loved coining idiosyncratic terms because he wanted to "avoid one word with too many meanings").† Rather than focusing on the design of methods to collect data, Tukey turned his attention strictly to the analysis of data.

---

* Manfred Schroeder, who encountered Tukey at Bell Labs, said Tukey's "human parallel process[ing]" was powered by his lunchtime consumption of six glasses of skim milk per day.
† Even when choosing among words already in circulation to represent new or modified concepts, Tukey leaned toward selecting shorter words and ones that were already employed for as few ideas as possible. For example, in *Exploratory Data Analysis*, he chooses "bin" to refer to intervals rather than "cell," since cell had more alternate meanings than bin. In a paper published after Tukey's death, Brillinger recognizes an unintended positive consequence of Tukey's unique fashioning of words: internet searches of Tukey terms surface to the top of search results.

Tukey began his speech by asking three questions of his audience: "What have our technical tools been? What are they today? What can we see of what they are to become?" He continued:

> The assessment of the future is always chancy. Who knows this better than a statistician? Yet experience has taught us that it is usually well to extrapolate so long as we go only a modest distance and do what we can to ensure adequate caution.... Accordingly, I shall focus on the future, saying little about the past, and less about the present.

He noted that statisticians have often had to possess a "split personality," since, although they work daily within a sandbox of numbers and symbols—"probably the most secure things in human life"—they also have to openly exercise caution at the interpretation and promulgation of their results, which stem from the uncertainties and variability inherent in real-world data. "[T]he tools of the statistician have been sharpened on the grindstone of algebra and hammered out on the anvil of mathematical models," he said.

Tukey then introduced the idea of marking time by eighths of a century (12.5 years) for the purposes of the lecture. For instance, the ASA, at the time of his speech, was ten-eighths old (125 years old). Why measure things this way? "Since we still learn to count on our fingers, by tens...." This brings to mind another of Tukey's rather esoteric methods of counting. He disliked using traditional tally marks since he believed that a mistake with tabulating could easily be made. So, he instead promoted the dots-in-a-box method that, coincidentally, was also a means of counting by tens (the method was an outgrowth of Tukey's stem-and-leaf plot, another form of organizing small data sets). Here's how it works: First, draw four dots as the vertices of a square: these four dots represent four tallies. Next, draw the four sides of the square, connecting the vertices: these four lines represent four more tallies, for a running total of eight. Finally, insert the two diagonals of the square: these two lines represent the final two tallies, adding up to ten total tallies.

Tukey's inventive tallying method wasn't created in a vacuum; there are alternative grouping methods—such as the Chinese tally count that groups counts by fives utilizing a Chinese character called the "cheng," suggested by K. H. Hsieh[*]—from which Tukey surely received inspiration. Nevertheless, Tukey's method is elegant, compact, and requires no

---

[*] The cheng is drawn using five interconnected lines, but the completed shape might not be immediately recognizable to Western eyes. More information can be found in the book *Principles of Medical Statistics* (2002) by Alvan R. Feinstein.

prior knowledge (e.g., what a particular Chinese character looks like when fully formed).

Tukey continued his speech, noting that thoughts of new ways to dissect and parse data should lead us naturally to machines—specifically, to then still-new electronic computers. "By two-eighths ago one could see the shadow of the programmable calculator on the outside of the window," and, then, "[t]here was a war, and a [John] von Neumann; it took only half an eighth to bring the program-self-modifying calculator to reality...." And this was followed by the idea of *software*, the notion that a piece of hardware need not be tethered to only one algorithm for life. Statisticians must leverage the capabilities of the computer and must do so quickly—lest the young will have scant interest in the field.

Tukey likely coined the term software; he is certainly the first to use the word, in the modern sense of the term (referring to computing), in print.* In a 1958 article entitled "The Teaching of Concrete Mathematics" (published in the *American Mathematical Monthly*), Tukey writes of a number of oppositions, such as pure mathematics versus applied mathematics (with teachers, he explains, feeling that the pure is superior to the applied, or "concrete," variety) and numerical versus algebraic computation (whereby "algebraic" he means symbolic manipulations which are not purely numerical in nature). Much of the "mechanics of computation, numerical and algebraic," take up a large proportion of students' time sans electronic aids, he writes. Tukey then transitions to lay out the distinction between software and hardware, with software having pride of place:

---

* There is continued controversy swirling around the etymology of the word "software"; there's certainly evidence of use of the term pre-1958, but it was synonymous with people who used electronic machines—viz., the proper functioning of the hardware (the electronic components) is dependent upon the software (people) who operate it. For Tukey's part, when his nephew asked him about "software" directly, he didn't take credit for its coinage but also did not say that the word had already been in use at the time he wrote the paper. Tukey's equivocal silence on the matter, his nonresponse—a tactic he would occasionally resort to when he didn't wish to go on the record with an answer—muddies the waters for historians of science.

What especially confused the issue, however, was the title of Tukey's *New York Times* obituary: "John Tukey, 85, Statistician; Coined the Word 'Software'"—the source of the *NYT* "software" claim came from a then-unreleased *The Yale Book of Quotations* (2006), assembled by researcher Fred R. Shapiro; in his book, underneath a passage of Tukey's containing the term, lies this equivocal statement: "Apparent coinage of the word *software*."

Numerical computation, through the centuries, has often faced up to reality and made things easier. The use of logarithmic tables, even by those who do not know how to recompute them, and of desk calculators and, now, electronic calculators, even by those who cannot repair them, has been a commonplace. Today the "software" comprising the carefully planned interpretive routines, compilers, and other aspects of automative programming are at least as important to the modern electronic calculator as its "hardware" of tubes, transistors, wires, tapes, and the like.

Tukey's point is that efficient software has made understanding the inner workings of these electronic calculators unnecessary. (In 1958, the term "computers" still more commonly referred to human beings who performed calculations, so his word choice of "calculators" here is actually synonymous with the way we use the word "computers" today. Also notice the scare quotes around the terms hardware and software in the block quote above—implying that these terms were not yet ubiquitous.) The time students spend doing hand calculations—this "avoidable labor"— can be freed up, courtesy of sophisticated software, to instead engage with higher-order mathematical problem solving and more broad concepts overall. Seems commonsensical now, but Tukey, recall, was proffering this radical proposal in 1958, with widespread personal computing still nearly two decades away.*

In his speech to the ASA, Tukey also put pride of place in the connection between hardware and *brainware*, the latter term meaning "the minds of those who know what is wanted" when examining data. And he excited his crowd by speaking of the potential of computer graphics to analyze data sets, observing that computers will become indispensable to the statistician because of their speed and ease of data visualization. He admonished his audience, though, by noting that he knew of no one using the visual-display capabilities of computers well, and by predicting that in the next eighth of a century statistics is going to depend heavily upon the capabilities of the computer because a computer could "fit the apparent desires of the data," rather than the other way around—a key theme of Tukey's still-developing framework of exploratory data analysis (EDA), a term which Tukey coined. (Roughly five years earlier Tukey had said, "We need not sit loosely in the saddle of data," perhaps his "first utter-

* A bit more than two decades later, in a paper contemporaneous with his retirement from Princeton, Tukey continued and extended the theme of his speech, detailing how computerized "expert systems" will pave the way for spending more time on calculations—which economically were becoming cheaper and cheaper to perform—and less time on theorem proving. Such numerical calculations could be utilized on an ad hoc, real-world basis, as opposed to theorem proving, which largely applied only to general cases.

ance on data analysis," according to then-graduate student Arnold Goodman.) The graphically intense EDA was presented in strict opposition to *confirmatory data analysis* (CDA),[*] another Tukey term, which in part involved performing traditional hypothesis testing to obtain *p*-values; in Tukey's view, CDA was formulaic and algorithmic and technique-driven and, as such, was tailor-made to *computerize*, especially by the early 1980s when small personal computers started appearing on desks in offices and homes around the world. CDA was an after-the-fact, post hoc approach, where data was gathered only after the key questions about the data were decided upon; controlled clinical trials, Tukey noted, were tailor-made for a CDA approach. CDA was the judge and jury. By contrast, the nonprobabilistic EDA let the statistician keep his or her eyes open to surprises in data; EDA was the detective searching for clues.

Tukey wasn't opposed to performing CDA; he wanted EDA and CDA to go hand in hand, but he also wanted others to give EDA its due. He felt that EDA was woefully underrepresented in the literature compared to CDA, so in the 1970s he wrote a book devoted almost entirely to EDA called *Exploratory Data Analysis*. Tukey believed there was no CDA without EDA, just as there was no need for a judicial system without detectives to notice and make sense of clues to crimes.

He wanted statisticians to be flexible "to the needs of the situation and the clues that the data has already provided." CDA must "[n]ot [be] a high priestess but a handmaiden," Tukey said in a speech entitled "Analyzing Data: Sanctification or Detective Work." David C. Hoaglin, one of Tukey's former students, elucidates the distinction between the complementary approaches: "The separation between exploratory data analysis and confirmatory data analysis allowed exploratory data analysis to proceed freely, without adherence to a unified framework, and assigned to confirmatory data analysis the systematic task of assessing the strength of the evidence." EDA relies on inductive thinking; CDA depends on deductive thinking. "[E]xploration involves finding as many clues as you can, whether or not they point to the right criminal," Tukey wrote. "And confirmation corresponds to the trial, whose aim…is to decide whether the desired degree of proof has been attained." Tukey always credited the time spent working with biometrician Charlie Winsor, with hundreds of

---

[*] The term CDA is, in effect, a retronym, since the practice of traditional statistics didn't need to be categorized in this way until Tukey fashioned EDA as a counterpoint. ("Analog clock" is an example of a retronym, since until the advent of the digital clock, the analog clock was called…a clock.) Tukey presents CDA in strict opposition to EDA, an approach to statistics that he argues for years wasn't respectable, wasn't "moral," and thus needed to be performed clandestinely. See Tukey's paper "Data Analysis: History and Prospects" (1984) for more details.

hours spent analyzing real-world data, as when he developed the "core of insight" that became EDA.

And to those who would warn of the pitfalls of computing, namely with respect to a lack of clarity, Tukey issued a warning: "The tool that is so dull that you cannot cut yourself on it is not likely to be sharp enough to be either useful or helpful." Stated differently, Tukey wanted statisticians to dive headlong into computers so they would have the opportunity to fully take advantage of the benefits, despite the risks. He even suggested the invention of a computer language devoted solely to data analysis, going so far as to say that he'd create it himself if no one else did.

About a decade after Tukey's ASA speech, in a short film from 1973, Tukey, stationed in a small room at the Stanford Linear Accelerator Center (SLAC), launches into a no-holds-barred talk—replete with statistical and physics jargon galore—of the newly commissioned PRIM-9 statistical computing hardware that he developed in an intense four-month span working with Mary Anne Fisherkeller, who rapidly implemented Tukey's ever-evolving thoughts on how to proceed; in fact, the system was developed in fits and starts, sans any sort of master plan, and came about as the result of much trial and error. Tukey credited Fisherkeller's speed at translating his oftentimes-nebulous ideas into practice as the key reason why the PRIM-9 was completed quickly and successfully.

Picturing, rotation, isolation, and masking—all to nine dimensions— accounts for the "PRIM-9" moniker. PRIM-9 is an "interactive display system for exploratory multivariate data analysis" developed at SLAC, according to the male narrator of the film. The narrator continued: "The development of PRIM-9 was a team effort. The key team members were: for optimism, innovation, and trial-and-error learning, John Tukey," who is shown smiling faintly, dressed in a rumpled dark suit with a maroon tie; Tukey's dual role of Princeton professor and Bell Labs employee was noted. Fisherkeller handled the implementation and programming of the system, while particle physicist Jerome H. Friedman (pictured on-screen sporting oversized sunglasses, a goatee, and an Afro, looking right at home as an extra in a *Shaft* movie)—along with a film editor and cinematographer—provided additional supports.

The film offers an immediate, visceral demonstration of Tukey's methods of teaching. His explanations are careful, deliberate, and methodical; with his unmistakable and pronounced Yankee dialect, he leads the viewer through the sophisticated (for the time) hardware and features of the PRIM-9. The statistical computing system, Tukey says, was developed to learn more about data—especially data generated from physics experiments (after all, the system was developed adjacent to a linear accelerator)—by looking at the "numerical aspects" in "more than two aspects [characteristics] at a time." (Particle physicist Jerome Friedman posited that although Tukey envisioned the PRIM-9 eventually working well with data sets from any discipline, he preferred to use data from physics, as opposed to fields like the social sciences, to highlight the many features of the PRIM-9, largely because of physics data's structured, multi-dimensional quality.) More significantly, though, the PRIM-9 permitted flexibility with visualization: a "pictorial examination and dissection of particle physics data, especially data involving several body final states…[through] picturing and rotation on the one hand, and on masking and isolation on the other." Masking helped to identify which data points needed to be isolated for in-depth examination. The PRIM-9's "pictorial system" went through a number of stages of trial-and-error learning before reaching its useable, finished state. In a contemporaneous article, Fisherkeller, Friedman, and Tukey summarize the power of the setup:

> By interactively applying picturing, rotation, isolation, and masking to his data, the user can, in particular, perform projection pursuit. That is, he can look for those views that display to him interesting structure. He can isolate structures so found and study them separately and/or remove them from the remaining sample, simplifying the search for still further structure.

In the film, we are next treated to a glowing image of green dots, clustered almost spherically with some outliers, on a fluorescent screen that rotate on a single axis: the basic idea was called "point cloud rotation," a new idea at the time that has since become standard in statistics software. The dots are data points, and the power of the PRIM-9 is quickly apparent to the viewer: using no more than a small beige keyboard (but looking nothing like a typical QWERTY keyboard layout) with four rows of eight buttons, horizontal and vertical axes can be chosen off any set of coordinate pairs, allowing for a near-infinite number of projection permutations of displays in however many dimensions necessitated by the data. A light pen, offering touch-screen capability, is also part of the interface package. As physicist Jerome Friedman noted decades later in an interview, "[Tukey] was very interested in human interfaces and he developed some really slick controls, especially given the crudeness of the equipment he had to work with."

Tukey is especially excited by the PRIM-9's ability to, as he says in the film, "move about," meaning rotate the projection of data to any desired viewing angle while simultaneously keeping some coordinates fixed: "Since we usually do not know just what we want, and when we do we will find it difficult to call for it in a general way, we need a way to move about." Rotation was controlled with three buttons: two for selecting co-ordinates and one for "driving the rotation"; the rotation-angle button had what Tukey called a "whoa-back" control, which directed the on-screen rotation/acceleration. In terms of the coordinates themselves,

> A rotation is specified by two integers i and j. These integers specify the current coordinate axes that participate in the rotation.... [I]f the axes that define the rotation coincide with the current projection axes, then the data points will simply move in circular orbits about their relative mean in the projection.

Wire-frame axes could also be added on-screen, helping one to see (cour-tesy of rotation) that the multidimensional "structure-less blurs" are in fact replete with structure, despite initial suppositions to the contrary. "To help in the interpretation of a particular projection, a display of the initial coordinate axes, as projected onto the current projection plane, is easily switched in and out of view." Tukey came to believe that the most important part of any statistical system like the PRIM-9 is the controls: clear, concise, easy to use control mechanisms invite the user to learn and explore, whereas clunky, clumsy, or overly complicated controls act as a barrier to effective analysis. To that end, while picturing, rotation, and isolation proved to be prescient—that is, replicated in future statistics software packages—masking died with Tukey, since it proved to be too complicated to use for nearly anybody but him.

Tukey's palpable enthusiasm in the film was clearly warranted, since most computers of the early 1970s were still only accessible via timeshar-ing hookups, only some of which had shed the teletypewriters (essentially, glorified text-only typewriters for input/output) in favor of clunky mono-chromatic cathode ray tube visual displays. The home computer revolu-tion was still several years away, with most people more familiar with computers of the cinema (like the HAL 9000 from *2001*) or the small screen (like the Robot from *Lost in Space*) than from any lived experience. The PRIM-9 display and user-friendliness were no doubt cutting-edge, yet still had a barrier to entry that left the system accessible only to the likes of the both intellectually gifted and academically credentialed, such as Tukey.

"One good idea is not enough; it is likely to take ten good ideas, or thirty, or even fifty!" Tukey explained in the fifth volume of the *Collected Works*, which focuses on graphics. He continued: "I hope I already held this view unconsciously before the work on PRIM-9, where Mary Anne Fisherkeller's skills made it possible to try something new each day or each second day—so I became conscious of how many steps—probably 30 to 50—we actually took together." The PRIM-9, one of the first in a line of computer-intensive algorithms to visualize and manipulate data sets, gave statisticians a one-way ticket out of Plato's Cave—from "you can see it, if you know how to look!" to "you can't miss it!"

But Tukey, even later in his life after computers became ubiquitous, faster, and easier to use, didn't always avail himself of their computational power; instead, he would reach for paper, pencil, and slide rule (although by the mid-1970s, he had an HP-45 scientific calculator at the ready, even speaking with Hewlett-Packard about ways to optimize the device). But he always maintained a fascination and interest in electronic computing; in fact, along with Brock McMillan, Tukey drew up designs on building a single-bit central processing unit, but never got around to actually constructing the device. When Tukey was a student at Princeton, he had built the musicologist Edward T. Candy a radio. By the end of World War II, Tukey had some experience using a punched card IBM, and perhaps also used a primitive IBM accounting machine to construct scatterplots. Tukey also helped John von Neumann finish building the computer he brought to the Institute of Advanced Study—by designing the electronic adding circuit for the machine; as Arthur Burks, a mathematician who helped design the ENIAC computer, explained,[*] "In [the circuit Tukey designed], each binary adder fed its carry output directly into the next stage without delay." Von Neumann said of Tukey, "There is this very bright graduate student, and the remarkable thing is that he does it all on milk."

In the 1950s, the German atmospheric scientist Hans A. Panofsky, influenced by Tukey's budding time series work, utilized the von Neumann computer for spectrum analysis; in turn, Tukey wrote that his interest in cross-spectra was "stimulated by Hans Panofsky's working on tower meteorology data from Brookhaven, using John von Neumann's new computer in Princeton." It was a symbiotic relationship.

In 1956, Tukey organized the Statistical Techniques Research Group (STRG); by the end of the decade the STRG, located at Gauss House on Nassau Street, was leveraging an IBM 650 mainframe computer regularly for calculations—perhaps the very first computer ever to reside on Princeton's campus.

But just because technology could calculate a particular statistical measure didn't mean that measure was ipso facto useful. Take the correlation coefficient, which measures the strength and direction of the linear relationship between two bivariate quantitative variables, for instance. Tukey found the correlation coefficient a very poor summary measure, a "dangerous symptom" of an undiagnosed disease, useful only in limited circumstances—such as when the "size of the units are devoid of meaning," since the correlation coefficient is scale-independent, as well as

---

[*] As relayed by David Brillinger.

when they serve as regression coefficients. But, Tukey wondered, if we use the correlation coefficient because we are not interested in the units of the variables, then how effective is our data analysis to begin with? The problem with the correlation coefficient, Tukey explained using charged but idiosyncratic language, is "an enemy of generalization, a focuser on the 'here-and-now' to the exclusion of the 'there-and-then.'" Charlie Winsor influenced his negative views about the correlation coefficient, Tukey admitted; Winsor even established an informal Society for the Suppression of Correlation Coefficients, which Tukey was quick to join.

Back to the film on the PRIM-9: After demonstrating the hardware, Tukey rises from his seat, walks over to a nearby blackboard, and delivers a pitch-perfect disquisition detailing the particle physics behind the data obtained at SLAC. Suddenly, Tukey morphs into his old friend Richard Feynman, illustrating the particle and force interactions after proton collisions using Feynman-like diagrams and formulas with vectors and dot products. After taking one more spin with the PRIM-9, Tukey lauds the future of such a statistical display system, but not before rather offhandedly coining yet more neologisms—like the *chewing-over programs* designed to sift through batches of numerical data—to emphasize the system's import. Tukey almost can't help himself to fashioning nomenclature when describing anything new; in his defense, however, he was so often at the forefront of statistics and technology in both the ivory tower and at Bell Labs that, like an early explorer, he had no choice but to conjure up names to describe concepts that had never before been encountered.

Out of the PRIM-9 spawned add-ons such as the *projection pursuit*, which consisted of an automated algorithm that optimized possible projections by maximizing the "projection index," thus offering data-rich displays of multivariate data. The projection pursuit came about as a result of discussions Tukey had with Jerome Friedman, the Afro-donning physicist. Friedman would sit and watch Tukey cycle through different visual displays on the PRIM-9, all the while wondering to himself: What makes Tukey believe that a particular picture is interesting? Friedman's specialty wasn't graphics; he was heavily involved with the analytical side.

"It seems that the pictures we like the most are the ones that have content," Tukey explained to Friedman, "they have a lot of small inter-point distances but then they expand over the whole thing." That notion, coupled with the optimization algorithms that Friedman had previously worked on at Berkeley, resulted in projection pursuit—and the publication of a 1974 article titled "A Projection Pursuit Algorithm for Exploratory Data Analysis," the only paper of Friedman's career that didn't require any revisions after the initial submission.

Besides projection pursuit, there were other ideas of Tukey's that had as their genesis the statistics software system, such as *cognostics*, where the computer sorts through and discards the least interesting displays,* leaving the potentially most interesting or revealing for human consumption; *draftsman's views*, utilized to display multivariate data sets (Paul Tukey, a cousin of Tukey's who also worked at Bell, wrote about draftsman's views); and *scagnostics*, a combination of the previous two ideas. And a decade before the PRIM-9 was even a glint in his eye, Tukey teased an idea for data analysis software that would be interactive in nature. "I know of no large machine installation," he wrote, "whose operations are adapted to the basic step-by-step character of most data analysis, in which most answers coming out of the machine will, after human consideration, return to the machine for further processing." The PRIM-9 was a baby step toward fulfilling the promise he envisioned.

In an *Annals of Statistics* article titled "John W. Tukey's Work on Interactive Graphics" published decades after the production of the film, Jerome Friedman, along with coauthor Werner Stuetzle, a professor at the University of Washington, reflects on the importance of the PRIM-9 system and how it came to fruition. (Friedman was also interviewed recently by *Statistical Science* about his collaborations with Tukey.) Needless to say, Friedman retrospectively accords the lion's share of credit to Tukey for the development of the PRIM-9. Multivariate data necessitated more than mere paper-and-pencil plots, Tukey realized by the early 1970s, so, in 1972, "PRIM-9, the first program to use interactive, dynamic graphics for viewing and dissecting multivariate data, was conceived by John during a four month [sabbatical] visit to the Computation Research Group" at SLAC. The head and originator of the Computation Research Group, William Miller, had set up Tukey's visit; Miller and Tukey were "close friends," according to Friedman. Back then, computer graphics applications were uncharted territory, especially in the realm of statistics problems, but Miller was fascinated with the technology and wanted to get a sense of the research possibilities by expert practitioners. So, he built the Graphics Interpretation Facility (GIF), a multimillion-dollar interactive graphics facility that was a significant drag on computing resources and was terribly cumbersome to use. But since the GIF was the only game in

---

* Here is Tukey in the thick of it, suggesting the use of cognostics: "…cognostics [will] help us rearrange our variables so that the initial view shows the most interesting k of them. Instead of simple scrolling, then, we might hold the first $k - 2$ (or $k - 3$, or $k - 4$) fixed and scroll the other 2 (or 3 or 1)."

town, the facility was utilized; to document the GIF in action, Miller in effect requisitioned a mini-movie studio: equipment for shooting 16 mm movies, complete with sound and other multimedia accouterments. What was missing was something to film.

When Tukey was due to arrive at SLAC, there was a distinct buzz in the air. Not because of his accomplishments as a statistician, but rather "because he was well known in computer science for having invented the Fast Fourier Transform," Friedman recalled. Yet Friedman, who had just arrived at SLAC himself, had no idea who he was. But that would change practically overnight, as the two "just hit it off."

After Tukey's initial four-month sabbatical at SLAC, he returned to a question from Friedman. "John," he asked him, "I think we ought to make a movie of this." Hence, the reason for the existence of the PRIM-9 movie—which was the first in a series of such short films set at SLAC, all produced by the newly christened Bin-88 Productions.

Statistician Peter Huber hypothesizes that Tukey first got the idea for the PRIM-9 from his visits to Berkeley, where biochemist Robert Langridge had set up shop with a newly installed experimental computer installation: a rudimentary graphics display running off of a Digital Equipment Corporation DEC-10 computer. Huber's wife, Effi, worked as a postdoctoral research associate in Langridge's molecular biology laboratory, where the new equipment was located. "Working with that installation convinced us that the combination of advanced graphics with a powerful general-purpose computer was more than the sum of the parts, and that it opened new pathways to data analysis in particular," he wrote. "Outsiders to Langridge's group were not permitted to use the equipment, but John Tukey repeatedly sneaked in to watch, and it must have inspired him to initiate the PRIM-9 project the following year, when he was on leave at SLAC in Stanford…."

Even though William Miller coordinated Tukey's long-term stay at SLAC, Friedman had been appointed as head of the Computation Research Group by the time of Tukey's arrival. Tukey spent the next decade, on and off, visiting SLAC, collaborating on graphical methods and multivariate analysis. For instance, Tukey returned to Stanford in 1979, only to discover that the GIF had been discarded in favor of the more advanced standalone ORION-1 workstation, complete with bitmapped color display and tracker ball, developed in part by John A. McDonald. Tukey devised a next generation system, called PRIM-81, from this primordial soup of computer technology. Unlike the previous iteration, the PRIM-81 saved previous states so that users could backtrack; these previous states were marked as "nodes." The PRIM-81 also featured transformations such as "twisting," which was a specific type of rotation with certain coordinates as pivot points that aided the user in visualizing particle physics data.

Tukey's involvement with SLAC began winding down in the early 1980s, as he neared retirement from Princeton. On sabbatical again, but this time traveling to Hawaii for a cousin's wedding with his wife in tow, he detoured to California at the urging of Elizabeth: she wanted them to take a quick vacation on the beach. Rather than booking a hotel, he stayed at the Stanford University campus, in the house of a professor who was also on sabbatical. Surprised that the home had a swimming pool, Tukey took advantage of the amenities: he would whittle away each morning by the pool, "writing out ideas—lots of ideas—about how to analyze high-dimensional data, usually written in cryptic words," which he hand-delivered every afternoon to a secretary at SLAC to transcribe, Friedman recalled. Even after leaving for Hawaii, Tukey continued to record his ideas, mailing them to Friedman from across the Pacific.

Not to put too fine a point on it, but the "PRIM" in PRIM-9 or PRIM-81 could have also stood for "primitive." But these statistical systems were markedly different than anything that came before them (although there is some precedent with the system for generating probability plots that Edward B. Fowlkes, who worked with Tukey at Bell Labs, had up and running by the late 1960s); as Friedman and Stuetzle explain, "To fully appreciate the revolutionary nature of PRIM-9 one has to view it against the backdrop of its time. When Statistics was widely taken to be synonymous with inference and hypotheses testing, PRIM-9 was a purely descriptive instrument designed for data exploration." It contained the seeds that spawned the multivariate statistics software packages of the future, such as XGobi, XGvis, GGobi, MacSpin, and Data Desk, as well as furthering Tukey's overarching goal of moving away from theory toward applications.

Friedman and Stuetzle conclude their piece on a personal note. "Working with John was a remarkable experience," they write. "He had the rare ability to think like a mathematician or like an engineer, depending on what the problem at hand required. His creativity was amazing and not constrained by conventions or by a fear of mistakes...." Tukey, Friedman explains, was much more interested in process and problem solving than in overarching theoretical frameworks; in that respect, he possessed an engineering mindset. In fact, Tukey rarely would divulge the whys behind what he was thinking or doing. As they built the PRIM-9, Tukey would issue Friedman directives: "Okay, here's a procedure: you do this, then you do this, then you do this, then you do that." Friedman was very inquisitive, however.

"John, okay, I understand that," the young physicist replied, "but why would you do this and this?"

"Well, you do this, then you do this, then you do this, then you do this."

"John, but why?"

After a hearty back and forth, Tukey would usually reveal, in detail, his "guiding principle," his reasoning behind the process-oriented, engineering-like set of instructions. Tukey showed himself to be driven by a pragmatic concern—Does the procedure work well?—rather than a need to identify and classify a theoretical approach systematically.

Moreover, Tukey "found joy in ideas and in solving technical problems, and not in the trappings of power and prestige," write Friedman and Stuetzle. By this point in his career, Tukey was a rare breed: humble to a fault, modest, and respectful to everyone despite his superior intellect and litany of accomplishments. With his prodigious intellect and vast connections, Tukey could have forged an empire, Friedman and Stuetzle claim, but he chose to exhibit humility and grace instead.

Today, of course, there are numerous computer languages with the requisite statistical bent that Tukey hinted at in his 1964 American Statistical Association speech, such as SAS, SPSS, S, and S's popular descendent R. Tukey directly influenced the development of the S programming language (recall that in the ASA speech he suggested the invention of a computer language for data analysis, even threatening to create it himself if no one else stepped up).

S was created at Bell Laboratories in the mid-1970s. Although not the first statistical computing language to come out of Bell, it was the first to be implemented, according to a historical eyewitness account of the language's development penned by Richard A. Becker of Bell Labs. Prior to the development of S, statistical computing was usually taken care of by the FORTRAN programming language: specifically, using the Statistical Computing Subroutines (SCS), a library of FORTRAN algorithms written for data analysis and manipulation. But using the SCS meant line-by-line coding was required to perform the simplest of statistical functions on a computer.

FORTRAN, a compression of the words FORmula TRANslation, is a programming language commonly employed for scientific and mathematical applications. Developed in the 1950s at IBM by a team of programmers led by John W. Backus, FORTRAN was the first of the high-level programming languages that would abstract away the particularities of the hardware from the user, allowing him to focus on solving the application problems rather than getting lost in the machinations of the machine (via either low-level machine language or the slightly less abstract but still mostly incomprehensible assembly code). FORTRAN, with its English-style words and variables, resembled algebra more than a then-prototypical computer language, fulfilling one of Backus's stated goals of building a language that "would make it possible for engineers and scientists to write programs for themselves on the [IBM] 704 [mainframe computer]." But another of his goals was laziness: he didn't think routines that kept popping up should have to be coded repeatedly rather than simply being packaged together.

So, while FORTRAN was certainly easier to use than the alternatives, it was still cumbersome, especially for recurring statistics problems. Why should a separate FORTRAN program have to be written to address each of even the simplest of data analysis queries? While the SCS library was excellent for large-scale simulation, such as of the Monte Carlo variety (a simulation style Tukey preferred, terming it "smart," that drew repeated random samples), it wasn't well suited to small-scale statistics, as Richard Becker explains:

> On the other hand, we did occasionally do simple computations. For example, suppose we wanted to carry out a linear regression given 20 x,y data points. The idea of writing a FORTRAN program that called library routines for something like this was unappealing. While the actual regression was done in a single subroutine call, the program had to do its own input and output, and time spent in I/O often dominated the actual computations. Even more importantly, the effort expended on programming was out of proportion to the size of the problem. An interactive facility could make such work much easier.

Furthermore, Becker writes, at Bell "we wanted to be able to interact with our data, using Exploratory Data Analysis [Tukey's] techniques…[since the] statistics research departments were heavily influenced by John Tukey and his approach to Exploratory Data Analysis." Thus, "[i]t was the realization that routine data analysis should not require writing FORTRAN programs that really got S going." Bell Labs, that hotbed of invention that was churning out revolutionary computing breakthroughs like the C language and the UNIX operating system, began work on yet another: flexible interactive statistical computing software, built by a team led by Becker, John Chambers—a Bell employee who was in the process of writing a book on a decade's worth of experience with statistical computing approaches, to be called *Computational Methods for Data Analysis*—and others. The result of this collaboration was S. Rich with features such as interactive graphics, the S statistical computing language was written in FORTRAN. It was all of a piece with what Tukey concisely described as the "Murray Hill tradition in data analysis [which had] long included aspects of 'plant your feet firmly on the ground, even if they do sink deep into the mud.'"

When John Chambers first met Tukey at Bell Labs, Chambers was deep into developing all sorts of software to model data; Tukey's interactions with him at Bell were mostly informal. Typically, Tukey would describe what he was working on at the time, and he would invite Chambers to "interact and comment on it." Chambers was honored at the invitations but also scared—he didn't want to be put in a position to have to "compete" with Tukey; after all, Tukey was so intellectually curious and gifted and full of energy, he would juggle three or four large projects simultaneously.

Nonetheless, Chambers accepted an invitation to sit in on several discussions about analysis of variance (abbreviated as ANOVA, which tests the equality of population means and was developed by Ronald Fisher) between Tukey and an Australian statistician. Chambers thought of it as a "great compliment" because he realized that Tukey would only have invited him if he were interested in his opinion; he already knew that Tukey commanded high respect as a teacher—his reputation preceded him. Although he never saw him interacting with his students, Chambers did notice that Tukey spoke differently amongst his statistics colleagues at Bell Labs than with colleagues in other disciplines. Moreover, Chambers noted that although Tukey could be clear and precise when speaking to the outside world, "when he was talking to his professional colleagues, a bit of mischief came into it—he took delight in inventing new words…and saying things in a way that he knew would rankle the audience. And believe me, it did." The British statisticians, he said, were often the least amused.

Interestingly, Chambers often found himself in opposition to Tukey's statistics worldview, having to defend "conventional statistics" (model-based, CDA-driven) "against what seemed to be John's dismissal of it," Chambers said. "[T]here may be a man for all seasons," Tukey explained, "but there isn't a [statistical] procedure for all purposes." Yet Chambers was hardly a proponent of approaching statistics in any sort of "conventional" manner; rather, Tukey was so extreme, so radical in his approach, that he made Chambers look like a stodgy, dogmatic conservative by comparison.

Ironically, though Tukey was clearly one of the biggest proponents of statistical computing in the 1960s and '70s, he didn't utilize computers very much for his work, and when he did, the results weren't necessarily useful. For instance, Chambers reminisced that while Tukey "[made] many contributions at the conceptual level," "John was never directly involved with programming himself." To Chambers, this was the most striking contradiction about the man: that someone who was so tied up in the computing revolution rarely, if ever, actually used one. There's no evidence that Tukey ever used the multitude of FORTRAN programs that were spawned by Cooley and Tukey's FFT algorithm, either.

Occasionally, though, Tukey would handwrite a computer program for others to code into a machine. Graduate student Alan M. Gross recalls the code of a FORTRAN computer program Tukey handed him, probably for an IBM 7090 mainframe; yet Tukey's code was nearly unintelligible. "FORTRAN ignores arguments that aren't used, so [Tukey] made each subroutine's argument list into a sentence with commas between the words," Gross said. "Typical John!" For his part, Jerome Friedman claims he never saw Tukey program a computer directly; rather he "wrote out his thoughts in a kind of pseudo-Fortran but he never actually sat in front of a terminal to execute code…."

Let's return once more to Tukey's 1964 ASA speech. Michael Tarter, who was there, said tellingly, "The banquet was part of the first meeting I attended after receiving my Ph.D. degree. As is no doubt common, buyer's remorse was beginning to set in. In [his] after-dinner speech [Tukey] predicted much of what has since then actually happened to our field and this was enough to dispel any doubts on my part concerning career choice."

This speech would not mark the last time Tukey would speak of the intersection of statistics and computers. He would go on to be the keynote speaker for the *On the Interface of Computing and Statistics* annual conference three times—in 1972, 1982, and 1986—with speech titles like "Another Look at the Future" and "The Interface of Computing: In the Small or in the Large?" But on this night, in 1964, his speech squarely hit the mark.

CHAPTER EIGHTEEN

Clashes, Criticism, ...

"I do not remember when I met John Tukey, but recall that I found
early encounters with him both frustrating and uncomfortable."
— Erich Lehmann

E ven with his legendary New Englander ethos which he prided
himself on, and his homespun, folksy, deliberate and spare manner—along with his quirks, such as drinking tall glasses of milk at
Princeton beer parties and filing papers in Ziploc bags—Tukey could be
almost overbearing and insistent when it came to getting his points
across. David Brillinger, arguably Tukey's best doctoral student (Tukey
was his doctoral supervisor from 1959 to 1961), recalls that many people
were afraid of Tukey. "For example, if they had a cockeyed idea, he didn't
mince words. He told me once that he thought the best way to get a scientific discussion going on something was to start an argument." Tukey
wouldn't hesitate to steamroll people just to argue a point; Tukey wasn't
afraid to pull out all the stops to win, to reach closer to whatever goal was
in his mind at the moment. Kaye Basford, a colleague of Tukey's in the
late 1980s, warmly relays a story about Tukey that nonetheless contains a
bit of an edge: "[Tukey] didn't [directly] make you feel inadequate when
you couldn't keep up with his line of reasoning. He would just give you
three of four of his papers to read and then expect you to understand his
viewpoint and discuss the pertinent issues the next morning."

Erich Lehmann, for a time, bore the brunt of a Tukey steamroll. Erich
Leo Lehmann, a Jewish statistician born in 1917 in Strasbourg, France,
obtained his doctorate under the supervision of the polymath Jerzy Neyman. Neyman, a key architect of many probabilistic and statistical methods (including confidence intervals), was born in 1894 in Bender, Moldo-
va, but he grew up in a Polish Roman Catholic family. He quickly took to
languages, learning at least five before he was ten years of age. But Neyman developed an interest in mathematics at the Kharkov gymnasium
and decided to pursue the discipline upon admission to Kharkov University. While there, World War I broke out, but Neyman was spared the
draft because of his poor eyesight. Probability—and, more specifically,

the work and unconventional ideas of statistician Karl Pearson—piqued his interest. But the end of Great War brought with it the start of the Russian Revolution and the beginning of health problems, like tuberculosis, for Neyman. It took several years and a long convalesce in Crimea, but he rose to the position of lecturer at Kharkov University, launching what would become a storied academic career. With the political situation tenuous, though, Neyman visited Poland to speak with the mathematician Wacław Sierpiński, which lead to a position at Warsaw University and the completion of a doctorate on probability applied to agricultural experiments, a subject in which Neyman had expertise.

Eventually, Neyman left Warsaw to study with Karl Pearson in London, an experience that left Neyman unfulfilled; instead, Neyman took to Egon Pearson, Karl's son. By the time Neyman shifted his work to Paris, he began collaborating with the younger Pearson, turning out papers on hypothesis testing that would have a far-reaching impact on statistics. Eventually, Neyman would land at University of California, Berkeley, and become "the driving force behind the [statistics] department. I have never had a similar experience again, an eruption of a place from sleepiness to bursting activity [when Neyman was present]," recalled Peter Huber, who spent the balance of his career at Berkeley.

After being under the tutelage of Neyman, Erich Lehmann contributed much to nonparametric (i.e., distribution-free) hypothesis testing. He also concurred with Kaye Basford: Tukey's rabid enthusiasm at coining new terms and spitting out strange-sounding acronyms (e.g., FUNOP, FUNOR, and FUNOM, which were types of plots discussed in FoDA)* made him that much more difficult to understand. Lehmann devotes a section to Tukey in his part memoir, part statistics primer *Reminiscences of a Statistician: The Company I Kept* (2007). While first lauding Tukey's many accomplishments—such as his split time between Princeton and Bell Labs, his high-level government work as part of the President's Science Advisory Committee, and his elections to prestigious academies (e.g., the National and American)—he pulls no punches in describing their interactions. "I do not remember when I met John Tukey," Lehmann writes, "but recall that I found early encounters with him both frustrating and uncomfortable." He continues:

> It was frustrating when he talked about what he was working on. I was, of course, interested. However, his conversation was sprinkled with new technical terms that he delighted in creating…, and unless one interrupted him constantly to ask for their meaning he was unintelligible, at least to me.

---

* FUNOP stood for "FUll NOrmal Plot," for instance.

The British statistician Maurice Kendall agreed with Lehmann, writing of the neologism *polykays*, which are a generalization of Ronald Fisher's *k*-statistics,[*] "we feel that there are limits to linguistic miscegenation which should not be exceeded."[†] Polykays were the fruits of a labor that began with a sabbatical taken from 1949 to 1950 courtesy of a fellowship from the John Simon Guggenheim Memorial Foundation. During the sabbatical, which took place at Princeton at first, Tukey found a spot to work in the Professor's Common Room at Fine Hall and proceeded to explore the "variance component in an unbalanced one-way design" by using "old-fashioned clumsy methods." Nearly a week of full-time algebraic manipulations followed, with Tukey becoming increasingly frustrated that the manipulations took so much work; in fact, correcting the errors in the algebra took even longer than performing the initial calculations themselves. Frustration became the mother of invention: namely, polykays, which Tukey later discovered were first arrived at by Paul L. Dressel in his 1940 University of Michigan doctoral dissertation.

But words like polykays grated on some people's nerves. Even Tukey's former student John A. Hartigan, who enjoyed Tukey's classes tremendously, was never sold on Tukey's incessant neologizing, realizing that it put up needless obstacles to communication among the uninitiated. Yes, the terms were attached to interesting new concepts and ideas in order to promote a sense of novelty, but why should the words have to be so mysterious, so foreign-sounding, so opaque?

Perhaps, in this one respect, Tukey's approach was similar to German philosopher Martin Heidegger's, who also had a penchant for fashioning new words out of whole cloth. As Sarah Bakewell writes in *At the Existentialist Café: Freedom, Being, and Apricot Cocktails* (2016),

> As his readers soon notice, Heidegger tends to reject familiar philosophical terms in favour of new ones which he coins himself….
>
> The effect is at once disconcerting and intriguing. Reading Heidegger, and feeling (as one often does) that you recognise an experience he is describing, you want to say, 'Yes, that's me!' But the word itself deflects you from this interpretation; it forces you to keep questioning….

Heidegger's reason for coining new terms, Bakewell concludes, is "to make the familiar obscure," to force us to rethink our assumptions about

---

[*] Get it? Many (*poly*) k's (*kays*)? Polykays generalize estimators like the sample mean and sample variance, coming in handy when distributions veer off from normality.

[†] "Linguistic miscegenation" since *poly* is of Greek origin while *kay* is Latin.

well-worn concepts or ideas. Likewise with Tukey, who wasn't content with reusing old tropes that had long since turned into passé clichés.

By 1951, things had improved between Lehmann and Tukey. Lehmann taught at Princeton for a semester, and, akin to a foreign language immersion program, he finally caught on to Tukey's unique way with words. Lehmann also found himself facing Tukey in a series of very competitive ping-pong games, which continued years later when Tukey made trips to the Stanford Linear Accelerator Center (e.g., his work with the PRIM-9).[*]

But understanding Tukey's language resulted in an unintended consequence: Lehmann came to realize how dismissive Tukey was of his (Lehmann's) work. Tukey saw a key difference between mathematical and theoretical statistics: the former was mostly a waste of time, while the latter was where important results could be achieved. Lehmann's work, of course, was of the mathematical variety. In explaining Tukey's issues with mathematical statistics, Lehmann quotes this passage of Tukey's taken from "Statistical and Quantitative Methodology" (1961):

> Mathematical statistics was once the knight in armor to save us from the dragon of ill-used descriptive statistics. This is did. Today it is the home of many respected colleagues, whose motivations are basically mathematical rather than scientific. Far less is heard of scientific statistics (which I like to call theoretical statistics), where the motivations are basically scientific. Yet the latter field is more important.

Tukey was again bringing into relief the distinction between the not-tethered-to-the-real-world, abstractions-for-abstractions'-sake style of pure mathematics—that which "value[s] its results in its own terms," appreciative of the "aesthetic nature of the results" in place of any real-life applications—and the context-based, utilitarian-driven approach of science, even if he presents this distinction in a manner replete with value judgments. (He clearly makes his home in science's corner.) "Science and technology," Tukey explained, "must avail itself of the aid of mathematics, yet dare not accept its attitudes."

---

[*] Tukey was an inveterate player of the game, oftentimes carrying around ping pong balls and a table-tennis paddle in his knapsack. Lyle V. Jones, the editor of several volumes of the *Collected Works*, played Tukey on occasion, and found the competition unrelentingly fierce. Once, with Jones seemingly coasting to victory, Tukey began talking to Jones about a "statistical issue we talked of last night." Engaging in conversation distracted Jones, resulting in a Tukey victory—and a reminder of Tukey's unparalleled multitasking abilities. Jones never beat Tukey in the game.

However, Tukey recognized that without the imprimatur of mathematics, statistics could come under fire: "it [statistics] has to look mathematical enough so that you are protected from criticism from your mathematical colleagues." Where did this imprimatur originate? Likely with the ancient Greeks, who possessed a strain of elitism toward mere applications of mathematics; their elitism was passed down through the generations to the mathematicians of the early to mid-twentieth century, who tended to cast aspersions on those utilizing mathematics for vocational-like purposes, such as in statistics and finance. Tukey had fought against this elitism for years by engaging in various tactics, like inserting mathematical proofs to encase his results with the patina of pure mathematics—after all, Tukey, with his doctorate in topology, was more than simply proficient at pure mathematics—but, ironically, he would come to develop his own sort of reverse elitism against mathematics for mathematics' sake. Although he knew his math, Tukey would frequently "put it aside" when approaching a statistics problem and instead say, "Here's what you do: take the data, do this, look at that," rather than conforming to any sort of mathematical model, according to John Chambers. After all, "Data analysis [was]…an antithesis of pure mathematics," Tukey wrote in "Data Analysis, Computation and Mathematics" (1972), a paper presented to mathematicians at Brown University.

The academic tension between Tukey and Lehmann thawed once Lehmann's nonparametric research became more methodological in nature—and thus Tukey finally looked kindly upon Lehmann's work. (Recall that a methodological approach to disciplines, such as in chemistry and topology, was a consistent theme running through Tukey's career.) Tukey and his wife Elizabeth even paid a visit to Berkeley as "guests of [the] department" that Lehmann's chaired. Fred Mosteller, appointed research professor at Berkeley and someone whom Tukey worked with often, arranged the visit. Tukey was set to deliver a series of Hitchcock Lectures (named for Charles M. Hitchcock, a physician who left a bequest to the University of California) on data analysis over the course of several weeks. He was not the first statistician to do so: decades earlier, Ronald Fisher was also a Hitchcock lecturer.

The late 1990s found Lehmann working at the Educational Testing Service (ETS) at Princeton, where he was once again in the regular presence of Tukey, who dropped by weekly to consult (Tukey's four decades of consulting at ETS earned him the Educational Testing Service Award in 1990). They would sometimes have lunch together. Only once during this time did Lehmann see Elizabeth; she was unwell, struggling with terminal cancer.

CHAPTER NINETEEN

...and Controversy: The Kinsey Affair

"Tukey was the worst."
— Clara McMillen

Much more confrontational and abrasive than his relationship with Erich Lehmann was Tukey's professional run-ins with the famed sex researcher Alfred Kinsey.

Kinsey was a very unconventional academic as well as being one of its most controversial. Alfred Charles Kinsey was born in 1894 in Hoboken, New Jersey, and from an early age had an interest in nature; that interest blossomed into him studying biology, where he earned a doctorate from Harvard in 1919. A year later, Kinsey landed at what was to be his academic home for the remainder of his career: Indiana University. There, as a professor of entomology and biology, he researched gall wasps until serendipity flew his way. While teaching a class called "Marriage and Family" in 1938, he developed an interest in sexual case histories and began the process of data collection that would consume the rest of his life. Here is how Matthew Crawford, in his book *The World Beyond Your Head: On Becoming an Individual in an Age of Distraction* (2014), describes Kinsey and his most famous publication, the *Kinsey Report*:

> The arrival of the first Kinsey Report was a very big deal in 1948.... On all sides, there was great emotional investment in the question of how representative the respondents in Kinsey's study were.
>
> Kinsey himself was an interesting character. He had previously been an entomologist, and relied on this fact to present himself as a man of science who just happened to have turned his disinterested gaze from beetles to human sexuality.

Tukey had already bumped elbows with some of the most controversial academics of the 1950s and '60s, including Noam Chomsky, with whom Tukey organized a linguistics seminar at the Institute for Advanced Study; in the early days of the IAS (the 1930s), "[t]hey were worried about keeping the nonmathematical statisticians out for a while," a fear that eventually subsided, according to Tukey. But the Tukey-Kinsey war of ideas turned personal. When the *Kinsey Report*—specifically, the 1948 work entitled *Sexual Behavior in the Human Male*—and its multitude of taboo topics first hit public awareness, Tukey was a member of the National Research Council. The *Report*'s impact was immediate, far-reaching, and consequential. The literary critic and public intellectual Lionel Trilling analyzed contemporaneously the "dramatic reception" that accompanied this publication "event":

> It is an event which is significant in two separate ways, as symptom and as therapy. The therapy lies in the large permissive effect the *Report* is likely to have, the long way it goes toward establishing the *community* of sexuality. The symptomatic significance lies in the fact that the *Report* was felt to be needed at all, that the community of sexuality requires now to be established in explicit quantitative terms.

This "sexual ignorance," contrary to the "universal involvement in sexual life" that was omnipresent in any Aristophanes comedy of the ancient world, was brought about by a society that has "atomized itself" through the effects of modern industrialization: neo-local residence patterns ripping the communal wisdom of society apart. Only through the availing ourselves of "statistical science" could we peel back the sexualized layers of our isolated society, Trilling explains.

But did the *Kinsey Report* actually establish this "community of sexuality" in a statistically rigorous manner? Tukey thought not. As part of a three-member committee assigned by the American Statistical Association to study Kinsey's work, Tukey almost immediately objected to Kinsey's sampling methods, which didn't even approach the most basic standards of random sampling (in principle, the ideal method of data collection).

In fairness to Kinsey, he had never intended this first *Report* to be his final word on the subject; the write-up was only considered provisional, a progress report of sorts before much more data—perhaps as many as 100,000 additional case histories—could be collected. Nonetheless, Kinsey's methodology in this progress report was suspect, having collected data using convenience sampling—i.e., gathering data most convenient to the researcher. Making matters worse, numerous individuals surveyed knew each other, further confounding the results. Plus, only those volunteering to describe in intimate detail their sexual predilections were considered, leaving a mass of what Nassim Nicholas Taleb has called "silent evidence" in its wake. Kinsey had his reasons for being so selective with his sampling, however. As Crawford explains, Kinsey was "a respectable professor in the Midwest, had sexual tastes that weren't very conventional, and his reports appear to have been motivated by a desire to reconcile these two facts"; in other words, the way he went about drawing inferences from his (suspect) data was self-serving, borne out of a desire to resolve a personal cognitive dissonance.

Similarly, Ronald Fisher didn't allow the data to speak for themselves when it came to his own predilections. Doubtless, the history of statistics could not be written without numerous chapters detailing the work and influence of Ronald Aylmer Fisher, who was born in 1890 in London, England. For instance, it was Fisher who popularized the idea of randomized, controlled experiments as a result of his analysis of data from crop experiments at the Rothamsted Experimental Station in England, which he presented in the book *The Design of Experiments* (1935).

Though he was a brilliant and farsighted researcher, Fisher stretched credibility by claiming that only well-designed experiments can definitively demonstrate a causative link between smoking and lung cancer. First, he thought that there was a publication bias: studies that demonstrated a negative effect from smoking tended to be published, while studies that didn't show such an effect were likely rejected. Second, he posited that there might be some gene X that, in fact, ties the variables of smoking and lung cancer together: the expression of gene X explains the positive relationship between the two variables, just as "the summer" is a tidy explanation for why more drowning deaths and more ice cream sold occur together. But his gene X correlation-isn't-causation argument wasn't the result of careful study, but rather an overactive imagination stumbling for something, anything, to self-justify a bad habit: Fisher loved smoking a pipe. Of course, experimenting on human beings in the context of smoking is infeasible, impossible, and (by any measure) immoral, so Fisher would never have a set of experimental results to convince him of the harmful consequences of his addiction.

A rival statistician and contemporary of Fisher's named Jerry Cornfield strongly disagreed with Fisher's self-serving conclusions. Instead of proposing a controlled experiment to investigate the effects of smoking, Cornfield examined many retrospective observational studies of smokers, finding the evidence that lung cancer caused smoking to be clear-cut and overwhelming.* Interestingly, F. R. Anscombe speculates that Tukey may have had a part in Cornfield's lung cancer-smoking research too, since he invited Cornfield to Princeton to work on statistical methods with Martin

---

* Specifically, the data satisfied the Bradford Hill criteria for causation, which are the standards that epidemiologist Austin Bradford Hill and medical researcher Richard Doll established in order to argue for causation *sans* direct experimentation: the association between the variables in question needed to be (1) strong; (2) consistent through time; (3) specific; (4) realistic; (5) responded to similarly in similar situations; and (6) backed up by other types of experiments.

Wilk and Frank Anscombe mere years before the publication of Corn-field's groundbreaking meta-study.

Regardless, cancer would claim Fisher a decade after he railed against the first published studies that strongly established a clear-cut causative link between tobacco smoking and cancer. Far from being a worthy sub-stitute to decision-making-by-morality or a "science of statistics and not of ideas" as Trilling had cast it, both Fisher and Kinsey had manipulated statistical science toward their own self-serving, unenlightened ends. One is reminded of the famous aphorism: "There are three kinds of lies," the British statesman Benjamin Disraeli said (as relayed by Mark Twain): "lies, damn lies, and statistics."

Alfred Kinsey had requisitioned financial support from the Rockefeller Foundation for his sex research. He worked closely with Rockefeller Foundation officer Alan Gregg, born in 1890 in Colorado Springs, Colo-rado. Gregg had become convinced of the importance of Kinsey's re-search after visiting him in Bloomington, Indiana, and witnessing Kin-sey's "extraordinary powers of persuasion," according to Kinsey biog-rapher James H. Jones in *Alfred C. Kinsey: A Life* (1997); Gregg ended up putting his career on the line to secure the funding as well as writing the preface to *Sexuality in the Human Male*. But Gregg had been tricked. As Jones explains,

> In Kinsey, [Gregg] thought they had found a metric-minded, Baconian scientist. [He] saw him as an instrument, a collecting machine who would compile the data others would use to develop social policies and pro-grams designed to control human sexual behavior. Instead, [he] had been co-opted by a genuine revolutionary, a man who intended to attack Vic-torian morality and to promote an ethic of tolerance.

Tukey, unlike Gregg, wasn't seduced by Kinsey or fooled by the gloss of scientific imprimatur.

The Rockefeller Foundation, stung by some of the early criticism of *Sexuality in the Human Male*, and hedging on whether to fund a companion volume focusing on females, welcomed professional scrutiny. The Com-mittee for Research on Problems of Sex of the National Research Coun-cil, which supported Kinsey's research financially, penned a letter to the American Statistical Association requesting "counsel regarding the re-search methods" of Kinsey. So, in 1950, the ASA, then headed by Sam Wilks, assembled a committee of statisticians to meet with Kinsey at his Institute for Sex Research at Indiana University, which Kinsey established in 1947, in order to statistically scrutinize his work. In addition to Tukey,

Frederick Mosteller and W. G. Cochran (designated the chairman) were selected for the assignment as well.

Charles Frederick "Fred" Mosteller was born in 1916 in Clarksburg, West Virginia. Probability theory turned into a lifelong interest at Carnegie Mellon, where a professor introduced him to mathematical problem solving. He earned a bachelor's degree and a master's degree from the institution before arriving at Princeton, where he was awarded his doctorate in 1946, which was co-supervised by Tukey. (The professor E. G. Olds was insistent that Mosteller go to Princeton.) At Princeton, Mosteller "sometimes sat with the mathematicians and physicists including Tukey, Richard Feynman, Bryant Tuckerman, and Charles Dolph."

During World War II, Mosteller's wife, Virginia, worked as a secretary to mathematician Merrill M. Flood, who co-developed the famous Prisoner's Dilemma problem; Flood helped to oversee the FCRO as well. Tukey's interactions with Flood during the latter part of the war point to a great mystery: Did Tukey have advance knowledge of the atomic bombing of Japan—even helping to plan it in some fashion? In the book *Prisoner's Dilemma: John von Neumann, Game Theory, and the Puzzle of the Bomb* (1992), author William Poundstone writes,

> During the war, mathematician John Tukey assigned Merrill Flood—who would later become co-discover of the prisoner's dilemma—to prepare a study on aerial bombing of Japan.... [Tukey] once hinted to Flood that it had something to do with the mysterious flash that had been reported in the New Mexico desert. The study was, of course, for the Manhattan Project.

Less than a month before the United States dropped two atomic bombs on Japan, a prototype was detonated in New Mexico. During this so-called Trinity test, the words of the *Bhagavad Gita* came to J. Robert Oppenheimer's mind: "Now I am become Death, the destroyer of worlds." Tukey's friend Richard Feynman witnessed the test, too. "It was a series from bright to dark, and I had *seen* it. I am about the only guy who actually looked at the damn thing," Feynman recollected. F. R. Anscombe ties everything together this way: "If Flood's recollection and Tukey's hint were accurate, then in July 1945 [by the time of the Trinity test] Tukey had finished the Nike study and was again serving the NDRC."* The intrigue is palpable: What did John Tukey know, and when

---

* The Nike wasn't decommissioned for some time afterward; the missiles, of which thousands had been constructed, met their end with the signing of the Anti-Ballistic Missile (ABM) Treaty in 1972, which permitted each signing party a scant one hundred antiballistic missiles spread over two ABM complexes.

did he know it? Attempting to get to the bottom of these questions is akin to engaging in a snipe hunt.

Regardless, we do know that Tukey, about five years later, did some calculations related to the thermonuclear hydrogen bomb, which, unlike the fission bombs dropped on Japan, generated a much more powerful fusion reaction. After Stanislaw Ulam—who taught Tukey topology decades earlier—and physicist Edward Teller sketched a design for the advanced weaponry in 1951, John Wheeler, a professor at Princeton, and a team of mathematicians were brought in to perform the necessary calculations to bring the bomb to life; Wheeler lured Tukey into the fold. The thermonuclear weapon was successfully tested in 1952 in Enewetak Atoll islands, located in the Pacific Ocean.

The test would not mark the last of Princeton's involvement with matters of nuclear research. Tukey lunched with a number of physicists in the early to mid-1950s, including, still, Lyman Spitzer, the now-retired "Führer." Spitzer was one of a team of physicists at Princeton, which also included Wheeler, who directed the team, and the German born Martin Schwarzschild, who worked on nuclear-weapons matters through the auspices of the university at the Forrestal Research Center; Spitzer, who started the project in 1951, called the nuclear research team "Project Matterhorn," named after a mountain in the Alps. Tukey, unsurprisingly, offered his own appellation for the lunch group of physicists: the "Chowder and Marching Society."

Fred Mosteller had a great number of intellectual interests and was a prolific writer; he authored many papers, including some with Tukey as coauthor. He also worked with Tukey on a number of projects, including one involving students' performance in various school districts through repeated surveying.

Sam Wilks was the editor for more than a decade of *The Annals of Mathematical Statistics*, a publication of the Institute of Mathematical Statistics (IMS), an organization which he helped found. Sometimes Wilks would slide an *Annals* research manuscript to one of his graduate students, such as Leo Goodman, to referee. But it was Fred Mosteller who became Wilks' assistant. Mosteller spent many all-night sessions with Wilks putting together issues of the journal that were usually triggered by an innocuous comment from Wilks such as, "I wonder if we shouldn't spend just a little time getting out the *Annals* tonight." (Later, while watching Tukey reviewing submitted papers for the *Annals* during a train ride—Tukey referred four papers from start to finish in the time it took the train to travel from Princeton Junction to Philadelphia—Wilks said that Tukey "ate those papers like popcorn.")* Wilks was invaluable to Mosteller's career—if not for Wilks, in fact, Mosteller may not have been anywhere near the successful statistician he ultimately turned into. In the spring of Mosteller's first semester at Princeton, Wilks asked if Mosteller had any summer plans. He told the statistician that he would "work on the road jobs as usual; otherwise I won't have funds to return to graduate school."

> Departing from his usual roundabout treatment of anything he was not pleased with, Wilks grumbled that this did not seem an effective way to become a professional statistician. He said he would be back to me in a few days. He returned with the opportunity of a summer job running IBM punch cards through a counting sorter for Professor Hadley Cantril, social psychologist and head of the Office of Opinion Research.

By the time Mosteller was deep into working on his thesis, Wilks and Tukey invited him to deliver a paper, on unbiased estimation,† at a statistics seminar they had organized. The talk was such a success that he was invited back for a follow-up session the very next week.

In 1948, Wilks published a book entitled *Elementary Statistical Analysis*. In the preface, he thanked three individuals for "helpful discussions": Albert Tucker, John Tukey, and Fred Mosteller. Having taught the course in which the book was based, as well as having an overriding interest in pedagogy (more on that below), Mosteller was in a unique position to be helpful in assembling *ESA*. In addition to creating homework problems, "I think my biggest contribution to this little blue book called *Elementary Statistical Analysis* was to think of the thumbtack as a device for giving a fixed but unknown probability," he recalled. "Wilks was enormously interested in applications, and was willing to work on them, and often did. Still, he felt that the mathematics was the real foundation to statistics," and *ESA* reflected that worldview.

Later in his career, Mosteller collaborated and wrote a book with U.S. senator Daniel P. Moynihan about early childhood education; by this point he had upended his approach to teaching statistics: from a top-down theoretical manner to one entirely data-driven. "So I got to thinking that there might be a way to teach a course in statistics using primarily data," he recalled. His dream was to be able to use interdisciplinary data sets to drive the teaching entirely.

---

* Mosteller relays Wilks' quote slightly differently: "He ate them up like peanuts!"

† An estimate of a population parameter that has zero bias, meaning that the difference between the estimator's expected value and the true value of the parameter should theoretically be zero.

Mosteller was one of the few statisticians that had a fair chance of being recognized by passersby on the street; he taught a televised class on probability and statistics in the 1960-61 TV season of the NBC program *Continental Classroom*, which was watched by more than a million people. The popularity of the show is all the more remarkable, considering that it aired in the morning—around 6:00 AM—so people had to make a point of waking up early to watch (of course, in the 1960s, viewers didn't have the option of catching an analog or digital playback at a later time). Some colleges even offered credit for taking the televised course.

The opportunity to star in *Continental Classroom* came about as a result of work Mosteller had done on a committee called the Commission on Mathematics for the College Entrance Exam Board. Al Tucker was on the committee, as were Sam Wilks, George Thomas, and Robert Rourke, who was a secondary school teacher. Teaching probability and statistics in the early grades was a major focus of the participants. Thus, the fruits of the committee's labors included a book, *Introductory Probability and Statistical Inference: An Experimental Course* (1959), that was designed for and written in part by elementary and secondary school teachers. After the committee disbanded, Mosteller, Thomas, and Rourke teamed up to write another book. Called *Probability with Statistical Applications* (1961), it served as the basis for the *Continental Classroom* television series.

Perhaps most notably, along with statistician David Wallace, Mosteller conducted a three-year study that attempted to get to the bottom of who, precisely, wrote twelve of the eighty-five *Federalist Papers*, since there was longstanding controversy regarding disputed authorship. They utilized techniques like sentence length and word frequency analysis, all with an overarching Bayesian framework, although they "had to invent Bayesian methods every step of the way" because the "Bayesian methods weren't ready." In their published report, entitled *Inference & Disputed Authorship: The Federalist* (1964), they determined that the author of the disputed papers was likely James Madison.

The last of the three ASA committee members assigned to study Kinsey's work was William Gemmell "W. G." Cochran, born in Rutherglen, Scotland, in 1909. He was brought onto the committee because of his expertise in randomization, the design of experiments, and sample surveys. Cochran had a sterling curriculum vitae, having developed many statistical methods throughout the course of his career, including the Cochran Q-Test. During the Second World War, Cochran was one of a number of statisticians to migrate to Princeton (others include Charlie Winsor and Paul Dwyer); there, he worked with Sam Wilks and moved his family into a large Princeton house shared with fellow statistician Alexander M.

Mood, who would win the Wilks Memorial Award decades later, and Mood's family.

The Cochrans and the Moods would host statisticians every Sunday afternoon at their home, complete with intellectual activities that included solving *New York Times* crossword puzzles, which Tukey enjoyed; in fact, he once mused that "[l]ife is like a double-crostic [a variant of a crossword puzzle in which the answers to clues reveal a quotation]; we can do far more than we know." Those afternoons also functioned as academic networking events, with mathematicians and statisticians alike benefiting (e.g., Tukey met George W. Snedecor, a leading proponent of applied statistics, in the garden adjacent to the house).

Kinsey and the three ASA committee members got off to a bad start. On the morning they were to meet, as Tukey, Mosteller, and Cochran were walking in the rain through the UI campus on their way to the Kinsey Institute, Mosteller began singing a fast-paced Gilbert and Sullivan song from the opera *H. M. S. Pinafore*, only recently learned by Mosteller, which Tukey and Cochran were quick to lend their voices to as well (they were both big fans of Gilbert and Sullivan, with Cochran a member of multiple singing groups). Kinsey, curt and reserved, directed them to a nearby office where they could work; no pleasantries were exchanged, and Kinsey left them. As the committee began setting up, Mosteller resumed signing the Gilbert and Sullivan tune, and the other two statisticians followed suit. Here is Mosteller, describing his shock at what happened next: "And so we started to sing this last verse, and the next thing we knew the door was being broken down and there was Kinsey and an army behind him of secretaries and others." Kinsey was furious; the din of the committee members' chorus could be heard through the entire Institute since the air ducts served as a sound conduit. Their behavior, Kinsey told them, was terribly inconsiderate.

Over the next week, tensions between Kinsey and the committee didn't thaw. Kinsey was dogmatic, stubbornly holding the line on his methods of data collection and analysis; he wasn't interested in listening to any suggestions or compromising on any points. "[Kinsey] believed that his way of doing it was likely better than the way anybody else wanted to do it," Mosteller explained. Part of the problem stemmed from how mathematicians do business: mathematically airtight arguments, rather than personalities, settle arguments. While Kinsey was a master debater and had a slick personality, he didn't possess the requisite statistical knowledge and was thus "in over his head," according to his biographer, James H. Jones. "[I]n mathematics," Mosteller added, "we are very used to very harsh arguments in which we don't pay any attention at all to the other person's feelings." The glint of mathematical truth can only be found at the edge of a pencil tip or a piece of chalk, no matter how anyone feels about it; in mathematics, pure logic serves as judge, jury, and executioner, and crying, whining, complaining, or sweet talking won't ever change that. Even though Tukey had his reservations when deferring to abstract mathematical methods, given a choice he'd take them over Kinsey's arm-twisting every day of the week and twice on Sunday.

Kinsey couldn't conclusively demonstrate, in any mathematically or statistically rigorous sense, the efficacy of any of his methods. Instead, as Jones notes, he consistently shifted the debate to the challenges inherent in sex research, thereby justifying his own solutions to the unique problem of excavating data on such a sensitive subject.

But then Kinsey and his small team of researchers interviewed the ASA committee members individually on their sex histories. Here, away from the realm of the quantitative, firmly in the milieu of qualitative research—where personalities and oral persuasion did in fact matter—Kinsey finally found his footing. The committee came to agree with Kinsey that a written questionnaire didn't permit the same sort of flexibility as an in-person clinical interview despite the potential for bias, and they were impressed with Kinsey and his team's "skillful performance" while interviewing.

Feeling like the tide was turning in his favor, Kinsey invited the committee members to dinner at his home. Kinsey's wife, Clara McMillen, cooked the meal. Kinsey held court on musical trivia. Nevertheless, despite the good intentions, the evening was an unmitigated disaster. Clara was annoyed at how inconsiderate the statisticians were toward her husband, as she revealed later in an interview from 1971. "I never fed any group of men that I would have so much liked to have poisoned," she recalled. "I just felt that here we invited them out for dinner, along with the associates, and I just felt that they were not very friendly. Tukey was the worst."

Indeed, compared to the inflexible Tukey, Mosteller and Cochran were practically Kinsey partisans. Tukey would give no quarter to Kinsey, never permitting any compromise in the realm of statistical theory or practice. He was Kinsey's perfect foil, which wasn't surprising given Tukey's general approach to investigation: "the best way to get the issues onto the table was to start an argument," according to Brillinger.

The written report the ASA eventually assembled took a long time to complete. Kinsey had, however, already attempted to adjust his research methods based on the committee's oral suggestions. The committee members and Kinsey touched base multiple times before the ASA published their report, meeting in various cities like Chicago and Princeton. Once, when returning to Princeton, Mosteller became so involved with the work that he exclaimed, "They couldn't pay me enough to do this. They couldn't pay me enough to do this."

And, as time passed, the meetings became less contentious and less argumentative, although Tukey continued to press his points—but relented a bit on some key items privately: Tukey believed that the perfect shouldn't be the enemy of the good, thinking that for Kinsey to completely wipe the slate clean and start over would be foolish since the sex data he had already collected was leaps and bounds better than anything ever before obtained on the subject.

Warren Weaver, the director of the Division of Natural Sciences at the Rockefeller Foundation, placed a phone call to Tukey in early 1951 in order to obtain his feedback about the committee's progress. He would have called Cochran, but Tukey "is closer by, and I have worked with him so long and intimately that I knew that he would talk to me pretty freely—probably more freely than Cochran would," Weaver wrote in a letter to Alan Gregg. "After all of this is said and done," Weaver continued, "Dr. Tukey remarked quite voluntarily that if he were in your [Gregg's] position he thinks that he would probably, although obviously reluctantly, go ahead with the project." Furthermore,

> Dr. Tukey said that if he were Dr. Kinsey himself, it is not at all clear to him that he would be willing to stop, wipe all of these years' work off the backboard, and start over…. It was certainly inferred in everything Tukey said that what Kinsey is doing is a substantial improvement over what anyone has produced or otherwise done in this field.

Tukey's acknowledgment of all this to Weaver was indeed reflected in the wording of the committee's final report: "The statistical and methodological aspects of [Kinsey's] work are outstanding in comparison to other leading sex studies." Even criticisms of Kinsey's sampling methods in the final report were restrained:

> Many of [Kinsey's] findings are subject to question because of a possible bias in the constitution of the sample. This is not a criticism of their work (although it is a criticism of some of their interpretations). No previous sex study of a broad human population known to us, medical, psychiatric, psychological, or sociological, has been able to avoid this difficulty, and we believe that [Kinsey] could not have avoided the use of a nonprobability sample at the start of their work.

Why was their language so tempered? Because Tukey had meditated on the issue and realized that he had perhaps been a bit too dismissive initially of Kinsey. But he still had grave concerns. As Weaver wrote to Gregg in 1951, "As an incidental point, Tukey remarked [to me on the phone] that after all of the very careful examination of this committee, he would be inclined to say that almost half of the statistical criticism of Kinsey was quite unwarranted, but that most of the other half was significant." In another letter, written several months later, Weaver relayed these concerns directly to the members of the Rockefeller Foundation. "My confidential conversations with two outstanding statistical experts [Tukey and Cochran] certainly led me to think that they view his sampling procedure with great concern," he said. "And they also indicated to me that they were not sanguine that Dr. Kinsey would understand their objections, would be interested in them, or would follow them."

Yet thanks to the machinations of Gregg, the ASA committee members, though they hadn't quite yet put the finishing touches on their final report, offered Kinsey an olive branch of sorts, writing a letter of provisional support for continued funding of Kinsey's work to the Rockefeller Foundation. But a preliminary report that the committee members had assembled, which was thick and full of technical details, was distributed not just to Kinsey, his research team, and the ASA, but also to officers at the Rockefeller Foundation. Kinsey was angry that he hadn't been given a chance to formally respond to the committee's thorny criticisms before the Rockefeller Foundation saw the preliminary report.

There was an even larger issue looming for Kinsey: that of the randomness in data collection—specifically random sampling, the process of selecting individuals randomly from the population of interest. As Weaver wrote to Gregg, "But on the much more basic issue of the original method of sampling, it is in the nature of the situation that no progress is possible at this stage...." He continued: "Tukey himself has pretty grave doubts as to whether useful and significant generalizations about the population as a whole can actually be inferred from the kind of samples which Dr. Kinsey used." Tukey was insistent on this point; indeed, he wrote that "it can be unethical, immoral, or even just plain wrong, to draw inferences from only part of the data."

Knowing that he had to prepare for an "upcoming battle with Tukey" about sampling methods (according to Jones), Kinsey decided to meet with pollster George Gallup and inquire about such procedures. Had it been tried on a national scale anywhere? And, if so, precisely how was it done? Gallup was surprised at the criticism Kinsey was being subjected to by the "'random sampling' boys," as he called them, thinking that most academics had softened their position on the issue since no, in fact, such random sampling on a nationwide scale had little precedent. So, to help Kinsey in his "battle with Tukey," Gallup and his assistant suggested arguments Kinsey could employ against the man with a "mania for random sampling."

In 1952, a meeting to decide the fate of Kinsey's past and future research took place at the Institute. As expected, the two stubborn bulls immediately locked horns over sampling methodology. "Everyone thinks that the data in other people's subjects are in better shape," Tukey once said, but he certainly didn't feel that way on this day. Exasperated by the heresies of Kinsey's data collection methods, Tukey brought the hammer down. Why not take a pin and plunge it into a telephone book repeatedly to obtain the sample? Heck, even a "random selection of three people would have been better than a group of 300 chosen by Mr. Kinsey," Tukey concluded. Which was theoretically correct—but, at the time, was underdeveloped in terms of practical implementations. Far from simply grasping at straws, that was just the sort of lifeline Kinsey needed in order to keep his project afloat.

"Statistical Problems of the Kinsey Report," published in the *Journal of the American Statistical Association* in 1953, lays bare the problems with Kinsey's sex research, although the committee is quick to note that "this report is confined to statistical methodology, and does not concern itself with the appropriateness or the limitations of orgasm as a measure of sexual behavior"—meaning that the statistics experts "discuss the Kinsey Report from the standpoint of statistical logic and from that standpoint alone," according to one contemporaneous reviewer writing for the *American Catholic Sociological Review*, "[t]herefore they do not consider certain weaknesses of the *Kinsey Report* that lie outside their field of specialization."

The committee members put aside an examination of qualitative methodology in favor of a narrower, quantitative scope. The questions they pose about the data, however, cut deep. For instance, Who is the population of interest? Is it all white males in the United States? If so,

> it would be a rather odd white male U.S. Population. It would have age groups, educational status, rural-urban background, marital status and all their combinations according to the 1940 census, but it would have more members in Indiana than in any other state, and it would have been selected to an unknown degree for willingness to volunteer histories of sexual behavior.

The committee deemed Kinsey's samples "deliberately disproportionate" to account for the differences between feasible sample collection (due to concerns such as geographical disproportion) and the population distribution.

Furthermore, how, precisely, could Kinsey obtain accurate information about people's sexual behaviors? The way the committee members saw it, he had three viable options: studying the behaviors live and in person (as Masters and Johnson would do, for different reasons, later on), from recordings, or from self-reports. Kinsey took the third option:

> The choice of reported behavior implies that the question: "On the average, how much difference is there between present reported and past actual behavior?" is seriously involved in any inferences about actual behavior which are attempted from [Kinsey's] results. The difference might well be large, leading to a large systematic error in measurement.

So why is random sampling of a population so important? According to the committee, the results obtained by a casual sampling of items from the host population will probably not result in a representative sample; in that case, application of even the most sophisticated mathematical tools won't bring the researcher any closer to the truth of the population of interest. Rather, bad sampling implies bad analysis as surely as garbage in implies garbage out.

If not random sampling, then, what kind of sampling did Kinsey perform? In using the example of a botanist gathering ten oak leaves each from a sample of one hundred oak trees to learn about the infestation of parasites in the entire population of oak trees, the committee cautions that the special type of formulas for analyzing this type of sampling, called "cluster sampling," don't apply to individuals independently selected at random from the population. "[Kinsey's] sample was, in the main, a cluster sample, since they built up their sample from groups of people rather than from individuals," they explain; each of Kinsey's "groups of people" are analogous to the ten oak leaves culled from each oak tree in a sample. Therefore, the standard and widely used statistical formulas—i.e., ones designed for individually sampling items—would lead to all sorts of errors if applied to data gathered from cluster samples (as seems to be the case in the *Kinsey Report*, since calculations of measures such as standard error were not adjusted to take into account the type of sampling performed). The committee argues that a straightforward probability (random) sample still could have been attempted, even among a restricted population, and even if that probability sample is of previous subjects.

Two years after the committee's final report was published, a symposium appeared in the *Journal of the American Statistical Association* with pieces by Kinsey and several other notables. After thanking the statisticians for constructive criticism and guidance, much of which he applied to his second volume on sexuality (focusing on females), he pointedly argued against the feasibility of probability (random) sampling. "Because of the sensitive nature of the subject involved, we do not believe that probability sampling is practical in any extensive study of human sexual behavior which attempts to survey the whole population of a large city, a state, or the United States," Kinsey wrote.

> Our primary problem, therefore, and the one which few of the reviewers of our work have adequately recognized, has been to discover some process by which we could persuade our subjects to divulge their sexual activities with such fullness and completeness as their memories would allow. To do this, we have had to give prime attention to establishing rapport and developing effective interviewing techniques. Only then has it begun to be possible to select the sample with which we wished to work.

Human beings are not insects in fields or tires on automobiles. Kinsey wasn't asking people about how many movies they attended per annum. He was asking human beings about sex. And in the final analysis, he felt, "the requirements of accurate sampling were antagonistic to the requirements for adequate reporting."

Many years later, after the storms had passed, Mosteller admitted that he admired how effective Kinsey was at arguing his points and standing up to Tukey; Mosteller viewed Kinsey as a "self-reliant scientist" who had some interesting ideas about how to compensate for the lack of randomness. "We took the whole thing we'd written and their team went over it in great detail, and we went over it line by line, so to speak," Mosteller said. "I was very glad that we did go over it in that manner, so [Kinsey] did have plenty of opportunities to point out places where we were perhaps giving innuendos in directions we didn't realize or perhaps saying something mistaken about what was going on." Mosteller admitted he respected Kinsey's devotion toward his work. With the benefit of hindsight, Mosteller was also a bit sheepish at Tukey's uncompromising approach toward Kinsey.

Even before the ASA published their final report (portions of which were quoted above), Kinsey had won the public relations battle by learning enough about sampling techniques—and what was and wasn't feasible—to confront the statisticians directly on their own turf. Plus, realizing that the *New York Post* was sniffing around trying to obtain a copy of the committee's preliminary report, Kinsey preemptively released a statement to the press that stressed the positive comments that the statisticians had made about his research as well as the many ways in which he was incorporating the committee's suggestions into his ongoing research into female sexuality. (Tukey suggested composing a much more critical, but proprietary, report than the general one released publicly, because certain technical issues weren't addressed sufficiently.) Although Tukey's former colleague Kaye Basford put a positive spin on Tukey's lack of tact by saying, "What a way to get the best out of people by having them strive to live up to those expectations!" his uncompromising behavior cost him in the Kinsey affair.

And that behavior stayed more or less consistent for the rest of his life. "Tukey very often, deliberately or not, overstated his points for the sake of argument," according to the statistician Peter J. Huber, who worked closely with Tukey in the early 1970s. Huber describes how "Tukey relished the presence of hard sparring partners" in the 1970-71 academic year at Princeton. He would "bounce his new ideas off us"—the "us" being Huber, the Swiss statistician Frank R. Hampel, and the Romanian-born Peter J. Bickel, an American statistician whose doctoral advisor was Erich L. Lehmann—and, if the group wasn't sold on one of Tukey's ideas, he might, just might, "retreat gracefully."

Although Tukey remained as obstinate as ever as he aged, he began to dismiss pure mathematics entirely, something noticed by Huber. "[Tukey] would rely on his intuition and profess open contempt for mathematics" as his interests shifted entirely to data analysis, Huber explained. Data analysis was a "performing art," Huber elaborated, not something easily written about but "rather, it is something you do." Tukey would sometimes even resort to proof—not mathematical proof, but proof by intimidation: "He would cow weaker discussion partners, including many of his graduate students, by the sheer weight of his authority (and unfortunately impress upon them that mathematics was unnecessary)." But, occasionally, "under duress he would produce nontrivial mathematical arguments." Were they formed off the top of his head, or had these arguments been percolating in his head for a while? Huber and company never got to the bottom of it. Regardless, as Huber notes, Tukey "used to change his focus of attention every few years…."

Tukey would need all the "hard sparring partners" he could find in the 1970-71 academic year at Princeton as he shifted his full attention to relatively unexplored territory: statistical robustness.

PART THREE

Life Among the Academics

CHAPTER TWENTY

The Quest for Robustness

"The floodgates were open, but the quality of the overflow was
generally low and sometimes appalling."
—Stephen Stigler

At a mathematics conference in 1960, statistician George Box got into a bit of a scuffle with John Tukey. Born in 1919 in Gravesend, England, George Edward Pelham Box, like Tukey, began his academic career by studying chemistry. Box thought himself an "accidental statistician," a nickname that stuck, because he learned statistics by analyzing the data obtained from the experiments he conducted during the Second World War on poison gases; after the war was over, he earned his doctorate in mathematical statistics from London University (his doctoral advisor was British statistician Egon Pearson, the son of famed statistician Karl Pearson and a dominating force in statistics in his own right).

Tukey and Box's dustup occurred over the notion of robustness: Tukey believed data sets could be altered (e.g., ignoring some points at the extremes, a process he called *trimming*), while Box thought that the data were sacrosanct—only the statistical model itself could be considered robust or not. Interestingly, the word "robustness" is a term that Tukey *didn't* coin—a fact that Box, a model-centric Bayesian famous for the pithy sentiment "All models are wrong, but some are useful," reminded Tukey when John Chambers, whom Tukey collaborated with at Bell Labs when fashioning the S computer language, adopted Box's aphorism as his own. Then Box pressed his point: because Tukey didn't arrive at the term, Box could have it mean anything he wanted it to!

Though Egon Pearson, not Box, was the first to study robustness (back in the 1930s), Box had indeed used the term first. On the opening page of a 1953 paper, titled "Non-normality and Tests on Variances," Box wrote,

> It would appear, however, that this remarkable property of "robustness" to non-normality which these tests for comparing means possess, and without which they would be much less appropriate to the needs of the

experimenter, is not necessarily shared by other statistical tests, and in particular is not shared by the tests for equality of variances....

Box described how Bartlett's test,[*] used to check the assumption of homoscedasticity (equal variances) prior to performing analysis of variance (abbreviated as ANOVA, which tests for the equality of population means), wasn't robust. "To make a preliminary test on variances," Box complained, "is rather like putting to sea in a rowing boat to find out whether conditions are sufficiently calm for an ocean liner to leave port!"

But was Tukey working on issues of robustness—albeit not explicitly calling them that—before Box? Box credited Tukey with doing so in a footnote—sort of: "Since writing the above a very interesting paper by J. W. Tukey (1948) has come to my notice which has many points of contact with the present paper and which expresses similar views to the above."

The paper Box's footnote referred to is called "Some Elementary Problems of Importance to Small Sample Practice," published in the journal *Human Biology*. In it, Tukey wrote of "a few problems concerning small samples whose solution would have considerable practical applications and which seem approachable by some combination of experimental sampling, empirical approximation, and, possibly"—here's where he hedged, unsurprisingly, since Tukey was averse to leveraging the traditional mathematical methods of theorem and proof unless he absolutely had to—"analytical investigation."[†]

The first of these problems, he said, was "connected with the behavior of *t* for non-normal distributions and the possibilities of finding an improved expression for use in such cases." The "*t*" in the paper referred to the *t* distribution that, unlike the normal (or Gaussian) distribution, is really a family of distributions, each one associated with a different sample size. At smaller sample sizes, the *t* distribution is symmetrical, low, flat, and stout, with thick tails; at larger sample sizes, the *t* distribution becomes rounder at the top, taller, and its tails skinnier, but it still stays symmetrical. In fact, the bigger the sample size, the more the *t* distribution begins to resemble the normal distribution. At an infinite sample size, the *t* and normal distributions are indistinguishable.

---

[*] Named after Maurice Stevenson Bartlett, whom Tukey would give credit for the independent co-development of spectrum analysis in the late 1940s.
[†] Interestingly, in census testimony from 1992, Tukey said that he only became familiar with robustness "in the more technical sense of the word" in 1958 (ten years after the publication of his paper in *Human Biology*), after publishing a joint technical report with Ted Harris, who had earned a doctorate in statistics at Princeton under Sam Wilks.

The normal distribution is the most important distribution in statistics, in large part because many real-world distributions tend to be normally shaped. Any normal distribution is symmetrical and bell-shaped (or mound-shaped), with its mean, median, and mode at the center. Only two numbers are necessary to describe a unique normal distribution: its mean and standard deviation. (Circles are also uniquely defined by only two numbers: the length of the radius and the location of the center.) The mean relays the normal distribution's placement on a horizontal axis, while the standard deviation describes the spread (or variability) of the distribution. The larger the standard deviation, the wider and shorter the normal distribution will be. Also, the normal distribution function is asymptotic to the horizontal axis, meaning that the distribution gets closer and closer but never actually makes contact with the axis from either direction.

The normal distribution is sometimes called the Gaussian distribution, after Carl Friedrich Gauss. But Gauss wasn't the first to describe its properties.[*] Rather, it was Abraham de Moivre, friend of Isaac Newton, inveterate gambler, and pioneer of probability theory, who first cast the mathematical parameters of the normal distribution. Later on, Karl Pearson wished to avoid naming the curve after any mathematician, so he called it "normal"—and the name stuck, though Sir Francis Galton had earlier termed the distribution normal.[†]

The t distribution is sometimes referred to as the Student's t distribution. To understand why, we have to go back to the turn of the previous century. In 1899, the Guinness Brewing Company,[‡] spurred by their new leader, Lord Guinness, hired a newly minted degree holder in mathematics and chemistry named William Sealy Gosset as part of a push at Guinness to bring greater scientific rigor and more stringent quality control to their production of beer. The inventive Gosset, a young Oxford graduate

---

[*] The Gaussian distribution is an instance of Stigler's law of eponymy (sometimes also referred to as the "law of misonomy"), which states that discoveries in science and mathematics aren't properly named for their creators. Rather ironically, Stigler's law is itself a member of this set, since Stephen Stigler didn't come up with the law (but he did popularize it).

[†] In *Exploratory Data Analysis*, Tukey said that to call the Gaussian distribution "normal" was misleading. He also said that the Gaussian distribution wasn't some sort of "physical law" that data sets must conform to, but rather a "reference standard" to which empirically collected data must be judged against. In the real world, data behaves in a variety of not-easily-mathematically-expressible ways, so it is helpful to know the approximate shapes of the distribution of the data points—normal-looking or not.

[‡] Of course, this is the same Guinness Brewing Company that originally published the *Guinness Book of World Records*.

holding degrees in chemistry and mathematics who was born in Canter-
bury, England, in 1876, rose through the company's ranks, solving all
kinds of brewing quandaries using sophisticated mathematical models.
But a problem arose: Gosset desperately wanted to publish his results,
but there were several company restrictions in place making publication
onerous. (Prior to Gosset's employment at Guinness, the company had
lost proprietary secrets through the publication of an article about brewing methods written by an on-staff brewer.) Around this time, Gosset
formed a secret friendship with Karl Pearson, the editor of *Biometrika*,
and began publishing papers—not under his own name, but that of a
pseudonym: "Student."

It was in one of those papers, "The Probable Error of a Mean" (1908),
that Gosset introduced the Student's t distribution. The reason the t distribution was necessary, Gosset realized, was to account for the additional
uncertainty imposed by the estimation of two parameters: the mean and
the standard deviation. But why not simply use the normal distribution?
Gosset explained his reasoning this way:

> Any experiment may be regarded as forming an individual of a "popula-
> tion" of experiments which might be performed under the same condi-
> tions. A series of experiments is a sample drawn from this population.

> Now any series of experiments is only of value in so far as it enables us
> to form a judgment as to the statistical constants of the population to
> which the experiments belong. In a great number of cases the question
> finally turns on the value of a mean, either directly, or as the mean dif-
> ference between the two quantities.

> If the number of experiments be very large, we may have precise infor-
> mation as to the value of the mean, but if our sample be small, we have
> two sources of uncertainty:— (1) owing to the "error of random sam-
> pling" the mean of our series of experiments deviates more or less widely
> from the mean of the population, and (2) the sample is not sufficiently
> large to determine what is the law of distribution of individuals. It is usu-
> al, however, to assume a normal distribution, because, in a very large
> number of cases, this gives an approximation so close that a small sam-
> ple will give no real information as to the manner in which the popula-
> tion deviates from normality….

Gosset adds that his "aim [in] the present paper ["The Probable Error of
a Mean"] is to determine the point at which we may use the tables of the
probability integral in judging the significance of the mean of a series of
experiments, and to furnish alternative tables for use when the number of
experiments is too few." Those "alternative tables" are built off of the t
distribution.

As David Salsburg explains in *The Lady Tasting Tea*,

> All of Pearson's work assumed that the sample data was so large that the parameters could be determined without error. Gosset asked, What happens if the sample were small? How can we deal with the random error that is bound to find its way into our calculations? Gosset sat at his kitchen table at night, taking small sets of numbers, finding the average and the estimated standard deviation, dividing one by the other, and plotting the results on graph paper.... It did not matter where the data came from or what the true value of the standard deviation was.... As Frederick Mosteller and John Tukey [later] point[ed] out, without this discovery [of the *t* distribution], statistical analysis was doomed to use an infinite regression of procedures....*

Later, statisticians such as Stanford's Bradley Efron demonstrated that the strict requirements of population normality that Gosset assumed weren't actually necessary after all, mainly because of the robustness of the *t* distribution—small departures from normality don't, in fact, adversely affect it.

Tukey, always prepared for any statistical problem, hid a table of *t* distribution values stuffed into his wallet—just in case.

Tukey, nonplussed by the exchange with George Box at the mathematics conference, penned a piece on robustness that was copied into the meeting's proceedings. Again, their somewhat antagonistic exchange occurred in 1960; back then, robustness generally referred to "insensitivity to assumptions...of the level of a test," according to Erich L. Lehmann. But Tukey, in the coming decades, worked hard to shoehorn the term robustness more toward his own liking, rather than Box's: namely, that of point estimation with respect to the "robustness of the efficiency of estimators," again according to Lehmann. Furthering this point, Lyle V. Jones, the editor of several volumes of the *Collected Works*, wrote, "Starting from the premise that it is better to be 'approximately right' rather than 'exactly wrong' Tukey searches for procedures that are resistant to common violations of those assumptions"; therefore, "he seeks solutions that aid in drawing meaningful conclusions and suggests procedures that give up little in efficiency." When pressed during census testimony in the last decade of his life, Tukey explained robustness as follows: "In the narrow technical sense, the idea [of robustness] is that rather than seeking a pro-

---

* In *Exploratory Data Analysis*, Tukey analyzes some of the data Gosset utilized in order to arrive at his groundbreaking results. See *EDA* chapter 17, COUNTS in BIN after BIN.

cedure that is optimum under narrowly specified conditions, one tries to find procedures which are very satisfactory under a variety of alternative specified procedures."

How efficient would certain statistics be in the presence of outliers? How well does a given sample represent its host population? These were some of the key questions that drove Tukey's exploration of robustness. Tukey ended up publishing a number of papers on the topic. The apogee of interest in robustness likely occurred during the "Princeton Robustness Year," also called the Princeton Robustness Study, which took place from the fall of 1970 to 1971. For the extended seminar, Tukey—who was teaching multiple courses at Princeton, doing research at Bell Labs, and, to top it all off, had just been appointed a member of the President's Commission on Federal Statistics—invited many statisticians interested in statistical robustness to Princeton, including Peter J. Huber and Peter J. Bickel, who visited Princeton for a year, as well as David F. Andrews and Frank Hampel, who were visiting from Toronto with recently obtained doctorate degrees in tow. The statisticians focused on robustness, including Tukey, were affectionately known as "robustniks."

The robustniks held meetings nearly every week, with additional meetings during time set aside for Tukey's seminars or at weekly colloquia. On top of that, in the fall semester, evening seminars featured time series robustness talks by students, too.

Officially, the robustness seminars began on September 21, 1970; on that day, Hampel gave a lecture, which stretched to the next day, on basic robustness concepts. The following week, Peter Huber followed suit, speaking on asymptotic aspects. Tukey was up next; he spoke about least squares generalized variance. In the first seminar of October, Peter Bickel discussed estimators. He was followed by Tukey, who lectured on the jackknife. Bell Labs' Louis Jaeckel spoke on the research he completed for his doctorate. Near the end of October, Bickel was up again, this time focusing on asymmetry. David Andrews was also given an opportunity to hold a talk. Tukey, Bickel, and Hampel led more talks in the months following. The fall semester wrapped up with a seminar on December 14, which did not center on a statistics topic, but rather on future directions of the robustness seminar itself.

On Christmas in 1970, David Andrews made a key suggestion to the other robustniks: to engage in simulation studies of robustness. Tukey wasn't sold initially, but, by the time the winter break ended, he was completely on board. Although there were topics besides simulation dealt with in the spring semester seminars—such as applied regression and various probability ideas—the bulk of the work was geared toward simulation.

Dozens of statistical estimators ended up being investigated using Monte Carlo simulation methods to see if the estimators targeted the true population values under a variety of circumstances. (Tukey had been talking about the usefulness of "smart" Monte Carlo since at least FoDA, if not before; Stanislaw Ulam originated the modern form of Monte Carlo, which came to him while he was playing solitaire during a period of convalescence.) A "Monte Carlo committee" was formed, which even included an undergraduate student named Bill Rogers who was especially adept at computing.

Ultimately, using simulation studies, there were more than ten thousand estimates obtained; small samples among thirty-two distributions were examined. The fruits of the robustniks' labors—including the groundbreaking simulation studies—were published in a book entitled *Robust Estimates of Location: Survey and Advances* (1972). The authors—Andrews et al.—cogently and succinctly open the book by summarizing the exploration that was undertaken:

> Estimation is the art of inferring information about some unknown quantity on the basis of available data. Typically an estimator of some sort is used. The estimator is chosen to perform well under the conditions that are assumed to underly [*sic*] the data. Since these conditions are never known exactly, estimators must be chosen which are robust, which perform well under a variety of underlying conditions.

The book, they write, is a "comprehensive, but not exhaustive" investigation of robustness; they then briefly touch upon the previous literature of robust estimation, noting the mix of the theoretical and practical, but also the more limited scope of study undertaken. Contrariwise, "[t]he significant advantages of this study," they assert, "are size and scope." To that end,

> A great variety of some 68 estimates were studied, some well known, others developed during this study; some hand-computable, others requiring a great deal of computer time; some suitable for sample size 5, others best suited to sample sizes over 100. In particular, trimmed means, adaptive estimates, Huber estimates, skipped procedures and the Hodges-Lehmann estimate are among the estimates considered.

Tukey was responsible for two of the book's chapters: the fifth and the sixth. "[N]umerical results are given for a variety of characteristics" in the fifth chapter, and, in the sixth chapter, "these results are analyzed in detail, introducing new methods for the summarization of such a large body of data." Tukey's influence was also acknowledged with respect to the development of effective Monte Carlo simulation techniques. In fact,

Tukey was so focused on these simulations studies that he planned to move past what he called "wave A"—the computations present in *Robust Estimates of Location*—to "wave B", "wave C," and beyond, with the help of Alan Gross. The results of some of these later waves appeared in publications through the 1970s and early '80s.

Frank Hampel, twenty-five years removed from the robustness study, reminisced in a written piece called "Some Additional Notes on the 'Princeton Robustness Year.'" Conventional wisdom has it that the only thing to come from the intensive year's worth of study using Monte Carlo simulation techniques was "robust estimates of location under symmetric longtailed distribution." Part of the problem, Hampel explains, is that *Robust Estimates of Location* offered little detail on the wide-ranging scope of discussions about the topic by the many statisticians involved—leaving only the "'hard' empirical numbers in the simplest possible situation" as a basis for understanding the "more powerful and penetrating concepts." Hampel relays an interesting anecdote involving himself and Tukey:

> After the first half of the semester [of the robustness year] there were gaps due to midterm break and also to a period when both Tukey and I had to stay in bed. This gave us the unique occasion for hour-long telephone conversations, during which I tried to convince Tukey that the Normal [distribution], as opposed to, for example, the Cauchy, plays a distinguished role in robustness theory.

By the second half of the first semester, Hampel says, the discussions became "heated," especially at Tukey's November talks, which centered on resistance, sensitivity curves, and regression analysis. As winter turned to spring, the focus shifted mostly to simulation studies, with the other ideas, such as regression, left unpublished even after being discussed in seminars. After the spring semester ended, Hampel recalls that *Robust Estimates of Location* was assembled in "an amazingly short time, thanks to the organizational talent of David Andrews," but, as a consequence of tight deadlines and faulty communication, the book went to print with a number of notable omissions and errors. For instance, a single outlier buried in the midst of thousands of numbers in the book was spotted and identified by Tukey, who was dumbfounded as to its origin: "What is going on?" he wrote in dismay. But this "outlier" was in fact nothing of the sort; rather, it was the result of an error in the reproduction of the manuscript. There were other printing errors as well, such as missing numbers in tables. In terms of the content, according to Hampel, the most striking and unfortunate omission was an analysis of the two asymmetric situations; the computer outputs of these simulations, which Hampel and Peter Huber worked hard to complete, simply didn't make it in time for the book's printing deadline.

Like Hampel, Huber also penned a piece, decades after the robustness study, which reflected on the accomplishments of the robustness year. "In robustness as in every other area he touched, John Tukey produced hundreds of original ideas, some brilliant, fundamental and lasting, some ephemeral," he said. For instance, Tukey also, around the same time as the "Princeton Robustness Year," gave a well-received talk on robust regression, but no follow-up studies resulted from it despite Tukey's best efforts.

But did Tukey inviting the robustniks to Princeton result in lasting ideas, or ephemeral ones? The response of the mathematical community to the Princeton Robustness Study was decidedly mixed. The historian and statistician Stephen Stigler writes that some saw the study as a "pathbreaking exercise…via ingenious advances in simulation technique and graphical exploratory data analysis," while others viewed it "as a fruitless exercise in self-indulgent ad hockery, beating a small and uninterestingly limited problem to death by computer overkill." Stigler finds elements of truth in both perspectives, noting that the robustniks underestimated the scope and complexity of the problems to be addressed at the time and thus resorted to simplifications of the function space. Plus, there was an unintended consequence after *Robust Estimates of Location* was released. Stigler, who was an editor at the *Journal of the American Statistical Association* (*JASA*) at the time, was met with a "deluge of simulation studies." "[I]t seemed like every statistician with a random number generator had a newly issued license to publish," he recalled. "The floodgates were open, but the quality of the overflow was generally low and sometimes appalling." And not just at *JASA*—other statistics journals were met a similar surplus of mediocrity. Regardless of the chain reaction they precipitated, Stigler gives Tukey and Huber, but not Box, the lion's share of credit for the maturation of robustness as a subdiscipline worthy of serious attention. Huber, following Tukey's lead, would next turn to data analysis.

Decades earlier, Stephen Stigler's father, George J. Stigler, a Nobel Laureate in economics, had his own run in with Tukey. During World War II, George Stigler was part of the Statistical Research Group (SRG), which operated out of Columbia University and supported Allied war efforts. "The SRG had an all-star cast," Stephen Stigler recently said at a talk. "They did a number of useful things, helping with statistical and economic analyses, but that was not all they did." Perhaps unsurprisingly, Tukey, via the FCRO, was also involved. Stigler relays how the two met:

> [Tukey] once drafted a paper on how to win the war. It found its way to my father for review, and his review was brief: "Professor Tukey has independently rediscovered much of economics up to 1820." Soon after Tukey showed up in my father's office, steam coming out of his ears.

But things soon resolved themselves, and Tukey and the elder Stigler formed a lasting friendship.

The robustniks, it should be noted, were all men. In the latter half of his career, however, Tukey would encounter and work with a number of women professionally, including in the subdiscipline of robustness. Which leads us to ask: Was John Tukey a feminist?

Bea Chambers, who worked with Tukey at Bell Labs in the math research department, didn't know what to expect when she first met Tukey. After programming a computer to produce some numbers for analysis, Chambers showed them to Tukey. He took a *coup d'oeil* at the printouts and said, "This won't do. There cannot be any negative numbers in the results."

"Why not?" she asked. For Chambers, a newly minted research mathematician, Tukey's formidable reputation didn't precede him (yet).

"SIT!" he told her. Tukey took the time to detail the problem. Chambers agreed that the numbers couldn't be negative but then explained to Tukey how she approached the problem. "Tukey pursed his lips for a few seconds, then, he looked at what I had done, told me what was wrong, told me how to correct it, gave me a little smile, and left," she recalled.*

If not condescending, Tukey was quite sure of himself with both Bea Chambers and Kaye Basford (a colleague of Tukey's in the late 1980s), both women.

Alan Gross, a graduate advisee of Tukey's in the 1960s, describes a scene of embarrassment (on Gross's part).

> I remember one time when he said he had to go to his home to get something for his wife who was spending the day at an auction. (I'm embarrassed now to say that.) I responded in mock horror, "What. You let her go to an auction alone?" His quiet, terse response [was], "She's selling." Little did I know then that Elizabeth was an antique dealer and professional appraiser, and John was a feminist, too.

Tukey, who lived through women's rapidly expanding workforce roles during and immediately after World War II, the ages of *The Feminine Mystique* and women's liberation movements as well as the Equal Rights Amendment, acquitted himself well on women's rights, though he wasn't marching on the picket lines; if not quite the feminist of Alan Gross's

---

* When Bea told Tukey that she had married John Chambers, whom Tukey worked with at Bell, he paused, smiled, and then said, "That's nice."

recollections, Tukey worked at a time when many of his male cohort refused to help or even deal with their fellow women professionals.[*]

Another of Tukey's students, Karen Kafadar, remembers a gruff but enthusiastic, collaborative, and intellectually generous man during their first meeting at Princeton. Kafadar arrived in New Jersey having already secured an undergraduate degree in mathematics and a graduate degree in statistics, both from Stanford in 1975; her master's thesis advisor was the American statistician and MacArthur Fellow Bradley Efron, who created the bootstrap resampling technique. After the chairman of the Princeton Statistics Department, Geoffrey Watson, told Kafadar that Tukey had "some project for [her] to work on," she "timidly approached Dr. Tukey following a 411 class (the famous 'undergraduate' course attended to by even full professors), introduced myself, and reported Watson's directive. He broke into a big grin and said, 'Wait here.'"

Shortly thereafter, he returned, sporting his "trademark black T-shirt whose pocket held the usual Bic 4-color pens," and faced Kafadar.

"Read this and then I think you'll see that we have a lot of computing to do," he said.

In her recollection, Kafadar pays special attention to the word "we" in Tukey's statement—which he pointedly used instead of "I"—realizing that "John Tukey chose his words very carefully." Kafadar admits that it took most of her first year at Princeton to even understand the assigned project.

Kafadar and Tukey had a fruitful mathematical relationship, and she earned her doctorate in 1979 under him. Her dissertation title was "Robust Confidence Intervals for the One- and Two-Sample Problem." Tukey's interest in robustness had rubbed off on his advisee.

Kafadar noticed the stirrings of an interest in robustness as applied to data analysis in Tukey's work from as early as 1962, with the publication of FoDA. After discussing how distribution-free, nonparametric methods are important first step toward examining "old problems in more realistic frameworks," he wrote that

> The development of a more effective procedure for determining properties of samples from non-normal distributions by experimental sampling is likely, if the procedure be used wisely and widely, to contribute much to the practice of data analysis.

---

[*] In *Exploratory Data Analysis*, Tukey sometimes writes "he or she" rather than just "he." But he also uses the term "housewives."

Stated differently, Tukey was calling for effective simulation to replace analytical, theory-based approaches; he was even hinting at such methods as far back as his 1948 paper cited by Box.

In 1960, two years before FoDA, "A critical leap forward into the development of robust methods [had] started with Tukey's paper, 'A Survey of Sampling from Contaminated Distributions,'" Kafadar claims, in which traditional estimators of the normal distribution, such as the sample mean and sample variance, were shown to significantly degrade (in terms of targeting the true population values) when the normal distribution was "contaminated." A contaminated normal distribution is really a "mixture" of normals, which is still symmetrical yet weighed down with heavier tails, thus facilitating the simulation of outliers. (In the Princeton Robustness Study, most of the distributions examined were scale mixtures of normal distributions.) "All available evidence and discussion," he explained, "leads the writer [Tukey] to believe that, although contaminated distributions are a thin representation of non-normality, they are an exploration of the most important area of non-normality." Also in "A Survey of Sampling from Contaminated Distributions," Tukey presented more robust alternatives to the sample mean and sample variance: the trimmed mean (a mean with extreme values on either end lopped off) and the *Winsorized variance* (a modification of the variance that accounts for extremes by manipulating percentiles of the distribution).

Why throw the traditional estimators overboard in favor of these modified ones? Because even with a distribution "contaminated" only slightly, the sample standard deviation no longer serves as the best estimator of its population counterpart. Stigler notes that this was a shocking result to statisticians at the time—well, at least all statisticians Tukey spoke to about it except for one: Ronald Fisher, who immediately realized, when he was asked about it by Tukey, that small contaminations had an adverse impact on traditional estimators.

The 1960 Tukey paper on contaminated distributions didn't appear as a standalone publication but rather as a contribution buried deep inside a volume entitled *Contributions to Probability and Statistics: Essays in Honor of Harold Hotelling* (1960) (Hotelling was an American statistician and economist). Tukey had waited years before publishing on contaminated distributions, although he worked out much of the theory during the war. As Mosteller notes in his three-page biography of Tukey presented in the *Collected Works*, "[H]is recognition of the sensitivity of the sample mean and standard deviation to contamination in the tails of distributions…were not published for decades, but many in the invisible college [i.e., word of mouth among statisticians at Princeton and elsewhere] were aware of that work." But Tukey's 1960 paper made enough of a splash to be required reading for anyone interested in robustness—which included Peter Huber.

Born in 1934 in Wohlen, Switzerland, Peter Jost Huber earned two degrees from ETH Zürich (Eidgenössische Technische Hochschule Zürichthe, or the Swiss Federal Institute of Technology) in mathematics: a diploma in 1958 and a doctorate in topology in 1961. Yet his journey to statistics was, by his own admission, circuitous. Huber found that whatever he studied in mathematics invariably led him from the more concrete to the more abstract, which worried him when he began exploring category theory: How much further abstract could he go? There would be nothing real remaining on the table to explore. At first, Huber thought the cure would be a turn to functional analysis. But the needs of the university would stymie that plan. At the time, ETH was in the search for a senior statistician; key names such as Erich Lehmann's came up as candidates for the position, but no one took the job. So, ETH looked to groom local talent instead, and about a year before landing his doctorate, several professors came to Huber, attempting to sell him on the possibilities of a career in statistics. Huber expressed interest, realizing that mathematical statistics was a subdiscipline of study adjacent to functional analysis.

Before ETH's hard sell of statistics to Huber, he worked with B. L. van der Waerden, the Dutch algebraist and historian of mathematics who taught at the nearby University of Zurich. Born in 1903 in Amsterdam, Netherlands, Bartel Leendert van der Waerden was best known for his work in abstract algebra. At the time, van der Waerden and Huber were assembling a book on ancient astronomy; he appreciated the elder mathematician's "direct" style of presentation. Van der Waerden had a "decisive influence" on Huber, since it was with van der Waerden's urging that Huber first began writing and publishing papers.

Huber was also intimately familiar with van der Waerden's work, having pored through his book of statistics for the *Die Grundlehren der Mathematischen Wissenschaften* series. In that book, van der Waerden had recommended readers peruse two other seminal works in the subject: Abraham Wald's *Statistical Decision Functions* (1950) and Joseph L. Doob's *Stochastic Processes* (1953). After ETH had come knocking at Huber's door, he took van der Waerden's advice and read the Wald and Doob tomes. And with the fervor of the newly converted, doctorate in hand, Huber had shifted away from pure mathematics to statistics. Not everyone was happy with the turn away from abstraction. Beno Eckmann, his doctoral advisor, urged Huber to remain in topology. Huber, though, went to California, landing a position in the statistics department at Berkeley.

When Huber and his wife Effi, an X-ray crystallographer, arrived at the San Francisco Airport in 1961, Berkeley graduate student Peter Nüesch greeted them. On the car ride to Berkeley, Huber told Nüesch that he was interested in working on a theory of robustness. Huber admitted he was greatly influenced by Tukey's "A Survey of Sampling from Contaminated Distributions," published the previous year. Huber would further explore Tukey's work in the Berkeley coffee room, which contained a collection of paper reprints.

But he wouldn't meet Tukey until 1963, during an East Coast trip—which was after Huber had finished writing a piece called "Robust Estimation of a Location Parameter," published in the *Annals of Mathematical Statistics* in 1964 and the most influential paper ever written on robustness, save for Tukey's 1960 effort. Tukey was very excited about meeting Huber, he told Brillinger, because of Tukey and Huber's shared mathematical background. "There is another topologist working in statistics!" Tukey exclaimed. Brillinger was responsible for running the Statistics seminar at Princeton at the time. So, Tukey implored his young charge: "Please invite him [Huber] to speak."

"What happens if the true distribution deviates slightly from the assumed normal one?" Huber asked in his landmark work, "Robust Estimation of a Location Parameter," observing that Gauss himself might have asked the question, "but which was, as far as I know, only raised a few years ago (notably by Tukey)...." Huber then answered his own question:

> As it is now well known, the sample mean then may have a catastrophically bad performance: seemingly quite mild deviations may already explode its variance. Tukey and others proposed several more robust substitutes—trimmed means, Winsorized means, etc.—and explored their performance for a few typical violations of normality. A general theory of robust estimation is still lacking; it is hoped that the present paper will furnish the first few steps toward such a theory.

"Robust Estimation of a Location Parameter" did in fact put an end to statisticians searching in the dark for effective robust measures in favor of arriving at optimal ones. As Stigler sees it, "If the newspapers of the day had covered such things, a headline might have read, 'The army of optimality has landed on the beach of applied statistics, and without visible resistance erected a large base camp.'"

Besides Tukey, Huber's biggest influence in writing his seminal paper was Berkeley's own Erich Lehmann—who, recall, had refused an invitation years before to teach at ETH. Lehmann was the former editor of the *Annals of Mathematical Statistics*, and he generously supplied Huber pointers on what, precisely, the journal was expecting in a submitted paper. Send the journal a paper that was too lengthy, Lehmann told him, so that they would recommend shortening it—which Huber could then begin working on as soon as possible.

The dominos leading to the Princeton Robustness Study fell quickly after the 1964 publication of "Robust Estimation of a Location Parameter." In 1968, at Berkeley, Frank Hampel put the finishing touches on his dissertation, which was called "Contributions to the Theory of Robust Estimation" and which built on Huber's work. One year later, also at Berkeley, the mathematician Louis Alan Jaeckel, with Lehmann as his advisor, completed a dissertation titled "Robust Estimates of Location," extending the ideas even further. Also in 1968, Huber published another paper, "Robust Confidence Limits," which lent him a sense of satisfaction that had been missing from his 1964 work. "I was never sure whether the theory of my 1964 paper was the real thing, but it did give the idea of robustness an element of respectability, which is all I could have hoped for," he said in an interview years later. "I feel more strongly, though, that the [1968] paper on robust confidence limits is the real thing."

The zeitgeist was now ripe for a robust examination of robustness, which would culminate several years later with the Princeton Robustness Study. And, throughout it all, still rattling around Tukey's head, was Charlie Winsor's sage admonition—that spark that had perhaps first ignited his interest in robustness: to "beware of extreme deviates, and, in particular, …beware of using them with high weights."

CHAPTER TWENTY-ONE

The Elders and Their Children

"Consequently bring pressure to bear on Gertrude [Cox]
if you dare, but not on me."
— Ronald Fisher, in a letter to John Tukey

John Tukey often referred to his dissertation advisees as his *children*. Karen Kafadar, who went on to a successful academic career at Indiana University and the University of Virginia and was recently elected to the presidency of the American Statistical Association, had seven "children" (advisees) of her own, giving Tukey, her academic father, even more *grandchildren* or *grand students*.* Tukey, for his part, never had any biological children.

Tukey's overriding pedagogical goal with his students was to develop and encourage their independent research chops; he was thesis advisor to 56 students, so he had 56 "children" and a still-growing list of "grandchildren." There was Karen Kafadar, of course, and John A. Hartigan, who would land at Yale, while Alan Gross and Arthur P. Dempster would make important contributions to algorithmic statistical theory at Harvard. There was Thomas Kurtz who, along with John Kemeny, would co-create the BASIC programming language at Dartmouth. There was *supposed* to be Melvin P. Peisakoff, who earned his doctorate in 1950, but, even though Tukey is formally listed as his doctoral advisor, the mentor-mentee relationship was akin to the Lefschetz-Tukey model: "I think I was supposed to be his advisor," Tukey reminisced, "but I was not at all convinced." Peisakoff was the exception.

And there was also Frederick Mosteller, perhaps Tukey's most successful student and certainly his greatest collaborator (Mosteller served as coauthor with Tukey on more publications than anyone else), who established Harvard's statistics department and whose statistical work had a great effect on public policy. Tukey didn't start out as Mosteller's thesis advisor; Sam Wilks did. But Wilks was "much in demand in Washington"—"though when he was [at Princeton], he was always willing to dis-

---

* Such students of students are typically called "descendants."

cuss technical problems"—so Mosteller would instead "would wander around the halls," swinging by to consult with Tukey, a man very intellectually "generous with his time and his ideas," on "late afternoons." Which rather quickly turned into a habit. Like Tukey, Mosteller believed that "one should behave as a scientist rather than a mathematician" when developing a statistician intuition. Interestingly, though, when Mosteller first met him and leaned forward to ask him a statistics question, Tukey was quick to reply, "I don't do statistics." Indeed—in the fall of 1939, when they first met, Tukey wasn't yet a self-identified statistician.

After various delays, including the war interlude in which he worked at a New York branch of the Statistical Research Group headed by John Williams, by the time Mosteller buckled down and finally finished writing his thesis, Tukey had become his de facto advisor as well as transforming himself into a statistician in earnest. As he was writing, Mosteller would seek out Tukey for suggestions, and Tukey would always consider the problem at hand and then suggest "something entirely different to work on," according to Mosteller. He "[tossed] off more ideas than I could use," Mosteller remembered. Whenever Mosteller got stuck, Tukey would help him move forward, finding new approaches with which to select relevant problems, even if they lead to entirely new questions. "Boundaries between disciplines, organizations, and people never lasted long in his mind, for he thought in terms of bridges, entrances, and opportunities," Mosteller reflected.

Throughout the course of the next year, everything started coming together for Mosteller, and his thesis practically began writing itself—save for one "terrible moment." When glancing through an issue of the *New Yorker*, Mosteller encountered a footnote of an article that coincidently mocked the wording of one part of his thesis by relaying the title of a related paper written by a Harvard statistician. Although the paper was indeed connected to what Mosteller was doing, it didn't affect the direction of his thesis, which he finalized in 1946. Mosteller was the first of Tukey's "children."

Before Mosteller decamped to Harvard to begin a consequential academic career of his own, both he and Tukey were invited to a conference at Lake Junaluska in North Carolina,* so they took a road trip together—with Tukey driving his 1936 wood-paneled station wagon, the "oldest living…most disreputable looking station wagon at Princeton," as Mos-

---

* More precisely, Tukey received special permission from the University of North Carolina—with its strange institutional setup of three statistics departments—to invite Mosteller.

teller described it. A passenger door had even once fallen off while Tukey was driving down Nassau Street in Princeton, resulting in the pink pages of an incomplete manuscript flying out. Tukey jumped out of the car and retrieved the pages, which were strewn all over the street.

Less than an hour into their long road trip to North Carolina, Tukey started regaling Mosteller with ideas for a paper on plotting binomial data atop a special kind of graph paper; incredibly, Tukey seemed to expect for them to finish writing the paper by the time they got back to Princeton. Indeed, as Mosteller remembers it, they began formally "drafting materials" on the ride back home. Their paper, "The Uses and Usefulness of Binomial Probability Paper," was published several years later; they would write many other papers together, including on quality control, a salient interest of Mosteller's.

They would also work together on the Kinsey affair, and, afterward, in the late 1960s, on the National Research Council (NRC) National Halo-thane Study (NHS), which investigated whether the anesthetic halothane was causing liver necrosis in people. Cases involving the deleterious effects of halothane caused enough of an uproar to result in a public controversy and ensure a formal government response. One case, for instance, involved a young woman who had accidently slit her wrists on a windowpane; after undergoing seemingly successful surgery, in which the anesthetic halothane was utilized, the woman died. The cause was hepatic necrosis—in effect, her liver shut down, the result of too many liver cells dying.

Roughly 50,000 hospital records were collected for the study, which documented 17,000 deaths. The statistician Stephen Fienberg, who worked on the NHS, recalls that "[t]he many statisticians involved in the halothane study brought a number of standard and new statistical ideas to bear on this problem," including log-linear models. But the NHS committee was so inspired and dependent on Tukey's judgment that they convened their meetings in whatever city Tukey happened to be in at the time, whether it was California, Arizona, or Princeton. This incessant traveling led them to thinking about how to rate hospitals, namely: How do you properly compare the outcomes of hospitals that take severe cases with ones that take less severe cases? "In the halothane work [Tukey] brought forward several fresh ideas, some of which have still not been fully exploited on other problems," Mosteller wrote in his autobiography.

The halothane study wasn't Tukey's first foray into health-related matters. Even in the early 1950s, he was advising the pharmaceutical company Merck on things like the design of clinical trials; over the course of the next five decades, he would publish nearly a dozen papers with scientists at Merck as co-authors. During brainstorming meetings at the company, the seat next to Tukey's was fondly referred to as "The batter's box."

The conference at Lake Junaluska had a number of mathematical luminaries in attendance, such as Ronald Fisher, who worked as a summer school teacher at the University of North Carolina. At conferences and talks, Tukey would typically find a spot in the back of the room and absorb his mind and hands with *knitting*—that is, multitasking by deploying his well-worn Bic four-color ballpoints to sketch out rows and columns of numbers in matrices, busily and productively analyzing data sets by hand while also devoting his attention to the goings-on in the front of the room.

Instead of knitting, sometimes Tukey would occupy himself with writing a paper, solving a crossword puzzle, or even just reading a newspaper. For example, the statistician Lyle V. Jones first encountered Tukey at a meeting of the American Statistical Association in 1952 in Chicago. When Jones entered the hotel auditorium with a lecture already in progress, he spotted a man seated at the back of the hall "studiously reading the *Chicago Tribune*, seeming to pay no attention to the speaker." Initially, Jones concluded that the man was a mere passerby who had taken a quick detour indoors to warm up from the chilly weather. But when the speaker concluded his remarks, the man in the back—of course, John Tukey—put down the newspaper and walked up to the podium, only to verbally tear apart the previous address. (Roughly a decade passed before Jones would have the opportunity to work directly with the Tukey. And even more time went by before Jones would begin assembling several volumes of the *Collected Works*.)

At Lake Junaluska, with Tukey watching from the back row, Ronald Fisher gave an especially impressive talk. Afterward, Fisher socialized with everyone, including the younger statisticians, in the evening, drinking beer and enjoying the festivities; he was in a visibly good mood and in good spirits throughout the conference, which was something of a rarity. Fisher treated Mosteller there like a contemporary; Mosteller almost felt like they were genuinely good friends. And Fisher always treated Tukey "very gently," never abrasively, Tukey remembered.

Adding to the fun at the conference was a large game of hearts, run in a third-floor dormitory and played by a number of academics such as Fred Stephan, David Duncan, Charlie Winsor, Tukey, and Mosteller; during the game, as he was playing, Tukey—who hated bridge, but loved hearts—was performing some mental combinatorics, figuring out all possible arrangements of players and dealer, ensuring that the ever-rotating "first player" was controlled for. By the end of the game, the consensus was predictable: Tukey was the most skilled player of hearts.

Less predictable was that the Lake Junaluska conference marked the start of a simmering intellectual feud between Fisher and Tukey that lasted for years and would lead to them ultimately cutting ties. Fisher was a proponent of fiducial inference, whereas Tukey was firmly on the side of Jerzy Neyman, who developed confidence intervals.[*] As explained by the Canadian statistician Donald A. S. Fraser, fiducial probability was proposed by Fisher in 1930 in order to obtain a probability distribution from observed data: "Fisher claimed that a fiducial probability statement had the same meaning as an ordinary probability statement," whereas "proponents of the confidence interval method claim that in this context probability statements concerning μ [the population mean] cannot be made," since the sought-after population mean either lies in the confidence interval or it doesn't. Put plainly, Fisher thought that Neyman's work was a rip-off of his own, because Fisher believed that confidence intervals were a mere generalization of fiducial intervals since both methods produced the same results for certain parameters.

Tukey's argument against fiducial distributions, and by extension against Ronald Fisher, connected the fiducial distributions to fiducial probabilities; his argument is complex, involving the search for counter-examples that would put into stark relief why Fisher was in error. In "Some Examples with Fiducial Relevance" (1957), Tukey lays bare his objective in language that is, rather typically for such technical papers, mostly impenetrable to a layperson:

> It has been believed by some…that—and R. A. Fisher [e.g., at the Lake Junaluska conference in 1946] has urged the desirability of determining whether—the distribution induced by a pivotal, sufficient and smoothly invertible set of quantities is unique…. If true, such uniqueness would be important in connection with the theory of fiducial probability.
>
> It is the purpose of this paper to present certain examples of particular interest showing that these conditions do *not* provide uniqueness.

---

[*] Lyle Jones summarized Tukey's reasoning this way: "Tukey emphasizes the importance of separating decision elements from conclusion elements in statistical methods. A test of significant difference is viewed as a qualitative conclusion procedure [i.e., reject or fail to reject the null hypothesis], while interval estimation is a quantitative conclusion procedure [i.e., a range of values which, with some confidence level, might contain the true population parameter]." Again, Tukey was especially concerned that tests of significance conflated procedures in which to make decisions with those used to arrive at conclusions.

Tukey notes that this notion of "uniqueness," and the conditions that permit it, is the lynchpin on which Fisher's fiducial argument stands. But Tukey breaks apart this lynchpin by carefully presenting counterexamples, conjured up by himself and other mathematicians, demonstrating non-uniqueness. He publicly presented this mathematization during the course of several talks for the Institute of Mathematical Statistics (IMS) (Abraham) Wald Memorial Lectures in 1958, which were held at MIT.* To a packed lecture hall, he offered only tentative statements about the fiducial argument. "I do not believe we have penetrated to the heart of the matter," he sadly concluded.

Tukey first developed an interest in Fisher's theories of statistical inference when he stumbled upon and then solved Fisher's "Problem of the Nile" (using the Ham Sandwich Theorem that he, along with Arthur Stone, had generalized); he later enriched his understanding of Fisher's singular contributions to statistics through the editing of a republication of some of Fisher's work in 1950. Furthermore, according to Tukey's former student Arthur Dempster, Tukey, heavily influenced by Fisher, pushed his students "to take a balanced view" with respect to British and American perspectives on statistics—depending on which side of the Atlantic you happened to find yourself on, approaches to the discipline were very different in many respects.

Tukey began corresponding with Fisher about the fiducial argument in the early 1950s; their missives to each other numbered in the dozens. Fisher invariably wrote to Tukey with thinly veiled sarcasm masquerading as politeness, addressing him as "My dear Tukey" or "My dear John" yet pedantically and defensively disagreeing with him on nearly every point while Tukey continued to needle him with questions and comments that couldn't easily be dismissed. Fisher, resorting to ad hominem attacks, criticized Tukey's "long screed about probability statements," and, at another point, implored Tukey to "get your bullheaded mind to stop and think." He even, in one letter, complained to Tukey about "your brother-in-law" (Frank Anscombe), who had criticized a book of Fisher's. Dempster summarizes the bulk of their exchange well: they "mostly [talked] past one another...."

At one point in the course of their lengthy correspondence, Fisher invited Tukey to England to visit with him and his wife. However, visiting

---

* Tukey was president of the IMS from 1960 to 1961. In that position, he laid the groundwork for a probability journal, called *The Annals of Probability* (complementary to the longstanding *The Annals of Statistics*, also published by the IMS), which was launched a decade later.

Tukey at Princeton proved more difficult; writing in February of 1951, Fisher warns Tukey of his limited time and his curious nature:

> As regards time, have mercy on my other interests: Remember that my mice need my attention and even the garden may produce things in May or June or July.... I believe if I were three months in all in your fine country it is about as much as I could do in one year. Consequently bring pressure to bear on Gertrude [Cox] if you dare, but not on me.

Tukey was hardly averse to traveling to England to meet with his interlocutor; he had visited the country before and would do so again in the years to come. For instance, in July of 1952, Tukey lunched in London with Lord Cherwell, who was Winston Churchill's science advisor during the Second World War. Tukey also went to England in 1955 and 1956, likely meeting with the British counterpart of the NSA: the Government Communications Headquarters (GCHQ), in Cheltenham, which retained the services of statistician I. J. Good. By this point Tukey was already a consultant with the Central Intelligence Agency (CIA)—the details of his work there are murky, but 1980s CIA Director William J. Casey wrote an appreciation, thanking Tukey for his report on the Strategic Defense Initiative (SDI, known colloquially as "Star Wars"), and 1990s CIA Director James Woolsey invited Tukey to join a Science and Technology Advisory Panel—and a member of the NSA Scientific Advisory Board (SAB), being invited to join the SAB, along with Sam Wilks and John von Neumann, only a month after the NSA's inception in November 1952; members of the SAB would convene semiannually with NSA scientists at Fort Meade in Maryland to discuss cutting-edge security-related technologies such as cryptography.[*]

Tukey and Fisher's correspondence ended abruptly after the former visited the latter at his home office in England. By this point, Tukey had pre-

---

[*] By the time he visited England in the mid-1950s, Tukey had already made multiple trips to the NSA—e.g., a two-day joint panel meeting held in 1954 at the personal invitation of William F. Friedman, executive secretary of the SAB. "It was the intention of the Board to staff these panels with eminent scientists who could be called upon for special service or consultation in matters of importance to the Agency," a historical study of the SAB reads. "It was proposed that formal meetings of the panels be very infrequent and that, as a general rule, panel members be called upon to serve only as their convenience permitted. In many instances, these panel members would represent NSA's sole contact with many major industrial concerns and educational institutions."

sented Fisher with counterexamples to the fiducial argument, and Fisher dismissed them as foolishness. So, Tukey traveled to England to offer some personal persuasion. He brought Elizabeth along on the trip. While dating, Tukey told Elizabeth that he, following Fisher's lead, would be devoted to arriving at more optimal methods with which to analyze data sets. But his comment, ostensibly designed to impress his future bride—after all, Tukey held Fisher in the highest esteem, having compiled an index of the master's work in 1950,* so Fisher must be well known—fell on deaf ears: Elizabeth replied that she had no idea who Fisher was.

In person with Fisher, Tukey went out his way to praise the master. The tact and deference he refused to show Alfred Kinsey he offered in spades to Fisher. Although he wasn't sold on the fiducial argument, Tukey said, the very fact that Fisher believed it made Tukey take a second look. "[Fisher] was unhappy that I took it seriously [simply] because he [Fisher] supported it (and I valued his judgment), rather than accepting its internal logic," Tukey later explained. "But rather than accepting the view that anything so logical should be unique, influenced also, no doubt, by my years as a mathematician, I attacked the uniqueness question through counterexamples."

Fisher was deeply unhappy with their exchange. He rose from his seat, trying to wrap up the conversation and simultaneously show Tukey the door. But Tukey's wife, Elizabeth, was deep in conversation with one of Fisher's daughters outside in the garden. So, instead, Fisher picked up his hat and cane and politely "went toddling out the door himself," Tukey recalled.† Although he repeatedly recounted these events in interviews later on in his life, Tukey never seemed to be too broken up by his and Fisher's falling out. After all, "whether or not we kick them in the face," Tukey once mused, "we must stand on the shoulders of others."

With Fisher out of his life, Tukey ultimately came to believe in a single unifying principle of fiducial probability: namely, that such unification was impossible. In the sixth volume of the *Collected Works*, he wrote, "Today I do not believe there is any chance of a successful single unifying approach to inference…." He continued: "This does not disturb me—growing partial understanding is all that we have seen in such fields as theoretical physics—and the problems of inference are broader and harder to experiment on…. Thus I have come to think belief in a unified

---

* As Peter McCullagh amusingly observes, the volume of Fisher's papers that were indexed by Tukey for publication by John Wiley & Sons purposely were arranged to have to most significant of the papers indexed using round numbers, like 10 or 20.

† It must be noted here that several secondhand accounts claim that Fisher in fact kicked Tukey out of his home rather than leaving first.

structure for inference as a dangerous form of hubris." In that same volume, editor Colin Mallows offers the reader a telling analogy: "Fiducial inference is to statistics what Fermat's Last Theorem is to mathematics."

Pierre de Fermat, a seventeenth century lawyer and mathematician, scribbled a fascinating mathematical statement of questionable validity in the margins of a reprint of Diophantus' *Arithmetica*:

> It is impossible to separate a cube into two cubes, or a fourth power into two fourth powers, or in general, any power higher than the second, into two like powers. I have discovered a truly marvelous proof of this, which this margin is too narrow to contain.

Fermat boasted of a "truly marvelous proof" that he never revealed—because even though he may have believed he possessed a proof, he was likely mistaken. Fermat's Last Theorem (technically, a conjecture) was finally proven true by Andrew Wiles of Princeton University some 350 years after Fermat wrote it down. Mallows compares Fermat's Last Theorem and Fisher's fiducial inference in this sense: "In both cases there are cryptic assertions by authors of unquestioned skill and depth, and the nagging suspicion that perhaps on this occasion the master has made a mistake."

The Lake Junaluska conference wasn't the only road trip Tukey and Mosteller would take together while Mosteller was still a student at Princeton. Once, Tukey drove him to Mattapoisett, Massachusetts, where Tukey's parents had settled in their old age. Upon arriving at the house, Adah was welcoming toward Mosteller. But she was also not pleased with her son. She asked him: When are you going to bring home a nice girl already? Eventually, of course, he did. "John's mother, a no-nonsense lady, finally got her wish that he marry a real nice girl," Mosteller recalled. At John and Elizabeth's wedding, Mosteller served as one of the ushers. Tukey's best man was Hendrik Bode, who had recruited Tukey to work with him at Bell Labs after World War II.

After Fred Mosteller spread his wings and became a mathematical leader in the 1960s, he and Tukey would arrange get-togethers at their respective summer homes: Mosteller's at West Falmouth, Massachusetts, and Tukey's second home near Cape Cod in West Port, Massachusetts, a location which the Tukeys had initially scouted by airplane. (During the academic year the Tukeys lived in Westport Point, Massachusetts, with Tukey buying an old sea captain's house there, in cash, around 1970.) It wasn't only mathematics that occupied their time. Tukey had quite the green thumb, and Mosteller's wife Virginia queried the statistician on all matters related to gardening as well as other "practical matters" in general.

Interestingly, despite Mosteller's impressive curriculum vitae, Tukey didn't consider Mosteller an individual of great mathematical ability—only of great ability overall. In fact, Tukey didn't even think Mosteller would make it to his second graduate year, believing the young man didn't have the requisite mathematical chops. Luckily, during the war, Mosteller realized that not every mathematical problem needed to be solved analytically; rather, simulation and approximation and even working out things by example could resolve a great many mathematical queries. Mosteller performed simulation studies with Wilks at that time (in addition to his duties as assistant to Wilks' *Annals* editorship), but such simulation was often bogged down by the primitive technology at hand.

Tukey and Mosteller ran into each other at Fine Hall and at meals—Tukey was often commiserating with Richard Feynman at graduate school dinners when Mosteller first saw him—but they didn't know each other especially well until after Tukey transitioned to a full-time statistics teaching role. During the war, Mosteller and Tukey worked together tangentially, on minor problems. For example, Mosteller wrote a paper dealing with moments of small samples (recall that moments describe the location and variability of statistical distributions: the mean is the first statistical moment; the variance is the second, while the skewness is the third and the kurtosis is the fourth), but the covariances (a measure of the dependence of two random variables) were left out. Mosteller ran the paper by Wilks, who immediately deemed it unsatisfactory without solving the covariance problem. But obtaining the covariances of order statistics was a very tough hill to climb, which defeated even automated calculating machines. One Sunday afternoon, Mosteller was socializing with Tukey and Winsor when he presented them with a problem: Wouldn't "it be nice if we had features of these order statistics, not just for the normal distribution [the bell curve], but for some other distributions"? So, Tukey figured it out. Mosteller published the paper, "Low Moments for Small Samples: A Comparative Study of Order Statistics," in 1947.

In the late 1970s, Tukey and Mosteller would publish a book together—*Data Analysis and Regression: A Second Course in Statistics*—that Tukey would fondly refer to as "the green book," because its cover and binding were printed in a solid shade of green. The green book came about as a result of a chapter on statistics the psychologist Gardner Edmund Lindzey asked Mosteller and Tukey to write for the second edition of Lindzey's book *Handbook of Social Psychology* (1969); Mosteller, along with Robert Bush, had previously written a chapter on statistics geared toward psychologists for the first edition of the book. But, for the second edition, Mosteller and Tukey ended up writing way too much: hundreds upon hundreds of pages. Lindzey radically pared down their submission, taking only the most relevant parts to include; afterwards, Mosteller and Tukey decided to build a new book, *Data Analysis and Regression,* around the excised material, focusing especially on regression analysis and exploratory methods.

Mosteller and Tukey, along with another of Tukey's former students, David Caster Hoaglin (who received his doctorate in 1971 under Tukey), made up the core members of what Tukey referred to as the "Cambridge Writing Machine." The moniker derived from Hoaglin's and Mosteller's successful recruitment of statisticians and mathematicians at Harvard (located in Cambridge, Massachusetts—hence the appellation) to write chapters for books on statistics. After all, as Tukey wrote in 1974, "[I]f present trends continue, an increasing fraction of all mathematicians will touch—or come close to touching—data during the next few decades," so much needed to be written and communicated to the masses about working with data. Hoaglin, Mosteller, and Tukey, in a brief but feverishly productive period, edited three books: *Understanding Robust and Exploratory Data Analysis* (1983), *Exploring Data Tables, Trends, and Shapes* (1985), and *Fundamentals of Exploratory Analysis of Variance* (1990). Along with *Exploratory Data Analysis* (1977), written solely by Tukey, and *Data Analysis and Regression: A Second Course in Statistics* (1977), penned by both Tukey and Mosteller, these five books became so indispensable that they tended to be referred to in conversation by their acronyms only: *UREDA, EDTTS, FEAV, EDA,* and *DAR,* respectively.

Another of Tukey's former students was David Ross Brillinger, who, like Mosteller, became a very successful statistician in his own right and was also probably John Tukey's biggest fan, freely admitting that he "watched Tukey like a hawk"—but he was certainly no sycophant. (Tukey seemingly had none of those, despite the great number of people who came to admire him.)

Tracing Swiss family roots going back at least to the 1400s, by the 1700s David Brillinger's distant relatives relocated to Pennsylvania and converted from Protestant to Mennonite. By the time of American Revolution, however, the Brillingers had made a home in Ontario, Canada. Born in 1937 in Toronto, Canada, when Brillinger was only seven months old, his father, who had aspirations of becoming an actuary, died of a cerebral hemorrhage; his maternal grandmother effectively took over raising him. Brillinger was an only child, so he formed close relationships with his cousins.

Some insurance money permitted Brillinger to attend a private boys' school for a while, until he was forced to transfer to the University of

Toronto Schools (UTS). He worked a number of odds jobs for money: small shop sales, caddying, prescription delivery, among others. At UTS, Brillinger realized he had a deep-seated love of sports—especially hockey, becoming a lifelong Toronto Maple Leafs fan—but possessed a natural ability at mathematics. In UTS mathematics teacher and school hockey coach Bruce "Nails" McLean, he found someone who personified both fields. McLean recognized Brillinger's talents at mathematics early on, so he let the young student work independently, at a table in the back of the classroom, delivering him books replete with math problems—including in statistics.

In order to graduate from UTS, students were required to pass a series of challenging high school exams. The set of math exams (focusing on algebra, trigonometry, and geometry) gave students a choice of solving any ten of twelve problems; Brillinger couldn't resist solving them all, and he ended up scoring over 100 percent on the exams, earning a scholarship in the process.

But he was just beginning to use his mathematical talents to earn money. As an undergrad at the University of Toronto (U of T), he won numerous math prizes—including the prestigious Putnam mathematical competition in 1958—snagging some substantial monetary awards, thereby helping to put food on the table.

Brillinger was fluent in both English and French; being bilingual allowed him to read some of the more interesting probability papers directly in French (France was home to many of the great probabilists of the time) instead of having to wait years for English translations. Though Brillinger graduated from U of T with a *bachelors honours* in pure mathematics, he attended all of the statistics courses at the university—even the actuarial classes. In fact, due to the influence of his father (whom he never knew but knew much about), Brillinger began leaning toward an actuarial career. Working in the actuarial profession, he reasoned, was a direct path to a middle-class lifestyle. Although Brillinger would eventually pass enough actuarial exams to earn an Associate of the Society of Actuaries (ASA) credential, he decided to settle upon becoming a statistician and an academic, since that would allow him to travel. Graduate school lay in the future, however.

After graduating from U of T, he sought adventure, as well as a chance to leave Canada, so Brillinger joined the Royal Canadian Navy. He ended up based on the West Coast and won yet another prize—this one for best navigational skills (the astronomy and trigonometry he had learned previously came in handy). The Navy also functioned as a sort of statistical proving ground: Brillinger was asked to count the number of messages sent by the fleet over a multi-year timeframe. Instead of physically counting every message—a tedious job which would have taken him years to complete by himself outright—Brillinger randomly selected one hundred messages, weighed them, calculated a weight-per-signal value, estimated the number of piles, and extrapolated from there.

By the summer of 1959, Brillinger had risen to the rank of Lieutenant, but he was finally ready to leave the navy for graduate school. He only submitted a single application: to Princeton. "It never even occurred to me to apply anywhere else," he recalled. Brillinger knew that Princeton was a haven for self-directed students: there, the ends mattered more than the means. A student could take any course of study that he wished; all that mattered was that you passed an oral exam[*] and wrote a satisfactory thesis.

When Brillinger first arrived at Princeton, he sought paid work—and landed on the doorstep of Sam Wilks. Wilks was busy proofing his book *Mathematical Statistics* and needed to check if all of the printed problems actually had solutions. So Brillinger was offered the gig. There was one problem Brillinger couldn't solve: finding a proof of the median and mean being jointly asymptotically normal. Wilks excised the problem from the final book proof. (Brillinger found a way to solve the problem years later.)

At Princeton, Brillinger was immediately drawn to mathematical statistics. By then, with the contributions of thinkers like Sam Wilks, William Cochran, Jerzy Neyman, George Snedecor, Gertrude M. Cox (she was the first woman to organize a Department of Statistics at a university, after working with Snedecor; her focus was on applications in the agricultural and biological sciences), Harold Hotelling (an American statistician and economist who studied with Ronald Fisher in England and was ultimately recruited to the University of North Carolina at Chapel Hill by Gertrude Cox), Abraham Wald (a Jewish-Hungarian mathematician who worked in the Statistical Research Group, led by W. Allen Wallis and operating out of Columbia University, during the war; posthumously, some of his statistics writings were strongly criticized by Ronald Fisher), and Albert Hosmer Bowker (who eventually rose to dean of Stanford, after establishing a

---

[*] The oral exam was called the "general exam"; it was typically taken at the completion of a student's first graduate year and covered four subfields of mathematics. In addition to the thesis, completion of the degree required demonstrating literacy in two foreign languages. As Leo Goodman recalled, "[F]or each of these languages, you had to demonstrate to a math faculty member of your choice that you had a reasonable ability to read ordinary mathematical texts that were written in the foreign language." Goodman didn't find the foreign language requirement particularly daunting, since students weren't expected to demonstrate fluency or mastery of the languages; plus, students were not being tested by language professors, but by mathematics professors.

statistics department at the institution) over the course of several decades, pursuing mathematical statistics was a viable academic option.

Becoming an expert in statistics allowed Brillinger to interact with many different kinds of people, which suited him well; a career instead spent in pure mathematics, in which he'd be working with a much smaller number of individuals, didn't have quite the same appeal for him, at least socially. The biggest factor swaying Brillinger toward the realm of statistics, however, was undoubtedly John Tukey.

"[Tukey] was so interesting generally and so much fun to watch," Brillinger remembered. Before he met Tukey, Brillinger was made aware of Tukey's esoteric habits, like drinking milk at beer parties and blasting Mozart or other classical music, usually baroque bass, repeatedly in his study from morning till noon while working (to be less of a disturbance, late in his life Tukey began using a Sony Discman, complete with earphones, that he had received as a Christmas gift from relatives in New Haven). When he attended his first class with Tukey, which was on time series analysis, Brillinger was confronted with even more personality quirks: Tukey's proclivity to eat apple pie and fish chowders for breakfast; his extreme care with money; his expression of New England sensibilities, which he took a special pride in; and his "'down-east' accent, offer[ing] few superfluous words," as one of Tukey's nephews characterized it. Brillinger also came to internalize Tukey's view of statistics as a science, rather than a math:

> I have found myself realizing that statisticians are the keepers of the scientific method. When a scientist comes up with something, what can they reasonably conclude? That appealed to me, to be able to get involved in many fields.

The Harvard statistician Arthur Pentland Dempster, who earned his doctorate under Tukey in 1956, added that Tukey's "most visible genius was mathematical, but science was in his psyche," and he chose to "[seek] ways to bridge the gap between mathematics and science."

Sitting in Tukey's time series course with Brillinger was David Freedman, who was a year ahead of Brillinger. It wouldn't take long for Tukey and Freedman to find themselves at loggerheads.

CHAPTER TWENTY-TWO

Making the Census Count

*"You will pardon me if I sigh, because the word quote assumptions
close quote in statistics is misleading and gives rise
to undue difficulty and it's I suppose all our fault."*
— Census testimony of John Tukey

David Amiel Freedman was born in Montreal, Canada, in 1938. He earned his Bachelor of Science degree from McGill University in 1958 and his doctorate from Princeton in 1960. Within a year, he landed at the UC Berkeley Department of Statistics. At first, Freedman was a dyed in the wool mathematical statistician and probabilist, hewing closely to theory—specifically, Bayesian theory.

The interpretation of probabilities has, for several hundred years, split mathematicians into one of several camps. Bayesians, for instance, put great stock in a subjective approach to probability that hinges on degrees of belief. Named in honor of the Presbyterian minister Thomas Bayes, Bayes himself explained how probabilities rely on subjectivism in a posthumously published paper called "An Essay Towards Solving a Problem in the Doctrine of Chances." Bayes' literary executor, Richard Price—a noted mathematician and demographer in his own right—discussed the motivations underlying Bayes' thinking:

> [Bayes'] design at first in thinking on the subject of it was, to find out a method by which we might judge concerning the probability that an event has to happen, in given circumstances, upon supposition that we know nothing concerning it but that, under the same circumstances, it has happened a certain number of times, and failed a certain other number of times. He adds, that he soon perceived that it would not be very difficult to do this, provided some rule could be found, according to which we ought to estimate the chance that the probability for the happening of an event perfectly unknown, should lie between any two named degrees of probability, antecedently to any experiments made about it; and that it appeared to him that the rule must be to suppose the chance the same that it should lie between any two equidifferent degrees;

which, if it were allowed, all the rest might be easily calculated in the common method of proceeding in the doctrine of chances.

Using Bayes, we don't approach the calculation of a probability tabula rasa; rather, we proceed with an initial probability in hand, "antecedently to any experiments made about it." This initial probability, of which there can be more than one, will need to be updated as we encounter new data. These revised probabilities are termed "posteriors"; any initial probabilities are called "priors." Bayes' Theorem, or Bayes' Rule, packages together these ideas in a tidy mathematical formula. Here is how Bayes himself summarized it (with his original italics intact):

> *Given* that the number of times in which an unknown event has happened and failed: *Required* the chance that the probability of its happening in a single trial lies somewhere between any two degrees of probability that can be named.

Subjective probability brings personal belief center stage; many mathematicians have argued that at least some subjective component to probability is inherent, is built-in—no matter what approach to probability one takes. Not everyone was sold on this, however. The economist John Maynard Keynes, in *A Treatise on Probability* (1921), wrote, "[I]n the sense important to logic, probability is not subjective. It is not, that is to say, subject to human caprice. A proposition is not probable because we think it so."

David Freedman, at first an acolyte of Bayesianism, began to turn skeptical, looking to explain real-world phenomena courtesy of a frequentist approach to probability rather than a Bayesian one. The problem with Bayes, he realized, was the assumption of prior probabilities. "My own experience suggests that neither decision-makers nor their statisticians do in fact have prior probabilities," he wrote.

> A large part of Bayesian statistics is about what you would do if you had a prior. For the rest, statisticians make up priors that are mathematically convenient or attractive. Once used, priors become familiar; therefore, they come to be accepted as "natural" and are liable to be used again; such priors may eventually generate their own technical literature.

Frequentism, contra Bayes, is a subset of an objectivist viewpoint: that probabilities exist empirically. A frequentist interpretation calculates the ratio of the frequency, or count, of a specific event to the number of times an experiment is repeated; the quotient is equal to the probability of the event occurring. Furthermore, as the number of trials of the experiment approaches infinity, the relative frequency of an event converges to the actual, or theoretical, probability of the event; this somewhat amorphous mathematical concept is called the law of large numbers.[*] The Swiss mathematician Jacob Bernoulli was the first to rigorously prove the law, but he had to settle on a key epistemological assumption in order to do it: "[We assume that] under similar conditions, the occurrence (or non-occurrence) of an event in the future will follow the same pattern as was observed in the past." Which leads us to some key problems with the frequentist approach, which might initially appear perfectly "objective." First, not all events are repeatable, ad infinitum, into the future; some arrive to us in the form of a single trial only. For instance, what was the probability of the Japanese bombing Pearl Harbor? Addressing the question with a frequentist approach makes no sense, since there is no way to conduct many trials—running through many World War IIs—of what was by its very nature a one-off event.

Second, the frequentist approach is hobbled by the reference class problem, recognized as far back as 1662 by Antoine Arnauld and Pierre Nicole in their probability treatise *Logic, Or the Art of Thinking* (probability is explicitly measured in print for the first time in this text). For example, when pondering the chances of your favorite sports team making a comeback in a championship game, you must consider the reference class—the group to which you're assigning potential trials. Would it be the set of all championship games ever played in the sport, or merely a subset demarcated by time or by type? Or would it be the games in which your favorite team and its championship opponent had already locked horns during the regular season? The reference class problem, then, is really one of classification. The mathematician John Venn eloquently summarized the problem more than a century ago. "It is obvious that every individual thing or event has an indefinite number of properties or attributes observable in it," he wrote, "and might therefore be considered as belonging to an indefinite number of different classes of things...."

---

[*] In what Stephen Stigler called a "heroic effort to gain a better understanding of chance," prior to the turn of the twentieth century evolutionary biologist Walter Frank Raphael Weldon rolled twelve dice an incredible 26,306 times, recording the frequencies of 5s and 6s of each throw. Weldon was trying to reconcile theory with real life, and his persistence permitted him a window into otherwise inaccessible mathematical ideas. Was a binomial model appropriate for the dice, or was some other model more effective? As Karl Pearson wrote of Weldon, "He had...a touch with observation and experiment rare in mathematics. In problems of probability, he would start experimentally and often reach results of great complexity by induction. Thus he was able to find out a number of problems relating to correlation between a throw of n dice...." Pearson, looking at Weldon's data, developed the chi-square test, one of the most widely used significance tests today.

Unlike Freedman, Tukey, who for most of his life was a frequentist, was never sold on, and ultimately never quite comfortable with, Bayesianism, but for a different reason than Freedman: largely because the theory attempts to capture and process all data related to the question of interest through a funnel, resulting in only one possible answer, only one valid a posteriori distribution (a distribution of posterior probabilities)—and thereby excludes any alternatives. Bayesians maintain a misguided "hope (or even a claim) that Bayesian approaches can also serve us well when we do not wish to draw on any source of information other than the data before us." But statisticians shouldn't have to "concern [themselves] with multiple answers," he said in the last decade of his life and should therefore ease off of trying "to look for *the* answer." Plus, Bayesians have "no really effective place for robustness," he said.

Nonetheless, Tukey was never opposed to using Bayes if a problem arose that the approach seemed well suited to solve; for example, perhaps without completely realizing it, Tukey and a team of statisticians utilized multi-stage Bayesian models to make election predictions for NBC from the early 1960s to the late 1970s. And in the *Collected Works*, Tukey admitted that if there's a need to pull together information from disparate sources and integrate it with collected data, such as with decision-making in business contexts or in pinning down the epochs in which ancient art pieces were constructed, a Bayesian approach might indeed be the best way to proceed, although there might be other options. Regardless, Tukey believed, attempting reflexively to use Bayesian techniques for every possible type of problem could only be deemed a significant failure of judgment.

David Freedman was a stringent opponent of statistically adjusting the census for undercounting, which put him in direct opposition to John Tukey, who was a proponent of statistical estimation of census counts to correct for miscounting. Freedman believed that adjustments would introduce new errors into the calculations.

The question of how best to take a census has a long pedigree. In ancient history—think of the Roman Empire, for instance—there was usually little distinction made between enumeration (counting) and statistics. In fact, as recently as two hundred years ago, talk of engaging in "statistics" meant merely the tabulation of census data by nations, perhaps even with an eye toward making decisions based on the data gathered; by the nineteenth century, though, statistics had become associated with probability theory in games of chance as well as scientific research.

Throughout recorded history, compilations of censuses usually have had two key objectives: taxation and conscription for military service.

Censuses date at least as far back to the time of the Old Testament: specifically, Numbers, one of the Books of Moses, in which some of the people of Israel—men at least twenty years of age (no children or women)—were counted to prepare for war.

The U.S. decennial census is hardly a true census, since it's not an exhaustive gathering of data from every member of the population. Who does the census miss? The homeless, the itinerant, undocumented workers, among many other groups. As Charles Seife eloquently explains in *Proofiness: How You're Being Fooled by the Numbers* (2010), billions of dollars are shelled out every decade for the express purpose of capturing a small segment of the U.S. population who either refuses or is unable to return census information cards. Although some sort of random sampling might seem to address the issue, the U.S. Constitution doesn't make things simple: the requirement for the census hinges on the word "enumeration," meaning "to count everyone" in the "several States." Interestingly, the U.S. Constitution Committee on Style chose to use the word "enumeration" for reasons of style rather than of substance. In addition, Seife notes, head counts of millions of people is in practice a process of estimation anyway.

Tukey was an active participant in the census debates of the 1980 and the 1990 censuses. From 1989 to 1991, Tukey was a member of a Special Advisory Panel advising the Bureau of the Census; he later said that, when all told, he had devoted "at least 20 full days and various other bits and pieces" to the census effort. He waded into a very politically fraught environment—congressional redistricting is a hotly contested affair by the major political parties, with such tactics as gerrymandering having a major impact on the results of elections both big and small—with the force of his great intellect not being enough to successfully navigate the choppy waters.

The basic point of contention centered on whether data from post-enumeration surveys (PES) should be utilized after the census results were compiled to help estimate how far off official counts were from actual counts. Only a small portion of the U.S. population received these comprehensive surveys—less than 400,000 people among 5,000 randomly selected blocks. The differential between the first pass (initial collection of census data) and the second pass among these randomly selected blocks would serve as a guide to estimating the undercount nationwide.

But these undercount estimates were not distributed equally among racial groups nor geographic regions. Thus, random selection of the blocks generated controversy: since there is variability when collecting data from a random sample, no matter how uniform the methods of selection, the results can be very different from sample to sample. Once the PES results were in, smoothing was implemented on the data, which also generated a fair share of controversy. In addition, there was a stigma attached to the PES: such surveys might appear as an admission of "guilt" that the census wasn't accurate on a first pass enumeration, requiring later estimates to bring it in line with the truth—which ultimately turned out to be an untenable position politically for many.

As reported in an article in the *New York Times*,[*] which effectively summarized the debate,

> Most experts agree that the 1990 census failed to ferret out about four million to five million Americans, a disproportionate number of them probably black, Hispanic, or Asian. Most also agree that the Census Bureau's statistical fix would better reflect the nation's total population.
>
> But they are deeply divided on the critical question of whether the adjustment would provide more accurate—and fairer—counts for individual cities and Congressional districts.

The racial issue was especially acute in the 1980 census, leading to much consternation as well as numerous lawsuits, which attempted to block any decisions made using the data. In 1989, the George H. W. Bush Administration went forward with plans to use a "dual-system estimator."

When Tukey spoke in support of post hoc census estimation before Congress, he discussed, in part, the empirical Bayesian techniques of borrowing strength that had served him well during his two decades of successful election predictions. In his 1991 testimony before the House of Representatives Census Subcommittee on the Census Count Review, Tukey noted that

> Adjustment of the census based on the post-enumeration survey, a more careful survey of a carefully drawn sample, as such is a measurement whose accuracy like that of all measurements, has limits.… First, the sampling uncertainty calculated by the bureau for the results of the different areas…and two, some sensitivity to exactly how the adjustments are calculated from the survey results. It is important that the sensitivity to reasonable choices is small, but it would be quite unrealistic to expect it to vanish.

Scaling up the quality of measurements is challenging, Tukey explained. To improve individual measurements more than 90 percent of the time—such as with the measurement/re-measurement of blood pressures of individuals or of the tolerances of machine parts—you must re-measure

---

[*] From August 6, 1991, as reported by Peter Passell.

with around 36 times the quality of the first measurement, which effectively renders the original measurement superfluous. (This notion—that "information on accuracy [does] not accumulate linearly with added data," as Stephen Stigler describes it—is usually referred to as the root-n rule. The rule was discovered centuries ago by Abraham de Moivre, emerging as a consequence of the normal approximation to the binomial distribution.) Instead of shooting for the moon, then, Tukey recommended simply re-measuring at the same level of precision, resulting in the same variability, and then averaging the original measurement and the new one; such a method will help the investigator arrive closer to the truth in roughly two-thirds of cases, he claimed. Analogously, repeated census measurements, at the same level of precision, will mostly get closer to the truth. That, along with smoothing out sampling fluctuations, Tukey said, "allows us to say with greater confidence that the [census] estimates are more accurate." Statistician David Hoaglin was retained to explore to impact of these statistical methods.

Back in 1980, Tukey continued, there were a proliferation of mathematical adjustment packages, but he couldn't determine which path forward was the most mathematically sound—so he recommended against adjusting the census then.* But by 1990, the technique of "prespecification" was available. Prespecification is "the best protection we know against much of the political pressures that might be involved in the adjustment process," he claimed. The details of the adjustment, as Tukey relayed in earlier testimony, should be set forth prior—or prespecified—to the data collection; he compared the process to his involvement in clinical trials, where the protocol had to be set forth in advance—and the results lived with after the experiments were completed.

---

* Tukey grappled in print with how such adjustments to the 1980 census might be effectively made; see, for example, the 1989 article "Adjusting the 1980 Census of Population and Housing," co-written with Eugene Ericksen and Joseph Kadane and published in the *Journal of the American Statistical Association*. As the authors of the article forcefully conclude, "Our major substantive finding is that the largest undercounts of the 1980 census occurred in central cities with large minority populations.... We believe that the Census Bureau creates political difficulties for itself when it ignores the undercount. The bureau will put itself in a better position by making its best effort, using available statistical and demographic methods, to adjust for the undercount." Even in 1985, Tukey wrote, "Demographic analysis has indicated differential undercounts for blacks (particularly for males) for the last few decennial censuses. The 1980 post-enumeration survey agrees, especially in central cities.... Such evidence of continuing inequity calls strongly, in my judgment, for remedial action."

Testimony in a lawsuit resulting from the City of New York suing the federal government in 1992 forced Tukey to elucidate the notion of pre-specification in greater detail. Prespecification protected the data from post hoc analytical tampering, otherwise "the choice of the method of analysis [could be] unduly influenced by the desires of one party [or] another." He continued:

> The usual technique for dealing with this is to prespecify the analysis in as much detail as one reasonably can. Now, this may mean prespecifying how you set about choosing the details of the analysis, it does not mean prespecifying the details. But once you do that, you have a clear prespecified answer which, in the clinical trial situation, may well be agreed on as the answer to the analysis of that trial.
>
> In the census situation the prespecification left two answers, the unadjusted enumeration and the adjusted enumeration, and an important reason for prespecifying things is to avoid dispersed attention and irrelevant controversy about other analyses that could have been done....

Tukey added, "[T]he importance of prespecification is that it really does greatly reduce the impact of prejudice and bias."

In their book *Who Counts: The Politics of Census-Taking in Contemporary America* (1999), authors Margo Anderson and Stephen Fienberg, who worked with Tukey on several projects and testified for the government about the census as well, summarize Tukey's positions on census adjustment. As long as there is ample prespecification, robustness—where "all of these [results] clearly indicated an absence of undue sensitivity, and so it was my judgment…that the adjustment was robust"[*]—and the statistical assumptions were met as best as possible, such adjustment procedures are valid. Therefore, block-level accuracy is not a significant problem after all.

An issue was raised, however, about the assumptions, which Tukey unpacked—with much annoyance—in his testimony as follows.

> You will pardon me if I sigh, because the word *quote* assumptions *close quote* in statistics is misleading and gives rise to undue difficulty and it's I suppose all our fault.
>
> You would be very wrong to think of assumptions as something like hypotheses in elementary geometry as things which were supposedly essen-

---

[*] In this portion of the census testimony, he also noted that David Hoaglin conducted some "alternative analyses" but the difference between his results and what Tukey obtained were marginal, hence leading to Tukey's conclusion that the adjustment was in fact robust.

tial to reach the conclusion…. There are *quote* assumptions which have helped to guide the choice of analysis…. If the real world were too far from those, the procedures would not be satisfactory. But typically the real world is not too far from these and the procedures are satisfactory.

He then spent the next several minutes unpacking the "assumption of homogeneity"—that the census undercount rates are identical within each defined subgroup. Even if such undercount rates weren't quite identical, he said, "the procedure [would still be] effective," especially with prespecification in the mix.

Grilled during cross-examination, when it was pointed out that the statistical smoothing methods lacked elements of prespecification, that there were coding errors when analyzing the data,* that there was "correlation bias," and that there were problems with some of the assumptions tied to the PES procedures, Tukey all but conceded "that the statistical procedures involved in the 1990 dual-system estimates have no assumptions" for inference, only "circumstances where they [the assumptions] work better and circumstances where they don't work as well as others." Tukey "all but conceded," rather than outright conceded, these points because the quotations in the previous sentence were those of the cross-examining attorney, Thomas W. Millet. Yet Tukey verbally agreed with Millet's phrasing of the issues surrounding the assumptions.

Millet and Tukey had a series of curt exchanges during cross-examination, including one in which the attorney handed the statistician a paper and told him, "I'm going to ask you to ignore my markings on this, Professor."

"That's easy," Tukey responded.

"I'm easily ignored," Millet challenged.

"I didn't say that," Tukey snapped back.

Another tempestuous exchange centered on the political implications of census adjustment by states, Millet noting that some states would be winners demographically, while others would be losers. And a third exchange, involving "fabrication rates," even had Judge Joseph M. McLaughlin delivering one-liners to defuse the tension. After Tukey replied to Millet that his "degree of surprise clearly depends on the day in which you ask me the question," the judge chimed in: "And the state of your digestion."

"We can't hope to eliminate political pressures [since] adjustment has important consequences. But focusing down to just the single choice…to

---

* Which potentially increased the nationwide undercount.

either not adjust or make the adjustment," Tukey testified in 1991, isn't an optimal path. Simply because we will never know the "best" method of adjusting the census doesn't mean we shouldn't proceed with an adjustment. All possible adjustments have inherent error. "I think in the adjustment issue we dare not let the best be the enemy of the good…. No one can ever know if they've made the best choice," he concluded, expanding the point in testimony a year later: "We would be glad to get perfection if we could, but in almost every situation that I know, probably every one, where adjustment is what one is considering, you are glad to improve things and you know perfection is never going to arise."

The Mayor of New York City at the time, David Dinkins, praised Tukey, saying, "I am grateful for your extraordinary contribution of time and intellect to this critical issue." But it was to no avail. David Freedman's philosophy of no census adjustment ruled the day. Freedman, who also testified about the census on multiple occasions, built his argument on several central ideas, including that the smoothing procedures were not, in fact, robust, and hence one smoothing procedure could result in a wildly different analysis than another, with no way to tell which procedure more closely reflected the truth. In addition, Freedman stressed that loss function analyses conducted by the bureau missed the mark.

Freedman also said that the PES itself was fraught with the potential for error. The Census Bureau had initially dispatched an army of half a million employees to take the first count, resulting in only about two percent of the population being uncounted—which was a significantly lower undercount than other recent decennial censuses, such as 1950's, Freedman noted. When asked if the census should be adjusted to correct for the "differential undercount," Freedman responded, "No, I do not. I don't think that that is really possible…. It is possible to do the arithmetic, but I don't think it is possible to do it in a way which gets you closer to the truth."

But why? Freedman pointed to three factors: sampling error, which arises when using a sample to represent a population; nonsampling error, which crops up due to issues besides taking the sample (such as survey wording or nonresponse bias); and "failures in the homogeneity assumption."

Robert A. Mosbacher, the Secretary of Commerce, sided with Freedman. We will not "abandon a 200-year-old tradition of how we actually count people," Mosbacher explained. As Fred Mosteller later noted, it's not enough to have good data to settle a policy question, since "policy implies politics, politics implies controversy, and the same data that some people use to support a policy are used by others to oppose it."

The dustup over the decennial census wasn't the first time that Freedman and Tukey were on opposite sides. As a graduate student, Freedman attended Tukey's time series course. The problems began when Tukey started sprinkling ill-defined, vague, and seemingly malleable terms into the lecture. Terms like *polyspectra*. Even simpler terms like *spectrum*. "What is the definition of 'spectrum'?" Freedman asked Tukey.

"Well," he began, "suppose you've got a radar transmitting signals up and it bounces off an airplane and a signal returns. So you see: well that's a spectrum."

The very next class, Tukey again began peppering his talk with the term. And Freedman still wasn't clear on what "spectrum" meant, so he raised his hand and asked Tukey to explicitly relay the definition.

"Well," he started, "suppose you have a sonar system and it bounces a signal off a submarine, or some such…."

Freedman, frustrated, had heard enough. He never attended the class again. Freedman and Tukey were on opposite sides in the census-adjustment debate not for reasons of statistical theory, but because their minds simply viewed the world differently: Tukey liked to keep things open-ended; Freedman, not so much. Freedman required rigor and precision in his definitions of terms. But Tukey appreciated vagueness and realized that the more effort you expended trying to define a term—since the process of definition is itself one of compromise—the more essential elements surrounding that concept may have dropped off, never to be recovered. "Far better an approximate answer to the *right* question, which is often vague, than an *exact* answer to the wrong question, which can always be made precise," he wrote in FoDA. False precision doesn't add to the storehouse of human knowledge, especially when the problems that data analysis helps us address are by their very nature typically nebulous and vague, with ill-defined borders.

Data analysis, in fact, moves forward by the search for approximate answers, just as science progresses through falsification and tipping points leading to paradigm shifts. As in science, data analysis also progresses by carefully evaluating and monitoring the tools at hand—both those that worked in the past, such as certain types of algebraic or analytic methods, and those that might be promising in the future—as well as the attitudes of the investigators, of which only the most cheerful, positive, adventurous, and optimistic approaches, especially when mathematical assumptions don't hold as expected, will do. Coupled with that optimism, however, also comes an overriding imperative to be honest, to be ready to face the limitations of techniques and procedures, to be willing to feel uncomfortable in the face of a tension between the possible and the impossible. Data analysis will never live in the space of the plane geometry of Euclid, will never be replete with a set of axioms and propositions and theorems arrived at deductively; rather, Tukey explained, "*data analysis is intrinsically an empirical science*" (his italics), with insights colliding with both experience and analogy to other similar situations—thereby producing technical advancement.

In FoDA, like in his census testimony, Tukey implored statisticians not to let the perfect become the enemy of the good by refusing to utilize certain statistical techniques merely because they were not completely mathematized or optimized yet (e.g., the Student's *t* distribution). What's more, Tukey felt that the search for the "best solution," rather than simply a good solution, was a fool's errand. In this, he was influenced by quantum chemist George Elbert Kimball, who wrote, "In my experience when a moderately good solution to a problem has been found, it is seldom worth while to spend much time trying to convert this into the 'best' solution. The time is much better spent in real research…."

As for David Freedman, he landed on his feet, going on to become a leader in applied statistics, contributing his analytical talents to public policy and the law, and always turning a skeptical eye toward theoretical models (mis)applied with little thought to reality.

CHAPTER TWENTY-THREE

Playing Favorites

"I really don't want a life like what you have and I am concerned about whether I want to be an academic."
— David Brillinger

Unlike David Freedman, David Brillinger immediately took to Tukey, and the feeling was mutual. Brillinger would tease him, despite their differing worldviews: Brillinger had a progressive bent, while Tukey was more conservative-minded. Some of their differences could be attributed to a generation gap, but not all of them.

Yet they were always very much in sync. Their connection was akin to Tukey's with Charlie Winsor, only this time in reverse: Tukey was now the elder statesman, and Brillinger the young and eager-to-learn talent. If Brillinger was riding too high about something, Tukey would cut him down to size. But if he was struggling, Tukey would offer him help and positive reinforcement. Tukey, traveling around the country, would unexpectedly phone Brillinger very early in the morning, beginning the call with: "I hope that I haven't woken you up." He would drive with Tukey to Bell Labs during the school year, since Brillinger had the "day-a-week job" at the Murray Hill site and Tukey split his time between Princeton and Bell; their conversations on these drives, some of which were in Tukey's beloved Mustang convertible—he also owned a truck affectionately called "The Monster"—were wide-ranging and fruitful. Tukey's graduate student Alan M. Gross, who also had memorable discussions during car rides with Tukey, concurred: Tukey never let a minute go to waste. Brillinger always felt like every paper he wrote, he wrote for an audience of one: John Tukey.[*]

---

[*] Brillinger wasn't the only Bell Labs employee who would hitch rides with Tukey. Harry Hart, a patent attorney at Bell, was also a resident of Princeton; on shared car rides to the Murray Hill campus, Hart would grill the statistician about the technical details behind the patents, to which Tukey would invariably supply the inquisitive lawyer with answers.

Brillinger was one of a number of Princeton graduate students to land summer jobs at Bell Labs. There, he made use of an IBM 701 mainframe computer; Brillinger already had some experience with an IBM 650 at U of T, but he had to program it in machine language, since FORTRAN hadn't been invented yet. The 701, though, had a FORTRAN compiler, so he whittled away his summer writing FORTRAN code for Tukey. Though Tukey was a leading proponent of computer use for data analysis, Brillinger never actually saw him program.

Brillinger and his wife, Lorie, whom he met at Princeton, had a self-described "warm relationship" with Tukey and his wife, Elizabeth. After having dinner at Brillinger's home, the two couples took a trip to the local zoo. Brillinger looked over at one of the animals, commenting that he had forgotten what it was. "Capybaras," a type of rodent, Tukey immediately answered. Then he was silent for a protracted period of time.

"Now John Tukey, don't you pretend that you haven't been asleep," Elizabeth said, breaking the silence.

"Well if Lorie hadn't made me such a good dinner, I wouldn't have been," he answered.

It was during Brillinger's time at Bell that he first heard Tukey speaking of data analysis. By the summer of 1960, he had a logged a year at Princeton under Tukey, and Brillinger decided to host a party at his home; Bell Labs employees, such as Ramanathan Gnanadesikan, Martin Wilk, and Tukey, attended. A discussion about the state of statistics ensued—namely, how mathematical statistics had quickly turned into the centerpiece of academic research in statistics departments, despite it being a hybrid discipline, not contributing to the mass of research in mathematics nor in statistics from the perspective of analyzing data. The assembled statisticians—Tukey termed a group of statisticians a *quarrel*—wondered: How could the analysis of data once again assume pride of place in statistics research? After all, luminaries like Fisher recognized the key role of data; Pearson did as well. At some point, however, there had been a shift. Could the ship be righted?

Tukey thought on the problem, remaining silent for a moment. Then he "snapped his head up," Gnanadesikan remembered, and said, "I think that what we are talking about is data analysis." Tukey would deliver a seminal talk on data analysis a year later, at the Institute of Mathematical Statistics' annual meeting in Seattle, which was expanded and published as FoDA in the *Annals of Mathematical Statistics*.

Tukey thought quite highly of David Brillinger, so much so that he coined an endearing unit of measurement called the *mini-Brillinger* (abbreviation: *mB*); effectively, this neologism told everyone a story: that Brillinger was the standard by which Tukey measured his other students. His advisee was so mathematically sharp, so quick to pick things up, that he finished his doctorate in less than two years. Ever humble, Brillinger claimed that the rapid pace was due more to the solvable nature of the problems Tukey posed—thankfully, he mused, Tukey didn't dump Fermat's Last Theorem on his lap!—rather than any preternatural skill on his part. Although Tukey was his role model, when Tukey asked him what he wanted to do with his life post-doctorate, Brillinger said, "I really don't want a life like what you have and I am concerned about whether I want to be an academic." Tukey responded by bringing up William "Willy" Feller as a role model: Didn't he have a good life?

William Srecko Feller, born in Zagreb, Croatia, in 1906, earned a doctorate from University of Göttingen summa cum laude at only twenty years of age, published a consequential treatise on probability theory less than a decade later, fled Hitler's Germany for the University of Stockholm, and shortly thereafter moved to the United States to work first at Cornell and then Princeton University, all the while continuing to contribute greatly to probability and snagging numerous honors in the process.

Yes, Brillinger agreed, Willy Feller had a good life. Maybe being an academic wasn't such a bad idea after all.

Eventually, though, Brillinger softly rebelled against Tukey, a man who needed mathematicians around him that he respected, such as Sam Wilks: Tukey pressed Brillinger to join the faculty at Princeton, but Brillinger demurred, wanting instead to stake out on his own academic territory. He eventually ended up on the faculty at Berkeley, after—for a short time—modeling his employment on Tukey's courtesy of a joint appointment: he became a lecturer at Princeton in mathematics while simultaneously working at Bell Labs as a Member of Technical Staff (MTS). As a lecturer at Princeton in 1962, Brillinger briefly worked with Tukey on complex election-projection forecasting for RCA/NBC.[*] Reflecting on his career decades later, by which point he had staked out that new academic territory in the form of "random process data analysis," Brillinger said that his time at Bell Labs was "the best job I ever had."[†] He added, "I can say that

---

[*] There is a black-and-white photograph capturing all the members of the 1962 election forecasting team in action: John Tukey, David Brillinger, Robert Abelson, Dick Link, David Wallace, and John Mauchly.
[†] Brillinger has called the time period 1960 to 1964 the "magic years" of Bell Labs, since so much of the statistical apparatus that is commonplace today—everything from statistics software to graphics—was, for the first time, given pride of place.

everything important about statistics that I ever learned, I learned at lunch at Murray Hill."*

Despite Brillinger's move to the West Coast, they remained close for the remainder of Tukey's life. They collaborated on a number of projects together. One in particular, on time series, really provoked Tukey's ire. In 1982, they co-authored "Spectrum Analysis in the Presence of Noise: Some Issues and Examples," at the invitation of the *Proceedings of the IEEE*. But the paper was rejected. They then submitted it to *J. Time Series Analysis*, but they rejected it as well. Tukey was upset: the writing had taken up a lot of time, time that could have been better spent doing other projects. (Ultimately, the piece appeared in the *Collected Works*.) A sympathetic academic referee from one of the journals mailed back the failed submission; among its pages was penciled in a curse word, which Tukey's loyal and longtime secretary at Bell Labs, Mary Bittrich, was determined to never let her boss see.

Their families remained close through the decades, too. Brillinger had two children with his wife Lorie: Jef and Matt. After a fifteen-year battle with a brain tumor and cancer, Jef, the older of the two sons, passed away, and Tukey called Brillinger to offer condolences. Countless tears punctuated the difficult phone call.

In the 1960s, Tukey especially wanted Brillinger around because the Princeton statistics department, a department that Tukey was integral to building, was dying slowly. Early on, Tukey wasn't concerned about the quality of students who passed through the graduate mathematics program, but he was worried that enough of these students would turn toward the study of statistics.

Joseph F. Daly, born in 1911 in Washington, D.C., was one of the first to earn a doctorate in statistics at Princeton, under Sam Wilks' supervision, after graduating from Catholic University. Daly became a statistician best known for his work at the U.S. Census Bureau, but, like Tukey, he hadn't come to Princeton for statistics; rather, Daly was lured in by Luther Pfahler Eisenhart, chair of the mathematics department, whose research focused on differential geometry. But Eisenhart was predisposed

---

* Indeed, lunches were where the intellectual wheels were greased. Consider, for a moment, how many lunches have already come up so far in this book: there was the "bit lunch" (when the term "bit" was coined), the "Chowder and Marching Society" lunches, the Lord Cherwell lunch, the Harvard Faculty Club lunch, and "The Quefrency Alanysis" lunch, to say nothing of the meals eaten with the Führocracy or the "1.9 meals a day" Tukey shared with the Winsors.

the year Daly arrived, resulting in Daly's serendipitous turn to Wilks and statistics.

Other students who were on "Sam's side of the hall" (Tukey's words) included Theodore "Ted" W. Anderson, born in 1918 in Minneapolis, Minnesota, who landed at Stanford after earning a doctorate at Princeton in 1945 and became a pioneer in multivariate statistics and econometrics; and David Votaw, a Texan who received a doctorate in applied mathematics at Princeton and ended up at Yale. During the Second World War, these two students were involved with the Wilks-led Statistical Research Group at Princeton (SGRP); Fred Mosteller and Leonard Jimmie Savage (known as Jimmie)—who was born in 1917 in Detroit, Michigan, worked with von Neumann during the war, and made major contributions to statistics, especially with his book *The Foundations of Statistics* (1954)—were connected with the associated research group at Columbia University (which was led by W. Allen Wallis and included, among other luminaries, Abraham Wald). By the end of the war, Tukey realized that Mosteller and Savage, who had learned to solve statistics problems on an incredibly tight deadline (and had many interactions on the first floor of a building on Columbia's campus, where the Princeton research group maintained an office, and on the tenth floor, where the Columbia research group resided), sounded so much alike from working together for so many hours that, from 1946 onward, if they were commiserating in the next room, you couldn't tell one from the other. They did, however, have different approaches to statistics. As Mosteller explained it, Jimmie Savage felt "that every new statistical problem has to be solved with new statistics," while Mosteller believed the reverse.

Mosteller and Savage continued to work together after World War II, having a memorable encounter with Milton Friedman, the twentieth century economist best known for advocating for free markets. Although Friedman was not a statistician by any means—he had accumulated experience with statistical methods during the war by working in Columbia's Statistical Research Group under Allen Wallis—but a man whose statistical judgment and sharp mind Tukey respected enough that if Friedman were in the audience during a lecture he was delivering, he would take extra care to dot the i's and cross the t's. Case in point: Friedman looked over a manuscript of Mosteller and Savage's and proceeded to savage it, marking it up with a thousand corrections. Mosteller and Savage weren't happy about the corrections, thinking twenty-two of them were in error. Friedman disagreed and fought them tooth and nail. "Well, you fellows really have a lot of good things to say," Friedman finally admitted, "and you ought to learn how to say them. There are some ways to learn how to write. Here are a couple of books that would do you a lot of good."

Mosteller and Savage, at first frustrated, found themselves indebted to Friedman. He helped them improve their editing skills.

CHAPTER TWENTY-FOUR

Statistics at Princeton

"How could you tell that to students? I would do it myself,
but I would shut and lock the office door first."
— Unnamed statistician speaking to John Tukey

A t no time in its two decades of existence was the Princeton statistics department ever particularly large. The department certainly posed no competition to its sister department, mathematics; in fact, Tukey was worried if there were "enough [statistics] thesis problems around to keep the trade running."[*] Of course, before there was a Princeton statistics department, students interested in pursuing statistics had to bubble up from the mathematics department.

In *A Princeton Companion* (1978), compiled by Alexander Leitch, Tukey lays out the history of statistics at Princeton. "Statistics at Princeton," Tukey explains, "was the creation of Luther P. Eisenhart and Samuel S. Wilks. Its history falls naturally into four periods: Wilks alone, World War II, postwar under Wilks, the early years as a department." It was Eisenhart who lured Wilks to Princeton in the early 1930s. Shortly after Wilks arrived, he got the ball rolling by offering a graduate course in statistics, but he was only an assistant professor, with limited access and opportunities available. A decade would pass before any additional statisticians were hired; meanwhile, Wilks was setting the early standards for statistical research, teaching, and supervision of doctoral students. "In those days," Tukey said, "the abnormal was the normal as far as statisticians were concerned…. [with people being] pushed by the seat of their pants." Back then, it wasn't about fashioning top-quality statistics courses; rather, the drive was toward retaining top-tier talent like Charlie Winsor, who had a doctorate in physiology, and attracting exceptional students, who would be self-directed enough to find statistics problems to research.

The war period had Wilks spending his energies as part of the National Defense Research Committee, with the focus being on "crucial applica-

---

[*] He said this in reference to the blossoming area of nonparametric statistics, but it could credibly be taken to be his attitude toward the discipline overall.

tions" designed to support the war effort, such as the work being done in Fire Control Research, of which Tukey and Charles Winsor were key contributors. Tukey wasn't directly involved with statistics education at Princeton until he wrapped up his activities at the FCRO. He then taught a statistics graduate course before ever even taking a Princeton statistics class.

Around this time, there weren't many professional avenues in which to pursue statistics outside of a strictly university classroom setting. The Institute for Advanced Study had a bias against inviting any nonmathematical statisticians, for instance. Of course, there was the ASA, which even had a biometrics (biostatistics) division. What's more, there was the possibility of membership in the Eastern North American Region (ENAR) of the Biometric Society.

At the first ENAR meeting, which took place in Washington, D.C., immediately following World War II, Tukey, along with Ronald Fisher and Arthur Linder (who was born in 1904 in Lausanne, Switzerland, and was a professor of mathematical statistics), shared a four-room hotel suite. (Tukey was anything but demanding when it came to travel accommodations, with an economic Travel Lodge being "quite sufficient," according to F. R. Anscombe.) Biologists spoke at the meeting; mathematicians spoke at the meeting; statisticians spoke at the meeting. There were many questions asked of the speakers; there was enthusiastic discussion. But one of the questions posed at lunch afterward was if the speakers had been treated unfairly. "The outcome of this [discussion]," Tukey relayed, "was that it was agreed that at a biometric meeting one was entitled to ask any question that one felt like." Several years later, Tukey rose to the position of council member of the Biometric Society.

The immediate postwar period saw administrative approval of a Section of Mathematical Statistics in the mathematics department at Princeton, which was a precursor to the standalone Department of Statistics. At first, the section consisted of Wilks, Tukey, and a visiting professor, but it expanded to include Francis "Frank" John Anscombe. Born in Hove, England, in 1918, Anscombe is perhaps most famous for his "Anscombe's quartet," a set of four data sets appearing in the 1973 *American Statistician* paper "Graphics in Statistical Analysis" that have identical descriptive statistics (sample sizes, means, variances, standard deviations, correlations, and even lines of best fit) but couldn't look more different when plotted on the coordinate plane, thus (literally) illustrating the importance of visualizing data sets rather than solely relying on their summary measures. "A computer should make both calculations and graphs. Both sorts of output should be studied; each will contribute to understanding," explained Anscombe. He also did critical work with the analysis of residuals, arguing for the importance of statistical computing.

In 1956, fresh off of an appointment at Cambridge University, Anscombe arrived at Princeton. Tukey was in favor of the appointment because he was itching for a colleague he could "talk to, not at." Anscombe married Phyllis Rapp, the sister of Tukey's wife, Elizabeth; Tukey thereafter referred to Anscombe as his "brother-in-squared-law," and, when either Tukey or Anscombe was asked of his occupation, they both told people that they "marry Rapp daughters." Less than a decade after his marriage, Anscombe was lured away to Yale University in order to establish a statistics department there.

Before long, the Anscombes had four children who often dropped by the Tukey house: Francis, Anthony, Frederick, and Elizabeth; at least one of those, as a young child, thought that Tukey was a mere employee of the phone company. Anthony once went sailing with his uncle, but the tide came in and tipped the boat over. "Your aunt doesn't need to know about this," Tukey told his nephew.

When Francis was around eight years of age, Tukey took him to a baseball game at Candlestick Park, home of the San Francisco Giants. Willie Mays, one of the greatest outfielders of all time, played in the game, which the Giants ended up losing to the St. Louis Cardinals by a score of 3 to 1. Mays was unflappable, however, catching balls no matter where they were headed. Tukey and Francis laughed at the sheer talent on display, bemused at how easy Mays made it all look without being flashy. Perhaps recognizing a kindred spirit, Tukey muttered to himself, "What a man."

The outbreak of the Korean War in 1950 saw Princeton turn yet again toward war-related activities, with mathematics professor Forman Sinnickson Acton, born in 1920 in Salem, New Jersey, heading the newly created Analytical Research Group, located at Princeton's Forrestal Research Center, designing military weapons. Acton was most interested in computers, however, and was the witness to a battle of wits between the brilliant Hungarian mathematician and computer science pioneer John von Neumann and John Tukey:

> I sat quietly in the corner of the office for about three-quarters of an hour while Tukey sat there, his back to the wall, sweating and trying to keep up with von Neumann. It was great fun. I didn't understand what they were talking about, but that didn't make any difference.

After the war, Acton earned a doctorate from the Carnegie Institute of Technology and eventually made his way back to Princeton, becoming a renowned computer science professor. He interacted with Tukey on many occasions—they both worked on the U-2 spy plane and Nike missile projects, for example—and Acton proved to be quite an idiosyncratic character. Mathematician Adam N. Rosenberg, one of Acton's most successful students* who later became a friend, recounted an especially enlightening interaction early on with his professor. "Besides learning my craft of numerical computing in his classroom in college, I remember one moment when he and I were sitting in a restaurant and he explained the nuances of a [sorting] method called a 'heapsort' on a napkin," Rosenberg, a self-described "industrial mathematician," said. "He drew pictures of binary trees with branches and roots and showed me how the method worked, why it worked, and why it was often better than some methods and sometimes worse than others."

In 1964, Sam Wilks passed away. His death served as the impetus to launch an independent statistics department at Princeton. In April of 1965, the Board of Trustees gave its approval for the establishment of the Department of Statistics on July 1, 1965. The department was given a "Coffee Room," similar to the traditional weekday afternoon tea in Fine Hall, which encouraged socialization between faculty and students.

In the 1966-67 academic year, Tukey was the department chairman, although he was splitting his time between Princeton and Bell Labs. John A. Hartigan joined the department, as did Michael D. Godfrey, who remained a (now half-time) member of the economics department. Godfrey owed Tukey a debt of gratitude; even though he wasn't one of his advisees, Tukey took the time to carefully pore through Godfrey's doctoral thesis. "John did two things," Godfrey recalled. "[H]e read it and wrote comments in red all over it (and sent it back within a few weeks—about the luckiest thing that ever happened to me), and told Oskar (Morgenstern) [the German economist and cofounder of game theory] about me." The upshot? "Thus, I went to Princeton."

In 1966-67, there were ten undergraduate majors of statistics as well as eight graduate students. When assembling the statistics department, Tukey came to realize that he had to do his best "fitting into the establishment. Probably straining the establishment a little, but not too much. A very delicate operation." Laying the groundwork for the department had caused Tukey great stress and many nights of fitful sleep; he got through

---

* Rosenberg, who has called John Tukey one of his heroes, graduated from Princeton in 1978 and went on to earn a doctorate from Stanford in Operations Research. He then, like Tukey, worked at Bell Labs—at the West Long Branch in New Jersey.

the "emotional trauma" (Elizabeth Tukey's words) of the department's gestation by working on his exploratory data analysis writings.

In 1970, Tukey handed over the reins of the statistics department to Geoff Watson, who facilitated its expansion and encouraged statistical computing. Geoff Stuart Watson, born in Bendigo, Australia, in 1921, was the head of the Princeton statistics department from 1970 to 1985. Snagging a doctorate from North Carolina State University in 1951, Watson had teamed with James Durbin at the London School of Economics to create the widely used Durbin-Watson statistic, a method for detecting autocorrelation (correlation present after a time delay),[*] which served as a boon for robust predictions in the dismal science. Watson also studied geologic (paleomagnetism) and environmental issues, and as chair helped to organize the "Princeton Robustness Year" from 1970 to 1971, but he wasn't treated especially respectfully despite capping off a successful career.

Peter Bloomfield was department chairman of statistics for a short time; he contributed to time series and regression analysis but wasn't particularly fond of being chair—so he decamped to North Carolina State. Donald McNeil, a strong hire in the early 1970s, flew the coop to Australia. Others left the institution as well.

By the mid-1980s the statistics department was devoid of exceptional senior talent save one: John Tukey. Forced into a mandatory retirement at age 70 in late June of 1985—he retired from Bell Labs in 1985 as well[†]— Tukey's absence sounded the death knell of a separate statistics department at Princeton University. By the end of that calendar year, the civil engineering department had absorbed what remained of the statistics department. By the time Tukey died, those remnants coalesced into Princeton's Committee for Statistical Studies.

Tukey's view of statistics education was multifarious and complex, largely because his own path to statistics was circuitous. After all, as he was fond of pointing out, he had multiple degrees in chemistry—but none in statis-

---

[*] Tukey also, unsurprisingly, contributed to the field of autocorrelation. In a paper, in which he noted that he "prefer[ed] to call [autocorrelations]…power spectrum analysis," Tukey enumerated the disciplines that might benefit from autocorrelations, such as communication engineering, cybernetics, economics, and oceanography, but he claimed that oceanographers treated autocorrelations as no more "than a means to an end" (Tukey developed that opinion after attending a conference held at Woods Hole in Cape Cod). It is with economics applications that Tukey saw autocorrelations as having the greatest potential impact.

[†] A decade later, AT&T spun off Bell Labs into Lucent Technologies.

tics. For one thing, he believed that if a graduate student was encouraged to do too much mathematics—and that student was aiming toward a degree in statistics—it might, in fact, be harmful to the student's future. Once, when walking past Fine Hall, Winsor made a snarky comment to Tukey about Sam Wilks: "[He] trains good mathematical statisticians and it's surprising how soon they become good statisticians"—the point being, there is a difference at being an expert at the theoretical underpinnings of statistics and practicing statistics in real-world settings; having a gut intuition for analyzing data was paramount.

Regardless, Tukey believed that satisfying mathematics requirements was critical for statisticians as well as for physicists, since a basic level of numeracy is necessary to navigate one's way through the technical journals in those disciplines. Plus, a grab bag of mathematical skills had to be mentally available to students so that they could practice what Tukey called "defensive mathematics," giving them the requisite imprimatur in fields that were still dominated by purists with little tolerance for the nebulous, difficult-to-codify "intuition" necessary for thinking properly about data.

As the statistician Herbert E. Robbins explained, "The statisticians of the past came into the subject from other fields—astronomy, pure mathematics, genetics, agronomy, economics, etc.—and created their statistical methodology with a background of training in a specific scientific discipline and a feeling for its current needs." Tukey worried that this migration of top-flight intellects from different disciplines toward statistics (as Tukey had been drawn from chemistry to mathematics to statistics) would never repeat, now that statistics as its own separate discipline had become codified, perhaps leading to dogmatism and ossification.

From a professor's perspective, instructing students in mathematics is straightforward, but teaching them data analysis is difficult, especially on the graduate level. After all, as Paul Velleman, one of Tukey's former students, explains, when making statistical judgments "[o]ur guiding principal should be that we seek truth about the world"; however, "This constant reference to understanding the world is one of the things that makes a Statistics course more difficult to teach than a mathematics course at a comparable level of technical sophistication." Another issue is the potential shame at presenting practical problems. One day, a statistician visiting at Princeton pulled Tukey aside after sitting in on one of his class lectures. The statistician, whom Tukey wouldn't name, was aghast that Tukey presented a practical approach to a statistical method rather than a purely mathematical one. "How could you tell that to students?" he asked Tukey incredulously. "I would do it myself, but I would shut and lock the office door first." Tukey attributed this statistician's fear of a public shaming to a larger issue: that of there being few agreed upon strategies, rather than mere tactics, to teaching data analysis.

Tukey did, however, push students to perform data analysis outside of the classroom via consulting and open invitations to practitioners. By the time the students are working on their doctorates, statistics consulting was an ideal proving ground for "the practical functioning of familiar techniques," as he wrote in "Discussion: The Role of Statistical Graduate Training" (1982)—if it was feasible. Which wasn't always the case, since not every statistics department had as deep a bench as Princeton's. Besides interacting with the faculty at Princeton, Tukey brought data analysis to life by inviting individuals to Applied Statistics Seminars who worked with real-world data yet didn't necessarily have solutions to the problems they spoke about (and were willing to field questions from the audience). He considered the Applied Statistics Seminars a kind of virtual statistics consulting laboratory, giving students exposure to the sorts of problems that can crop up outside the academy as well as giving them the chance to interact with people who are better versed in the origins of the data than they (the students) are; after all, Tukey said, a "consultant is a man who thinks with other people's brains." At these seminars, which started in 1946, he told his students to not hold back asking questions or making comments, no matter their confidence with the material at hand. Likewise, the speakers weren't required to have solutions to any of the problems.

To further enrich their understanding of statistics, Tukey would recommend that his students read a publication like the British *Journal of the Royal Statistical Society*—specifically, pre-1948 issues of the journal, which were called *Supplement to the Journal of the Royal Statistical Society*, and which Tukey read early on in his career (in addition to the British journal *Biometrika*); from these one could get a good sense of "what people were doing or had been doing" over the years (or the past forty years, in the case of when Tukey first read *Biometrika*), even though there were differences in the ways that British and American statisticians practiced and honed their craft.

PART FOUR

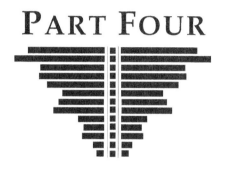

Exploratory Data Analysis

CHAPTER TWENTY-FIVE

The Development of
Exploratory Data Analysis

"Writing the limited preliminary edition of *Exploratory Data Analysis*
was a necessary relief from finding myself a part-time (at the
University) chairman of a new university Department of Statistics,
as was teaching from it to a mixed class of undergraduates."
— John Tukey

Finally freed from having to teach pure mathematics, Tukey was now able to offer a freshman course in exploratory data analysis (EDA) in the spring of 1968. An early draft of his book of the same name served as the (Xeroxed) text for the class in 1970 and 1971; there were a total three preliminary versions disseminated from 1970 to 1976. A number of colleagues, including David Hoaglin and Leonard M. Steinberg, read through these preliminary volumes, offering Tukey guidance and suggestions. After receiving editorial help from Mosteller that resulted in excising about half of the material from the preliminary edition, as well as financial support from the Army Research Office in Durham, North Carolina, and from Bell Labs, *Exploratory Data Analysis* (*EDA*)[*] was finalized and published as a first edition, and packaged with a distinctly bright orange cover, in 1977. "Writing the limited preliminary edition of *Exploratory Data Analysis*," Tukey reminisced, "was a necessary relief from finding myself a part-time (at the University) chairman of a new university Department of Statistics, as was teaching from it to a mixed class of undergraduates." Tukey followed up *EDA* by releasing *Data Analysis and Regression: A Second Course in Statistics*, its cover wrapped in green binding, with Mosteller as coauthor, only several months later.

---

[*] Henceforth, references to Tukey's *Exploratory Data Analysis* will be designated with the moniker *EDA* (in italics); general references to exploratory data analysis, as developed by Tukey but extended by others, will be denoted by EDA (not in italics).

Oftentimes the tandem of books were referred to solely by their cover colors: *EDA* was the "orange book," while *DAR* was the "green book."

EDA was dedicated to Charles Winsor as well as to Edgar Anderson, a botanist whom Tukey had assisted with data analysis two decades before. Winsor and Anderson were "data analysts both, from whom the author learned much that could not have been learned elsewhere," Tukey wrote.

By the end of his life, Tukey had become best known for EDA (even by 1975, prior to the publication of the first edition of *EDA*, EDA was the focus at the American Statistical Association's annual meeting), but, as David C. Hoaglin notes, "data analysis played a major role in his work from early on indeed. I don't think it would be an exaggeration to say that most of John's contributions to statistics involved or grew out of problems in data analysis." *Exploratory Data Analysis*, which unsurprisingly didn't contain techniques of confirmatory data analysis and other, by then, pro forma methods of inferential statistics, was an outgrowth of what Tukey had already written about on data analysis, much of which is present in two volumes of his copious *The Collected Works of John W. Tukey*. For example, as far back as 1949 Tukey published a now-famous paper entitled "One Degree of Freedom for Non-Additivity," reprinted in the seventh volume of the *Collected Works*, that addresses the mathematical difficulties inherent in analysis of variance (termed ANOVA, which tests for the equality of population means) when testing for interactions between variables in a two-factor experiment; this effort was only one of Tukey's many contributions to the development of ANOVA (also noteworthy is his Tukey's Honest Significant Difference test, a multiple comparison test which provides a researcher with specifics regarding where significant differences between means may lie, as well as the *hat matrix, H*, used with both ANOVA and regression).* ANOVA, he said in the last decade of his life, was around ninety percent exploratory—"no matter what the books and professors pretend." *EDA* also took cues from FoDA and papers like "Data Analysis and Statistics: An Expository Overview" (1966).

To some extent, prior to the publication of *EDA*, exploratory data analysis was an emerging science in a "pre-paradigm" state, in the Kuhnian sense of the term; post-publication, all the important elements of EDA would coalesce into a unifying set of principles.

---

* He kept the problem that spawned "One Degree of Freedom for Non-Additivity" buried "in his pocket" for more than two years until the path forward became clear to him.

The orange book is truly without peer, falling somewhere in between a textbook and a conversational set of prescriptions or recipes, although it mostly evades even these sorts of simplistic classifications. On the one hand, there are chapters divided in sections, with each section having a set of review questions, but, on the other hand, the review questions themselves are always concatenated together in a single paragraph, rapid-fire style. The questions themselves are a mix of the definitional and the algorithmic, but they are not numbered and their answers are not printed anywhere in the text. Here is a representative example from the first chapter, section 1C: Scratching down numbers:

review questions

What is a batch? What is an example of a set of numbers that is not a batch? Why do we use bold figures? What choices have we in making a similar effect with pencil or pen? What are two ways of tallying numbers?

There are "PROBLEMS" for some sections as well—and "PROBLEMS" and "More Problems" and "Some more problems" and "Still more problems" that close out chapters—and they also don't have answers printed in the text, perhaps because not all of the questions have only one answer. The problems were designed to be completed using only pencil and paper; a handheld calculator wasn't strictly necessary. Tukey cautions teachers not to assign too many of the problems, since solving them can be especially laborious for students; he also pleads with teachers not to take off too much credit for minor errors in arithmetic.[*]

Each chapter of *EDA* begins with about a page of introduction and justification for the statistical techniques forthcoming, followed by an index itemizing the chapter's subsections and graphs. Tukey writes important sentences and subtopic headings in bolded font.[†] Some of those subtopics are written in the form of questions; all are printed in mostly lower case. Nearly all chapters end with a section called How far have we come?, which summarizes the important points of the chapter.

To set off the importance of a term or idea, Tukey usually places the term or idea alone on a line. For example, from chapter 14, section 14F: Rematching and strength of relationship, "a comment":

---

[*] Most arithmetic errors, in Tukey's view, were caused by failing to note or mistakenly flipping the signs of quantities. As a fix, he recommends circling negative values.

[†] He implores readers to employ bolding in graphs and other displays made by hand. Such bolding can take the form of the use of multiple colors of ink or even pen ink brought into relief by pencil figures. Seizing the reader's eyes must always be a paramount goal of displays, argues Tukey.

In most cases, we expect to find the ends of the

actual middle

"somewhere between"—either between the most positive trace and the horizontal median OR between the horizontal median and the most negative trace.

Tukey often inserts parentheticals under the guise of these sorts of "a comment" subsections; such "comments" mostly center on elucidating procedures rather than on clarifying concepts.

The orange book overflows with graphs, which are called "exhibits." Most of them have the appearance of being drawn by hand—obviously furthering a key theme of the book: that of the importance of constructing pictures to visualize data sets. (In fact, the pictures were all drawn with straightedge and pen.) The book is also packed with tables of numbers corresponding to a wide variety of real-world situations as well as some suited for mathematical conversions. Most of the formulas Tukey uses in *EDA*, such as the slope equation of a line, are usually not too complex to work through by hand. Occasionally more complicated formulas, usually involving logarithms and square roots, take center stage, especially when dealing with large counts of data; in those cases, Tukey offers the reader some calculation tricks, even describing how to employ a slide rule.[*]

A variety of characters and symbols are used throughout the text as well. For instance, a "*" represents a "place filler" (e.g., 5322**** could be any number between 53220000 and 53229999; these place fillers help to counteract false precision); a "#" stands for a "count" (the frequency of some category); a ">" connotes a "skip mean" (essentially, the arithmetic average of two numbers, used in place of them in order to smooth data); and alphanumeric characters, like "h" for "and a half" (so 6.5 becomes 6h, for example), have many special meanings—such as for data coding schemes. There are uppercase letters corresponding to some of the summary measures that Tukey frequently employs when working with batches of data, such as M for the median, H for the hinges, and E for the eighths.[†] Much ink is spilled on rounding, "cutting" (chopping off

---

[*] See *EDA* chapter 15, Counter fractions, section 15G: Easy froots and flogs with a slide rule (optional).

[†] Although it is now common practice to summarize a batch of values or a data set by using summary measures like the mean and median, this wasn't always the case. In *The Seven Pillars of Statistical Wisdom*, Stephen Stigler discusses how, prior to the widespread use of the arithmetic mean, a single "good" observation was selected to be representative of a set of values. By the

extra digits),[*] and placeholders. Of course, this is to say nothing of the many neologisms; luckily, a glossary is included at the end of the book to sort through them. Tukey also frequently either prints words in all uppercase or bolds them for emphasis.

Tukey's conversational style in the orange book, though often inviting, can at times be grating and jarring to read; he writes discursively and elliptically, with a strange mix of informality and technical jargon, capped off by the occasional reference to fiction or pop culture (e.g., Linus' security blanket from the *Peanuts* comic strip serves as an analogy to a statistics concept). And it's rare to go more than a couple of sentences in *EDA* without encountering double hyphens, which are meant as a stand in for the long dash (also called the—wait for it—"em dash"). There is also frequent repetition of words. To get a better sense of the style of *EDA*, consider this representative passage, culled nearly at random, from the twentieth chapter, section 20A: Binnings vs. distributions:

> ...Rather more have simple formulas for one or two of the three. Others have not very simple formulas--some of these are quite important--or even quite complex formulas for one or two or three of the triad: representing function, density, or cumulative. This will not bother us here because--at least in analyzing data--we will always do one of two things....[†]

On the first page of the preface, Tukey throws the reader right into the fray: exploratory data analysis is about "understand[ing] what you CAN DO before you learn to measure how WELL you seem to have DONE it." Stated differently: don't count your chickens before they hatch. In the preface, Tukey also sets the stage for the many techniques he'll present throughout the book, all designed with one overriding purpose: to hear what the data seem to be telling you. These techniques won't necessarily be easy to understand or to master, but they will mostly involve pared down arithmetic calculations and the drawing of simple graphs to represent data sets, all in an effort to shed facile assumptions and allow deep dives. Isolated examples of real-world data, he writes, will be used to illus-

---

time of Carl Gauss two centuries ago, use of the arithmetic mean was commonplace, with many arguing for its supremacy. Tukey also writes about this idea.

[*] This is in contrast to "cutting values," or numbers that chop a data set into slices. For example, the cuts could be at the locations in a distribution corresponding to the lowest possible scores for earning letter grades of A, B, C, and D.

[†] All remaining passages quoted from *EDA* will use a "—" symbol for the long dash rather than a "--" so stylistic consistency with the rest of this book's text is maintained.

trate the techniques. If the methods we use reduce complexity while also serving as an effective, simpler description of the data and peeling back layers in the process, then we're on the right track. He adds that the pictures of data we construct should be overtly revealing of the unexpected, the surprising, the heretofore hidden. As Heraclitus said, "If we do not expect the unexpected, we will never find it."

That being said, however, we must avoid falling into the confirmatory data analysis trap: beginning our analysis by concluding what generalizations can be made from the sample of interest to the host population. With CDA comes a certain kind of dogmatism that the investigator must work hard to shake; the descriptive statistics that arise from an EDA well practiced can teach the investigator much about the data, too. Tukey signed off on the preface—which was the last section of the book he wrote—on Christmas, 1976.

Tukey took the perspective that assembling *EDA* was the culmination of a multi-year-long research project: gathering together strands of what already existed of EDA, along with stitching in statistical methods out of whole cloth. He packed the book with a great many statistical techniques, not all of which satisfied him; too many of them, he said, were suboptimal or inefficient. At least eighty percent efficiency among all the techniques had been his (unfulfilled) goal.

Despite the inefficiencies, two *EDA* displays in particular caught on like wildfire, whether by "folklore" (as Huber characterizes it) or in print. The first display, called a *stem-and-leaf plot* or simply a stemplot, was especially effective at organizing small sets of data; the stemplot is a frequency distribution with granular detail. By cutting the last digit of each data point—call these digits *leaves*—the remaining digits of the data serve as the *stems* of the plot; leaves are placed in ascending order next to their associated stems, which are arranged to the left of a solid vertical line. Sometimes two- or even three-digit leaves could form effective displays; sometimes stems with place fillers (e.g., 5**) could be useful, too. He even presents iterative methods for checking to make sure that no errors in stemplot construction have been made.

Tukey conceptualized the stemplot as a "simple improvement on an ancient graphic display of distribution information," where numerical digits replaced X's as the leaves. There are a great many variants of Tukey's basic stemplot, like the back-to-back stemplot and the *stretched* (or split) *stemplot*, which allow for the comparison and widening of the scale of data sets, respectively. *Squeezed stem-and-leaf plots* widen the scales even further. Even paired data points can be plotted on a stem-and-leaf plot. Oftentimes, odd effects appear when stemplots are constructed, such as triangular arrangements of leaves that follow what Tukey identifies as the "abnormal law of large numbers."[*] If the number of values in a batch is excessive, then he suggests using the dots-in-a-box method of tallying by tens in place of inserting individual leaves.

The second influential display, called a *box-and-whisker plot* or simply a boxplot,[†] works especially well for large data sets. The boxplot is one of a number of graphs built off of "standard summaries," or numbers or graphs that may summarize data sets well but at the expense of hiding the sort of granular detail that might reveal surprises in data (stemplots can show such surprises). Tukey builds the case for the importance of the boxplot in the second chapter of *EDA*, called Easy summaries—numerical and graphical.

First, he says, it makes sense to consider the extremes and the median as critical values in any batch of data; from there, he discusses various methods of "ranking" values, introducing a new term called the *depth*, which is the least rank (the placement or location) of a data point. There are "interpolated ranks" as well. But the median and the extremes by themselves don't provide the investigator with enough information; hence, we need to find the *5-number summary*[‡] of a data set: the minimum, median, maximum, and the first and third quartiles, which are the medians of the lower and upper halves of the data set, respectively; instead of quartiles, Tukey calls them *hinges*, which are obtained effectively in the same way and are easy to calculate by hand.

Why be restricted to only five numbers? Tukey subdivides data sets even further in *EDA*: by halving into eighths and sixteenths, resulting in 7-number and 9-number summaries, respectively. The data analyst can continue halving, ad infinitum, if deemed necessary.

Antecedents of the 5-number summary were present in a 1949 unpublished paper of Tukey's. Look even further back in the statistical literature, however, and you'll find a similar idea in the work of British statistician and economist Arthur Bowley at the turn of the last century. Arthur Lyon Bowley, born in 1869 in Bristol, England, wrote one of the first statistics textbooks: *An Elementary Manual of Statistics* (1909). In the book, he details a type of 7-number summary:

---

[*] He implies that he didn't coin this term. Recall that the (non-abnormal) law of large numbers, by the way, is a key probabilistic idea: as a process is conducted more and more times, the empirical (experimental) probability of the process converges to the theoretical (true) probability.

[†] "Boxplot" is consistently written out by Tukey in a two-word, non-concatenated form: "box plot."

[‡] Most, but not all, of the time, Tukey writes the number 5 in place of the word five, as in "5-number summary" instead of "five-number summary." The latter form is now more commonly used.

Suppose we wish to test the knowledge of a large class of students (say 100). We might by some very simple examination, or by consulting the teacher, place them roughly in order of intelligence, and then examine in detail, say Nos. 1, 10, 25, 50, 75, 90, 100 (the maximum and minimum, median, quartiles and two deciles). Thus a good estimate could quickly be obtained, and the relative ability of two similar classes quickly judged. [A footnote to this paragraph reads in part, "The deciles are the values which divide a group into ten equal parts, in the same way as the quartiles divide it into 4."]

Bowley offered up graphical displays similar to stemplots as well but, according to Spyros Missiakoulis of Hellenic Open University, the Greek writer Phlegon produced a primitive stem-and-leaf display almost two thousand years ago in his book *On Long-lived Persons.**

The 5-number summary, Tukey explains, can be organized in tabular form into a rectangular arrangement called a *letter-value display*, which denotes the sample size of the batch and the depths (respective locations) of the median and hinges as well. By comparing the depths of the median, the hinges, and the extremes in a letter-value display, the investigator can get a sense of the shape of the distribution (e.g., is it positively skewed, with a tail on the right? Or vice versa? Or is it symmetrical?). In addition, measures of spread such as the range (the distance between the extremes) and measures of center such as the *trimeans* (similar to the median, but that take into account the hinges) can be easily obtained from the letter-value display.

The letter-value display leads us naturally to the boxplot, which plots the 5-number summary of a data set. When making such graphical plots, Tukey recommends using tracing paper or acetate for an overhead and slipping a page of graph paper underneath while drawing. In fact, Tukey spends paragraph after paragraph in *EDA* talking about the characteristics of various types of graph paper, akin to an oenophile painstakingly recounting the qualities of certain wines. To construct a boxplot, "We draw a long, thinnish box that stretches from hinge to hinge, crossing it with a bar at the median," Tukey writes. "Then we draw a 'whisker' from each end of the box to the corresponding extreme." This is currently termed a "skeletal boxplot"; Tukey referred to it as a *free-form box-and-whisker plot.* Boxplots can also be made to highlight some of the values at the extremes (not just the minimum and maximum points), by simply extending the whiskers to the near-extreme values and plotting and label-

---

* See the article "Phlegon's Stem-and-Leaf Display" (2018) printed in *The American Statistician.*

ing the remaining points beyond the span of the whiskers. From there, it is a short jump to what is now called a "modified boxplot" but what Tukey called a *schematic plot*, which formally demarcates outliers in the data as well. Modified boxplots are sketched as follows: two "boxes" enclose the quartiles and share a side with the median, while the "whiskers" extend from the quartiles to either the maximum values, or the lowest or highest non-outlying values in the data set. (In Tukey's schematic plot, the whiskers are drawn with dashes, each terminating at perpendicular crossbars, unlike with free-form boxplots, in which whiskers were constructed using solid lines.)

"One reason for the box" of a boxplot, Tukey wrote, "was to emphasize the middle half of the distribution, to emphasize 'central clumping.'" A boxplot does nothing to reveal the number of observations in a data set, however, or in any portion of one. Yet side-by-side boxplots (Tukey calls them parallel schematic plots) could be especially effective at comparing batches, as Tukey demonstrates in *EDA* with data relaying the densities of nitrogen that were gathered by Lord Rayleigh (birth name: John William Strutt) near the turn of the twentieth century.[*] Tukey also proposed the *wandering schematic plot* in *EDA*, which wrapped hinge and median traces around a convex polygon. No matter the variation, though, boxplots can never offer visual displays of data at the granular level of detail like stemplots or dotplots, which brings us to a key theme of *EDA*: graphs can show generalities or granular detail of a data set, but usually not both.

At first, not everyone was sold on the boxplot. For instance, the Yale statistician Edward Tufte wrote a book, *The Visual Display of Quantitative Information* (1983),[†] that offered a "stripped plot" its place—one that was devoid of the horizontal elements of an up-and-down boxplot. Tukey thought Tufte's plot, unlike his own, didn't give the proper emphasis to certain aspects of a data set, but nonetheless offered a compromise version, complete with wrapped-down ends and dashes and dots, in his 1990 essay "Data-Based Graphics: Visual Display in the Decades to Come." The tremendously detailed justifications offered in this essay for every graphical decision—even considering such factors as how a reader's eyes

---

[*] See exhibit 11 in chapter 2 of *EDA*.

[†] Tukey had a complaint with the book's title, thinking it should have instead been *The Visual Display of Quantitative Phenomena* (which was the name of a past research proposal of Tukey's) or even *The Visual Display of Phenomena with Quantitative Roots*, underscoring Tukey's emphasis on the notion of qualitative phenomena being center stage with numerical information serving merely as supporting cast.

will sweep through the segments of a plot, and for what purpose*—show a careful, deliberate, incisive mind in action despite Tukey having long since passed middle age.

Since *EDA*'s publication, there have been a number of proposed modifications to boxplots, suggested by people besides Tukey, such as revising parameters for the extremes (e.g., box widths proportional to percentiles), drawing the plot as a multicolored solid object instead of with multiple lines, and visually denoting the number of data points in the quantiles (i.e., the equally sized groups, such as quartiles or quintiles) and distribution skewness. With the aid of computers, multidimensional boxplots are also easy to generate.

Though the boxplot is probably Tukey's best-known graphical creation, he certainly didn't invent it out of whole cloth; rather, sometimes Mary Eleanor Spear is awarded credit for its design. In 1952, Spear published a book called *Charting Statistics* that displayed the "range bar": a horizontal line, spanning the length of the range of a data set, intersected by a box with vertical sides at the quartiles along with a vertical bar denoting the placement of the median. Stated differently, the range bar was a proto-skeletal boxplot. Though Tukey greatly refined the idea, hung a series of neologisms on it, and brought it into widespread use, he is more accurately termed the boxplot's midwife rather than its father.[†] Perhaps because of the scope of his many other accomplishments, it is rare to encounter published articles or books that don't give Tukey sole credit for the boxplot's creation.

One source that doesn't attribute boxplots solely to Tukey is *Principles of Medical Statistics* (2002), by the epidemiologist Alvan R. Feinstein. In the book, Feinstein writes, "The 'invention' of the box plot is regularly attributed to John Tukey, who proposed it in 1977, but a similar device, called a *range bar*, was described in 1952 in a text by Mary Spear."

Yet others studying the historical record, most notably the "statistically minded geographer" Nicholas J. Cox of Durham University in England,

---

[*] At the end of the 1980s, William Cleveland wrote in detail of this and other kinds of visual decoding, as well as the ascendance of real-time graphics on computer screens (and their manipulation with then-novel peripherals, like the mouse), related to John Tukey's work in the introduction to the fifth volume of the *Collected Works*. Cleveland also discussed ways in which Tukey's earlier work presaged later dynamic graphical displays (e.g., the PRIM-9 as an antecedent of the "brushing" technique).

[†] You might wonder: If Tukey didn't invent the boxplot, then why does it feature so prominently as a visual motif throughout this book? My justification is that Tukey is so closely tied to this particular display, which he refined and popularized, that its repeated use here is warranted. And most people (incorrectly) believe he invented it anyway.

have traced the antecedents of the boxplot well beyond Mary Eleanor Spear. Cox fingers an article on statistical graphics by Kenneth W. Haemer, published in *The American Statistician* in 1948, as a key source of inspiration for Spear, also noting that "dispersion diagrams [were used] in geography and climatology" as early as the 1930s. More overarching influences stretch back even further—namely, to Francis Galton, who understood the importance of graphical displays of data. Nonetheless, "[d]espite this earlier history, my guess is that box plots would not now be nearly so popular without Tukey's reinvention and propaganda," concludes Cox.

Perhaps the statistician Edward Tufte was harsh on Tukey because he knew that Tukey hadn't invented the boxplot yet had typically received the credit for doing so. Tufte wrote a 1990 article titled "Data-Ink Maximization and Graphical Design" for the journal *Oikos* that reproduced Spear's range bar design and compared it to Tukey's extremely similar boxplot design from the orange book. While this could be a case of (nearly) simultaneous invention, it seems more likely that Tukey encountered Spear's range bar—either in *Charting Statistics* or elsewhere—and the elemental design gained a foothold deep in his subconscious.

For his part, Tukey never mentions Spear or Haemer as inspiration for boxplots in *EDA*. Tukey's feelings toward Tufte, however, were rather equivocal; criticizing Tufte in the fifth volume of the *Collected Works*, he wrote, "Display, including graphics, should be a cause of impact, not merely a testbed of archeology! (Here I part company with my friend Edward Tufte…particularly with his emphasis on reducing 'ink' so long as 'information' is preserved—with no attention at all as to whether *impact* is preserved.)" When someone introduces someone else as a "friend" before launching a broadside (in print or elsewhere), there might be no love lost between them.

CHAPTER TWENTY-SIX

Discovering Surprises in the Data

"The dog did nothing in the night-time.
That was the curious incident."
—Sir Arthur Conan Doyle

In general, EDA is very inductive, very much about "discover[ing] surprises in the data," Tukey wrote, adding that "[e]xploratory data analysis is an attitude, a state of flexibility, a willingness to look for those things we believe are not there, as well as those we believe to be there."

EDA was more than simply a modern way of performing descriptive statistics. Tukey thought of exploratory data analysis as active "detective work," and he said so in *EDA*. "[Tukey] believed the exploration of data is best carried out the way a detective searches for evidence when investigating a crime. Our goal is only to collect and present evidence. Drawing conclusions (or inference) is like the deliberations of the jury," according to Michael Sullivan, author of the textbook *Statistics: Informed Decisions Using Data, 4th ed.* (2013). A nearly-contemporaneous review of *EDA* by the experimental psychologist Russell M. Church relays the same sentiment: "The approach of exploratory data analysis is described [in *EDA*] as being detective in character. It is a search for clues. Some of the clues may be misleading, but some will lead to discoveries."

Indeed, Tukey begins the first chapter of *Exploratory Data Analysis* with this line: "Exploratory data analysis is detective work—numerical detective work—or counting detective work—or graphical detective work." The data analyst, he explains, "needs both tools and understanding." He then compares the unique sets of skills and contexts that detectives in London operate with as compared to detectives in other locales, such as Paris, the American West, or the Australian Outback: one couldn't be easily transposed from one location to another yet still remain equally effective. Nevertheless, there are certain general techniques that all detectives abide by. Likewise, different fields of study may require different mindsets and approaches to the analysis of data, but there are certain "general understandings" that hold true no matter the field.

Tukey sets up the fifth chapter of *EDA*, called Plots of relationships, by discussing one of Arthur Conan Doyle's most famous Sherlock Holmes tales: "The Adventure of Silver Blaze" (1892). In the story, Holmes investigates the murder of a racehorse's trainer as well as the horse's disappearance, all of which took place the night before a race. After conducting his investigation, the master detective realizes something critical: no one that he interviewed had heard the watchdog bark. The Scotland Yard detective asks Holmes, "Is there any other point to which you would wish to draw my attention?"

"To the curious incident of the dog in the night-time," Holmes replies.

"The dog did nothing in the night-time."

"That was the curious incident."

Holmes' brilliant insight that eluded the Scotland Yard detective (and Dr. Watson) was this: The very fact that the dog was silent implied that it knew the killer.

"The moral [of the curious incident] is clear," Tukey explained in *EDA*. "[W]e ought to judge each occurrence against the background of— or a background derived from—other 'nearby' occurrences" in data. That Tukey felt comfortable with a detective-work paradigm is no surprise, considering his love of detective, mystery, and adventure novels: he collected them throughout his life, eventually bequeathing his entire collection to Brown University—some 12,000 books.

The scientist-as-detective, the mathematician-as-scientist: Tukey's wide range of interests, as well as his sheer genius, allowed him to see one process as another, to connect seemingly disparate disciplines, to make mathematical metaphor. Tukey, whose academic background was in chemistry, engaged in a bit of alchemy when he transformed his next love—mathematical statistics—into a science. "Exploratory data analysis can never be the whole story, but nothing else can serve as the foundation stone—as the first step," he wrote. As Peter J. Huber notes, one of Tukey's favorite stories was *The Three Princes of Serendip*, which could serve as a suitable metaphor for his approach: like the eponymous princes who, via clues, sagely piece together the whereabouts of a camel they had never before encountered, Tukey was open to surprises and serendipity while performing data analysis. His mother Adah, over the course of thousands of hours of homeschooling, had instilled in her son an open-mindedness to learning-through-discovery, which served Tukey perfectly as he developed the intuition and methodology behind EDA; in fact, an argument could be made that the development of EDA proceeded along the inductive lines it did precisely *because* of the style of learning Tukey became comfortable with as a child.

There was more to *EDA* than simple data displays, although Tukey's predilection throughout the book was toward the visual (the fewer the grid marks and numbers printed on axes, the better)—since graphs can help give the researcher a sense of the data, especially when performing comparisons—and the notion of comparison, in all its guises, is one of the most important themes running through the book. In general, Tukey said, graphs should be purposely designed "to reveal the unexpected" and "to make the complex easier to perceive," but the statistician should be judicious with his choice of what, precisely, to turn into a visual display. When a simple numerical summary is more than sufficient but a graph is produced nonetheless, what results is overkill—of the whole being less than the sum of its parts. Yet if the simplest possible numerical summary of a data set contains a mountain of numbers, perhaps a cogent graph is needed. "There is no excuse for failing to plot and look (if you have ruled paper)," Tukey wrote. Plotting could take many forms, such as with level lines, level curves, level traces, and middle traces, coupled with sliced co-ordinates. He added that contrary to the old saying, usually attributed to politician Al Smith, that "no matter how thin you slice it, it's still baloney," the choices an investigator makes when constructing the slices affects the resulting traces and regression line.[*]

In *EDA*, Tukey elucidated the overarching purpose of graphs when performing EDA. A visual display must facilitate both in the search for phenomena and the absence thereof, similarly to how a prospector might hunt for gold if he also searched for the absence of gold as well. Graphs must be constructed in such a way as to permit us to see the unexpected. But, Tukey added, "[g]raphs should report the results of careful data analysis—rather than be an attempt to replace it," and no one graph should be expected to reveal everything about a data set. After all, the interpretive qualities of the brain, facilitated by the "picture-examining eye," can adjust for surprises in data. The best graphics have a sense of immediacy—of striking the reader instantaneously with its impact when he "put[s] eye to paper," perhaps even causing him to think differently about the data at hand. Yet if one graph doesn't suffice to communicate the particular phenomena under scrutiny, then using two is preferred.

---

[*] For more, see *EDA* chapter 14, Looking in two or more ways at batches of points.

CHAPTER TWENTY-SEVEN

A Graphical Touch

*"[I]n graphics we use the work of [William] Playfair and Tukey
without citation — indeed often without knowledge of their
contributions, because they are so basic to our understanding
that we cannot easily imagine the world without them."*
— Howard Wainer

The Purdue statistician William S. Cleveland, who worked for Bell Labs early in his career, was instrumental in getting the Wadsworth Publishing Company not only to publish Tukey's *Collected Works*, but to do so with Tukey still in a position to help assemble, comment on, and add additional written responses to the massive project. With the first volume published in 1984, and additional volumes appearing regularly over the next decade, the set of *Collected Works*—containing published and unpublished papers, lectures, and book manuscripts—are a bit of a misnomer, since they hardly feature everything Tukey wrote (e.g., work from the last decade and a half of his life as well as his numerous contributions to robustness are not present). There are a total of eight volumes: two volumes are on time series, two on the philosophy and principles of data analysis, one on graphics, one on mathematical ideas, one on factorial analysis and analysis of variance, and one on multiple comparisons. The complex text layout (in Palatino font) for the *Collected Works* was, unsurprisingly, processed on computers at Bell Labs, running on a UNIX operating system.

Cleveland, swimming in Tukey's work for years, was in a rather unique position to make near-definitive judgments about Tukey's contributions. For instance, he apportioned Tukey the lion's share of credit for the ascendance of graphical methods for data analysis—and especially for almost single-handedly overcoming the "bias against devoting research energy to data display because the methodology of graphics lacks a heavy infusion of formal probabilistic inductive inference, which for many decades had been the sacred banner of statistics," he wrote in 1988. Although some nineteenth century mathematicians, such as Adolphe Quetelet, created graphical displays, it was Karl Pearson, Ronald Fisher,

Jerzy Neyman, and Egon Pearson who tipped the scales toward probabilistic inductive inference (in the form of confidence intervals and hypothesis testing), consequently engendering the "bias" against visual displays of data Cleveland wrote about in the *Collected Works*. Not to say that there were no graphical methods developed in the twentieth century prior to Tukey's synthesis of EDA, but such methods were deemphasized in favor of numerical methods, Cleveland argues, until the pendulum swung back the other way.*

Tukey's graphical displays, not only in *EDA* but elsewhere, receive a thoughtful treatment in the article "Graphical Visions from William Playfair to John Tukey" (1990) by Howard Wainer, a statistician who received his doctorate from Princeton (but not under Tukey). Playfair, born in 1759 in Fife, Scotland, was an engineer and economist who first conjured up statistical displays such as bar charts† and line graphs. Wainer begins his article by noting that modern physicists rarely cite Newton, since his work and results are so woven into the tapestry of the modern world that we take them for granted. "Similarly," Wainer continues, "in graphics we use the work of Playfair and Tukey without citation—indeed often without knowledge of their contributions, because they are so basic to our understanding that we cannot easily imagine the world without them."

Wainer sees three points of agreement with the approaches of Playfair and Tukey. First, the impact of the graphics on the reader must be a consideration. Second, understanding graphs will not always be automatic. To that end, Wainer posits that there are two types of good graphs: a "strongly good graph," which is immediately penetrable to the reader, and a "weakly good graph," which is revealing only if it is understood correctly; as Tukey wrote, "A picture may be worth a thousand words, but it may take a hundred words to do it," meaning that sidebar commentaries, with verbal descriptions explaining the visuals, may be necessary in order to fully flesh-out the meaning behind the graphics. And third, a graph can reveal otherwise non-obvious information: "The greatest value of a graph is when it forces us to see what we never expected," Tukey wrote (quoted

---

* Unfortunately, in volume five of the *Collected Works*, Cleveland pointedly writes that Tukey is to be commended for "inventing a large number of [graphical] methods...[like] box plots, stem-and-leaf diagrams...." However, as discussed previously, Mary Eleanor Spear probably invented boxplots, and Tukey's invention of stemplots is of questionable provenance at best.

† Tukey explored why bar charts retained a high degree of popularity into the late twentieth century. Discounting their geometric truthfulness or their ease at facilitating good numerical estimates from the viewer, he points out the numerous ways that bar chars allow for comparisons: between counts and relative frequencies, among others.

by Wainer).* As Tukey and his fifth cousin, the statistician Paul A. Tukey (who worked for Bell Labs as well), wrote in a joint paper, "There is nothing better than a picture for making you think of questions you had forgotten to ask (even mentally)." Together, they also wrote about the "draftsman's display" and the "window plot." (Tukey's first cousins from his mother's side of the family included Clayton Tasker, who lived in Jekyll Island, Georgia, and Wilder A. Tasker, who lived in New Bern, North Carolina.)

Tukey and Playfair didn't agree on everything. For instance, Tukey maintained that comparing curves on the same chart is typically difficult, resulting in differences between curves being rendered obscure or hard to detect. Playfair didn't hesitate to churn out curve-difference charts, however, such as one on the balance of trade between England and the East Indies. And Tukey may have loved apple pie at breakfast, but he was not sold on pie charts, created by Playfair in the early 1800s but later made famous by Florence Nightingale's mortality studies of the Crimean War; she had improved upon a circular plot of William Farr's, which tracked by month the devastating cholera epidemic in mid-eighteenth-century England, by packing together wedges whose areas corresponded to mortality data. "There is no data that can be displayed in a pie chart, that cannot be displayed BETTER in some other type of chart," Tukey sneered.

Tukey also put forth maxims about graphics, summarized eloquently by Wainer, that bear mentioning. First, the purpose behind the construction of a particular graphical display needs to be clear.

Second, the graphical display shouldn't merely be a rehash of the data points themselves; "'Reading off numbers' is NOT the point of a graphic," Tukey wrote (quoted by Wainer).† "If we want numbers, we can do

---

* Tukey was writing this at a hinge moment in the history of computer hardware—when complex graphics not only became feasible but also relatively easy for the non-programmer to generate. Hence, he recommends that programs displaying statistical graphs hew closely to WYSIWYG (what you see is what you get) between what's shown on the monitor and what's output on the printer.

† When Tukey wrote a word entirely in capital letters, it was usually for reasons of emphasis; sometimes, however, he would use uppercase in place of a mathematical symbol. For instance: "given = fit PLUS residual," which describes the relationship between an actual value and the associated predicted value in a data set that helps to classify the behavior of points in a plot. "Notice that we have pictured 'plus' by writing it out in capital letters—thus giving it its proper emphasis instead of using a single unobtrusive symbol." Another example: "max MINUS min." Too often, Tukey explained, nonmathematicians might skim over or not even notice the subscripts or the symbols of mathematical operations. He also was quick to add psychological theory as

better by...going to a conventional table." After all, numbers are only the supporting cast for the central actors in the drama: qualitative phenomena.

Third, complex computation should serve as support for a graphical display, not the other way around; we can't fall into the "tabula rasa fallacy" trap, which puts the onus on the visual display to reveal everything in the data; such displays should instead complement the computation.

Fourth, adding color to graphs is generally unhelpful, redundant, or even distracting because graphs can easily become unbalanced visually.[*] In general, we should seek to avoid cluttered visuals (Tukey lists a number of germane recommendations, such as turning one picture into two if necessary as well as avoiding shapes that are open, or unconnected), even, if necessary, stealing ideas from contemporary graphic designers like Jacques Bertin, a French cartographer whose work (such as the 1967 book *Semiology of Graphics: Diagrams, Networks, Maps*) Tukey tremendously respected, to those as far back as Leonardo da Vinci. Working with the PRIM-9 graphical display system had taught Tukey that when constructing graphics, one or two iterations is not enough; rather, as many as forty to fifty versions may be required to achieve the desired results.

Fifth, and perhaps most important, the "absence of phenomena is itself a phenomenon!" To illustrate this notion, Wainer uses the example of Abraham Wald's research during World War II. Wald's key contribution during the war involved the analysis of American fighter planes that returned to base littered with bullet holes. When the Statistical Research Group was asked where the airplane armor should be installed—figuring that the areas of the plane that looked like Swiss cheese, such as the fuselage, were being targeted the most with artillery—Wald had an insight: the planes that needed to be examined weren't the ones that returned safely, but the ones that were shot down. Interestingly, the planes that returned had few bullet holes near their engines, leading Wald to suggest that the missing planes—the ones that didn't return—were hit with artillery fire around their engines, which were therefore vulnerable.

---

justification, noting that capitalization forces readers to slow down their mental processing just enough to absorb additional information.

[*] Texas Instruments would seem to disagree with Tukey: they added color displays to their popular series of TI-84 graphing calculators several years ago, allowing for color-coded boxplots.

CHAPTER TWENTY-EIGHT

Hunting for Wild Shots

"It is easier to carry a slide rule than a desk computer,
to say nothing of a large computer."
—John Tukey

I n *Novum Organum*, Francis Bacon wrote, "For whoever knows the
ways of Nature will more easily notice her deviations; and, on the
other hand, whoever knows her deviations will more accurately describe her ways." Although Tukey was hardly the first mathematician to
formally lay out a procedure to identify these "deviations," or outliers, in
data—nineteenth century mathematicians such as William Chauvenet
(called Chauvenet's criterion), and Benjamin Peirce[*] and his son, Charles
Sanders Peirce (called Peirce's criterion), did so, as did mathematicians in
the twentieth century, like Frank E. Grubbs (called Grubbs' test for outliers)—Tukey's unique approach didn't require assumptions about the underlying population distribution. Past approaches usually hinged, one way
or another, on the assumption of population normality. But "REAL
DATA OFTEN FAIL to be Gaussian [normally distributed] IN MANY
WAYS," Tukey and Brillinger wrote in a paper (their capitalization, obviously done for emphasis).

The search for outliers required a model. What Tukey first termed *wild
shots* (he interchanged the term with "outliers," "blunders," "large deviations," and "spotty data") fifteen years earlier in FoDA became what is
today informally referred to as the "outlier test."[†] He was especially influ-

---

[*] Stephen Stigler writes that Benjamin Peirce, "In 1852[,] published the first
significance test designed to tell an investigator whether an outlier should be
rejected…. The test, based on a likelihood ratio type of argument, had the
distinction of producing an international debate on the wisdom of such ac-
tions…."

[†] Tukey's methodical look at "spotty data" in FoDA bears little resemblance
to his approach in *EDA*, since in the former he assumes a host population
whereas in the latter he doesn't. Plus, the intended audience for each work is
different—he expects those reading FoDA will have a strong mathematics
background whereas such background knowledge is optional for *EDA*.

enced in this by Winsor: by the time Tukey met him in 1941, Winsor "had already developed a clear and individual philosophy about the proper treatment of apparent 'wild shots.'" Winsor didn't excise the outliers from a data set. Rather, he replaced the outlying values by their nearest non-outlying values. Tukey described this technique as Winsorizing a data set, or simply as Winsorization. In FoDA, Tukey also notes that since outlying data points may in fact reveal useful information, outputs and plots of data should come in two varieties: those with "cleaned-up observations," and those with the outliers left intact.

Tukey's outlier test has uses beyond simply the construction of schematic plots; the notion of flagging for outliers was to invite second looks rather than to summarily disregard such data points. (In *EDA*, Tukey refrained from using the word "outlier.") He conjured up *fences* to capture appropriate bounds for outliers; data more than 1.5 times the *H-spread* (hinge-spread, or distance between the hinges; effectively the same as the interquartile range, which is the distance between the first and third quartiles) constituted the *inner fences*,* whereas data more than 3 times the H-spread formed the *outer fences*. Values beyond an outer fence were classified as "far out"; values lying only outside a fence were "outside"; values barely inside the inner fences were termed "adjacent." A tabular form of display, called a *fenced letter display*, summarized the fences and outside values of a batch. And, on a schematic plot, far out values (i.e., the extreme outliers) would be labeled in uppercase letters, while outside values (i.e., not-too-extreme outliers) would be labeled in lowercase.

But where did these multiplier values of 1.5 and 3.0, designated by the letter *k* in *EDA*, originate from? David Hoaglin explains:

> John did not arrive at 1.5 and 3.0 by setting up some sort of theoretical calculation. That step came later, as a form of evaluation, when we were working on *UREDA* [*Understanding Robust and Exploratory Data Analysis* by Tukey, Hoaglin, and Mosteller, published in 1983). Boris Iglewicz [a Temple University biostatistician, who was a member of the institution's statistics department since 1969] proposed that we study the performance of the fences for data from the Gaussian [normal] and some heavier-tailed distributions.

In the 1970 (pre-publication) version of *EDA*, Tukey had originally proposed *k* values of 1.0 (called *side values*) and 1.5 (called *three-halves values*). The constants evolved to the now-familiar 1.5 and 3.0 by the 1977 pub-

---

* Note that in "Data-Based Graphics: Visual Display in the Decades to Come" published thirteen years after *EDA*, Tukey writes that the inner fences are "defined to fall at '2.5 × one hinge MINUS 1.5 × the other hinge')."

lished version of *EDA*. For convenience, Tukey coined a special name for 1.5 multiplied by the H-spread: the *step*.

Besides outlier tests, there were a number of other EDA techniques designed to needle and poke and prod at data, all in an inductive, experimental, empirical manner, as free as possible from assumptions about distributions and the like. There is the somewhat nebulous concept of *resistance*, which more or less refers to statistical measures that are not affected by outliers or, equivalently stated, an insensitivity to small sample changes; resistance is "the property of being little influenced by changes, possibly large, in a small fraction of the data," as Tukey wrote in "Data Analysis: History and Prospects" (1984). For instance, the mean is attracted to outliers in data—it is pulled toward them—so the mean would not be considered a resistant measure. But the median, which is found in the middle of a data set (if the data are in order), is considered resistant, since outliers, if they exist, would be located at the extremes, not the middle. Likewise, the interquartile range is resistant, while the range—the distance between the minimum and maximum data points—is not resistant, since the minimum and/or maximum could be outliers themselves. Hoaglin defines resistance as "insensitivity to localized misbehavior," and outliers certainly fall under the rubric of "misbehavior."

"Exploratory data analysis isolates patterns and features of the data and reveals these forcefully to the analyst." Toward that end, *EDA* also spills ink on residuals, an essential element of model diagnostics. In a 1963 article coauthored with brother-in-law Frank Anscombe, Tukey claims that "[p]robably the single most important reason for calculating residuals is to detect outliers, observations that have such large residuals, in comparison with most of the others, as to suggest that they ought to be treated specially." In *EDA*, Tukey mathematically expresses residuals as follows:

$$\text{residual} = \text{given value MINUS summary value}$$

or, more specifically,

$$\text{data} = \text{fit PLUS residuals}$$

The "summary value" of a univariate quantitative data set[*] might be, for instance, a measure of center like the mean or median—essentially, any

---

[*] The collection of numerical data of a single variable from individuals. For example: the weights of students in a class. Univariate data can be plotted using a histogram, a boxplot, a stemplot, or a dotplot.

measurement that neatly summarizes the batch. Residuals can be calculated off of two-way tables as well.

With bivariate quantitative data sets,* viewing plots of residuals—or differentials between the actual paired data points and the predictions, or fits, of those same paired data points—can help data analysts determine if the mathematical model being fit to the data (e.g., linear, exponential, and the like) is, in fact, a good fit. If the fit is poor, though, then *scale transformations* of the data set may help; such transformations—Tukey called them *re-expressions*, which he decided was the "safer term"†—whether they be power, logarithmic, or square root, in effect restate paired data on a different scale without changing the inherent relationship between the data points, thus (hopefully) allowing for more fruitful analysis and effective prediction. "If—often by so simple a change as taking square roots, or logarithms—we can eliminate most of these nonlinearities by a more appropriate choice," he explained, "we will be able to see much more deeply in these phenomena…." In a book review of *EDA*, James R. Beniger explains that "[f]or Tukey, all scales—even counts—are completely arbitrary, and choosing a scale is like purchasing dime store eyeglasses: you are free to try out several, and to take the ones that help you best to see."

Among the suggested re-expressions, logarithms (abbreviated simply as "logs") tend to be the most useful in the widest variety of situations,‡ while square roots tend also to be effective. For instance, in *EDA* Tukey reproduces a data set obtained from early studies of radioactivity completed by Stefan Meyer and Egon von Schweidler; he straightens out plots

---

* The collection of numerical data of two variables from individuals. For example: the heights and weights of students in a class. Bivariate data can be plotted using a scatterplot, where the explanatory/factor variable (the predictor) lies on the horizontal axis and the response variable (the predicted) on the vertical axis.

† Tukey believed that the term "re-expression," unlike "transformation," had the built-in implication of an apology coupled with a recognition that a redo—a re-transformation—must be in order.

‡ Taking a logarithm is the mathematical inverse of exponentiation. When the base of a logarithm is not given, we assume that the logarithm is base 10 (termed a "common logarithm"). Note that Tukey goes out of his way in *EDA* to make a key point: since logs turn multiplication into addition, and addition is always preferable to multiplication because of its simplicity (remember: all techniques in *EDA* were designed to be performed by hand), logs help us avoid having to make multiplicative comparisons (e.g., the circumference of Jenna's head is half that of her little sister Carolyn's: take the log of both of their circumferences, and then adjust the results additively for the purposes of easy comparison).

of radioactivity versus time by taking logarithms of the data. Another example in *EDA* is of U.S. population data, obtained from the U.S. Census between 1800 and 1950,[*] which requires a two-part transformation: from 1800 to 1870, a logarithm is taken of the population counts to straighten out the data, while for 1870 to 1950, no transformation is necessary (when no transformation is applied, this is termed *identity*). Checking the slopes of the lines passing through several pairs of points of paired data clearly reveal radical differences in the shape of the plot through time.[†] As Karen Kafadar notes, Tukey called such multipart transformations *hybrid re-expressions*. A number of other paired quantitative data sets, such as distance to stop versus speed of automobiles and vapor pressure of water versus temperature, are also given a thorough treatment in *EDA*, with Tukey methodically documenting his reasoning for each re-expression (whether the transformation is applied to the explanatory variable, the response variable, or both).[‡]

But what could serve as the motivation behind transforming nonlinear data into a more linear form? Tukey presents three reasons, as recapitulated by experimental psychologist Russell M. Church: "(a) A transformation may be selected to produce a symmetrical distribution, (b) it may increase the similarity of the spread of different sets of numbers, and (c) it may straighten out a line." Some data sets are difficult to compare without transforming them first, such as atomic weights of two elements (e.g., see exhibit 6 of the third chapter of *EDA*). Deciding which transformations to implement in order to "straighten" the data out (i.e., linearize the data) is made somewhat systematic by utilizing *Tukey's ladder*: go "up" the ladder for power functions (e.g., squaring, cubing, and so on) or go "down" the ladder for logarithms (represented as the zeroth power) followed by reciprocal power functions. Chapter 3 of *EDA* presents the shapes of all these simple functions graphed on the same coordinate axes. Whether to travel up or down Tukey's ladder is largely determined by the shape of the scatterplot (which displays the paired data on a coordinate axis): "move on the ladder of expressions in the direction in which the curve bulges," Tukey instructs, and *EDA* includes an exhibit displaying four quadrants, with differently oriented "curve bulges" in each of them (e.g., "hollow upward," "hollow downward," and so forth) along with ladder-traveling instructions contained within each quadrant. Neverthe-

---

[*] Variations in population counts seen in the U.S. Census, especially the farther back in time one goes, may be due more to data collection methods than to actual population change.

[†] See *EDA* chapter 5, Plots of relationship, as well as the start of chapter 6, Straightening out plots (using three points), for the full details.

[‡] Refer to *EDA* chapter 6, Straightening out plots (using three points).

less, as Church notes, "[T]here are complex relationships that cannot be transformed into a straight line" due to the variability inherent in real-world data, no matter what mathematical transformations are performed—even accounting for the more exotic ones on offer in *EDA* such as *folded square roots*.

So, in summary: Raw data frequently didn't conform to the stringent assumptions required for conventional, CDA-style statistical inference, so transforming these data might help with satisfying the conditions necessary for inference, might assist in "bending the data nearer the Procrustean bed of the assumptions underlying conventional analyses," Tukey said. The "Procrustean bed" reference was a not-so-oblique reminder of Tukey's disdain for rigid statistical models, for putting the mathematical theory in front of the statistical practice akin to the proverbial cart being placed before the horse. Of course, not all paired data could be straightened out by climbing or descending the ladder, at which point applying *smoothing* methods came into play and

$$data = fit\ PLUS\ residuals$$

got reworked, becoming

$$given\ data = smooth\ PLUS\ rough$$

Techniques such as smoothing and *resmoothing*, which replace scattered data points with smooth curves by using *smoothers* (i.e., smoothing data with such techniques as running medians and iterated smoothing, among others), and the median polish, which is an iterative robust process performed on data in two-way tables, were also integral parts of *EDA*. In fact, a significant portion of *EDA* deals with *median smoothers*, like a *3R* or a *3RSS* or a *3RSR* or even a *3RS3R* (i.e., running medians of limit length 3, iterated until convergence, splitting of horizontal stretches of limit length 2 or 3). There was even a *3RSSH3RSSH3!*[*] And if a smoother was essentially being applied twice, like *3RSS,twice*, this was termed *twicing*. Tukey also coined the term *hanning* (verb: to *hann*), a smoothing procedure that used simple arithmetic, naming it after the Austrian meteorologist Julius von Hann, who made a habit out of smoothing weather data.[†]

In general, *smooths* could be made even smoother by a bit more polishing, all in an effort for readers not to be distracted by *little* or *minor wiggles*

---

[*] See *EDA* chapter 7, Smoothing sequences.
[†] Von Hann "often used 1/4, 1/2, 1/4 to smooth meteorological series," Tukey wrote. Interestingly, these are the same values that were used by Richard Hamming to smooth Budenbom's radar tracking data.

in displays—which could be counteracted by *blurring the smooth*—and which should have an impact built on immediacy, inescapability, and *interocularity*. Sometimes smoothing across a "break" (area of discontinuity) made sense; other times, if the investigator perceived the "break" to be a significant discontinuity in the data, smoothing was to be completed in chunks called *broken smooths*.

As was his wont, Tukey introduced scads of new vocabulary words for the reader to digest in *EDA*. Besides hinges and fences and sensitivity curves, there were *flogs* (or "folded logarithms," used for graphing proportions) and *fflogs* (doubly folded logarithms) and *batches* (used in place of "samples," although they weren't quite the same thing: a batch of values had some sort of commonality) and *froots* (or "folded square roots"), as well as graphical procedures like *untilting*, to consider as well. Even as early as the original, 1970 Xeroxed edition of *EDA*, the *sensitivity curve*, a type of jackknife sampling procedure, appeared.

And there was so much more to *EDA*. For instance, tables displaying data in tabular form, such as two-way tables which present two qualitative (categorical) variables simultaneously, featured prominently,[*] as did the *bag plots* which display the bivariate median in bivariate quantitate data. There were *forget-it plots*, where the horizontal coordinates served to straighten out all of the lines so the reader could focus in only on the vertical information, rather than anything horizontal. There were also *rootograms*, similar to histograms[†] except that the square roots of the frequencies, rather than the frequencies themselves, are employed.[‡] (Unsurprising that he fashioned the rootogram, since Tukey always urged his readers to "first reach for some kind of square root" whenever dealing with counts from a data set.) And there was the *completed rank*, or *c'rank*, which took as its point of departure Zipf's law, originated by the linguist George Kings-

---

[*] See, for instance, *EDA* chapter 10, Using two-way analysis, where data in two-way tables are analyzed using residuals (with the median as the summary value) in the form of row-PLUS-column and row-TIMES-column analyses, with single vertical bars (|) and double vertical bars (||) demarcating counts from medians and residuals, respectively. Tukey abbreviates the word "effect" as *eff* when examining row and column effects: as in, *row eff* and *col eff*. Also, two-way plots of residuals are coded, using seven symbols to categorize the magnitude of each residual, allowing for quick visual judgments. Tukey even details the ins and outs of three- and more-way tables, too.

[†] Histograms are bar charts of quantitative, rather than qualitative, data. A histogram separates a range of values into identically sized groups, displaying the frequency or percentage of data points falling into each group.

[‡] Rootograms even came in several varieties, such as *hanging rootograms* and *suspended rootograms*.

ley Zipf to predict the frequency of words in print, but refined and expanded with *half-octave* calculations as well as displays such as *octave bins*.

The final chapter of the book, called Postscript, is divided into several parts: a discussion of the computerization of statistical techniques and purposeful omissions of *EDA*, rounded out with an executive summary of topics. The most interesting section is 21A: Our relationship to the computer. Here, Tukey memorably calls society's shift to computerization "culturally rapid but humanly slow," calling to mind Alvin Toffler's notion of "future shock": rapid change in an incredibly compressed timeframe. Tukey went from using a hand-crank desk calculator[*] to assisting von Neumann "a little" (more than a little—he was being humble in *EDA*) on his embryonic computer ten years later. Yet even by 1962, in FoDA, Tukey wasn't sold on the power of computerization, at least in statistics; he downplayed its uses, explaining that, for the most part, the computer, though important, has not been vital.[†] In addition, he wrote of the machine's lack of convenience—"It is easier to carry a slide rule than a desk computer, to say nothing of a large computer," he scoffed—and, though he wasn't opposed to the automation of "standardizable" statistical procedures for laypeople performing data analysis per se, he felt that such types of automation could be decoupled from computerized automation, as evidenced by the fact that he didn't even mention computers when discussing the idea of automated examination of data. Five years after FoDA, at a conference at the University of Wisconsin in Madison, Tukey's equivocation on the role of computers in statistics was on full display. For evidence of this, look no further than the title of his talk: "Is Statistics Comput*ing* Science?" If he had to ask…

In *EDA*, Tukey defends his strictly paper-and-pen-and-pencil approach by noting that the techniques can all be performed by hand regardless, mostly without the need even for a handheld calculator; in addition, he writes, the computing power necessary to do a serviceable job at statistics wasn't widely available regardless, and certainly unavailable to the layperson. Remember, he wrote *EDA* more or less simultaneously while doing work on the PRIM-9 and its successors, so, in Tukey's mind, any useful manipulation of data using computers was far from ready for

---

[*] Which Tukey had in common with Ronald Fisher. According to Besse Day, who worked with Fisher for over a year, "[A]ll he [Fisher] had learned he had learned over the (then hand-cranked) calculating machine."

[†] For instance, he details Hotelling's T^2 procedure, which requires an arithmetically complex matrix inversion. If one has access to a computer to perform the mathematical inversion, great; if not, there are a set of "quick" alternative procedures performable by hand. Lacking a computer won't stop the statistician dead in his tracks. He also writes of the inevitability of more and more graphs being "drawn" by computers.

home use. The PRIM-9 was bulky, specialized equipment; Tukey likely couldn't conceive of anything compact and powerful enough to do the job, despite the fact that by 1977, the year of *EDA*'s publication, the home computer revolution was afoot. *Byte* magazine famously called the three major plug-and-play computer releases of that year the "Trinity": the Tandy TRS-80 Model I, the Apple II, and the Commodore PET, all of which were more than capable of statistical manipulation, courtesy of a bit of creative software design, of course. But writing software wasn't in Tukey's wheelhouse—far from it. Though he paid some lip service to the background importance of computers in the writing of *EDA*, the biggest misstep in this otherwise brilliant book is its failure to anticipate how much the practice of statistics would change due to the ubiquity of computers. Even when game planning what a second book on exploratory data analysis might look like in the Postscript, Tukey details refinements of techniques already presented in *EDA*, only halfheartedly suggesting that perhaps a computer program might assist in calculations or in the construction of scatter diagrams.

Paul Velleman notes that when *EDA* was first published, no commercial statistics software used the words "data analysis" in promotional materials. But twenty years later, such desktop software advertised "data analysis" up front and center as a key selling point. Many of the methods in *EDA* had become the needs of users of statistics software, in spite of Tukey's intentions. Arthur P. Dempster concurs with Velleman, explaining that although "little attention [is] paid in his writing to the increasing importance of massive computing power in exploring data, and he has little to say about the role of big models that appear to be necessary if complex phenomena are to be understood as a whole," Tukey's "simple tools…survive especially through widely used plots provided in statistical software packages." The legacy of *EDA* largely persists in the one place Tukey didn't anticipate it would: the computer.

Before moving on, let us pause to note some ironies. Tukey's statistical intuition was second to none, and he railed against the programmatic and cookbook-like uses of CDA-style inference—yet he fashioned tools in *EDA* that were rather easily reducible to computer algorithms. Tukey foresaw the statistical uses of computing, such as in his 1964 ASA speech, where he even threatened to write a statistics computing language himself—yet his most famous book encouraged hand calculations to the exclusion of all else. Tukey was a pioneer in statistical graphics and computing in general, with the development of the PRIM-9 and the FFT algorithm among his greatest accomplishments—yet in daily life he was practically a luddite, making sure to avoid computers and acquiescing to "program" in pseudo-FORTRAN only if absolutely necessary. The cognitive dissonances are overwhelming.

CHAPTER TWENTY-NINE

Critical Reaction to *EDA*

"[EDA] is a tragic failure, and the failure is major, not minor."
— Andrew S. C. Ehrenberg

Because he mostly failed to anticipate the imminent computerization of statistics, thinking it way beyond the horizon if it were to even happen at all, Tukey consciously made every effort to keep the calculations in *EDA* as simple as possible, using basic arithmetic (even lines could be "added" and "subtracted"). To that end, the notion of "halving"—of employing repeated divisions by two in a variety of circumstances—frequently came into play. Order statistics such as medians, and intermediate order statistics obtained by halving and then having again, featured prominently. The 5-number summary is a direct result of the idea of halving: a batch containing two extremes is chopped into two at the spot of the median, and then these halves are halved again, resulting in the hinges (quartiles). If one wanted to continue halving the halves, one could do so.

Many EDA techniques, such as the iterative procedures, are tedious to do by hand—despite Tukey's claims in *EDA* that calculations only require a straight edge, tracing paper, a set of index cards, a four-color pen, maybe a pencil (to contrast with pen ink, if only a single-color pen is available), and some graph paper, but no calculator or computer—are a natural fit for computer algorithms and thus rapidly became standard on a variety of statistics software, including on then-nascent graphing calculators (e.g., boxplot displays on first generation Texas Instruments graphing calculators). Tukey would find ways to shed as many calculations as possible; consider the *lomedian* as an example. Whereas the classical median is obtained in one step for an odd number of values in a batch—it's simply the middle number (when the data are ordered)—an even number of numbers necessitates finding the arithmetic average of the middle two data points. The lomedian works identically to the classical median in the case of a batch with an odd number of values; if there are an even number of data points in the batch, however, the lesser of the middle two is taken—and therefore no averaging is required.

Yet despite the shortcuts and the rules of thumb, computers were best suited to performing the calculations, but Tukey wasn't particularly satisfied with a machine-driven approach to EDA. "I know of no large machine installation whose operations are adapted to the basic step-by-step character of most data analysis," Tukey complained, "in which most answers coming out of the machine will, after human consideration, return to the machine for further processing." To begin remedying this, the Princeton statistics department installed a Digital Equipment Corporation PDP 11-40 computer on-site, with Michael Godfrey implementing EDA as a software package called SNAP-IEDA. The pro-computation approach to statistics—statistics being "essentially a branch of Applied Mathematics," in the words of Ronald Fisher—was decades ahead of the data-mining explosion of the 2000s, which from the start had EDA's fingerprints all over it, even if the response to *EDA* at the time of its publication was a mixed bag.

Take a book review for the *Journal of the Royal Statistical Society* penned by the British statistician Andrew S. C. Ehrenberg, for example. While praising the "good points" in the book, such as the stem-and-leaf display, he also labels *EDA* "a tragic failure, and the failure is major, not minor. The book seems misconceived in its expository style"—as such, it is "impossible to dip into," he adds—"in much of its contents, and in its general aim, i.e., in the idea of exploratory data analysis as such." Ehrenberg is put off by Tukey's approach to CDA as well: "He pays lip-service to inference ('One of the great intellectual products of our century'), but nowhere suggests how one might get on to that stage of analysis (in those cases where it might be needed)." He also calls many of the techniques in *EDA* "self-indulgent inventions still waiting to be seriously tested." He vociferously complains about the tedious calculations that need to be completed in order to obtain many of the summary measures, even questioning the efficacy of certain types of these measures that use medians—since the median is a one-off, unable to be utilized when aggregating multiple data sets. Most tellingly, Ehrenberg mostly dismisses EDA entirely, calling the Tukey approach to EDA "bunk," because the overwhelming majority of the time when we analyze data sets, we are consciously or subconsciously comparing them to similar such data sets we've already encountered from whatever source population they happen to have come from. Thus, practically, most of the time we are engaging in "comparative data analysis," Ehrenberg maintains, not exploratory (read: first time seeing) data analysis. EDA is a tabula rasa approach to data, which is an exceedingly rare situation to find oneself in—unless one is a "dilettante or statistical consultant."

In contrast, Jeffrey B. Birch from the Virginia Polytechnic Institute, who wrote a review of *EDA* for the *Journal of the American Statistical Asso-*

ciation, saw things quite differently. The book was "worth the wait," he begins the article, replete with examples and explanations of techniques that "should appeal to those with limited formal training in statistics." Birch, unlike Ehrenberg, praises Tukey's many uses for the median because of the measure's robustness and resistance to outlying values. Birch also singles out *EDA*'s treatment of bivariate situations, such as with fits, residuals, and re-expressions, as especially ingenious. "*EDA*," he concludes "contains many worthwhile techniques that could be a valuable addition to every applied statistician's tool box."

What of non-statisticians in fields like the social sciences? How did they greet *EDA*? "There is little doubt that [*EDA*] is an important book," writes Charles W. Mueller, an associate professor of sociology at the University of Iowa. "It is an innovative approach to descriptive statistics, an area which has been given a back seat for some time by both instructors of statistics and social science researchers." Unfortunately, however, "most researchers trained in 'traditional' statistics will find the book difficult and frustrating reading." Therefore, "the contents of the book should be communicated to social science researchers, but the book itself will not do the trick for the majority of researchers."

In *Contemporary Sociology*, James R. Beniger of Berkeley also speaks positively of *EDA*. "Even beyond technique and strategy," he explains,

> much of the book's appeal lies in its implicit challenge to prevailing statistical fashion.... *Exploratory Data Analysis* is a call for statisticians to return to their roots in nineteenth century social statistics, to a time when "statisticians only explored," meaning simply "looking at data to see what it seems to say."

Beniger also relays this interesting fact: "Upon formal publication last spring, *Exploratory Data Analysis* had already been acknowledged and cited more often than are most books during their entire lifetimes in print."

Not everyone found the book painful or difficult to read. Beniger wrote that Tukey's style is "positively charming" and the illustrations especially effective at "capturing the simple joy of statistical discovery." John F. Osborn of the London School of Hygiene said, "As a whole the book is very thorough and, apart from the unfamiliar vocabulary, the style is 'chatty' and easy to read." The British statistician Florence Nightingale David penned a short review of *EDA* in which she concluded that Tukey's book is "interesting in that it encourages the learner to think what he/she is doing instead of learning by rote" and "enjoyable to read."* And two reviewers for the journal *Technometrics* wrote, "The material, at times intricate, is made easily accessible by the conversational style and the extensive use of examples…. The presentation of the material is usually clear in spite of a highly individualistic style." *EDA*, they concluded, is "one of the most stimulating books to appear in statistics for some time…. [W]e look forward to the sequel on confirmatory data analysis."

That sequel would never come.

---

* In the piece, F. N. David, as she was usually known, refers to World War II as "the second German war," perhaps as a result of the disruptions the two World Wars caused to her life. David was born in 1909 in Ivington, England; the Great War interrupted her early schooling. By 1931, she had earned a degree in mathematics from the Bedford College for Women. After failing to get hired as an actuary due to gender discrimination, she turned to Karl Pearson at University College, who hired her as his research assistant. A year before the Second World War, David obtained her doctorate. She assisted the Allied war effort with her statistics acumen, analyzing the effects of bombs. Two decades later, she left England and settled in the United States, joining the Department of Biostatistics at the University of California, Riverside.

CHAPTER THIRTY

Exploratory Data Analysis Practiced as Ritual

"Neither exploratory nor confirmatory is sufficient alone."
— John Tukey

One thing Tukey would not abide by was considering *EDA* as a primer for a general, overarching theory of data analysis. There was a purposeful vagueness to his detective, inductive approach. The problem with having a data analysis strategy too formulaic is nicely summarized by Tukey in his 1980 article "We Need Both Explanatory and Confirmatory." First, he lays out this flowchart of a typical paradigm for engineering and science:

Question → Design → Collection → Analysis → Answer

This programmatic design—which is confirmatory, rather than exploratory, in nature—seems logical and comprehensive, but it is far from airtight and leaves much unstated and implicit. For instance, Tukey notes, how are the questions themselves formulated? What types of questions in the "general area" have been already asked and are being asked? What is the scope of the question of interest? Science, and engineering, "DOES NOT BEGIN WITH A TIDY QUESTION" (his capitalization, again obviously for emphasis). "Finding the question," Tukey explains, "is often more important than finding the answer."

There are further things for the researcher to consider, such as: What are the real-world constraints? What did similar sets of data reveal (if any exist)? What sort of study design is possible and efficient? Is there sufficient randomization in the study? Will the data collection be scrutinized for departures from patterns? How are the nuts and bolts of the analysis managed? These are not trivial concerns; rather, they lie at the heart of what Tukey saw as the problem with the normative, programmatic, strictly confirmatory approach: since there so much flexibility required, when implementing what seems to be confirmatory, "we need to do a lot of exploratory work," he writes. Thus, "[n]either exploratory nor confirmatory is sufficient alone. To try to replace either by the other is madness. We need them both." David Brillinger agreed strongly with his mentor, noting that "[s]tatisticians are the keepers of the scientific method. We say whether the scientists can reasonably draw that conclusion from the data they have. We do both exploratory and confirmatory data analysis, so we lose very few arguments."

In "We Need Both Explanatory and Confirmatory," Tukey also mentions the problem of multiplicity, an issue that he was, as his career neared its end, becoming interested in again anew. Recall the issue: How can we perform multiple significance tests while controlling for the fact that some of these tests will result in finding statistical significance purely by chance alone? Also recall that Ronald Fisher considered a significance level of five percent sufficient, meaning a p-value less than or equal to five percent connotes statistical significance in a hypothesis test. Perform multiple hypothesis tests, all at the five percent significance level, and the chances of rejecting at least one null hypothesis are given by $1-(0.95)^n$, where n is the number significance tests. Thus, the probability of making a Type I error—rejecting the null hypothesis when the null is in fact true—increases dramatically with each additional test; in effect, Tukey says, we become "hostages to fortune." When the problem of multiplicity arises, it always requires due consideration.

EDA necessitates an attitude of flexibility, a "reliance on display, NOT a bundle of techniques," that Tukey didn't wish to see turn too formulaic or algorithmic or formalized, casting out intuition in favor of the dogmatism inherent in mathematical proof; while he thought there might be a number of valid *theories* of data analysis (such as that offered piecemeal by statistician Colin Mallows; born in Great Sampford, England, in 1930, Colin Lingwood Mallows was invited by Tukey in 1956 to teach for a year at Princeton as part of the Statistical Techniques Research Group, and then worked at Bell Labs from 1960 to 2000. When he traveled with Tukey in London, Mallows was amazed that Tukey had less trouble navigating the notoriously serpentine London streets than he did), he was adamant against there being *the* theory of data analysis.

To that end, when asked how, precisely, an instructor should teach EDA, Tukey only offered this advice: "I guess my only answer is that is 'Whatever way a really interested teacher wants to teach it!'" When asked to whom EDA should be taught, he relayed examples that covered a gamut of possibilities, from a graduate course instructed by Harvard's David Hoaglin to a high school course. Tukey was afraid of EDA turning into a ritual, into a grab bag of set algorithms. He had expressed similar concerns years before, when writing specifically about data analysis in FoDA, comparing the teaching of only a single one-sample statistical procedure—avoiding discussing the relative merits and demerits of numerous procedures with the same host population—to instructing doctors to dispense only a single pill to address their patients' ailments: aspirin. Such thinking, both with data and doctors, necessitates operating under a number of assumptions which may be both narrow and unrealistic. At the time, Tukey was also concerned about two related ideas, the over-emphasis on optimization and the drive to produce "official" results (CDA-style), which might further sanctify data analysis.

Tukey also complained about the dangers of resorting to rituals when practicing EDA in "Exploratory Data Analysis: Past, Present, and Future," a report compiled for Princeton and presented at the University of Maryland in 1993 as part of their "Year of Data" program. "The environment of attitude being pushed by statisticians…[is] that EDA was being developed [to be] rigid, protective, and optimistic," he said. "One was supposed to be led to the procedures to be used by deriving them from a model, which means from assumptions. The true applicability of the assumptions was hardly ever in question." EDA, as properly practiced, had shed a model-based approach: "procedures [should be] legitimized by showing that they worked rather than being derived from a 'model,'" Tukey explained. And not only were models given short shrift—the theory of probability also mostly didn't make the cut, with Tukey explaining that "much that was useful in the analysis of data could be done without any mention of probability."

EDA, Tukey preached, required the statistician, mathematician, or scientist to recognize that even in the face of results shown to be statistically significant courtesy of CDA methods, "some things had in fact happened by chance." Thus the danger of hypothesis testing using a five percentage point significance level, or, indeed, any significance level: satisfy the threshold of the test, and we've granted imprimatur to the effects, even if they were solely the result of chance; but declare the data "nonsignificant" and we fall into a trap of considering the results equivalent to "zero" or "as all exactly alike." How can we dig ourselves out of this binary opposition, out of this significance test fallacy?

First, Tukey said, by recognizing that "appearances need not be significant to be relevant and worth some attention." And second, by using confidence intervals, even though they may cause "pain to both mathematicians and investigators to recognize, explicitly, the presence of uncertainty"—something that these professionals, by lazily relying on significance testing, expressly wish to avoid doing. After all, transitioning from a point estimate (a single sample value estimating a population parameter) to a range of values, Tukey said, "involves admitting (particularly to ourselves) that there is uncertainty about what value certain summaries are trying to describe!"—especially since "[s]ummaries can be very useful, but they are not the details."

The Stanford professor of statistics and former magician Persi Diaconis warns of the dangers inherent in EDA in "Theories of Data Analysis: From Magical Thinking Through Classical Statistics" (1985), arguing that performing rituals brings the statistician dangerously close to magical thinking—the process of attributing causation to events with no obvious or verifiable link, akin to the South Pacific cargo cults' ritualistic behaviors and incantations that were designed to "summon" supplies and food, even going so far as to build runways for ostensibly Western planes to land and deliver them goods. A much more nefarious historical example, not offered by Diaconis, is described cogently by Peter Hayes in his book *Why? Explaining the Holocaust* (2017):

> By the late Middle Ages, a correlation between social crisis and the slaughter and expulsion of Jews had become firmly established. Whenever adverse developments occurred that people could not otherwise account for, they identified Jews as the agents of Satan who had caused the problems. Massacres of Jews followed the Italian famine of 1315-17 and the outbreak of the Black Death in the Rhineland in 1347, for example.

Of course, the Jewish persecution reached its apotheosis with the Nazis. "Nazi ideology was a witches' brew of self-pity, entitlement, and aggression," Hayes explains. "It was also a form of magical thinking that promised to end all of Germans' postwar sufferings, the products of defeat and deceit, by banishing their supposed ultimate cause, the Jews and their agents."

But how does magical thinking relate to exploratory data analysis? "At one extreme," Diaconis writes, "we can view the techniques of EDA as a ritual designed to reveal patterns in a data set." He continues:

> Thus, we may believe that naturally occurring data sets contain structure, that EDA is a useful vehicle for revealing the structure, and that revealed structure can sometimes be interpreted in the language of the subject matter that produced the data. If we make no attempt to check whether the structure could have arisen by chance, and tend to accept the findings as gospel, then ritual comes close to magical thinking.

Classical statistics, or CDA, practiced properly helps one to avoid falling into the trap of magical thinking by deciding "upon models and hypotheses *before* seeing the data." But, as Diaconis noted in a speech given to a meeting of the American Psychological Association, Tukey "discusses the use of classical statistics as a ritual for sanctification." Diaconis was specifically referring to Tukey's speech "Analyzing Data: Sanctification or Detective Work" (1969), where Tukey insists that data analysis needs to be both confirmatory and exploratory, and EDA requires flexibility "for adapting what is calculated—and, we hope, plotted [graphically]—both to the needs of the situation and the clues that the data has already provided." However,

> [W]e dare not…let [confirmatory data analysis] be an imprimatur or a testimony of infallibility. "Not a high priestess but a handmaiden" must be our demand….
>
> The Roman Catholic Church is a long-lived and careful institution. It has long held that sanctification was only for the dead—indeed only for those dead for an appropriate period. I believe, and I urge you to feel, that sanctification of data is equally only for dead data—data that is only of historical importance, like Newton's apple.

Diaconis explained that cutting a path between the Scylla of mathematical statistics and the Charybdis of magical thinking when analyzing data requires a persistence of habit and a flexibility of mind.

In addition, in "Theories of Data Analysis: From Magical Thinking Through Classical Statistics," Diaconis discusses the importance of science, arguing that science progresses by "combining exploration with fresh attempts at confirmation." Science also progresses through replication—the collection of data from independent researchers which confirms or refutes previously held theories. But replication isn't always possible; sometimes a single observation or sample is all there is available (e.g., oftentimes in geology). Tukey terms this *uncomfortable science*, a way of systematically drawing inferences from whatever data we can despite the lack of replication. For his part, Diaconis relays the example of Bode's law, which mathematically models the distances of the planets to the sun. Although the formula works, there is not enough data—not nearly enough planets—to test predictions; Bode's law might instead simply be a "numerological artifact," a model that nearly conforms to the relatively few observations at hand but would fall apart if met with a much larger data set. Diaconis suggests ways to compensate for having to perform uncomfortable science, such as not publishing with p-values or involving probability in calculations of any kind, examining parallel situations so as to "borrow" analyses, or using distribution-free statistical techniques such as bootstrapping, among other remedies. He also points out that a number of statisticians, including George Box and Arthur Dempster, applied Bayesian techniques within EDA. (For his part, Box, like Tukey, recognized that the effective practice of mathematics wasn't necessarily correlated with the effective practice of statistics—and "in some cases [the two are] actually antithetical.") Tukey was less sold on the power of Bayes' theorem, which relies on an approach that modifies a researcher's subjective initial probabilities in the face of incoming data. "Bayesian techniques assume we know all the alternate possible states of nature," Tukey said, which is unlikely under most real-world circumstances. After all, as Tukey wrote in *EDA*, "In dealing with distributions of the real world, we are very lucky if…we know APPROXIMATELY how values are distributed…."

Not everyone hopped on the EDA bandwagon. Eytan Adar, an associate professor of electrical engineering and computer science at the University of Michigan, wrote a detailed online posting about how "EDA" is an unartful term, taking especial umbrage at the word "exploratory" and its root word, "explore." "I've banned the word 'explore' from all project proposals in my…class. No explore. No exploration. No exploratory." Adar explains how a single word has led to a major misunderstanding:

> I got to have lunch with John Tukey many years ago. We talked about birding. I wish we talked about "Exploratory Data Analysis." For all the clever names he created for things (software, bit, cepstrum, quefrency) what's up with EDA? The name is fundamentally problematic because it's ambiguous. "Explore" can be both transitive (to seek something) and intransitive (to wander, seeking nothing in particular). Tukey's book [*EDA*] seems to emphasize the former—it's full of unique graphical tools to find certain patterns in the data: distribution types, differences between distributions, outliers, and many other useful statistical patterns. The problem is that students think he meant the latter.
>
> Somehow that term has given students, and some professionals, the license to be totally imprecise about what they were building, and (more critically) how to evaluate whether it worked. If you're not seeking anything in particular, any tool that lets you meander through data is perfectly reasonable.

The unboundedness of "exploration" turns data analysis into a kind of Rorschach test. Yes, Tukey urged us to be open to surprises (a "willingness to find some happenchance phenomena"), but that openness needs to be tempered with having some structural idea of what might constitute a surprise, rather than having no expectations about what the data will show (a "happiness in finding phenomena with some continuing reality").

In addition, one must look beyond the data when gathering information and forming conclusions. To allow for all of this flexibility, data analysis required what he called "guide*zones*" rather than "guide*lines*" (his italics).

Continuing this line of thought, in "John W. Tukey as 'Philosopher'" (2002), even Tukey's former student Arthur Dempster launches a salvo or two at his old mentor. Although it might have been obvious to Tukey when a particular statistical analysis was successfully completed or even useful to begin with, Tukey "unwisely assumes" it's also apparent to everyone else—but there is hardly more agreement on statistical matters than in most other avenues of life, so alternative approaches need to be thoroughly examined. Furthermore, Dempster criticizes Tukey's repeated unwillingness to provide "top down," or deductive, explanations for a variety of EDA techniques. Finally, Dempster finds little evidence of Tukey considering the wider historical currents of EDA or addressing how advances in statistics perhaps served as an impetus for reconsideration of issues in science.

CHAPTER THIRTY-ONE

Unpacking Statistics 411

"No amount of observations of white swans can the allow the inference that all swans are white. But the observation of a single black swan is sufficient to refute that conclusion."
— David Hume

Besides teaching courses focusing on EDA, Tukey also offered a general course in statistics aimed at undergraduate seniors called Statistics 411. With enough instructor notes to fill up a filing case—which they did, in his Princeton office—Tukey regaled his students with a buffet of statistics topics as the course evolved through the years; he was not the only professor to teach it, but he was undoubtedly considered the best.

The course, which Karen Kafadar called "famous," wasn't only attended by undergrads—Henry Braun, a Princeton professor, took Stats 411 with Tukey six years in a row in order to stay abreast of new approaches toward data; graduate students also took it—but Tukey, who arrived to class each day with papers inside his trademark Ziploc bags, made sure to have the undergrad seniors sit right up front so he could "answer *their* questions before I answered anybody else's," he recalled, lest those students might be crushed by "moral pressures." The emphasis in Stats 411 was not on the mathematics behind the statistical methods, but on utilizing the statistical methods in the real world, which can be messy and in which assumptions for inferential procedures don't always necessarily hold true.

Tukey also occasionally taught a course at Princeton called Advances in Data Analysis, which, unlike Stats 411, was geared toward engineers and scientists. Both the Stats 411 and the Advances courses had content related to multiple comparisons, which Tukey wrote about early on in his career, and then again at the very end.

Whenever he taught regression in these classes, Tukey always had a maxim by William Cochran at the forefront of his mind: Regression is "the worst-taught part of statistics."[*] To Cochran, the problem with regression was that one could easily be lulled into a sense of complacency with the procedures and formulas, churning through seemingly valid answers despite data collection methods or the chosen variables themselves being suspect. Tukey concurred, calling such regression analysis "seductive and dangerous." Sure, we might be able to fit a line to such data if it appears relatively linear when graphed on a scatterplot, but can we reliably predict the data set's marginal change: the amount of increase of the y variable for every one unit increase in the x variable? Or would we be making claims that would result in faulty extrapolation?

Tukey thought back to his mentor Charlie Winsor, who arrived at an especially relevant example. Looking at U.S. Census data from the first half of the twentieth century, suppose x represents the percentage membership in Protestant evangelical churches (by state) and y represents the out-of-wedlock birthrate (by state). Though the relationship between the variables was strong—as y was larger, so was x—could we therefore conclude that increasing x would thereby increase y? Hardly so. Lurking variables, or what Tukey called *surrogates*, such as location and demographic makeup, are much likelier to explain the association, which is not a cause-and-effect one regardless. Thus, while an x-y plot of churches and the out-of-wedlock birthrate might be a wonderful description of a data set, it doesn't inform us about prediction, of how we might go about understanding the impact of changing one variable on the other. As Tukey noted in *EDA*, "Even when we see a very good fit—something we know has to be a very good summary of the data—we dare not believe that we have found a natural law."

In the article "Exploratory Data Analysis: Past, Present, and Future," Tukey relays the results of N. Gross's study of school principals: Gross found a strongly negative association between performance as principal and the number of graduate courses taken in educational administration. But having a principal simply take no such graduate courses likely wouldn't result in he or she becoming a more effective principal; there is a limit to how far extrapolation can be reasonably taken. Though Tukey doesn't use this example, consider the relationship between vehicle weight, x, and miles per gallon (MPG), y: the heavier the vehicle, generally speaking, the lower the MPG. But extrapolate too far—for example, reducing a vehicle's weight to a single pound, resulting in an MPG in the thousands!—and results go off the rails.

The philosopher David Hume wrestled with the idea of extrapolation centuries before Tukey was born. Relying on past events to form predic-

---

[*] Tukey reflected that despite this truism, multiple regression methods continue to been employed by investigators without abandon.

tions on future events isn't necessarily sound strategy, yet we quite naturally extrapolate from past experiences all the time. Commonly referred to as the "problem of induction," Hume famously presented the example of the black swan as an instance. Europeans since time immemorial had only encountered white swans, until finding the black variety while colonizing Australia. "No amount of observations of white swans can the allow the inference that all swans are white," Hume said. "But the observation of a single black swan is sufficient to refute that conclusion." Hume also noted, "[T]he sun will not rise tomorrow is no less intelligible...and implies no more contradiction than the affirmation that it will rise," meaning that just because the sun has risen on countless previous mornings, this fact, in and of itself, offers us no guarantee about what will happen tomorrow morning.

Any reasoning through pure induction can be spoiled with the advent of a single counterexample, like a black swan; that's why when performing hypothesis testing we fail to reject the null hypothesis, rather than "accept" the null hypothesis—failing to reject is a hedge against future disconfirming observations, against encountering a black swan.* Of course, this notion connects directly back to what Karl Popper said about the scientific method. Recall his words: "A scientific idea can never be proven true, because no matter how many observations seem to agree with it, it may still be wrong."

---

* Which ties into modern medical diagnostic tests as well. The acronym NED, or no evidence of disease, is used rather than END, or evidence of no disease, because not finding evidence of a disease doesn't imply its absence in a human body: the absence of evidence (a weak statement) is not evidence of absence (a strong statement). Science can't prove a negative.

PART FIVE

The Post-Retirement Years

CHAPTER THIRTY-TWO

Statistics at Sunset

*"I'm glad to see that you are training your baby
to be good in Data Analysis."*
— John Tukey, addressing Luisa Fernholz

One of the most consequential professors ever to sit in on Tukey's Statistics 411 Data Analysis course was Luisa Fernholz. Born in 1941, Luisa Turrin Fernholz was interested in mathematics at a young age, having completed a world tour of graduate studies in the subject at the Scuola Normale Superiore in Pisa, Italy, immediately after snagging a master's degree in mathematics from the University of Buenos Aires, Argentina, all while still in her twenties. (Her father, Vanilio Turrin, owned a steel foundry in Buenos Aires.) Before reaching the age of thirty years old, while still living in Pisa, she met and married Robert Fernholz, who was teaching at the University of Buenos Aires; he also specialized in mathematics, earning degrees from Princeton (as an undergraduate) and Columbia (as a doctoral student), and used his expertise in the mathematics of finance to found INTECH Investment Management. They gave birth to two sons, Ricardo and Daniel, who both earned doctorates themselves.

Fernholz changed her career path in her thirties, shifting toward studying statistics. By the late 1970s, she had earned a doctorate in statistics from Rutgers University in New Brunswick, studying under Robert Harold Berk; her thesis is titled "Topics in Mathematical Statistics and Probability Theory," and deals with statistical ideas far afield from the applied, data-driven approach Tukey pioneered. By 1979 she had secured a teaching appointment at the University of Pennsylvania.

In the spring of 1980, she delivered a seminar lecture at Princeton's statistics department, "present[ing] some mathematical results that used Fréchet and Hadamard derivatives to derive certain asymptotic results," she explained. John Tukey was in the audience. Though she had never been a student of his, nor even ever met him before, she was nonetheless very worried: his reputation preceded him in a number of ways. Not only was he famous for the FFT algorithm, EDA, et cetera, et cetera, but he was also well known to not give quarter to anyone in a seminar talk—he would sometimes appear to fall asleep, then surprise the speaker with a sharp, pull-no-punches question—especially when that talk revolved around the theoretical, mathematical side of statistics. Yet during Fernholz's lecture, not only did Tukey not fall asleep, but he also made a pointed and especially useful comment about empirical distribution functions. Things went so well, in fact, that Fernholz was invited to join Princeton's statistics department as an instructor. She stayed in the department for four years. Auditing Tukey's Stats 411 course during that period opened her eyes to "a new reality of statistics." Pregnant with her second son while taking the class, Tukey's sparkling wit shined through courtesy of this comment to her: "I'm glad to see that you are training your baby to be good in Data Analysis."

By the mid-1980s, Fernholz landed at Temple University, where she eventually became a Professor Emerita of Statistics. But her connections to Princeton didn't end when she left the institution in 1984. In the mid-1990s, she became a member of the Advisory Council for the Department of Mathematics at Princeton. At around the same time, she also became one of Tukey's last major collaborators.

Working with Tukey, Fernholz remembered later, was more like slipping into the "realm of surrealism." She collaborated with him when he was between the ages of eighty and eighty-five. Despite his protestations in a contemporaneous interview (in part with Fernholz) that he wasn't as quick of a reader as he once was, Fernholz was startled at how fast Tukey could calculate the results of algorithms, such as a jackknife-variant called the *multihalver*, mentally, holding scores of numbers in his head almost always without resorting to paper and pencil or electronic crutches like calculators. She would hand him reams of computer output, and he would immediately spot latent patterns hidden in the masses of digits on the pages, all the while spouting off new ideas and making connections so quickly as to leave even a sharp intellect like Fernholz overwhelmed. Tukey would sketch out diagrams and flowcharts for her, drawing by carefully pressing his multicolor pens on his standby yellow pads, and the pages would be bursting with complexity. And he wouldn't hesitate to call Fernholz, no matter the day or the hour, to run by exciting new approaches to whatever research problems they were currently in the thick of.

Tukey's way of speaking to Fernholz was so dense, so exhaustive, so farsighted, that she had to pore through each of his sentences with a fine-tooth comb, picking out the nuggets of wisdom, sorting through the old and the new neologisms, and translating the idiosyncratic notation. There was much detail in what he said, yet he still managed to use as few words as possible. Understanding what Tukey was talking about, as statistician

Erich L. Lehmann realized decades earlier, was no easy task, requiring one's complete concentration. But Fernholz adapted to the Tukey idiom well. She found herself audiotaping the man during work meetings, later transcribing and loosening the bundled complexities packed tightly into his words. And those words kept pouring out until his final days.

Through his influential talks, publications—some solo, many with coauthors, of which he had more than one hundred—commiserating with fellow statisticians, and, of course, teaching hundreds of students, Tukey ultimately achieved one of his major goals: a move of the statistics discipline, as a whole, away from a pure, mathematical statistics-based approach, toward a more balanced approach. In an article from 1986 entitled "Sunset Salvo"—named after a comment by a retired executive vice president at Bell Labs, who, unlike most academics, actually retired (hence the "sunset")—Tukey puts his finger on the pulse of the state of statistics, finding that "[o]verall, things have become more diversified—more mathematical, more admittedly data analytic, more admittedly graphically displayed—and we can hope for continuing diversification; we need to struggle to keep this diversification balanced." But the struggle wouldn't be to ensure more mathematical-style, theoretical output; rather, the struggle will be to "emphasize all the other directions," "pointing from mathematical statistics toward data analysis." "Sunset Salvo" details the many ways that this "struggle" can successfully be staged, such as relying more on randomization, using effective and relevant displays, recognizing the limitations of a lack of independence in data sets, and shifting the paradigm toward realizing that satisfying stated statistical assumptions for inference is very difficult—leading the way for alternative assumptions to be considered. Tukey also pushed, in the piece, for *jackknifery* as a means to deal with many levels of uncertainty in the underlying distributions of collected sample data.

"Sunset Salvo" also functions as a readymade primer for constructing graphical displays, with Tukey carefully instructing the reader what is and what is not effective visually. For example, while a log–log plot of data points might feed all-too-easily into an "O, see how straight!" sales pitch—since the data assemble into an almost artificial-looking diagonal line—and plotting confidence intervals might improve matters, what such a graph really needs to show is not where the answers *should* be, but where they *cannot* possibly be, moving (and improving) the analysis from an overall fuzziness to only endpoints that are fuzzy. And an author of statistical papers should never assume that his readers are omnipotent by only inserting titles for axes, for instance; instead, a full-blown sidebar commentary is often necessary to inform readers of the origin and meaning of the graphics. Beyond graphical displays, Tukey proffered rules of thumb centering on confidence intervals and measurement error. "Sunset Salvo" fired shots across the bow of a variety of other targets, too; as usual, Tukey's aim was true.

CHAPTER THIRTY-THREE

Still Keeping Busy

"He always knew just the right thing to say
to make his students feel better."
—Karen Kafadar

In their chapter on the Princeton statistics department which appears in the book *Strength in Numbers: The Rising of Academic Statistics Departments in the U.S.* (2013), David Hoaglin and Karen Kafadar describe how intellectually generous Tukey was with students, always being "readily approachable and willing to discuss statistical problems, from the point of view of those presenting them, and to offer suggestions," even in the most unusual of circumstances, such as while birding (his many birding expeditions may have "really [been just] an excuse to discuss statistics," according to biostatistician Byron "Bill" Brown; to that end, Tukey could often be found at Brigantine Unit Edwin B. Forsythe National Wildlife Refuge in New Jersey watching birds and relaxing by the water), and in fields that weren't within the scope of his research interests. Recall that Fred Mosteller benefited greatly from Tukey's accessibility and generosity, bouncing thesis ideas off the elder statistician who wasn't even (as of yet) his doctoral advisor. But, as with many things, Tukey's quirky personality surfaced when it came to where he would meet students:

> [S]ometimes at his office in Fine Hall, but more often while chopping wood or doing yard work at the Tukey's home, or at the filling station while his tires were being rotated, or even during trips to Spain, England, or Austria—his students learned to be efficient in their requests for his time and adaptable to meeting him wherever he was.

The time constraints were partly due to his Bell Labs work, and partly because of the many independent projects he took on. He was spread thin: in the words of David Brillinger, Tukey was "half-time in Princeton, half-time at Bell Labs and half-time in Washington," which led to him scheduling some classes to meet four times a week but only actually running these classes on the three weekdays that happened to fit into his busy schedule, or instead setting class times to go for two hours instead of the standard hour and fifteen minutes.

Yet Tukey's intellectually generosity oftentimes knew no bounds. Full of ideas, Tukey simply "threw them out, and let others work on them," Kafadar remembers.

> Many of them have taken people 20 or 30 years to work out why they perform so well. Consistent with that characteristic, he never used his own name for his ideas, procedures, or methods. They were always the "Duckworth test", or the "Bruceton test", or "Winsorization", or "decigalt" ("for Francis Galton,* who started so many things").... The other characteristic of his personality that always impressed me was his constant encouragement to his students.... He always knew just the right thing to say to make his students feel better.

More than simply not taking credit for his own ideas by refraining from affixing them eponymous labels, Tukey would often do the mental heavy lifting, behind the scenes, for projects that needed desperately to get done. He was always quick to inquire among his colleagues: What are you up to? What are you working on? Not to steal their ideas, but to further their thinking, to get closer to answers, to advance the state of knowledge. He did have a pragmatic reason, too: he enjoyed and benefit-

---

* Sir Francis Galton, born in 1822 in Birmingham, England, was one of the most creative and controversial figures in mathematics. He came up with the statistical ideas of correlation and regression to the mean. When visiting a livestock fair for fun in the early 1900s, Galton witnessed a bizarre game hundreds of people were playing: they would each guess the weight of a slaughtered ox. Galton was surprised to find that, though no single person guessed the correct weight exactly, the averages of their guesses (specifically, the median; the mean ended up being even closer to the truth), was very close to the mark: "the middlemost estimate expresses the *vox populi* [the voice of the people], every other estimate being condemned as too low or too high by a majority of the voters." This idea of using aggregate responses from people, contemporarily called the "wisdom of crowds," or crowdsourcing, has been found to be at least as good as responses originating from any individual in the group.

No discussion about Galton would be complete without mentioning his darker accomplishments: he also arrived at the notion of eugenics, publishing the book *Hereditary Genius* in 1869 which argued that the British government should "[prevent] the more faulty members of the flock from breeding." Thus, Adolph Hitler was indirectly one of his greatest admirers—the dictator was inspired by the eugenicists who applied Galton's ideas, namely, Americans Charles Davenport and especially Madison Grant, whose *The Passing of the Great Race* (1916) heavily influenced *Mein Kampf* (1925).

ed from professional collaborations—a significant portion of Tukey's corpus is collaborative, rather than solo, work—since his mind was so active, and he jumped from one topic to another so quickly, that he didn't want to get bogged down in some of the details of publication (submitting repeated revisions and so forth). Tukey would draft a paper, signing it "_____ and J. W. Tukey," and then seek out a collaborator who would refine the work and take charge as lead author—leaving Tukey to move on to whatever other ideas were percolating in his head; he would even maximize his time when handwriting papers and correspondence by having his "pen never [leave] the page," according to his nephew, F. R. Anscombe.

In the 1960s, there was a call to compile a statistical citation index, a first-of-its-kind massive undertaking that presaged modern knowledge databases. Tukey wrote how to go about such an undertaking in the 1963 article "A Citation Index for Statistics and Probability," and then proceeded to turn his words into reality: Tukey headed a team of eminent minds to compile the articles—including Jim Dolby and Ian Ross—but "did a lion's share of the grunt work," said then-student Alan Gross, which ultimately amounted to keypunched entries filling roughly 120 file drawers. "Everywhere he went in those days, he had 10 or 15 side-inches of journals under his arm," Gross remembered. "He would attend seminars, and spend the whole time copying references out of said journals onto data entry sheets." Gross's description of *side-inches*, by the way, pays homage to another of Tukey's neologisms: the *side-foot*, which measures a stack of printed computer output—"When I said we should be using computers by the foot, I did not mean by the running foot of output paper. I meant, rather, by the 12 inches of thickness of stacks of printout" that statisticians are calling the *side-foot*, Tukey said—but which was, by and large, a term that never gained any traction.

Even if the heavy lifting of a project wasn't exclusively of the mental variety, the relentless Tukey would often intercede to finish the task. In the late 1970s, Tukey was called to action by a citizen group near Princeton. The group was up in arms about how traffic patterns would be affected by a proposed development. Research, in the form of traffic counts, was required. Phyllis Marchand, a member of the group who later went on to become a successful mayor of Princeton Township, remembers:

> Imagine my surprise when Professor John Tukey, the Donner Professor of Science at Princeton University, and one of the most influential statisticians came over and offered to do the job. [Marchand had met him in the 1970s, prior to her run for mayor.] A man who could command

hundreds of dollars an hour for statistical consulting and analysis had agreed to sit in a lawn chair and count cars as they passed by. John Tukey, with all his fame, volunteered his expertise, and without calculators, computers or any fancy technology, sat on a chair at the designated spot on Route 206 and with a pad of paper and a pencil counted the cars and trucks as they traveled past. I smile as I think of that image.

Marchand also fondly recalls how active both Tukey and his wife were in donating their time and energy into "raising money and raising consciousness about environmental sensitivity, quality of life, and historic preservation" at Princeton. Elizabeth even became the First Chair of the Princeton Township Historic Preservation Commission.

In 1974, Tukey was even granted an opportunity to speak as his quasialma mater, New Bedford High School. In the speech, he touched on several key themes that were embedded in much of his writings and work: the double-edged sword of technological progress, the need for balanced judgment, the necessity of avoiding the siren's song of easy answers to complicated questions, and the civic responsibilities of every citizen of the United States.

> We all recognize that crossing the street is dangerous—and that living our lives on a single block is unacceptable. That riding in an automobile is dangerous, but that walking everywhere is rarely a solution. We try to balance our risks and our gains, our costs and our benefits…. Each of you has the opportunity to be a single small voice speaking out—both in conversation and when you vote—for balanced judgment and for people who will strive for balanced judgment.

Then he exclaimed, "The Chinese have a curse: 'May your children live in interesting times!'" There won't ever be a shortage of societal problems to tackle. But the problems we face as a society will neither disappear nor get worse but will change, he added. The difficulty arises in adapting to the changes that come in the wake of "interesting times."

University of Chicago Professor Peter McCullagh, no stranger to interesting times, takes the long view when it comes to assessing Tukey's academic contributions. Tukey had some successes, such as with multiple comparisons and especially with spectrum analysis; in addition, establishing data analysis as a breakaway discipline achieved some measure of success. But neither Tukey's work on robustness nor his push to integrate the techniques of exploratory data analysis within the framework of how all statisticians practice the discipline never met a full realization, nor did demand for the textbook *EDA* necessitate it having many printings or editions. McCullagh also points out a significant missed opportunity, something Tukey *didn't* do but perhaps should have: putting the foundations of statistical inference on solid mathematical footing—despite this being a task he seemed especially well suited for, given his background in topology.

Misses aside, Tukey's dominant influence through much of the twentieth century, McCullagh argues, was just as much due to the force of his idiosyncratic personality—and the "good theatre" that invariably attended to his public performances—as to the importance and utility of his statistical results.

CHAPTER THIRTY-FOUR

Down to One

"I do not plan to stop thinking or working."
— John Tukey

The end, when it came, found Tukey's mental powers almost as strong as ever, but he was emotionally devastated. He had lost his wife Elizabeth several years before (on January 6, 1998), after cooking and caring for her as much as he possibly could before having to resort to hiring professional health care providers. She had suffered with metastatic breast cancer for years. During her hospital stays, he diligently sat her bedside, yellow pad in hand, working out mathematics, likely to help him cope with the incredible stress. (Tukey sketching out results on his yellow pad during Elizabeth's protracted illness was a depressing inversion of a prediction her father had made to his future son-in-law during the courtship: that he would "whip out a yellow pad and not waste any time" while waiting for her at the altar.)

Elizabeth had always considered herself and her husband "a team," able to accomplish much more together than they ever could apart. She had made great personal sacrifices for her husband. Speaking at Tukey's 80th birthday celebration at Prospect House at Princeton on the night of June 19, 1995, Elizabeth directed a telling comment at Frances Baker (née Burrill), the wife of William O. Baker, one of Tukey's oldest friends: "As the wife of another dedicated workaholic I understand the selfless love and devotion, accommodation and deprivation required to 'keep them on the road.'"

The Tukeys would not celebrate their golden wedding anniversary together. After 48 years of marriage, Elizabeth passed away. At her eulogy, Tukey heartbreakingly said, "One is so much less than two." Roughly two years later, all her art and antiques, her Asian ceramics and botanical drawings, her antique American furniture spanning the life of the nation—all of it was sold.

In the years before her death, Tukey had hardly stepped off the gas pedal. After retiring from Princeton in 1985, and being granted the role of Senior Research Statistician and Donner Professor of Science *Emeritus* (in 1976, six years after the stepping down as chair of the statistics department, he was appointed the Donner Chair), Tukey turned his attention to new ventures. "When I formally retire," he once mused, "I do not plan to stop thinking or working. I plan to continue to provide both new techniques and new annoying-but-true statements." He was as good as his word.

Post-retirement, Tukey directed professional energies into consulting for the Xerox Palo Alto Research Center, or PARC. It was at PARC that Ethernet, object-oriented programming, and graphical user interfaces were invented and demonstrated in 1979 to a very young and very cocky CEO of Apple, Steve Jobs; he passed on the first two innovations in favor of the third—GUIs—resulting in the Apple Lisa and Macintosh possessing the slickest interfaces to ever grace home computing.

Tukey was very productive at PARC, managing to score a series of patents, all collaboratively submitted with other Xerox employees, mostly centering on software algorithms, such as searching through and organizing digital documents. By this point in his life, he had received a number of prestigious honors, including the Sam S. Wilks Award of the American Statistical Association, the Institute of Electrical and Electronic Engineers (IEEE) Medal of Honor (Mosteller attended the 1982 awards banquet, which took place in Boston, as did Elizabeth; the honor citation reads, "For his contributions to the spectral analysis of random processes and the fast Fourier transform algorithm"), the National Medal of Science in Mathematical, Statistical, and Computational Sciences (in 1973, presented to Tukey personally by President Nixon; Jerzy Neyman is another statistician who won the award), the Deming Medal from the American Society of Quality Control (in 1983), and the James Madison Medal from Princeton (in 1984)* as well as being elected to the Royal Society of London and the American Philosophical Society (he served as its vice president from 1974 to 1977; after his death, his corpus of papers ended up with them)—not to mention a host of honorary degrees from the likes of Case Institute of Technology (his first, awarded in 1962), the University of Chicago, Brown University (his alma mater awarded him a doctor of science degree in 1965), Yale University, Temple University, Waterloo University (in Ontario), and, least surprising of all, Princeton University.†

---

* It was in his acceptance speech for this award that Tukey quipped, "Like those who have stood here in earlier years, I am deeply honored to be here. Unlike them, I cannot talk of returning, for I enjoyed the Princeton Graduate School so much that I have not yet left it."

† When asked during census testimony in 1992 how many honorary degrees he had thus far acquired, Tukey—a man who was extremely precise in his language, especially when it came to matters quantitative—uncharacteristically imprecisely replied, "About five."

Although it took until 1998 for it to happen, Princeton's ceremony citation captures the professional spirit of the man well: "A self-described 'miscellaneous type' in an age of specialization." When asked what his fields of specialization were in a census adjustment hearing in 1992, he said, "I have a collection of fields of specialization, really rather than one…. [S]ome of them are time series, robust techniques, exploratory techniques, graphical techniques, probably I should add analysis of variance, seasoned with other topics to taste, such as regression."

Tukey's professional interests had remained relatively consistent, if not more refined and better developed, since the post-World War II *American Men of Science* biographical listing. Even by the first edition of the comprehensive *World Who's Who in Science: A Biographical Dictionary of Notable Scientists from Antiquity to the Present*, published in 1968, Tukey was strictly classified as an American statistician who studied "mathematical, theoretical, and applied statistics," although the paragraph-length biography also took a more historical view: "point set topology; military analysis; [and] fire control equipment" were also listed as his interests.

CHAPTER THIRTY-FIVE

The Greatest Symposium

*"Paul Velleman was arguing about statistics being a science.
I would tend to think it would have been more accurate
to say science-and-technology."*
—John Tukey

On June 19 and 20, 1995, to celebrate his 80th birthday, a two-day symposium was held at Jadwin Hall in Princeton University in honor of John Tukey, where Tukey's contributions were the focus of the talks.* Besides his wife, there were approximately one hundred of "John's friends, students, and colleagues," according to David Brillinger, some of whom followed Elizabeth's lead in giving short speeches and tributes to the man. There were thirteen individuals who spoke in detail on a statistics topic as well. Luisa Fernholz had set the ball in motion, making sure to contact as many potentially interested parties as possible; Brillinger and Stephan Morgenthaler assisted her.

Morgenthaler and Henry Braun served as chairs for the first day of the symposium, which began at nine in the morning and didn't end until nearly seven o'clock in the evening. Twenty- to thirty-minute lectures were given by John Chambers, William Cleveland, George Easton, Frank Hampel, John Hartigan, Karen Kadafar, Colin Mallows, and Paul Velleman. The day concluded with a video of an interview with Tukey. The next morning had David Hoaglin taking over as chair for the ceremonies, with presentations by David Brillinger, David Donoho, Leo Goodman, Fred Mosteller, and Roy Welsch, capped off with a panel discussion with Tukey himself.

Two years later, Brillinger, Fernholz, and Morgenthaler published a Festschrift, a collection of writings packaged together in tribute of an ac-

---

* Tukey also participated in several extensive interviews during the two-day event, which helped to paint a richer picture of his life. A video, filmed two years prior and produced by BellCore and the American Statistical Association, of a personal conversation between John, Elizabeth, and two statisticians, was also shown at the symposium.

ademic. Called *The Practice of Data Analysis: Essays in Honor of John W. Tukey* (1997), the book assembles papers and other materials (such as an extended interview with Tukey as well as Elizabeth's dinnertime speech) stemming from the symposium. For example, mathematician Christopher A. Field's contribution is entitled "Estimating Abundances for a Breeding Bird Atlas," a paper that serves as a tacit nod to Tukey's love of birding; Brillinger and Alessandro E. P. Villa submitted a piece called "Assessing Connections in Networks of Biological Neurons," which orients the reader with a quote of Tukey's we encountered earlier: "The stronger the qualitative understanding the data analyst can get of the subject matter field from which his data come, the better—just so long as he does not take it too seriously"; Kafadar's "Geographical Trends in Cancer Mortality: Spatial Smoothers and Adjustment" combines together two of Tukey's longstanding interests, techniques for epidemiology and smoothing data—thereby separating the signal from the noise. "The Tennessee Study of Class Size in the Early School Grades," penned by Mosteller, focuses on another of Tukey's perennial concerns: teaching. Observing that Tukey "worked for many years on the National Assessment of Education Progress [NAEP] designing not only the sampling scheme for the nation's school children but also many special analyses," Mosteller makes sure to note how vital Tukey's contributions to the study of American schooling were not only to the Tennessee study, but to assessment and school improvement overall. (Tukey started at the NAEP in 1965 and was intimately involved with a number of advisory committees.)

Tukey came to refine his view of statistics as a science. In an interview late in his life, Tukey said, "Paul Velleman was arguing about statistics being a science. I would tend to think it would have been more accurate to say science-and-technology." In that same interview, Tukey was pessimistic about the state of affairs of statistics, lamenting that in this "period of academic retrenchment" some university statistics departments are going to dissolve—in part, he said, because there weren't enough "analogs of me [Tukey]" to innovate statistically and pedagogically and then publicly document those innovations, but also since there was an incongruity of the rollercoaster life of the statistician who deals with (and in) uncertainty and yet relies on the certainty of mathematical tools to perform his task. Pressed for any regrets, Tukey sidestepped the question but nonetheless expressed dissatisfaction that he didn't do more to expand the options available to statistics postdocs.

In his last half-decade of life, Tukey was still very much involved in the academic community, "was able to work with statisticians in the Princeton area as well as correspond with other statisticians all around the world, and he also continued some of his consulting work," as Luisa Fernholz recalled. She, her husband, and their children frequently availed themselves of his and Elizabeth's company. Such family gatherings were gateways to surely the most enjoyable and edifying intellectual discussions in the tri-state area, with her sons perhaps benefiting the most: Tukey would regale them with discussions on everything from arboriculture to quantum computers.

In that last half-decade, Tukey would also involve himself in a court case that had larger implications. Specifically, the case brought a question of social justice into relief: Were African Americans more likely to be given a death sentence than white defendants? To investigate this issue of potential prejudice, a proportionality review in *State of New Jersey v. Loftin* (1996) was conducted, with a special master, the retired New Jersey appellate judge Richard S. Cohen, appointed to the position. Cohen sought out John Tukey to assist in the review. After weeks upon weeks of careful analysis, here is what Tukey reported back to the court:

> The "relentless conclusion" is that, so far as these analyses go, there is no definite evidence of racial bias in penalty trials. Since the other analyses usually considered include far too many factors to be trusted, we must conclude that there is no relentless evidence of bias in penalty trials.

In a chapter he penned for the book *Social Science, Social Policy & the Law* (1999), criminologist David L. Weisburd explained, "Judge Cohen and Professor Tukey took the position that the instability caused by including too many variables [in a regression analysis] was so great that it was necessary to reduce their number." But reducing their number resulted in new mathematical models that ultimately didn't reveal clear-cut evidence of racial bias.

CHAPTER THIRTY-SIX

His Working Boots Stayed On

"Do you know who this man is?"
— Luisa Fernholz

By 1997, Elizabeth's health was declining rapidly, and Tukey, rather than traveling to Washington Road in Princeton to meet with Fernholz at his office at 408 Fine Hall, insisted that they collaborate at his house, simply because he didn't want to leave his wife alone. Tukey and Fernholz usually set up shop in the Tukeys' dining room, which contained a large table that rapidly became strewn with papers. Other meetings took place in the library or even the kitchen, which, suiting Tukey's practical nature, was outfitted with 1950s vintage items— including the original refrigerator. If the fridge still works fine after all these years, Tukey asked, then why purchase a new one?

Once Elizabeth became seriously ill, the Tukeys hired professionals to help with the upkeep—of both the house and of the Tukeys themselves. A woman named Khris Quicksall, hired by Elizabeth, was the best of them, and stayed on to assist Tukey as his housekeeper for several years. Described by Fernholz as a "friendly and warm person," Quicksall had a "devotion to both John and Elizabeth [that] had earned her John's respect and affection," one of the few silver linings for Tukey in a profoundly difficult time.

During this difficult period, Tukey saw fit to memorialize his parents by endowing a scholarship at Bates College, which they both attended, in their name. But the Ralph H. Tukey and Adah Tasker Tukey Scholarship Fund was saddled with almost comically complex criteria:

> Given by Dr. John W. Tukey, Donner Professor of Science Emeritus at Princeton University, in honor of his parents, Dr. Ralph H. Tukey and Adah Tasker Tukey, graduates of Bates College in the Class of 1898, providing a scholarship during the senior year of undergraduate study, the recipient to be selected from the upper 2 percent of his or her class in academic standing, based upon the scholastic records of the class at the end of the first five semesters of undergraduate study, with first pref-

erence for demonstrated scholastic excellence in mathematics or the classics or some other field of academic study in the natural sciences.

In early July 2000, only several weeks after his eighty-fifth birthday and his last professional consulting trip,* Tukey suffered a stroke; he had just wrapped up several days' worth of discussions with Kaye Basford about the analysis of two-way tables. "Although not in top physical condition, he was in good spirits and positive about the future," she remembered.

After being discharged from the Robert Wood Johnson University Hospital in New Brunswick, New Jersey, he was placed at the Merwick Care & Rehabilitation Center in Princeton for a recovery regimen. Slowly, he began to walk again. Fernholz was able to speak to him several times about statistics, and he seemed anxious to get back home. Tukey's long-time secretary, Mary Bittrich, had called numerous contractors, all in an effort to reconfigure Tukey's house by putting the bedroom and studio on the same floor so he could resume his life's work: statistics. David Brillinger spoke with him, and Tukey asked his former student: Do you have a statistics problem for me to consider?

But by July 25, Tukey was back in the hospital, placed in a double room with a semiconscious young man.

Tukey joked with his nurse there about statistics, telling her he was a statistician. She told him that she had studied modes and medians in school years ago.

Tests were conducted. Tukey lost consciousness from the drugs he was administered. Unlike after his stroke, the prognosis wasn't good.

Fernholz visited him, struggling to locate his room in the confusing layout of the hospital. Although the nurse there told her that "[h]is condition is reversible," Fernholz wasn't convinced. He didn't look well. "Do you know who this man is?" she asked her. The nurse knew he was a statistician but didn't realize he was a polymath of the highest order. So Fernholz said, "[H]e is much more than a statistician. Please make sure that he'll be well cared for."

Fernholz then called Bittrich, telling her to get someone to the hospital immediately to keep vigil. Quicksall was on her way, she said; in addition, Phyllis Anscombe (Elizabeth's sister) and other family members would be arriving shortly.

Shortly after midnight the next morning, Fernholz got a call from Quicksall. Tukey had suffered a heart attack.

---

* On June 1, 2000, he visited Merck and took part in discussions about highly technical, proprietary biological ideas such as microarray databases and Taq-Man Gene Expression Assays.

The polymath was no more. He had died "with his working boots on," F. R. Anscombe said.

John Tukey's funeral service was conducted on the afternoon of July 31, 2000, at Trinity Church on Mercer Street in Princeton. He was buried with his wife at the nearby Princeton Cemetery (Tukey's parents, Elizabeth's parents, and the Anscombes are also buried there). A single, simple headstone memorializes both of their lives. Immediately beneath their names are these three words: "United in Marriage." And the following verse, written by the English poet George Crabbe, is chiseled into the lower half of the stone:

A Marriage Ring

The ring, so worn as you behold,
So thin, so pale, is yet of gold:
The passion such it was to prove—
Worn with life's care, love yet was love.

Tukey was taken with another English poet who lived several generations before Crabbe: Richard Lovelace. "Stone walls do not a prison make," Lovelace writes in the poem "To Althea, from Prison," "Nor iron bars a cage:"

Minds innocent and quiet take
That for an hermitage.
If I have freedom in my love,
And in my soul am free,
Angels alone, that soar above,
Enjoy such liberty.

Tukey designated that haunting passage as his epitaph.

EPILOGUE

Fifteen years later, on September 18, 2015, Princeton University threw a 100th birthday celebration in honor of Tukey. The conference, which "focus[ed] [on] Tukey's scientific legacy and his enormous impact on modern statistics and data science," gathered together a number of mathematicians to speak on Tukey's impact who "either worked directly with Tukey or are in his direct academic lineage." Of course, many whom Tukey worked closest with had already passed away: Charles Winsor in 1951, Ronald Fisher in 1962, Sam Wilks in 1964, Jimmie Savage in 1971, Solomon Lefschetz in 1972, Henry Scheffé in 1977, Hendrik Bode in 1982, Richard Feynman in 1988, Ralph Boas in 1992, Albert Tucker in 1995, Lyman Spitzer in 1997, Arthur Stone in 2000, Claude Shannon in 2001, Bryant Tuckerman in 2002, Frederick Mosteller in 2006, and Erich Lehmann in 2009. James Cooley would die only several months after the conference.

But Yoav Benjamini was there, as were Persi Diaconis, Luisa Fernholz, Jerome Friedman, Karen Kafadar, and Stephan Morgenthaler, among many others. The centennial was held in McDonnell Hall—which is part of mathematics department and is adjacent to Fine Hall—with a reception and poster session in the Frick Chemistry Laboratory Atrium; fitting that the conference was held in those particular locations, given Tukey's start in chemistry and his migration to mathematics and then statistics.

Benjamini spoke about Tukey's final paper, published posthumously, which unpacked two seemingly unrelated concepts on multiplicity that Benjamini proceeded to link together by using the scientific concept of replicability. Diaconis talked about Tukey's deep background in mathematics, illuminating "Tukey's love-hate relationship" with math. Fernholz spoke of Tukey's life and legacy, while Friedman recounted Tukey's work at the Stanford Linear Accelerator Center. Kafadar sketched out examples of methodology inspired by applications from Tukey's work. "Because of his wide range of consultancies in industry and government, John Tukey contributed much methodology motivated by real problems," she said. Her talk detailed examples involving "two-dimensional smoothing, errors in variables, clustering, spectrum analysis, and multiple comparisons," while Morgenthaler's focused on Tukey's contributions to multiple comparisons. Others speakers presented on topics like big data, EDA in bio-medical research, and hierarchical models for predictions.

The keynote was given by David Donoho, a professor of statistics at Stanford who was a student of Tukey's as an undergraduate. He spoke about the emerging field of data scientists, contrasting them with applied statisticians—and discussing if there's any real difference between the two. "To a statistician," Donoho explains in a paper based off of his presentation, the modern "definition of statistics seems already to encompass anything that the definition of Data Scientist might encompass, but the definition of Statistician seems limiting, since a lot of statistical work is explicitly about inferences to be made from very small samples—this been true for hundreds of years, really." He argues that Tukey's "The Future of Data Analysis" was prescient, correctly predicting that "something like today's Data Science moment would be coming"—a moment predicated on the somewhat circular notion that "Data Science [is] the science of learning from data." FoDA, recall, was published in *The Annals of Mathematical Statistics* in 1962. Whereas

> [o]ther articles appearing in that journal at the time were mathematically precise and would present definitions, theorems, and proofs[,] John's paper was instead a kind of public confession, explaining why he thought such research was too narrowly focused, possibly useless or harmful, and the research scope of statistics needed to be dramatically enlarged and redirected.

Tukey cogently argued that data analysis wasn't a branch of theoretical mathematics, it was instead a scientific field of study. Its formal mathematical underpinnings weren't the point; in fact, Tukey wrote in FoDA, "Data analysis can gain much from formal statistics, but only if the connection is kept adequately loose." Thus, Tukey set in motion the modern data science paradigm, since data scientists needed new tools, such as graphical ones, to successfully grapple with data sets that are quite different in magnitude from the much smaller data sets of the past—making, in some cases, qualitatively different approaches to statistics necessary, although Donoho seems to suggest that the difference between big data and merely large data sets is solely one of degree, rather than of kind. Regardless, Donoho describes the implications of data science on statistics, such as computer applications developed for big data as well as pedagogical approaches to data science.[*]

---

[*] Tukey wasn't the only observer who saw the writing on the digital wall. Critic Marshall McLuhan realized that the age of big data was upon us—way back in 1964. "We have reached a similar point of data gathering," he wrote in *Understanding Media: The Extensions of Man*, "when each stick of chewing

In a seminal talk at Berkeley in 2012, Jeffrey Hammerbacher, who is known for organizing the first data analysis team at Facebook as well as coining the term data scientist (though he adamantly denies that), sketched out a history of data science, starting with Ronald Fisher's design of experiments and ending with the work of contemporary computer scientists. In between, however, was the man Hammerbacher pointedly called "the first data scientist": John Tukey. Though Tukey never called it "data science," in FoDA he wrote, "All in all, I have come to feel that my central interest is in data analysis." As Steve Lohr, author of *Data-ism: The Revolution Transforming Decision Making, Consumer Behavior, and Almost Everything Else* (2015), explains it, "To Hammerbacher, Tukey was the founding father of the 'data-first' ethos, a kind of Copernican shift in discovery and decision making. The data-first proponents, he explains, are 'starting with the data and seeing what it tells them instead of starting with a hypothesis and seeing what they can learn." Which is exactly what Tukey wanted: a turn away from CDA in favor of EDA.

"Undoubtedly, the swing to exploratory data analysis will go somewhat too far," Tukey predicted in "Exploratory Data Analysis as Part of a Larger Whole" (1973). "However: *It is better to ride a damped pendulum than to be stuck in the mud*" [his italics]. But it took a generation to get there, helped along by, quite bluntly, the disappearance of old statisticians and the appearance of new ones—an observation made by the Dutch physicist Hans Kramers with respect to revolutions in physics, stated poetically by Max Planck ("science advances one funeral at a time"), and paraphrased by Tukey late in his life as he looked toward the future* of his own discipline.

But what of big data? Tukey saw it coming. In a 1965 paper co-written with Martin B. Wilk, "four influences" that impact data analysis were elucidated. Theoretical approaches to statistics were the first consideration. The other three—the fast-paced developments in the field of computers, the increasingly common gathering of massive amounts of data in all walks of life, and the "accelerating emphasis on quantification" in an ever-growing number of fields—constituted the remaining essential ingredi-

---

gum we reach for is accurately noted by some computer that translates our least gesture into a new probability curve or some parameter of social science. Our private and corporate lives have become information processes just because we have put our central nervous systems outside us in electric technology."

* Tukey wrote about prospective data analysis of the year 2005, which he did not live to see come to fruition.

ents in a recipe for cooking up big data. Notably, warned Tukey and Wilk, just because mountains of data were collected didn't necessarily mean that fruitful analysis could proceed apace: one obstacle to such analysis, for instance, was that what appeared simple at first glance might turn out to be much more complex upon closer inspection. Another obstacle was the lack of standardization and relative inaccessibility of the electronic equipment to analyze the copious amounts of data—but recall that Tukey and Wilk were writing in 1965. All the pieces of the big data puzzle hadn't yet fallen into place and wouldn't for decades to come.

How would Tukey have handled the analysis of big data today? One clue comes from an interview with Peter Huber, who worked closely with Tukey several times in his career. An issue with using computers to pore through large data sets, Huber explains, is "that the statistician of old times who analyzed data by hand would notice if something was amiss, whereas the modern statistician sees masses of data filtered through computer manipulations [that] may conceal data problems." Tukey was clearly a "statistician of old times."

Another clue comes from a paper Tukey wrote coinciding with his retirement from Princeton in 1985. In it, Tukey warned of the hubris that attends to the gathering of more and more data without limit to obtain an answer, and he urged statisticians to counteract undue feelings of confidence using an *antihubrisine*—effectively, an antihistamine for the ego inflammation caused by hubris—offering his audience one more clever neologism in the process. His point: the answers a statistician seeks may not be contained or revealed within the data, even if mountains more of it are collected. In our era of rampant data collection and analysis, Tukey proffered humility as an antidote to an overconfident mindset. Sometimes the answers aren't at an arm's length, he says; sometimes our reach exceeds our grasp; sometimes we all just have to live with healthy-sized dose of uncertainty. Sage words that, coming from Tukey, were simply par for the course.

All told, Tukey's reach never quite seemed to exceed his grasp. So perhaps it is the title of Donoho's keynote address that best characterizes Tukey's contributions and place in history: "John W. Tukey: Scientist, Oracle, and Prophet."

CODA

In May of 2015, several months before Tukey's 100th birthday celebration at Princeton, nearly 200,000 students sat for the Advanced Placement Statistics examination, with tens of thousands more having enrolled in the AP Statistics course. It was a typical year for high schools in the United States.

The AP Statistics exam, administered annually by the College Board since 1997, covers a vast swath of mathematical content. According to the most recent *AP Statistics Course Description*, the AP Stats course is designed for "secondary school students who wish to complete studies equivalent to a one-semester, introductory, non-calculus-based, college course in statistics." To that end, content is organized thematically; the first of four major themes is

Exploring Data: Describing patterns and departures from patterns

with the other three themes centering on probability, simulation, sampling, experimental design, and statistical inference.

The AP Statistics exam, which students have three hours to complete, is divided into two parts: a multiple-choice section, of which there are forty questions, and a free-response section, containing six questions. Students are permitted the use of graphing calculators. On the 2015 AP exam, seven of the multiple-choice questions were exploratory in nature, with two involving the analysis of boxplots. And two of the six free-response questions were also exploratory—one of which necessitated analyzing a graph of parallel boxplots, while the other required that students construct a side-by-side stemplot. All told, questions involving exploratory data analysis techniques that Tukey pioneered or promoted constituted around twenty percent of the examination.

EDA was undeniably mainstream and, with many of these hundreds of thousands of students going on to pursue careers in mathematics, statistics, science, engineering, psychology, or sociology, the work that John Tukey took a lifetime to develop, refine, and popularize will continue to live on.

RESOURCES

The pages that follow list the key resources that were used in researching and writing this book. For online materials, in addition to associated websites, the authors, dates, and source publications are provided (if available).

Books

Agresti, Alan, and Meng, Xiao-Li. (2013). *Strength in Numbers: The Rising of Academic Statistics Departments in the U.S.* New York: Springer.

Anderson, Margo, and Fienberg, Stephen. (1999). *Who Counts: The Politics of Census-Taking in Contemporary America.* New York: Russell Sage Foundation.

Andrews, David. (1972). *Robust Estimates of Location: Survey and Advances.* Princeton, New Jersey: Princeton University Press.

Bakewell, Sarah. (2016). *At the Existentialist Café: Freedom, Being, and Apricot Cocktails.* New York: Other Press.

Boas, Ralph, et al. (1995). *Lion Hunting and Other Mathematical Pursuits: A Collection of Mathematics, Verse, and Stories by Ralph P. Boas, Jr.* Providence, Rhode Island: American Mathematical Society.

Bowley, Arthur. (1909). *An Elementary Manual of Statistics.* London: Richard Clay & Sons.

Brillinger, David (ed.). (1984). *The Collected Works of John W. Tukey, Volume I, Time Series: 1949-1964.* London: Chapman & Hall.

Brillinger, David, et al. (1997). *The Practice of Data Analysis: Essays in Honor of John W. Tukey.* Princeton: Princeton University Press.

Cheney, Oren. (1915). *General Catalogue of Bates College and Cobb Divinity School, 1863-1915.* Lewiston, Maine: Bates College.

Cleveland, William (ed.). (1988). *The Collected Works of John W. Tukey, Volume V, Graphics: 1965-1985.* New York: Chapman & Hall.

Cochran, William, et al. (1954). *Statistical Problems of the Kinsey Report on Sexual Behavior in the Human Male.* Washington, D.C.: American Statistical Association.

Cox, David (ed.). (1992). *The Collected Works of John W. Tukey, Volume VII, Factorial & ANOVA: 1949-1962.* New York: Chapman & Hall.

Crawford, Matthew. (2015). *The World Beyond Your Head: On Becoming an Individual in an Age of Distraction*. New York: Farrar, Straus and Giroux.

Debus, Allen (ed.). (1968). *World Who's Who in Science: A Biographical Dictionary of Notable Scientists from Antiquity to the Present, First Edition*. Chicago, Illinois: Marquis-Who's Who.

Dodge, Yadolah, and Whittaker, Joe. (1992). *Computational Statistics: Volume 2: Proceedings of the 10th Symposium on Computational Statistics, COMPSTAT, Neuchâtel, Switzerland, August 1992*. Heidelberg, Germany: Physica-Verlag.

Ellenberg, Jordan. (2014). *How Not to Be Wrong: The Power of Mathematical Thinking*. New York: Penguin.

Ewick, Patricia, et. al. (1999). *Social Science, Social Policy & the Law*. New York: Russell Sage Foundation.

Feinstein, Alvan. (2002). *Principles of Medical Statistics*. Boca Raton, Florida: Chapman & Hall/CRC.

Feynman, Richard, and Leighton, Robert. (1997). *"Surely You're Joking, Mr. Feynman!" (Adventures of a Curious Character)*. New York: W. W. Norton.

Gardner, Martin. (1988). *Hexaflexagons and Other Mathematical Diversions: The First "Scientific American" Book of Puzzles and Games*. Chicago, Illinois: University of Chicago Press.

Gertner, Jon. (2012). *The Idea Factory: Bell Labs and the Great Age of American Innovation*. New York: Penguin.

Gleick, James. (1992). *Genius: The Life and Science of Richard Feynman*. New York: Vintage.

Green, Judy, and LaDuke, Jeanne. (2009). *Pioneering Women in American Mathematics: The Pre-1940 PhD's*. Providence, Rhode Island: American Mathematical Society.

Harari, Yuval. (2017). *Homo Deus: A Brief History of Tomorrow*. New York: HarperCollins.

Hayes, Peter. (2017). *Why? Explaining the Holocaust*. New York: W. W. Norton.

Johnson, Lyndon. (1967). *Public Papers of the Presidents of the United States: Lyndon B. Johnson, 1966*. Washington, D.C.: Government Printing Office.

Jones, James. (1997). *Alfred C. Kinsey: A Life*. New York: W. W. Norton.

Jones, Lyle (ed.). (1986). *The Collected Works of John W. Tukey, Volume III, Philosophy and Principles of Data Analysis: 1949-1964*. London: Chapman & Hall.

Jones, Lyle (ed.). (1986). *The Collected Works of John W. Tukey, Volume IV, Philosophy and Principles of Data Analysis: 1965-1986*. Monterey, California: Wadsworth & Brooks.

Kapur, Jagat. (1973). *Thoughts on Nature of Mathematics: A Collection of Nine Hundred Thoughts of the Greatest Mathematicians and Scientists*. Delhi: Atma Ram & Sons.

Kennedy, Gavin. (1983). *Invitation to Statistics*. Oxford: M. Robertson.

Keynes, John. (1921). *A Treatise on Probability*. London: Macmillan.

Klein, Daniel. (2015). *Every Time I Find the Meaning of Life, They Change It: Wisdom of the Great Philosophers on How to Live*. New York: Penguin.

Kline, Morris. (1980). *Mathematics: The Loss of Certainty*. New York: Oxford University Press.

Kotz, Samuel, and Johnson, Norman (eds). (1992). *Breakthroughs in Statistics Volume II: Methodology and Distribution*. New York: Springer.

Lehmann, Erich. (2007). *Reminiscences of a Statistician: The Company I Kept*. New York: Springer.

Leitch, Alexander. (1978). *A Princeton Companion*. Princeton, New Jersey: Princeton University Press.

Lohr, Steve. (2015). *Data-ism: The Revolution Transforming Decision Making, Consumer Behavior, and Almost Everything Else*. New York: HarperCollins.

Mallows, Colin (ed.). (1990). *The Collected Works of John W. Tukey, Volume VI, More Mathematical: 1938-1984*. London: Chapman & Hall.

McElreath, Richard. (2015). *Statistical Rethinking: A Bayesian Course with Examples in R and Stan (Chapman & Hall/CRC Texts in Statistical Science)*. Boca Raton, Florida: Chapman & Hall.

Mosteller, Frederick. (2010). *The Pleasures of Statistics: The Autobiography of Frederick Mosteller*. New York: Springer.

Mosteller, Frederick, and Tukey, John. (1977). *Data Analysis and Regression: A Second Course in Statistics (1st ed.)*. New York: Pearson.

Nasar, Sylvia. (1998). *A Beautiful Mind*. New York: Simon & Schuster.

Offit, Paul. (2017). *Pandora's Lab: Seven Stories of Science Gone Wrong*. Washington, D.C.: National Geographic Press.

Pearson, Karl. (1906). *Walter Frank Raphael Weldon 1860-1906: A Memoir Reprinted from Biometrika*. Cambridge, England: Cambridge University Press.

Pook, Les. (2003). *Flexagons Inside Out*. Cambridge, England: Cambridge University Press.

Poundstone, William. (1992). *Prisoner's Dilemma: John von Neumann, Game Theory, and the Puzzle of the Bomb*. New York: Doubleday.

Rosenberg, Adam, and Kemp, Sid. (2003). *CDMA Capacity and Quality Optimization*. New York: McGraw-Hill.

Salsburg, David. (2001). *The Lady Tasting Tea: How Statistics Revolutionized Science in the Twentieth Century*. New York: Henry Holt and Company.

Seife, Charles. (2010). *Proofiness: How You're Being Fooled by the Numbers*. New York: Penguin.

Shapiro, Fred (ed.). (2006). *The Yale Book of Quotations*. New Haven, Connecticut: Yale University Press.

Stigler, Stephen. (2016). *The Seven Pillars of Statistical Wisdom*. Cambridge, Massachusetts: Harvard University Press.

Sullivan, Michael. (2013). *Statistics: Informed Decisions Using Data, 4th ed.* New York: Pearson.

Trilling, Lionel. (1950). *The Liberal Imagination: Essays on Literature and Society*. New York: New York Review of Books.

Tukey, John. (1940). *Convergence and Uniformity in Topology*. Princeton, New Jersey: Princeton University Press.

Tukey, John. (1977). *Exploratory Data Analysis*. Reading, Massachusetts: Addison-Wesley.

Tukey, John, et al. (1965). *Restoring the Quality of Our Environment: Report of the Environmental Pollution Panel President's Science Advisory Committee*. Washington, D.C.: The White House.

Ulam, Stanislaw. (1976). *Adventures of a Mathematician*. New York: Charles Scribner's Sons.

Wang, Zuoyue. (2008). *In Sputnik's Shadow: The President's Science Advisory Committee and Cold War America*. New Brunswick, New Jersey: Rutgers University Press.

Print Articles

Anscombe, Francis. (2003). "Quiet Contributor: The Civic Career and Times of John W. Tukey," found in *Statistical Science*, Vol. 18, No. 3, pp. 287-310.

Anscombe, Francis, and Tukey, John. (1963). "The Examination and Analysis of Residuals," found in *Technometrics*, Vol. 5, No. 2, pp. 141-160.

Aspray, William, and Tucker, Albert. (1985). "Interview with John Tukey," found in *The Princeton Mathematics Community in the 1930s*. Transcript No. 41 (PMC41), Princeton University.

Becker, Mark. (2009). "A Conversation with Leo Goodman," found in *Statistical Science*, Vol. 24, No. 3, pp. 361-385.

Becker, Richard. (2000). "A Brief History of S," for AT&T Bell Laboratories.

Beniger, James. (1978). "Review: *Exploratory Data Analysis* by John W. Tukey," found in *Contemporary Sociology*, Vol. 7, No. 1, pp. 64-65.

Benjamini, Yoav, and Braun, Henry. (2002). "John W. Tukey's Contributions to Multiple Comparisons," found in *The Annals of Statistics*, Vol. 30, No. 6, pp. 1576-1594.

Birch, Jeffrey. (1978). "Review: *Exploratory Data Analysis* by John W. Tukey," found in the *Journal of the American Statistical Association*, Vol. 73, No. 364, pp. 885-887.

Bode, Hendrik, et al. (1949). "The Education of a Scientific Generalist," found in *Science*, Vol. 109, pp. 553-558.

Box, George. (1953). "Non-normality and Tests on Variances," found in *Biometrika*, Vol. 40, No. 3/4, pp. 318-335.

Brillinger, David. (2001). "John Tukey and the Correlation Coefficient," for the *On the Interface of Computing and Statistics* conference.

Brillinger, David. (2002). "John Wilder Tukey (1915-2000)," found in the *Notices of the AMS*, Vol. 49, No. 2, pp. 193-201.

Brillinger, David. (2002). "John W. Tukey: His Life and Professional Contributions," found in *The Annals of Statistics*, Vol. 30, No. 6, pp. 1535-1575.

Brillinger, David. (2006). "Discussion [of Colin Mallows' Paper]," found in *Technometrics*, Vol. 48, No. 3, pp. 325-327.

Brillinger, David. (2014). "…How Wonderful the Field of Statistics is…," found in *Past, Present, and Future of Statistical Science* (Xihong Lin et al., eds.). Boca Raton, Florida: CRC Press, Taylor & Francis Group.

Buja, Andreas, and Künsch, Hans. (2008). "A Conversation with Peter Huber," found in *Statistical Science*, Vol. 23, No. 1, pp. 120-135.

Canby, Edward. (1980). "Audio ETC," found in *Audio,* Vol. 64, No. 12, pp. 8-14.

Chamberlin, Thomas. (1965). "The Method of Multiple Working Hypotheses," found in *Science*, Vol. 148, No. 3671, pp. 754-759.

Church, Russell. (1979). "How to Look at Data: A Review of John W. Tukey's *Exploratory Data Analysis*," found in *Journal of the Experimental Analysis of Behavior*, Vol. 31, No. 3, pp. 433-440.

Cooley, James. (1987). "The Re-Discovery of the Fast Fourier Transform Algorithm," found in *Mikrochimica Acta*, Vol. 3, pp. 33-45.

Cooley, James, and Tukey, John. (1965). "An Algorithm for the Machine Calculation of Complex Fourier Series," found in *Mathematics of Computation*, Vol. 19, No. 90, pp. 297-301.

Cooley, James, and Tukey, John. (1993). "On the Origin and Publication of the FFT Paper," found in *Current Contents*, Vol. 33, No. 51-52, pp. 8-9.

Cox, Nicholas. (2009). "Speaking Stata: Creating and Varying Box Plots," found in *The Stata Journal*, Vol. 9, No. 3, pp. 478-496.

Dempster, Arthur. (2002). "John W. Tukey as 'Philosopher,'" found in *The Annals of Statistics*, Vol. 30, No. 6, pp. 1619-1628.

Diaconis, Persi. (1985). "Theories of Data Analysis: From Magical Thinking Through Classical Statistics," found in *Exploring Data Tables Trends and Shapes* (D. Hoaglin et al., eds.). New York: John Wiley.

Donelan, Mark, and Cardone, Vincent. (2003). "Geophysicists: Willard J. Pierson, Jr. (1922-2003)," found in *Eos, Transactions, American Geophysical Union*, Vol. 84, No. 42.

Ehrenberg, Andrew. (1979). "Review: *Exploratory Data Analysis* by John W. Tukey," found in *Journal of the Royal Statistical Society. Series C (Applied Statistics)*, Vol. 28, No. 1, pp. 79-83.

Ericksen, Eugene, et al. (1989). "Adjusting the 1980 Census of Population and Housing," found in *Journal of the American Statistical Association*, Vol. 84, No. 408, pp. 927-944.

Fernholz, Luisa. (2003). "Remembering John W. Tukey," found in *Statistical Science*, Vol. 18, No. 3, pp. 336-340.

Fernholz, Luisa, and Morgenthaler, Stephan. (2003). "A Conversation with John W. Tukey and Elizabeth Tukey," found in *Statistical Science*, Vol. 15, No. 1, pp. 79-94.

Fernholz, Luisa, and Morgenthaler, Stephan. (2003). "A Conversation with John W. Tukey," found in *Statistical Science*, Vol. 18, No. 3, pp. 346-356.

Fienberg, Stephen. (2014). "Statistics in Service to the Nation," found in *Past, Present, and Future of Statistical Science* (Xihong Lin et al., eds.). Boca Raton, Florida: CRC Press, Taylor & Francis Group.

Fisher, Nicholas. (2015). "A Conversation with Jerry Friedman," found in *Statistical Science*, Vol. 30, No. 2, pp. 268-295.

Frasier, Donald. (1968). "Fiducial Inference," found in the *International Encyclopedia of Social Sciences*, published by the Macmillan Company and the Free Press, pp. 403-406.

Friedman, Jerome, and Stuetzle, Werner. (2002). "John W. Tukey's Work on Interactive Graphics," found in *The Annals of Statistics*, Vol. 30, No. 6, pp. 1629-1639.

Furfey, Paul. (1955). "Reviewed Work(s): Statistical Problems of the Kinsey Report on Sexual Behavior in the Human Male," found in *The American Catholic Sociological Review*, Vol. 16, No. 3, p. 219.

Halmos, Paul. (1988). "Some Books of Auld Lang Syne," found in *A Century of Mathematics in America, Part I* (P. Duren, ed.). Providence, Rhode Island: American Mathematical Society.

Hartigan, John. (2003). "A Memory of John Tukey as a Teacher," found in *Statistical Science*, Vol. 18, No. 3, p. 341.

Hoaglin, David. (2003). "John W. Tukey and Data Analysis," found in *Statistical Science*, Vol. 18, No. 3, pp. 311-318.

Howell, David. (2000). "Scheffé Test," found in *Encyclopedia of Research Design, Volume 1* (N. Salkind, ed.). Thousand Oaks, California: SAGE.

Huber, Peter. (1964). "Robust Estimation of a Location Parameter," found in the *Annals of Mathematical Statistics*, Vol. 35, No. 1, pp. 73-101.

Huber, Peter. (2002). "John W. Tukey's Contributions to Robust Statistics," found in *The Annals of Statistics*, Vol. 30, No. 6, pp. 1640-1648.

Kafadar, Karen. (2003). "John Tukey and Robustness," found in *Statistical Science*, Vol. 18, No. 3, pp. 319-331.

Kettenring, Jon. (2001). "A Conversation with Ramanathan Gnanadesikan," found in *Statistical Science*, Vol. 16, No. 3, pp. 295-309.

Kinsey et al. (1955). "The Cochran-Mosteller-Tukey Report on the Kinsey Study: A Symposium," found in *Journal of the American Statistical Association*, Vol. 50, No. 271, pp. 811-829.

Mallows, Colin. (2003). "John Tukey at Bell Labs," found in *Statistical Science*, Vol. 18, No. 3, pp. 332-335.

Moore, David. (1993). "A Generation of Statistics Education: An Interview with Frederick Mosteller," found in the *Journal of Statistics Education*, Vol. 1, No. 1.

Morgan, Samuel. (1998). "Richard Wesley Hamming (1915-1998)," found in *Notices of the AMS*, Vol. 45, No. 8, pp. 972-977.

Mosteller, Frederick. (1964). "Samuel S. Wilks: Statesman of Statistics," found in *The American Statistician*, Vol. 18, No. 2, pp. 11-17.

Mueller, Charles. (1980). "Review: *Exploratory Data Analysis* by John W. Tukey," found in *Administrative Science Quarterly*, Vol. 25, No. 4, pp. 700-703.

Osborn, John. (1978). "Review: *Exploratory Data Analysis* by John W. Tukey," found in the *Journal of the Royal Statistical Society. Series A (General)*, Vol. 141, No. 4, pp. 548-549.

Panaretos, Victor. (2011). "A Conversation with David R. Brillinger," found in *Statistical Science*, Vol. 26, No. 3, pp. 440-469.

Pétard, H. (1938). "A Contribution to the Mathematical Theory of Big Game Hunting," found in *The American Mathematical Monthly*, Vol. 45, No. 7, pp. 446-447.

Roland, Alex. (1986). "Introduction," found in *The Papers of the President's Science Advisory Committee, 1957-1961*. Bethesda, Maryland: University Publications of America.

Scheffé, Henry, and Tukey, John. (1944). "A Formula for Sample Sizes for Population Tolerance Limits," found in *The Annals of Mathematical Statistics*, Vol. 15, No. 2, p. 217.

Scheffé, Henry, and Tukey, John. (1945). "Non-Parametric Estimation. I. Validation of Order Statistics," found in *The Annals of Mathematical Statistics*, Vol. 16, No. 2, pp. 187-192.

Shannon, Claude. (1948). "A Mathematical Theory of Communication," found in the *Bell System Technical Journal*, Vol. 27, pp. 379-423, 623-656.

Smith, Terry, and Griffin, Malcolm. (1980). "Review: *Exploratory Data Analysis* by John W. Tukey," found in *Technometrics*, Vol. 22, No. 1, pp. 129-130.

Speed, Terry, and Nering, Evar. (1985). "Interview with Albert Tucker," found in *The Princeton Mathematics Community in the 1930s*. Transcript No. 39 (PMC39), Princeton University.

Straf, Miron, and Tanur, Judith. (2013). "A Conversation with Stephen E. Fienberg," found in *Statistical Science*, Vol. 28, No. 3, pp. 447-463.

Stigler, Stephen. (1978). "Mathematical Statistics in the Early States," found in *The Annals of Statistics*, Vol. 6, No. 2, pp. 239-265.

Student (Gosset, William). (1908). "The Probable Error of a Mean," found in *Biometrika*, Vol. 6, No. 1, pp. 1-25.

Thibodeaux, Michael. (1979). "The Lighter Side," found in *The Two-Year College Mathematics Journal*, Vol. 10, No. 4, pp. 266-269.

Tuddenham, Read. (1962). "The Nature and Measure of Intelligence," found in *Psychology in the Making* (L. Postman, ed.). New York: Knopf.

Tufte, Edward. (1990). "Data-Ink Maximization and Graphical Design," found in *Oikos*, Vol. 58, No. 2, pp. 130-144.

Tukey, John. (1957). "Some Examples with Fiducial Relevance," found in *The Annals of Mathematical Statistics*, Vol. 28, No. 3, pp. 687-695.

Tukey, John. (1958). "The Teaching of Concrete Mathematics," found in the *American Mathematical Monthly*, Vol. 65, No. 1, pp. 1-9.

Tukey, John. (1962). "The Future of Data Analysis," found in *The Annals of Mathematical Statistics*, Vol. 33, No. 1, pp. 1-67.

Tukey, John. (1974). "Mathematics and the Picturing of Data," found in *Proceedings of the 1975 International Congress of Mathematics*, Vol. 2, pp. 523-531.

Tukey, John. (1980). "We Need Both Exploratory and Confirmatory," found in the *The American Statistician*, Vol. 34, No. 1, pp. 23-25.

Tukey, John. (1985). "Estimating the Population in a Census Year: 1980 and Beyond: Comment," found in *Journal of the American Statistical Association*, Vol. 80, No. 389, pp. 127-128.

Tukey, John. (1986). "Sunset Salvo," found in *The American Statistician*, Vol. 40, No. 1, pp. 72-76.

Tukey, John. (1987). "Comment [of "Dynamic Graphs for Data Analysis"]," found in *Statistical Science*, Vol. 2, No. 4, pp. 383-385.

Tukey, John. (1990). "Data-Based Graphics: Visual Display in the Decades to Come," found in *Statistical Science*, Vol. 5, No. 3, pp. 327-339.

Tukey, John. (1991). "The Philosophy of Multiple Comparisons," found in *Statistical Science*, Vol. 6, No. 1, pp. 100-116.

Velleman, Paul. (2008). "Truth, Damn Truth, and Statistics," found in the *Journal of Statistics Education*, Vol. 16, No. 2.

Wainer, Howard. (1990). "Graphical Visions from William Playfair to John Tukey," found in *Statistical Science*, Vol. 5, No. 3, pp. 340-346.

Wigner, Eugene. (1960). "The Unreasonable Effectiveness of Mathematics in the Natural Sciences," found in *Communications in Pure and Applied Mathematics*, Vol. 13, No. 1.

Online

Biographies

"Salomon Bochner" (2004) by J. J. O'Connor and E. F. Robertson for the MacTutor History of Mathematics Archive

http://www-history.mcs.st-andrews.ac.uk/Biographies/Bochner.html

"David R. Brillinger, Honorary Member" (2010) for The Statistical Society of Canada

https://ssc.ca/en/awards/2010/david-r-brillinger

"William Gemmell Cochran" (1996) by J. J. O'Connor and E. F. Robertson for the Mac-Tutor History of Mathematics Archive

http://www-history.mcs.st-andrews.ac.uk/Biographies/Cochran.html

"Luther Pfahler Eisenhart" (2005) by J. J. O'Connor and E. F. Robertson for the MacTutor History of Mathematics Archive

http://www-history.mcs.st-andrews.ac.uk/Biographies/Eisenhart.html

"William Srecko Feller" (2016) by J. J. O'Connor and E. F. Robertson for the MacTutor History of Mathematics Archive

http://www-history.mcs.st-and.ac.uk/Biographies/Feller.html

"Scientist at Work: Richard L. Garwin; Physicist and Rebel is Bruised, Not Beaten" (1999) by William J. Broad for the *New York Times*

http://www.nytimes.com/1999/11/16/science/scientist-at-work-richard-l-garwin-physicist-and-rebel-is-bruised-not-beaten.html

"Solomon Lefschetz" (2003) by J. J. O'Connor and E. F. Robertson for the MacTutor History of Mathematics Archive

http://www-history.mcs.st-andrews.ac.uk/Biographies/Lefschetz.html

"Harold Calvin Marston Morse" (2003) by J. J. O'Connor and E. F. Robertson for the MacTutor History of Mathematics Archive

http://www-history.mcs.st-andrews.ac.uk/Biographies/Morse.html

Walter Munk, the "Einstein of the Oceans" (2015) by Kate Galbraith for the *New York Times*

https://www.nytimes.com/2015/08/25/science/walter-munk-einstein-of-the-oceans-at-97.html

"Jerzy Neyman" (2003) by J. J. O'Connor and E. F. Robertson for the MacTutor History of Mathematics Archive

http://www-groups.dcs.st-and.ac.uk/history/Biographies/Neyman.html

"Leonard Jimmie Savage" (2010) by J. J. O'Connor and E. F. Robertson for the MacTutor History of Mathematics Archive

http://www-history.mcs.st-andrews.ac.uk/Biographies/Savage.html

"Henry Scheffé" (2015) by J. J. O'Connor and E. F. Robertson for the MacTutor History of Mathematics Archive

http://www-history.mcs.st-andrews.ac.uk/Biographies/Scheffe.html

"John W. Tukey: 1915-2000" by Karen Kafadar for Statisticians in History

https://ww2.amstat.org/about/statisticiansinhistory/index.cfm?fuseaction=biosinfo&BioID=14

"John Wilder Tukey" (2004) by J. J. O'Connor and E. F. Robertson for the MacTutor History of Mathematics Archive

http://www-history.mcs.st-andrews.ac.uk/Biographies/Tukey.html

Obituaries

"Forman Acton, Pioneer in Early Computing, Dies" (2014) by Steven Schultz for *Princeton University News*

https://www.princeton.edu/news/2014/03/14/forman-acton-pioneer-early-computing-dies?section=topstories

"Forman S. Acton" (2014) by Adam N. Rosenberg

http://www.the-adam.com/adam/formanacton/index.html

"Theodore W. Anderson, a renowned scholar in mathematical statistics and econometrics at Stanford, dies at 98" (2016) by Kathleen J. Sullivan for *Stanford News*

http://news.stanford.edu/2016/09/23/theodore-w-anderson-scholar-mathematical-statistics-econometrics-dies/

"Noted Statistician Francis J. Anscombe Dies" (2001) for the *Yale Bulletin & Calendar*

http://archives.news.yale.edu/v30.n9/story11.html

"Hendrik Wade Bode" (1989) by Harvey Brooks for *Memorial Tributes: National Academy of Engineering, Volume 3*

https://www.nap.edu/read/1384/chapter/11#51

"Albert Hosmer Bowker, Former Stanford Dean, Department of Statistics Founder, Dies at 88" (2008) by Hayley Rutger for the *Stanford News*

https://news.stanford.edu/news/2008/january30/bowker_obit-013008.html

"Renowned Statistician George Box Dies at 93" (2013) by Jill Sakai for *University of Wisconsin-Madison News*

http://news.wisc.edu/renowned-statistician-george-box-dies-at-93/

"In Memoriam: George W. Brown" (2005) by Alex M. Mood and Lyman Porter

http://senate.universityofcalifornia.edu/_files/inmemoriam/html/georgewbrown.htm

"Kai Lai Chung, Emeritus Math Professor, to be Remembered at Nov. 6 Gathering" (2009) by Janelle Weaver for the *Stanford News*

https://news.stanford.edu/news/2009/october19/kl-chung-memorial-101909.html

"James William Cooley Obituary" (2016) for the *New York Times*

http://www.legacy.com/obituaries/nytimes/obituary.aspx?pid=180576599

"Gertrude M. Cox, 1900-1978" (1990) for the *Statisticians in History* (reprinted from *The American Statistician*, Vol. 44, No. 2)

https://ww2.amstat.org/about/statisticiansinhistory/index.cfm?fuseaction=biosinfo&Bio ID=2

"Joseph Daly, Ex-census Official, Dies" (1987) for *The Washington Post*

https://www.washingtonpost.com/archive/local/1987/09/13/joseph-daly-ex-census-official-dies/26fd2771-c202-4a76-88e9-806f3c7d0972/?utm_term=.65760153618f

"Statisticians in History: Florence N. David, 1909-1993" by Megan Kruse for the American Statistical Association

https://ww2.amstat.org/about/statisticiansinhistory/index.cfm?fuseaction=biosinfo&Bio ID=3

"Memorial: Paul Sumner Dwyer" (2011) by Cecil C. Craig and Phillip S. Jones for the *University of Michigan Faculty History Project*

http://um2017.org/faculty-history/faculty/paul-sumner-dwyer/memorial

"Richard Feynman Dead at 69; Leading Theoretical Physicist" (1988) by James Gleick for the *New York Times*

http://www.nytimes.com/1988/02/17/obituaries/richard-feynman-dead-at-69-leading-theoretical-physicist.html?pagewanted=all&mcubz=3

"Noted statistician David Freedman has died at 70" (2008) by Robert Sanders for *UC Berkeley News*

http://www.berkeley.edu/news/media/releases/2008/10/20_freedman.shtml

In Memory of Joe Hodges (2014) for the Department of Statistics at Berkeley by Peter Bickel and Erich Lehmann

http://statistics.berkeley.edu/memory/joe-hodges

"Harold Hotelling, 1895-1973" by Megan Kruse for the American Statistical Association

https://ww2.amstat.org/about/statisticiansinhistory/blocks/dsp_biosinfo.cfm?BioID=7 &pf=yes

"Lindsay, Robert Bruce" (1993) by Martha Mitchell for the *Encyclopedia Brunoniana*

https://www.brown.edu/Administration/News_Bureau/Databases/Encyclopedia/search.php?serial=L0120

"Donald Percy Ling" (1984) by Brockway McMillan for *Memorial Tributes: National Academy of Sciences, Engineering, Medicine Volume 2*

https://www.nap.edu/read/565/chapter/34

"Obituaries: Brockway McMillan" (2016) for *The Ellsworth American*

http://www.ellsworthamerican.com/obituary/brockway-mcmillan/

"Mathematical Theorist Frederick Mosteller" (2006) by Adam Bernstein for *The Washington Post*

http://www.washingtonpost.com/wp-dyn/content/article/2006/07/24/AR2006072401080.html

"Memorial: Paul Smith Olmstead '19" (2017) for the *Princeton Alumni Weekly*

https://paw.princeton.edu/memorial/paul-smith-olmstead-%E2%80%9919

"Dr. Robert Clay Prim" (2017) for the IT History Society

http://www.ithistory.org/honor-roll/dr-robert-clay-prim

"Richard Scammon Dies at Age 85" (2001) by Richard Pearson for *The Washington Post*

https://www.washingtonpost.com/archive/local/2001/04/29/richard-scammon-dies-at-age-85/a71e6ee4-c97c-4bce-b877-8f05732da86a/?utm_term=.cfd23deaebbf

"Lyman Spitzer, Jr. (1914-1997)" for the National Aeronautics and Space Administration (NASA)

https://asd.gsfc.nasa.gov/archive/hubble/overview/spitzer_bio.html

"Statistician, Longtime Faculty Member James Thompson Dies" (2017) by Patrick Kurp for Rice University News & Media

http://news.rice.edu/2017/12/07/statistician-longtime-faculty-member-james-thompson-dies/

"Albert W. Tucker, 89, Pioneering Mathematician" (1995) by Sylvia Nasar for the *New York Times*

http://www.nytimes.com/1995/01/27/obituaries/albert-w-tucker-89-pioneering-mathematician.html

"Obituaries: Bryant Tuckerman" (2002) for the Society for Industrial and Applied Mathematics

http://www.siam.org/news/news.php?id=464

"Statistician John W. Tukey Dies" (2000) from the Office of Communications of Princeton University

https://www.princeton.edu/pr/news/00/q3/0727-tukey.htm

"John Tukey, 85, Statistician; Coined the Word 'Software'" (2000) by David Leonhardt for the *New York Times*

https://www.nytimes.com/2000/07/28/us/john-tukey-85-statistician-coined-the-word-software.html

"John H. van Vleck – Biographical" for the Nobel Prize Website

https://www.nobelprize.org/nobel_prizes/physics/laureates/1977/vleck-bio.html

"David L. Wallace, Statistician Who Helped Identify Federalist Papers Authors, 1928-2017" (2017) by David Mercer for *University of Chicago News*

https://news.uchicago.edu/article/2017/10/25/david-l-wallace-statistician-who-helped-identify-federalist-papers-authors-1928

"Geoffrey S. Watson, 76; Wrote Statistics Formula" (1998) by Ford Burkhart for the *New York Times*

http://www.nytimes.com/1998/01/18/nyregion/geoffrey-s-watson-76-wrote-statistics-formula.html

"Joachim Weyl, 62, Mathematics Dean at Hunter College" (1977) for the *New York Times*

http://www.nytimes.com/1977/07/23/archives/joachim-weyl-62-mathematics-dean-at-hunter-college.html?mcubz=3

"Obituary: Martin B. Wilk, 1922–2013" (2013) for the *IMS Bulletin Online*

http://bulletin.imstat.org/2013/05/obituary-martin-b-wilk-1922-2013/

Articles

"The Fantastic Foresight of Katherine MacLean" (2014) by Andrew Liptak for Kirkus Reviews

https://www.kirkusreviews.com/features/fantastic-foresight-katherine-maclean/

"Banning Exploration in My Infovis Class" (2017) by Eytan Adar

https://medium.com/@eytanadar/banning-exploration-in-my-infovis-class-9578676a4705

"50 Years of Data Science" (2015) by David Donoho for the Tukey Centennial Workshop

http://courses.csail.mit.edu/18.337/2015/docs/50YearsDataScience.pdf

"Keepers of the Flame" for the New Zealand Institute of Mathematics & Its Applications Newsletter, *NZIMAges*

https://www.stat.berkeley.edu/~brill/Papers/NZIMAges0001.pdf

"Christopher Hone Receives 2010 Rapp Prize for Academic Excellence"

http://ecosystems.psu.edu/alumni/newsletters/2010/sum-vol10-1/students/rapp-prize

"History of Statistics at UCLA: Statistics at UCLA — 1939 to 1998" by Don Ylvisaker

http://statistics.ucla.edu/about/statistics-at-ucla/

"Four Faculty Members Recognized for Outstanding Teaching" (2003) from the Office of Communications of Princeton University

https://www.princeton.edu/pr/news/03/q2/0603-teaching.htm

"Luisa Turrin Bride in Italy" (1970)

http://www.nytimes.com/1970/06/05/archives/luisa-turrin-bride-in-italy.html

"Can't Count on Numbers; The Elaborate Effort to Adjust the Census by Using Statistics Adds Up to Ambiguity" (1991) by Peter Passell for the *New York Times*

https://www.nytimes.com/1991/08/06/us/can-t-count-numbers-elaborate-effort-adjust-census-using-statistics-adds-up.html

"Kinds of Bootstraps and Kinds of Jackknives, Discussed in Terms of a Year of Weather-Related Data" (1987) by John Tukey for the U. S. Army Research Office

http://www.dtic.mil/dtic/tr/fulltext/u2/a184495.pdf

"Historical Study: The National Security Agency Scientific Advisory Board, 1952-1963" (1965) by Anne S. Brown for the NSA

http://www.governmentattic.org/4docs/NSA-SAB52-63_1965.pdf

"Warren Weaver's final statement on RF support for Kinsey" (1951)

https://rockfound.rockarch.org/digital-library-listing/-/asset_publisher/
yYxpQfeI4W8N/content/warren-weaver-s-final-statement-on-rf-support-for-
kinsey?inheritRedirect=false&redirect=https%3A%2F%2Frockfound.rockarch.org%2
Fdigital-librarylisting%3Fp_p_id%3D101_INSTANCE_yYxpQfeI4W8N%26
p_p_lifecycle%3D0%26p_p_state%3Dnormal%26p_p_mode%3Dview%26p_p_col_id%
3Dcolumn-1%26p_p_col_pos%3D1%26p_p_col_count%3D2%26p_r_p_564233524_
tag%3Dnational%2Bresearch%2Bcouncil%2Bcommittee%2Bfor%2Bresearch%2Bin%2B
problems%2Bof%2Bsex

Interviews, Speeches, Seminars, and Personal Recollections

"James W. Cooley, an Oral History" (1997) conducted by Andrew Goldstein for the IEEE History Center in Hoboken, New Jersey

http://ethw.org/Oral-History:James_W._Cooley

"The Work of John Nash in Game Theory: Nobel Seminar" (1994)

https://www.nobelprize.org/nobel_prizes/economic-sciences/laureates/1994/nash-lecture.pdf

"Claude E. Shannon, an Oral History" (1982) conducted by Robert Price for the IEEE History Center in Hoboken, New Jersey

http://ethw.org/Oral-History:Claude_E._Shannon

"Memories of John W. Tukey" (2002) compiled by David R. Brillinger for Bell Labs

http://ect.bell-labs.com/sl/tukey/tributes.html

"People are Different" by David Brillinger

https://www.stat.berkeley.edu/~brill/tukeyfinal54.pdf

"Stephen M. Stigler Talk at 'Stigler in the 21st Century'" (2017) by Stephen Stigler for the 40th Anniversary of the George J. Stigler Center for the Study of the Economy and the State, Chicago Booth School of Business

https://research.chicagobooth.edu/-/media/research/stigler/pdfs/gj-stigler---steve-stigler-speech.pdf?la=en&hash=95CAF11D3A9A58031E471790C1B732402670F46E

"Summary of Warren Weaver's Conversation with John W. Tukey" (1951)

https://rockfound.rockarch.org/digital-library-listing/-/asset_publisher/yYxpQfeI4W8N/content/summary-of-warren-weaver-s-conversation-with-john-w-tukey

"John W. Tukey 100th Birthday Celebration at Princeton University—September 18, 2015"

https://csml.princeton.edu/tukey

"John W. Tukey 100th Birthday Celebration at Princeton University—September 18, 2015: Speakers, Titles, and Abstracts"

https://csml.princeton.edu/sites/csml/files/media/tukey_conference_talk_abstracts.pdf

Historical and Geographical Documents of Interest

Ronald A. Fisher Correspondence with John W. Tukey

http://hdl.handle.net/2440/68070

The Bell System Technical Journal (1963), Vol. 42, Issue 4

10.1002/j.1538-7305.1963.tb04055.x

"Princeton in the Nation's Service" (1902), an address delivered by Woodrow Wilson

http://infoshare1.princeton.edu/libraries/firestone/rbsc/mudd/online_ex/wilsonline/indn8nsvc.html

"David Brillinger – Scientific Ancestors Chart" by Victor Panaretos

https://www.stat.berkeley.edu/~brill/ancestors.html

"Robert D. Eddy Papers, 1935 – 1982" for the Tufts Digital Library

https://dl.tufts.edu/catalog/ead/tufts:UA069.001.DO.MS168

"Biographical Memoir of Raymond Pearl, 1879-1940" (1942) by H. S. Jennings for the *National Academy of Sciences of the United States of America Biographical Memoirs (Volume XXII)*

http://www.nasonline.org/publications/biographical-memoirs/memoir-pdfs/pearl-raymond.pdf

Destination New Bedford: New Bedford is Rich in History (2018)

http://destinationnewbedford.org/history/

New Bedford High School Main Webpage (2018)

http://nbhs.newbedfordschools.org/

Unveiling 54th Regiment Walkway (2016) for the New Bedford Whaling National Historical Park

https://www.nps.gov/nebe/learn/news/unveiling-54th-regiment-walkway.htm

"Tukey's Bridge, Portland, ca. 1900" by the Maine Historical Society

https://www.mainememory.net/artifact/20248

New Bedford Library: Special Collections

http://www.newbedford-ma.gov/library/special-collections/

Bates College: Vital Statistics (1997)

http://abacus.bates.edu/pubs/mag/98-Winter/vital.html

Photograph of the John and Elizabeth Tukey Headstone

https://www.findagrave.com/memorial/33609825#view-photo=149836993

Photograph of the Ralph and Adah Tukey Headstone

https://www.findagrave.com/memorial/33609872#view-photo=149837069

* Note: Although the website ancestry.com offered a number of unique details about John Tukey and his family, much of the material seemed either superfluous or inappropriate to include: e.g., social security numbers, home addresses at various points in time, income figures, records of passenger manifests, marriage certificate numbers, and the like. Such information was only used to confirm general biographical timelines.

Miscellanea

The Mathematics Genealogy Project

http://www.genealogy.ams.org/

The Census Trial (1992)

http://www.stat.ucla.edu/census/

College Board AP Statistics Course Description (Effective Fall 2010)

https://apcentral.collegeboard.org/pdf/ap-statistics-course-description.pdf?course=ap-statistics

Luisa Turrin Fernholz: Professor Emerita of Statistics at Temple University, Department Webpage

https://astro.temple.edu/~fernholz/

"Karen Kafadar *Curriculum Vitae*" (2017)

http://statistics.as.virginia.edu/sites/statistics.as.virginia.edu/files/KAFADAR_cv17uva.pdf

Videos

PRIM-9 (1973), filmed at the Stanford Linear Accelerator Center by Bin 88 Productions

http://stat-graphics.org/movies/prim9.html

History of the FFT with James Cooley and John Tukey (1992), from the Plenary Session Presentation at the International Conference on Acoustics, Speech, and Signal Processing

https://www.youtube.com/watch?v=o-UUudjFR1Y&t=1113s

The 1990/1991 Census Testimony, recorded by C-SPAN

https://www.c-span.org/person/?johntukey

John Chambers, Founder of S and R-core Member: Brief Reminiscences of John Tukey (2014)

https://www.youtube.com/watch?v=UBMCqwa4UEI

Stu Hunter: Recollections of John Tukey (2013), an interview of J. Stuart Hunter by Lynne Hare

https://www.youtube.com/watch?v=zirh9z6T9N0

Richard Feynman: Fun to Imagine (1983), the BBC Series

https://www.youtube.com/watch?v=Cj4y0EUlU-Y

Vintage RCA Computers—A Brief Look at the RCA 501—History Archives (2015) by the Computer History Archives Project

https://www.youtube.com/watch?v=mbV1t0JFyug

ACKNOWLEDGMENTS

First and foremost, I must thank the three mathematics professors who did so much to spur my research interests: Ned, Louis, and Carlos. I would also like to thank the two professors—one an English professor, the other an education professor—who helped shape my writing style and my ability to engage fruitfully with ideas: namely, Tom and Lisa.

On the day John Tukey died, I was a fresh-faced and naïve twenty-year-old college graduate finishing my second month of full-time work as an actuarial analyst. I never met Tukey, although I had been exposed to some of his work, since my undergraduate concentration was in actuarial science—a course of study replete with statistical theory and practice. Having been given an opportunity to teach statistics at my alma mater years later, pointedly introducing Tukey and his myriad accomplishments to undergrads closed the circle.

Along with John Kemeny and Thomas Kurtz, whom I've written about previously in *Endless Loop* (the third book of my BASIC programming language rehabilitation project), John Tukey became one of my intellectual heroes. He has never ceased to be a fount of wisdom for me. For instance, Tukey said, "[W]hether or not we kick them in the face, we must stand on the shoulders of others." Certainly when writing about a deceased subject he or she has never met, a biographer is forced to rely on the works of others, to stand on the shoulders of giants—and, when it comes to Tukey, no one is taller than statistician David R. Brillinger, undoubtedly his greatest biographer as well as a former doctoral student and colleague of Tukey's. Without the yeoman's work of David Brillinger, this book—which, despite its relatively slender size, was enormously difficult to write, taking me years to research and assemble, all the while having to repeatedly remind myself to stay levelheaded and not slip into hagiography—would have been impossible to finish. In his definitive biographical article about Tukey, entitled "John W. Tukey: His Life and Professional Contributions" and published in *The Annals of Statistics* in 2002, Brillinger prefigures the critical role his own work might play in any potential Tukey biography by writing, "This article touches on some aspects of [Tukey's] educational and professional life, perhaps to serve future biographers." The article, only one among a corpus of documents he penned about Tukey, has indeed served me well, especially from an organizational standpoint. The writings of statistician Frederick Mosteller, a former student and colleague of Tukey's, and F. R. Anscombe, Tukey's nephew, as well as Tukey's in-depth interviews, of which there are only a handful extant, were also invaluable to the development of this manuscript, as were countless other summary works and interviews of mathematicians and statisticians.

I'd especially like to thank Nicholas Cox of Durham University who, in a sharp, incisive, and thorough book review, not only directed me to a number of gaps in my research and errors in my first manuscript, but also explained how to correct them. Though Cox's unsolicited public review was, quite frankly, a bitter pill to swallow, I came to tremendously value his many corrections and suggestions because my singular goal when writing this book was to arrive at the closest version of the truth of Tukey's life and times, not to protect my fragile ego.

In a previous book, I justified my choice of topics this way: "I write books I wish were available to read but am unable to locate on the bookshelves." This sentiment holds especially true with ADVENTURES OF A STATISTICIAN. Quite frankly, I was waiting—and hoping—for someone to take the reins and write the first book-length biographical treatment of John Tukey, a singular man whose accomplishments certainly merit a much wider recognition among the lay public. I waited over a decade for such a book to appear. While my patience ran out, my own research began. (Unlike Stanislaw Ulam, who wrote *Adventures of a Mathematician*, and Richard Feynman, who co-wrote *"Surely You're Joking, Mr. Feynman!"*, the closest Tukey came to offering anything autobiographical were nuggets embedded within his statistics writings, such as "The Future of Data Analysis," as well as in a handful of transcribed oral interviews. As F. R. Anscombe observes, Tukey wasn't one to write much about himself.)

So I've done the best I possibly could to pull together the many disparate threads of John Tukey's life and work, and I hope that, through my efforts, I have honored him and the many he influenced and inspired. Any mistakes, oversights, omissions, or misstatements in the text are unintentional but are also entirely my responsibility.

ABOUT THE AUTHOR

Mark Jones Lorenzo, who has written books on statistics, mathematics, and computer programming, is a teacher. He lives in Pennsylvania with his dogs.

Printed in Great Britain
by Amazon

47591647R00200